Modernist aesthetics have been identified with a sense of cultural crisis, defined by its distance from an ideal of unified, 'undissociated' consciousness attributed to primitive man. This original study of the problem of consciousness in modern poetry examines the struggle towards that ideal of 'unitary' subjective experience, through close readings of British and Irish poets from Hardy and the Georgian poets, through D. H. Lawrence, Edward Thomas, Yeats, Eliot, MacNeice and Auden, to Ted Hughes. Hugh Underhill argues that the poetry's emphasis on inner states and 'the experience itself' under-represents the extent to which the crisis is socio-historically determined. Acknowledging the Romantic inheritance of a myth of 'poetry', Underhill embraces both modern poetry's resistance to positivist reductions of the mystery of consciousness, and the clarification of poetry's socio-cultural role (co-ordinating 'inner' and 'outer' worlds) provided by contemporary theories of subjectivity and the text. The problematic status of any notion of the unitary in the twentieth century is shown to give space at least for experiencing indeterminacy as a field of creative choice and freedom.

THE PROBLEM OF CONSCIOUSNESS
IN MODERN POETRY

THE PROBLEM OF CONSCIOUSNESS IN MODERN POETRY

HUGH UNDERHILL

Department of English, La Trobe University

CAMBRIDGE
UNIVERSITY PRESS

Published by the Press Syndicate of the University of Cambridge
The Pitt Building, Trumpington Street, Cambridge CB2 1RP
40 West 20th Street, New York, NY 10011–4211, USA
10 Stamford Road, Oakleigh, Victoria 3166, Australia

First published 1992

Printed in Great Britain at the University Press, Cambridge

A catalogue record for this book is available from the British Library

Library of Congress cataloguing in publication data

Underhill, Hugh.
The problem of consciousness in modern poetry / by Hugh Underhill.
p.   cm.
Includes bibliographical references
ISBN 0 521 41033 9 (hardback)
1. English poetry – 20th century – History and criticism.
2. Modernism (Literature) – Great Britain. 3. Consciousness in
literature. I. Title.
PR605.M63U53 1992
821'.91091 – dc20   91-32360   CIP

ISBN 0 521 41033 9 hardback

To my parents, Aileen and Arthur

Contents

Preface

I first gave my attention to the topic of this book while writing a Ph.D. thesis in the early 1970s at the University of Kent at Canterbury, and some material survives from that project. The book also incorporates versions, somewhat revised, of a number of published articles. 'From a Georgian Poetic to the "Romantic Primitivism" of Robert Graves and D. H. Lawrence' appeared in *Studies in Romanticism* (Winter 1983), 'The "Poetical Character" of Edward Thomas' in *Essays in Criticism* (July, 1973), and 'Edward Thomas: A Special Case?' and 'Ted Hughes. Medicine Man and Maker' in *Meridian. The La Trobe University English Review* (May 1983 and May 1989 respectively). I am grateful to the editors of these journals, and to the Trustees of Boston University in the case of the *Studies in Romanticism* article, for permission to reprint this material. Two further articles from which more minor adaptations have been made are cited in notes. Acknowledgement is also due to the King's School, Canterbury, for kindly allowing the use of quotations from manuscript letters by W. H. Davies to Edward Thomas, held in its library.

   I have inevitably incurred various other debts: to the University of Kent and in particular Mr E. B. Greenwood; to La Trobe University, Melbourne, for granting me various periods of leave and to the advice and encouragement of my colleagues in the English Department, in particular Max Richards, who read some of the work in stages, David Rawlinson, John Barnes and John Wiltshire; to the department's secretarial staff; and to Les Harrop for much helpful discussion and collaboration. I wish especially to record my feelings of gratitude to my friends and former teachers Professor John Lucas, Dr Allan Rodway and Dr George Parfitt.

Introduction: the inward revolution

'Consciousness is an end in itself', wrote D. H. Lawrence in his provocative late work *Apocalypse*. At least, so it was, he imagines, for the earliest civilizations, before man's arrogant 'mental consciousness' got the upper hand and set in motion the long process of misdirection which has culminated in the disaster of modern life. Now, '[w]e torture ourselves getting somewhere, and when we get there it is nowhere, for there is nowhere to get to'.[1]

'The old pagan process of rotary image-thought' (p. 46) inhered in a way of being which fulfilled the individual, which allowed him to exist at one with his fellows and his surroundings. There was a perfect unity of the outer and the inner life, an absence (I quote now from Cleanth Brooks) of that 'split between the subjective and the objective' which plagues modern mankind, none of that 'chasm between the life of the emotions and attitudes within the poet and the universe outside him ... that so much troubled the Romantic poets'.[2] That objections arise to any such notion of an original 'wholeness' of consciousness is a point I shall come to. But the terms in which Lawrence talks of this supposed original consciousness of civilized man are remarkably like those often seen as endeavouring to address a modern *crisis* of consciousness. The ancients had, says Lawrence,

a great depth of knowledge arrived at direct, by instinct and intuition, as we say, not by reason. It was a knowledge based not on words but on images. The abstraction was not into generalisations or into qualities, but into symbols. And the connection was not logical but emotional ... Images or symbols succeeded one another in a procession of instinctive and arbitrary physical connection – some of the Psalms give us examples – and they 'get nowhere' because there was nowhere to get to, the desire was to achieve consummation of a certain state of consciousness, to fulfil a certain state of feeling-awareness. (p. 42)

A completed thought was the plumbing of a depth, like a whirlpool, of emotional awareness, and at the depth of the whirlpool of emotion the resolve formed. (p. 44)

This kind of knowledge was what the oracles offered:

They were supposed to deliver a set of images or symbols of the real dynamic value, which should set the emotional consciousness of the enquirer, as he pondered them, revolving more and more rapidly, till out of a state of intense emotional absorption the resolve at last formed ... (pp. 44–5)

Compare this with the way we have been encouraged to read modern poems. The obvious example, *The Waste Land*, has often been seen as possessing an Imagist or symbolic 'logic' of its own. The narrative 'links in the chain' are suppressed, but the poem arises out of a unified source at a deeper level of consciousness, by a process which Eliot himself described when discussing what he called 'the auditory imagination'. The poem 'gets nowhere' in the sense that it does not have a consecutive structure, but images and motifs revolve and revolve in patternings which finally form a 'resolve' or meaning. (*Four Quartets* does this much more overtly.) Moreover, in the present century it has been widely proposed that something like 'rotary image-thought' is the intrinsic mode in which the human mind works. Consciousness is analogous with a stream or flow (or at other times a deep pool); 'logic' is an artificial tidying-up of consciousness which may have necessary specific functions, but also involves a disastrous fragmenting of 'unity of being' – it leads to a 'dissociation of sensibility'. And so the modern poem is merely an attempt to re-instate and enact the true nature of human consciousness. It often seeks to reach back to some original, more 'completed' kind of thought or knowledge, not hopelessly lacking coherence like modern knowledge. It is a 'plumbing of a depth'; the 'auditory imagination' involves 'sinking to the most primitive and forgotten, returning to the origin and bringing something back, seeking the beginning and the end'. In discussions of modern poetry, whether or not of the expressly 'Modernist' kind, we keep coming upon some such series of propositions. The twentieth-century poet does indeed assume the role of oracle.

There are two things to be noted, and then left aside for the moment. First, in this way of envisaging, symbols are not arbitrary signs which derive any meaning they may have from their relationships with other signs (Lawrence turns that on its head, it is the *relationships between* symbols that are 'arbitrary'); they reach back to an 'origin', which can in some sense be recovered. Second, this account of a modern poem such as *The Waste Land* pushes into the background its overt intertextuality: its exemplary demonstration, not of unity or closure, but of a relational structure of plural items, items themselves retrieved from pre-constructed systems or discourses, but which are then arranged or disposed by its maker to 'make it new', make a new thing, not a recovered thing.

Lawrence and Eliot, one might think, are two writers little in sympathy. But this is conspicuous about modern writers. They insist in extreme and even perverse ways not only on their difference from 'ordinary' people but on their difference from each other. Idiosyncrasy is nursed and cherished. And in one way, this is as it should be – that writers should resist the depersonalizing uniformity which societies are always foisting upon themselves (not a new thing but given new scope and dimension by modern technologies), which is then represented as natural and necessary, and which condemns the individual to 'inauthentic' existence. Writers, it would appear, have always, in a dual way, mirrored and been formed by yet also contested their worlds. But in the modern period the result, it has often been observed, is an unprecedented isolation and fragmentation in our cultural life, and of the artist from the populace at large. So that paradoxically what unites Lawrence and Eliot and makes each in some sense typical is their very isolation, their extreme and intense concentration on an art of the subjective. It follows from this – and perhaps hardly needs to be said – that there are many kinds of modern poet; there is no mould into which all can be fitted. Nevertheless, it is a task of the critic to offer an account of such patterns, to systematize such relationships, as can be discerned. A significant number of talented poets in the twentieth century have encountered more than usual difficulty in coming to terms with, and experiencing a secure sense of identity within, their time and place. They have felt at odds with what they have taken to be the prevailing values of their society or civilization, unable to share in any sense of community, or to conceive of the here and now or of the historical dynamics at work in it as meaningful and real. As a consequence, they have sought reality and meaning elsewhere, turning to notions such as Lawrence's of an original whole, shared human consciousness, and to the value to be found in subjective life. One notes how Lawrence's formulations – his valuing of something which is *an end in itself*, his rejection of the effort to get *somewhere* and insistence that there is in reality *nowhere to get to* – entail the notion that social action and involvement in history are without meaning. He opposes to history a 'real dynamic value' of another kind. This exploration of subjective life is a matter both of gains and losses: on one side of the account, it is a corrective and an extension of range, opening up possibilities which in earlier periods faith in a rational and objective consensus about god-given dispensations may have kept closed off. But it also often leads to misrepresentations of our modern situation, to exaggeration of the valuelessness in the modern world of public and social roles, though one might have thought these legitimate and indeed inevitable areas of human expression. In such poetry there is indeed a dissociation of sensibility: inner life overwhelms communal experience, self-realization outweighs engagement with 'history'. And the question arises as to what kind of transcendent 'truth' can be said to reside in subjectivity, whether it can be accorded this value as a sort of metaphysical absolute, if, as is often now supposed, subjectivity is itself culturally and historically constituted.

The problem, while incipient much earlier, crystallized at around the time of the Industrial Revolution, and as such is at the heart of what it is sometimes useful to see as a continuous Romantic-modern tradition. I have chosen for discussion a number of poets who exemplify this problematic, but have attempted, as I suppose will be obvious, to be neither comprehensive, nor definitive in the treatment of individual poets: I have tried to strike a balance between sufficient detail in presenting each case to establish the reality of the 'problem' and enough breadth of example to figure the larger pattern. I have also tried to set against acute cases of the problem, others who suggest means of alleviation. In doing so, I hope I will not appear prescriptive. I am more concerned to conduct an argument about what poetry peculiarly *does*: to suggest that in order to do its work it depends upon realizing a world we experience in immediate terms (which is not at all to say that it merely effects recognitions, affirms given truths: the most interesting kind of poem always turns out to be a new thing, not a recovered thing), and that if it withdraws too far into some otherworld of the imagination or of subjective being it ultimately ceases to be of effect or to seem to matter to us. Poetry itself, because concrete, drawing on empirical experience, and because it works with language, which is nothing other than a social and historical practice, does not allow the escape from history. It follows that for a poet to be 'modern' must mean in some sense or another, however broadly interpreted, to be in touch with 'the modern world'. I should interject here that since all discussions such as this must adopt arbitrary boundaries, I confine myself, with certain notable blurring at the edges (Yeats, Baudelaire, some brief comments on R. S. Thomas and Robert Frost), to poetry in England, however relevant other poetry might be. Nor have I attempted to discuss any poet born later than circa 1930. Though I think the 'problem' I've indicated continues to exercise some sway, the map of 'modern poetry' undoubtedly looks different when redrawn to include poets younger than that.

One of the things Lawrence wanted to claim in *Apocalypse* was that objective and subjective consciousness were originally one, and that such oneness may be found recorded in myth. The powerful attraction of myth goes hand-in-hand with the modern interest, on the one hand, in buried forms of consciousness or the 'unconscious', and on the other, in attempts to synthesize new kinds of 'order' (a spin-off from the systematizing efforts of nineteenth-century comparative religion and mythology). The more one looks, in fact, the more the two impulses appear interdependent. In his well-known remarks in connection with Joyce's *Ulysses* about the necessity of the mythic method, Eliot seems to offer myth as a means of transcending the subjective to achieve impersonal order. But it seems to me that more often than not the opposite is the case: the resort to myth, for twentieth-century poets, is a means of reinforcing subjective isolation. In their anthology *The Modern Tradition* Ellman and Feidelson pointed to a correlation between 'exploration of the heritage of myth' and a failure to realize 'public, communal and historical' relatedness:

Modern exploration of the unconscious mind and of the heritage of myth has been part of a larger concern with the distinctive qualities and value of subjective life. But if the Unconscious is primarily a personal subjective world for Freud, it is primarily super-personal for Jung; and if the forms of myth are closely related to the private visions of symbolist poets, they are also public, communal and historical. Subjective life at its most intense is personal and private, wholly individual, and the value of subjective reality in this sense is a modern article of faith. The individual persona has turned round upon himself, seeking to know all that he is and to unify all that he knows himself to be. The totality of self has become the object of an inner quest. This cultivation of self-consciousness – uneasy, ardent introspection – often amounts to an almost religious enterprise.[3]

Certainly what characterizes much of the poetry I want to discuss is 'uneasy, ardent introspection', as well as, in one way or another, a peculiar sense of consciousness as *an end in itself*, of a kind hard to find in thought and writing before the present century. Herbert Read's *The True Voice of Feeling* included an account of Lawrence's attempts at expressing in verse 'the immediate, instant self',[4] and located a large, general movement in English poetry, initiated by Wordsworth and more particularly Coleridge, towards varieties of 'organic form', a movement which unites both Romantics and Moderns in a continuous evolution. I cite Read's book particularly because his title catches that preoccupation of poets during the last two centuries with the 'plumbing of a depth ... of emotional awareness', a preoccupation about which they have been intensely, and ever-increasingly *self*-conscious. Obviously there was 'feeling' in poetry of earlier periods, but it entered the poetry as part of something else, not as an avowed 'truth' in itself. Ellman and Feidelson comment:

A first principle of self-consciousness is that nothing, however inglorious or unpleasant, should be ignored. Jean-Jacques Rousseau's *Confessions* is the prototype of many later examples of the elevation of candour into a prime virtue. Rousseau premised his book upon his capacity to be wholly honest with himself and the reader. (p. 685)

Thus a man who was much a product of the Enlightenment (the Enlightenment putting in place, as it did, the preconditions for the Romantic) helped set in motion a continuous 'post-Enlightenment tradition that connects the nineteenth and twentieth centuries'[5] to culminate in the subjectivism of much modern poetics – the self-consciousness, the ardent introspection, the effort of the poet 'to be wholly honest with himself and the reader', his anxious quest for coherent identity ('totality of self') in the face of a society which is felt to deny him role or status. There comes into being what Virginia Woolf in *A Room of One's Own* referred to as 'this enormous modern literature of confession and self-analysis' (Grafton Paperback, 1971, p. 50; 1st edn 1929) Quite logically, the more self-consciousness heightens, the more intensely a need for unity of consciousness is felt, since self-consciousness is *ipso facto* both a process of analytical fragmenting of consciousness, and an awareness of separation from otherness. The 'immediate, instant self' clearly implies an instability in subjective consciousness, that it mutates from instant to instant, is extraordinarily difficult to pin down and totalize. And in conjunction with this, the writing of the poem too, the act which arrests and makes a whole of some otherwise unstable fragment – some phase or mood – of consciousness, in a society which has no place for poets, comes to function as an end in itself (and as such, an heroic act). And one can see here another attraction of myth, for myth, in Barthes's analysis, 'fixates', 'does away with all dialectics ... organizes a world which is without contra-dictions'.[6] Myth also, with its essentialist or archetypal content, reaches back; resists, and releases the subject from, the merely contingent realities of history, isolates him in a world, by definition, 'mythic'. This operates even where the twentieth-century self-consciousness necessitates irony in its use of myth; the purpose is to signify an absence of the mythic absolute as what is wrong with our civilization. Thus, in all these aspects, there indeed takes place an 'almost religious enterprise', but one which is, in seeking totality, fraught with contradiction.

In a well-known book of some years ago Frank Kermode elucidated an interdependence of the 'Romantic Image' – of which I take Lawrence's 'rotary image-thought' to be a version – and the seeming disablement of the Romantic poet for public life, social participation:

These two beliefs – in the Image as a radiant truth out of space and time, and in the necessary isolation or estrangement of men who can perceive it – are inextricably associated ... The artist's devotion to the Image developed at the same time as the modern industrial state and modern middle class. From the beginnings of Romantic poetry, the artist has been ... 'malade de sa différence avec son temps' ... Some difference in the artist gives him access to this – an enormous privilege, involving *joy* ... But the power of joy being possible only to a profound 'organic sensibility', a man who experiences it ... must be lonely, haunted, victimised, devoted to suffering rather than action ...[7]

Oscar Wilde was speaking from the crest of a very actual historical wave when he wrote in *The Critic as Artist:* 'We might make ourselves spiritual by detaching ourselves from action, and become perfect by the rejection of energy.'[8] As the nine-teenth century progressed, the most available social stance an artist could adopt became paradoxically that of 'inaction'. The Romantic–Symbolist–Modernist preoccupation may be with the inner life, but this represents a kind of continuing inverted dialogue with the 'outer' world. A certain psychopathology, the Romantic accidie, is expressly a response to an age which stressed 'industry', a revolutionary challenge to it. The 'real contribution' of Lawrence's poetry, M. L. Rosenthal has said, 'was to transpose the perspectives of political and social revolution into private, inward terms'.[9] There is 'nowhere to get to', consciousness is 'an end in itself'; history, then, is an illusion, an unreality. Lawrence, as I shall discuss, was one of the great deconstructors of a certain level of bourgeois myth, and far from wanting to 'fixate', rejected all absolutes and finalities, but the 'real dynamic value' he sought was an inner one, 'at the depth of the whirlpool'. All meaningful action and resolution – all meaningful dialectic and change – are enacted as inner drama, or interpersonal only in the private sense of some attempted knowing of inner being by inner being. 'We have got clean out of history – we are not today living in history', wrote Wyndham Lewis.[10] Intervention in history is neither possible nor meaningful: 'There is no way in by history's road', says a poem by Robert Graves. T. S. Eliot's *Four Quartets* is a work very much *about* history, but very peculiarly so, stressing a condition in which 'here and now cease to matter'. 'History may be servitude, / History may be freedom' says the poet, by which he means that we can either, to our detriment, be enslaved by history, or learn from it the only worthwhile lesson it has to teach: that history doesn't matter. Edward Thomas spoke of himself as 'pure of history', and he is a figure to whom I shall devote a chapter as presenting in peculiarly heightened form the Romantic-modern concentration on the historyless 'experience itself'.

Yet can a movement that denies the importance and even reality of 'history' be revolutionary? Shelley's intention, Marilyn Butler has said, 'was to *dramatize* the intellectual, exploring the hazards of his life, like sterility, loneliness, ineffectiveness and self-pity, and the temptations, such as Byron's cynicism and Rousseau's worldliness'. That is, we must distinguish between incapacitating indulgence in those 'Romantic' traits and the controlled artistic representation of them. Shelley and Peacock show 'reluctance to countenance the poet's withdrawal into privacy', and the concept of a duty to society, a duty if possible to achieve action, recurs in the writing of Tennyson, Browning, Arnold and George Eliot. On the whole they are uneasy with the openly 'Romantic', that is, other-worldly, argument; and so, of course, were Wordsworth and Cole-ridge. Even the case they [Peacock and Shelley] made in 1814–17 for the contemplative life had a social connotation, and was frankly and positively committed to politics. It is one of the peculiarities of polemic, that both sides lay claim to the same virtues and the same ground; and one of the ironies of literary history, that even writers of the more 'Romantic' position in the second decade of the century should have acepted what we now feel to be a classical or utilitarian premise, that the poet is bound by society's claim on him.[11]

But, granting what is said here about the peculiarities of polemic, aren't 'sterility, loneliness, ineffectiveness and self-pity' necessarily counter to the achievement of action? Isn't it just that troubled, guilty sense of art as otherworldly and opposed to 'society's claims' which produces such damaging confusions in, say, Tennyson's poetry? Doesn't Arnoldean 'culture' have at its root the nostalgic desire for withdrawal from 'the strange disease of modern life'? Whatever might be said of Browning and George Eliot, I shall present cases which seem to show the seductions of the 'otherworldly' often winning out in that polemic and that history of which Marilyn Butler speaks. After all, almost anything one writes does have, in some sense, a social or political 'connotation', but to write in advo-cacy of the contemplative life can hardly be quite the same thing as committing to paper the Communist Manifesto. Cer-tainly many of the Romantic poets were deeply concerned with social ideals, and in Book II of *The Prelude* Wordsworth appealed to 'The great social principle of life'. However, not only does he here give a very special twist to the notion of the 'social principle', but we perceive in it, I think, a version of the paradox or irony endemic to Romanticism. This involves the disposition to experience opposites as aspects of the same organic whole, in a fluid, irresolvable interdependence: Wildean paradox merely pursues the logic of this. In a very peculiar way, Wordsworth can conceive of solitude and 'a wise passiveness' as pursuit of the 'active universe' and the 'social principle of life'. (Passiveness: the will cannot, and should not, be interposed in this 'natural' flux; it is not the same thing as man-made systems.) Another way of suggesting the problem is to point out the tension involved in *writing poems* apotheosizing 'solitude': a poem assumes somebody is being addressed. It takes place, especially once published, in a process of social transaction. Eventually, because its contradictions are irresolvable, the Romantic tradition leads to an impasse. Raymond Williams has usefully stated the effects of this for modern writing. The poet may wish to 'achieve action', but his very social idealism, so recurrently finding embodiment in versions of myth (and Shelley was a chief protagonist of this), ends in disconnecting him from the unideal states of 'actual human societies':

Given the facts of isolation, of an apparently impassable subjectivity, a 'collective consciousness' reappears ... This is the 'collective consciousness' of the myth, the archetype; the 'collective unconscious' of Jung. In and through the intense subjectivities a metaphysical or psychological 'community' is assumed, and characteristically, if only in abstract structures, it is universal; the middle terms of actual societies are excluded as ephemeral, superficial, or at best contingent and secondary. Thus a loss of social recognition and consciousness is in a way made into a virtue: as a condition of understanding and insight. A direct connection is then forged between intense subjectivity and a timeless reality ... Not only the ordinary experiences of apparent isolation, but a whole range of techniques of self-isolation, are then gathered to sustain the paradoxical experience of ultimate collectivity which is beyond and above community. Social versions of community are seen as variants of the 'myth' – the encoded meaning – which in one or other of its forms is the only accessible collective consciousness.[12]

Again a Romantic-modern paradox: meaningful 'collectivity' is felt to exist only 'beyond and above community'. But how can this be so?

It is to this formulation in Williams's *The Country and the City* that much of the present book is addressed. Without wishing to make this an all-inclusive scheme (which it isn't), I shall see country and city as representing a symbolic antithesis in twentieth-century writing, especially among English poets. Schematically speaking, nature suggests images of timeless continuity and recurrence; urban life breaks the natural rhythm, makes time matter, accords worth to historical process. That I move, in a general way, from rural to urban poets suggests a movement in the course of the present century from the forging in poetry of 'a direct connection ... between intense subjectivity and a timeless reality' to a poetry which attempts a more direct relationship with history. Moreover, where Romantic doctrine often has it that the country is the place of organic community, poets come to *feel* the countryside as echoingly empty, and it is slowly admitted (or rediscovered) that cities too can be the locus of the life of a community. This is always a complicated matter. Despite Dickens in the novel, it took an expatriate American, T. S. Eliot, to show the English how to make poetry out of the city, yet as much as or more than any country poet, he was one of those who took the city to symbolize alienation and who proposed some timeless 'other reality'. And I finish with Ted Hughes as a poet who in the second half of the century resists the movement, even seeks to reverse it, re-investing in the 'Romantic primitivism' with which the book begins. However, a counter-current makes itself felt when Louis MacNeice announces at the outset of his book *Modern Poetry*: 'The poet, therefore, in a sense is man at his most self-conscious, but this means consciousness of himself as a man, not consciousness of himself as a poet.'[13] And again: 'I shouldn't think it worth it to become an over-specialized human-being.' MacNeice is resisting the idea of the poet as special or different, the oracular voice disengaged from history, as well as obsessively concerned just with subjective being, with inner and emotional experiences. The poet is the whole person, *plurally* conscious, appropriating value for idiosyncratic 'private visions', but also the person in the street (MacNeice being indeed chiefly a city-dweller), taking his or her place in what is 'public, communal and historical'. *That* existence is not necessarily inauthentic and complacent, one's socio-historical identity is an essential aspect of one's reality.

That is a poet speaking, some fifty years ago. It is now common to see 'the poet' as much less a self-determining agent than MacNeice no doubt thought himself. Yet in a sense he is endorsed, for in many quarters it is now axiomatic that there is no identity which is *not* socio-historical, which is other than a cultural construction. That is what the Romantic myth of the poet obscures. I've quoted from Marilyn Butler's *Romantics, Rebels and Reactionaries*, which opposes the view of a homogeneous 'Romantic Movement' in which a solipsistic preoccupation with self-expression isolated the poet from his society and excluded him, a 'special' being, from concern with politics and social action. History too is writing, and can be miswritten: this, properly rigorous, recuperates history by deconstructing a vague sense of 'the age' and a notion of the tyrannical sway of an ineffable 'Romantic Imagination'. Nevertheless, I want to contend (arguments of this sort having a way of doubling back on themselves) that the Romantic ethos extended its power relentlessly. There is a risk in assuming a 'Romantic-modern tradition', as if the protean literary imagination ever made such neat historical fits, and 'tradition' these days comes under suspicion as one of many imposed unities holding in place undeclared ideological assumptions. Moreover, that Romantic and modern can't simply be hitched together, since the modern is most obviously defined in terms of discontinuity with the past – after all, what does the word mean? – I take as given. T. E. Hulme, for example, set himself expressly to explode the Romantic myth, and historically, each periodic call for a 'new poetic', for the jettisoning of outworn diction and forms, has something of that deconstructive character. But it is against this clear discontinuity that the need to perceive *continuities* presses, and I suppose that this is a recurring human need; I see no reason to quarrel with T. S. Eliot's 'No poet, no artist of any art, has his meaning alone.' That, indeed, is virtually to say that meaning only arises within systems of relationships, or that literary works are always intertextual. The same principle underlies a statement such as Allen Tate's that 'Poetry does not dispense with tradition; it probes the deficiencies of a tradition. But it must have a tradition to probe.'[14]

So one can speak of a tradition; and it involved, I think, the kind of 'Romantic conflict' once succinctly generalized by A. E. Rodway as 'conflict between the poets and their society as well as conflict within the poets themselves'.[15] And it is observable that this conflict, failing resolution in any but the most tentative ways, often enough led to withdrawal to see this as characteristic: the conflict crystallizes most sharply as a contradiction between ideals of social relatedness and of transcendent self-isolation. Much of the evidence does support Kermode's proposition that the kind of artist who perceives 'the Image as a radiant truth out of space and time' is 'devoted to suffering rather than action'. Later I shall cite Baudelaire's assertion of a 'modern' aesthetic explicitly defined by 'suffering'; in many poets what appears a positive talent for suffering functions as part of the disabled relationship with 'history'. Even in the case of Lawrence, whose restlessness might appear to have little to do with 'inaction', the iconoclastic pursuit of *joie de vivre*, raised to the level of a mission, was to become frustrated by the sufferings his own experiences entailed and to culminate in a vehement ahistoricism.

It is perhaps the case that by writing at all, or at any rate by making his work public, a poet in some sense inserts himself into history. The idea that the choice, in Yeats's phrase, is between 'perfection of the life or of the work' might itself be seen as Romantic exaggeration; Yeats himself, indeed, was a public figure of a sort, and arguably some responsibility in a poet other than that to his art benefits his work. But it would be silly, of course, to require that poets should be highly active individuals. In the traditional distinction of *vita activa* and *vita contemplativa*, the discipline of poetry is bound to belong largely to the second. It is a problem again clarified by Barthes, who theorizes all reflective language as inevitably tending to mythic distortion; it is only the language of work or action, language which is 'operational, transitively linked to its object' (*Mythologies*, p. 145), which does not distort. Of all the poets I discuss, it seems to me Auden who has most adequately addressed this; without adopting a simply propagandist stance (poems, it is clear, are distinguished from kinds of discourse which aim directly to incite or move us to action), he conceived of the writing of poetry as embedded in a circuit which incorporates action, and held (speaking of Yeats again) that at least in one sense the poet *acts*: 'there is one field in which the poet is a man of action, the field of language'. If I say that poems need a language which engages both transitive and intransitive, active and reflective states, what I am arguing is that poems otherwise forfeit some of their claim upon us. For a poet's work to claim to transcend acting-in-history is to suppress elements of its own production and dynamics, to perpetuate those effacements and contradictions inherent in the Romantic-modern tradition. And since history is our concrete condition, if we want, as the Romantics and Moderns (Lawrence not least) certainly did, to change that condition, we have to negotiate with history, we can't simply absent ourselves.

However, I have stressed the gains, as well as the losses, arising from the poetic exploration of subjective consciousness. Auden once wrote that 'the private life and the emotions are facts like any other, and one cannot understand the public life of action without them'.[16] If we assert that modern poetry needed to re-include the 'middle terms of actual human societies', we must also give full recognition to the question which modern poetry has insistently set before us: what kind of worthwhile 'community' can there be, or for that matter, what kind of social action or 'revolutionary' course can be worth contemplating, that does not accord a place and value to inwardness, 'feeling-awareness', the facts of 'subjective' life? And when we come to individual cases – when we test the generalizing abstractions against the complex signifying and affective operations of actual works of art – we encounter quiddity, the specialness of each poet's achievement, the insatiable pursuit of idiosyncratic possibility. The critic here finds himself problematically making incursions into the realm of 'mind' or 'psychology', and into biography, but the details of a writer's life, as well as what can be ascertained about his 'thought' and his 'psychology', seem available to be 'read' just as is the text itself (in chapter 5, I shall borrow the awkward term 'the psychobiographical approach'). The peculiar psychological states manifested by poets are a materially determinative factor in their art; the tension beween the empirical individual who lives a life, writes letters to friends, and generally provides materials for biographies, and the impersonal stylizations which are his or her poems always begs critical investigation. Why did this person rather than another write this text with its idiosyncrasies of style and preoccupation at this particular time; why are no two poems ever exactly alike; do authors not *know* what they are doing? These are questions not easily set aside and it is hard to deny that addressing them extends our knowledge in useful ways. While this study opposes the notion of 'author' as transcendental subject possessed of oracular authority, releasing himself from history, the poets chiefly discussed impress me with their powers as 'makers', and that role of the poet, as 'maker', is endorsed. It is, after all, the *art* (the state of complex formal textuality for which that term may stand as well as any other) which brings into uniquely intelligible focus those historical, cultural, ideological or material conditions which generate a writer's productions, and I shall assume the reality of the creative imagination and the validity of examining, not to say celebrating, its operations and achievements. How to theorize 'imagination' I acknowledge as a problem, but it is not just an idealist phantom; its concrete functioning, like that of 'mind' or psychology, seems to me inescapable.

Am I after all, then, lending weight to the Romantic privileging of a visionary and synthetic power of 'Imagination', the ineffability of 'the poem', the 'almost religious' truths intuited by an autonomous, suffering subject? To a metaphysics of closure and withdrawal – returning to the *origin*, the quest for *totality* of self, the '*consummation* of a certain state of [*undissociated*] consciousness' – by means of which negotiation with history is evaded, and the options for active choice among open and plural realities are denied, a metaphysics enabled by the authority of authorship?

It is in the nature of the literary work, I suggest, to seek unity, 'closure', not so much, or primarily, out of a quest for an idealist order (political, spiritual, imaginative or whatever), though under pressure the quest may become this, but because without ordering our lives and the world which impinges on them, we cannot live,[17] but at the same time to express or signify the disorder, the contradiction, the plurality which are the concrete condition of our lives and our world. Whenever this plural drama failed to find resolution it tended to be seen by traditional formalist criticism as a fault – a failure in the artist to unify his material. But *The Waste Land*, I earlier ventured, is exemplary in its anticipation (whatever Eliot himself may have 'intended' and whatever coherent organization – 'a resolve at last formed' – critical readings may offer or find wanting) of our present theories of the nature of consciousness and view of our epistemological fate. The most interesting, the most inexhaustibly challenging and involving, works – those, perhaps, which evince the fullest powers of 'making' in the writer (here I gingerly step into the minefield of 'value') – will be those which least suppress the dynamics of this full and plural drama. I have drawn on Frank Kermode for my discussion of the isolation of the modern poet; his later book *The Classic* foreshadows my present point:

> In fact, the only works we value enough to call classic are those which, and they demonstrate by surviving, are complex and indeterminate enough to allow us our necessary pluralities ... It is in the nature of works of art to be open, in so far as they are 'good'; though it is in the nature of authors, and of readers, to close them.[18]

Much more recently Kermode has conceded that this does not dispose of the question 'of the way in which value is attributed to one text rather than to another. I think I rather missed that out, as if there were certain things which had, inherently, this capacity for fruitful plural interpretation, and of course, that's begging the whole question.'[19] For the sake of rigour, one must assent, yet I share Kermode's sense that some works are more worth talking about at length, and more open to doing so, than others, and I shall proceed on this assumption.

To put the problem of consciousness at the centre of an account of modern poetry is to reflect a sense of consciousness – so much so that it may come to be seen as 'an end in itself' – as the only certain domain in a world wholly made up of relativities, a world whose epistemological faith has become the denial of absolutes, essences, transcendent ideals. However, we have already seen that the notion of expressing 'the immediate instant self' implies the instability of consciousness itself; Lawrence's original consciousness which pursued 'depth of knowledge' through images and symbols succeeding 'one another in a procession of instinctive and arbitrary physical connection' no less suggests an unstable process: it is only, as I shall shortly discuss, *the experience itself* which can be trusted. If the Lacanian account of consciousness is accepted, the notion of a 'whole' or 'undissociated' or 'original' consciousness, and that it can be given verbal expression, is a fallacy, since at the very moment of entry into language a split in consciousness eventuates. Consciousness is inseparable from language, which both modifies consciousness by tidying and ordering it, and is acquired, only permitting a self constructed on its paradigms. Truth can't be only *in* the self, since that self is a construction; subjectivity can't escape history because it is constituted *by* history. We can't assume an 'I' without the ideological package which comes with it. This 'I' anyway is only a kind of stable centring of the flux of consciousness, organizing for the individual a provisional subjectivity; it is not co-terminous with consciousness. As so many modern poets have been perplexedly aware, multiple selves are possible; even the self is not something fixed to set over against an incoherent outer world. These problems help account for just how profoundly 'uneasy' the introspection is, how obsessively the fact of being conscious (and split from 'nature', set over against otherness) is itself felt to entail suffering: the problem of consciousness often comes to seem, then, the dominant concern of the modern poem.

However, if more than one self is possible, the self governed by a prevailing ideology is not incontestable: the liberating and meaning-creating act – it is in Auden, again, that I will find this understanding most fully explored – is to choose. To choose is to empower oneself, to perceive ideological options, to insert oneself into (not take flight from) history. To conceive of reality as irreducibly plural is to grasp an inescapable dialectic between subjectivity and history – history shapes us and we shape it. The *langue–parole* distinction expressly permits the creative ambiguity that while language speaks us, while we are produced by sets of forms and conventions, we also speak language, meaningfully choose and fashion, perform infinite variations and explore infinite possibilities. Imagination is a function of intelligence which perceives both openings and connections, which invents, and which also enables sympathy or empathy, a means of defeating determinism. Lacan's mirror-phase in the making of the self, which functions to exclude the 'other', while it theorizes the irreversible process of alienation, also supposes the latency of connection – that the 'split' in self, and by extension the 'split between the subjective and the objective', can be reached across. Human vision is not narcissistically confined to contemplating mirror-images: imagination, it might be said, is the power to conceive of otherness, and, if not to coalesce with it, which is impossible, to connect with it. It makes 'community' workable, and is what enables works of art to arrange their pre-existent materials into new and unique configurations.

It follows that the critic too can perform creatively, be empowered by the process of selection (of project, materials, approach), discrimination, judgement. The institution of criticism is variable. Critical methods and approaches had already multiplied in the course of our century before the new theories, the *nouvelle critique*, mounted their challenge; the critic had to be judicious in his use of these, and the newer perspectives only extend the options, adjust imbalances, and sharpen awareness. This is not to gloss over radical, sometimes disorientating, disagreements, but argument and counter-argument have always been the structure and incentive of enquiry. The more open field, the less dogmatic centre, seem to be enabling; that is, providing the older dogmas and distortions are not supplanted by new. A certain pluralism of critical means may facilitate elucidation of necessarily dialectical relationships; in our present case, it is not a question of the visionary and mysterious *or* the concrete social and natural worlds, of subjective 'totality' *or* engagement with history, for either/or terms have no independent meaning, only signify in relation to each other. And if these balancings, together with what I have said here about the unique powers of human consciousness, may suggest a humanist leaning, a pluralist criticism may also enable those of us who feel the need to recuperate a humanist reading of our texts, while being on our guard against the closures and suppressions, the so-called logocentrism, of the older humanist criticisms; that is, without evading the problematics of humanism.[20]

If I reach for a currently fashionable term, it is because it is the precise one for my needs. It will be seen that I am talking about 'pluralism' on three overlapping planes: a plurality in consciousness itself, the openness of the text to plural readings, and pluralism of critical means and approaches. Part of my case is that pluralism, in the making of the text and in criticism as in consciousness itself, counters dogma and corrects distortion. But pluralism 'leaves everything as it is', I have seen it said.[21] Is, then, pluralism a prescription for the inaction or inertia I am presenting as a problem? This assumes that only one course of action (or one critical method, or one aesthetic prescription) can be the right one, the logic of which, as Auden insisted, is totalitarian. I shall cite Auden's point that action only makes sense in the context of a plural reality; that, in his term, a 'monist' position is a quietist one; it implies necessity, disallows the freedom of choice and commitment. None of these pluralisms is without problems (I don't conceive of any of them as anarchically without constraints), but the immediate concern of this introduction is to establish frames within which the business of the book may be got on with. The argument, therefore, is that the poetry which seems to matter most to us is likely to be that which encompasses something like the plural consciousness Louis MacNeice was proposing – but which has proved remarkably elusive in the poetry of our century, not least, as I shall discuss, for MacNeice himself. My project is to insist on the validity and importance of that quiddity and idiosyncrasy, of those subjective understandings, which the Romantic tradition exalts, and at the same time that there is no such thing as immunity from 'history' or escape from the fact that concrete social and material contingencies do shape the productions of individual artists. My point, in fact, is that it is at the intersection of the two, in the complex interaction of the problematical 'I' and extra-personal pressures, that poetry acquires its capacity to work and to matter.

From Georgian origins to 'Romantic primitivism': D. H. Lawrence and Robert Graves

I

Critics have long been anxious to keep good poets uncontaminated by the term 'Georgian'. There are grounds for this, as I shall touch on later, but Georgianism was not only one thing. C. K. Stead noted that 'a chorus of critics begins its remarks on D. H. Lawrence's poetry by saying that he was "not a Georgian"', then added:

In so far as all poets are individuals, no poet is a Georgian – or a Metaphysical either. But the characteristics which mark off the Georgians from their immediate predecessors are shared by Lawrence, Graves, Owen and Sassoon: a rejection of large themes and of the language of rhetoric that accompanied them in the nineteenth century; and an attempt to come to terms with immediate experience, sensuous or imaginative, in a language close to common speech.[1]

'Immediate experience', 'a language close to common speech' – these phrases denote key ideas and I will return to them. Pound's Imagists may soon have looked more innovative, but the Georgians were just as clearly 'marked off from their immediate predecessors'.

In the beginning they seemed dramatically so, to their editor – 'this volume is issued in the belief that English poetry is now once again putting on a new strength and beauty' – and to the public and reviewers, notably Lawrence himself in an article on 'The Georgian Renaissance': 'But we are awake again, our lungs are full of new air, our eyes of morning. The first song is nearly a cry, fear and the pain of remembrance sharpening

away the pure music. And that is this book.'[2] Other contemporary reviewers found 'a wholesome revolt against poetic *clichés*,
a desire for directness and simplicity both of feeling and expression ... [a] consuming interest in life',[3] and referred to the
Georgians' 'acceptance of individual whims and wayward
fancies in place of firm philosophical ideals' (Stead, p. 81).
Georgian poetry was by its nature untheoretical, partly a
revolt against the nineties Aesthetes, against the conscious
formulation of a programme or an aesthetic; a consequent lack
of sharp definition helped lead to its decline after that initial
phase of excitement (especially from 1917 on). But these
reviewers' responses to *Georgian Poetry*, including Lawrence's,
can be seen as recognitions of a poetry of subjectivity and
'direct experience' running in a main stream from the Romantics to the modern. Edmund Gosse put his finger on this in
another review:

In short, they are willing to stretch to its extremest limit the
emotional consciousness of the intellect. It is obvious that this distinguishes poets of the Georgian group from their predecessors, and
leads them to an excess of subjectivity which is in direct opposition to
the objectivity which marked the poets of the close of the Victorian
age. (Rogers, p. 76)

The objectivity, that is, of decidedly uncentral figures such as
Alfred Austin and Henry Newbolt. It's certainly the case that
what immediately preceded Georgianism would have made
almost anything appear refreshing.

It might seem convenient to reserve 'Georgian' for a vein of
lyric poetry – quiet, craftsmanlike, often on rural subjects –
typified by such names (not all in the original anthologies) as
A. E. Housman, de la Mare, W. H. Davies, Edmund Blunden,
Andrew Young. I will comment on some of these in a later
chapter. But this vein is narrow in range and, though not
always unmodern in sensibility, mainly traditionalist in its
allegiances. Actually, Georgian poetry had a wider focus. It
engaged and manifested a central modern problem: how to
express and assert value for the inner life and the life of the
senses in a world experienced as impersonal and dehumanized,
lacking palpable warmth and vitality. Lawrence's new

awakening is longed for; there are restatements of a mythic theme already endlessly restated by the Romantics, of rebirth or rising again, something subjectively experienced rather than validated by the material realities of a social or historical situation (usually, in fact, expressly in opposition to them). Often, too, Georgian poetry recorded the inertia and directionlessness which are in part an inevitable consequence, deeply rooted in Romantic psychology, of an intense subjectivity, and in part the symptom of an incapacity to relate to actual modern conditions – despite the 'consuming interest in life' which is paradoxically itself an index of 'subjectivity' (because 'life' is what *I myself* experience, as opposed to the abstract structures of the public and social worlds). It conforms, that is, to the scheme outlined in my Introduction and my concern in this chapter will be to examine the consequences of this in the work of two poets who were at first associated with the Georgian movement, D. H. Lawrence and Robert Graves. They are important here both because of the way they each exemplify the problematical flight into the timeless and the subjective and because of the striking insights into the nature of consciousness their singular talents elicit. I first need to examine the Georgian phenomenon more closely, and to say a little about the centrality of Hardy.

The shortcomings of Georgian poetry are well known. It lacks the *élan* of the Sitwells' *Wheels* – that self-consciously avant-garde riposte to the Georgians – or the clarity and direction of the Imagist anthologies. Yet beside both of these the *Georgian Poetry* volumes have a certain weight and substance, a resistant nub of complexity. One might note, to start with, the recurring emphasis on haunting and phantasmagoria, which allows poems by non-contributors (Hardy, Edward Thomas, Wilfred Owen) to be linked with Sassoon's 'Haunted' (*Georgian Poetry 1916–1917*, p. 47) and with many poems by Graves, Rosenberg, Harold Monro, Blunden and de la Mare. And to be haunted, one might say, is almost a defining characteristic of modern poetry. The emphasis is often associated, of course, with war experience, and it's striking that an editor of Edward Marsh's position in the Establishment should give

the war poetry of Sassoon, Graves and Robert Nichols so large
a place in the third and fourth volumes. But from here one can
trace a much more general interest in elusive mental states and
painfully subjective experience of a kind which suggests an
anxious failure to relate to the outer world and a turning
inward in search of sustenance or meaning. This is by no means
always the complacent acquiescence or feeble escapism sometimes attributed to *Georgian Poetry*; a result of dealing with
painful material such as this is that lyric fluency – 'pure music'
– is largely avoided. It can't be easily accommodated to gen-
eralizations about the anthologies reflecting, to adapt R. H.
Ross, the 'literal-minded, middle-class ... worldly' outlook of
the reading public at which they were aimed.[4] We find
repeatedly that what we have in place of 'large themes', 'firm
philosophical ideals', 'the objectivity ... of the Victorian age',
is poetry of the moment and of a Paterian or William Jamesian
flux or 'stream', registered and defined by the intently self-
conscious voice. '[T]ruth to life', in this subjective sense, is
crucial. '[T]ruth to life, the quality which, for want of a more
precise term, one is compelled to call realism' is what R. H.
Ross finds the 'first concern' of *Georgian Poetry* (p. 47). Certainly it often appeared as literalness or banality. But Robert
Graves is loyal to his Georgian origins when he 'scorns as
academic any poetry which is more concerned with style ...
than with saying the honest truth',[5] whereas for the proto-
Imagist T. E. Hulme (Imagism was a *stylistic* revolution)
'subject doesn't matter'.[6] In Imagist 'direct treatment of the
thing', the *thing* tended to be of secondary importance; I shall
take this up briefly in a later chapter. Subject indubitably
mattered for Lawrence and he hardly belongs at all with the
Imagists despite appearing in Imagist as well as Georgian
anthologies. Georgian emphasis on content rather than on
theory, or style, or experiment with form and technique, was a
re-emphasis of the Wordsworthian principle of closeness to
experience and directness of expression.

It points forward as well as back. Edmund Gosse noted 'a
desire to render the texture of poetry more plastic, more
sensitive, more independent of mediocrity'; he found work

'haunted ... by the poignant and feverish hopes of individuals
... an ingenuousness, sometimes a violence, almost a rawness in
the approach to life itself' (Rogers, p. 75). Here is the recipe
for an art of the extreme, fashionable later in the century, for
poetry 'written immediately out of the jangle of agonized
nerves'.[7] The war poets – we have the evidence of their note-
books and letters as well as the poems – constantly examined
their own states of mind even in the midst of their ordeals: 'the
sensitivity of the poet', says Ross, 'was kept alive, laboriously,
deliberately' (p. 171). This is a further stage in Romantic
self-consciousness, a further concentration of meaning in
consciousness itself, as is Lawrence's immediacy, getting the
experience down, as it were, in a liquid and white-hot state.
'Not the fruit of experience, but the experience itself, is the
end', wrote Pater; compare Owen's 'every poem ... should be
a matter of experience'.[8] There comes to seem a necessary
connection between subjectivity, 'immediate experience' (it
can't really be immediate unless you have experienced it your-
self), and 'a language close to common speech' (language
removed from common speech will tend to be removed from
immediate experience). I don't overlook the extent to which
Pater's own language is unlike ordinary speech – Edward
Thomas, who can be aligned with what I am here characterizing as having its origins in the Georgians, had perceptive things
to say about this in his 1913 book on Pater – and in this respect
Pater is a prototype of Modernist obscurity and aloofness from
the reader rather than of Georgian concern with 'truth to life'
and communicability. But his remark bears on the sense of the
fruit of experience having become, in the modern world, discredited. The emphasis is on the felt quality of one's *own*
experience, exactly as it is, exactly at the moment it is known
(experience may include the act of recollection, though seldom
in tranquillity; the troubled act of recollection itself is often the
focus of the poetry because remembrance is so centrally
involved in the establishment of a sense of subjective coherence) and on how that might deliver up a new constellation of
meaning – a new vision or awakening (new because utterly
singular and personal) – to replace the disintegrated outer

reality (where experience is no longer felt to have a teleology, to bear fruit in meaningful relationships of cause and effect). Ultimately, indeed, what is being felt, however obscurely, is some falseness even in given subjectivity; for Lawrence in particular, the endeavour becomes to achieve a *new self*. The tenacity of what is represented by at least the first part of this formula is evident later in the century when Philip Larkin, who had in many respects sloughed off the Romantic inheritance, writes: 'I feel that my prime responsibility is to the experience itself, which I am trying to keep from oblivion for its own sake.'[9]

How, then, do Lawrence and Graves develop these traits latent in Georgianism, and what connections can be made between these, again, two very different poets? The 'realistic', prosaic aspects of the Georgian poetic (prose is closer than 'poetic diction' to immediate experience) contribute to steering each poet's verse away from Modernist expressive means, and help create the directness and lucidity of their writing. For them, the complex arrays, the overt intertextuality, which Modernist poetry manipulates can only get in the way. But Georgian realism – here the usefulness of Ross's term ends – was superficial and reductive, itself a version of a 'Romantic essentialism' which David Perkins identifies in the Georgians: an interest in the simplifyingly 'elemental', the supposed 'real' elements of human behaviour and feeling.[10] As I shall indicate, the work of Lawrence and Graves, particularly of the latter, is affected by this yearning for the essential or elemental, but not with the Georgian reductiveness. We find in them an intensely Romantic stress on experience itself and on the visionary flight or reawakening, but this is integrated with a genuine realism, especially of a psychological kind. Both poets, different as they are, manage to combine psychological realism and directness and lucidity of expression – communicability – with an often esoteric, or at any rate very singular, kind of vision and experience. Lawrence stretches language precariously: 'Poetry is a matter of words', he wrote, '... and still it is something else.'[11] Both feel the constraints of language, but without Eliot's chafing sense that words will not do what the poet wishes of them; the intensest Modernism ultimately longs to take poetry out of the realm of mere linguistic signification altogether. The more intractable problem is that 'experience itself' cannot, by almost any definition, be art; art *works upon* experience. Lawrence and Graves attempt to meet this problem in different ways, which distinguish their poetic methods as expressionist and formalist. Lawrence's method is a further development of the Romantic principle of organic form. Graves imposes shape *on* his experience; his Romantic material is refracted through classical form. If this can't escape contradiction – if Lawrence seeks to disrupt the formal discourse which poetry *is*, though that is only what all making it new must do, and if Graves's formalism finally runs against making it new – these methods embody alternative strategies in the face of the extreme states their poetry has to deal with.

For polemical reasons the notion of the Georgian brief lyric has gained much currency, but this is odd, since, as Edward Thomas remarked, so many of the poets were 'represented either by narrative or by meditative verse',[12] or used forms in one sense or another dramatic. These forms can be seen as attempting either to make the subjective states objective and manageable, or to distance experience which is all too immediate. Lawrence himself wrote what (in his Foreword to the *Collected Poems* of 1928) he called 'imaginative or fictional' verse as well as his more 'immediate' poetry; the two kinds, in a sense opposed, may mingle in the same poet, as they do in Hardy and in Edward Thomas. Sandra M. Gilbert's *Acts of Attention* (Ithaca and London, 1972) represents this as a confusion of selves in Lawrence, out of which must emerge the new self. Graves, we might say, was anxious only to keep the self in place; he wholly adopts a strategy in which, if it is not too much a paradox, direct experience becomes formalized so that it may be obliquely handled; painful subjective states are made tolerable. Lawrence's essential endeavour, on the other hand, is to stay as close to the subjective experience as possible and bearable, not to remove or distance it, to submit to it pliantly and eagerly, to register and explore it as minutely as can be done.

II

Gordon Bottomley can be considered a core Georgian – one of those around whom Marsh built his anthologies (he appeared in all but the last). To some extent his work is characterized, like that of the other core Georgians, by a gentlemanly dillettantism with which the passionate dedication of Graves and Lawrence to realizing themselves through their writings has little connection; by derivative literariness; and by the essentialist 'realism' of his verse-play *King Lear's Wife*, a kind of realism which Lawrence found repulsive.[13] Occasionally, however, he produced something like the 1907 lyric 'Netted Strawberries', a kind of writing, I suggest, which has elements in common both with Lawrence and with Hardy.

'I am a willow-wren', the poem opens. It has the look of those simple nature lyrics often stereotyped as Georgian, the verse evoking the willow-wren's world with a certain unpretentious skill. The connection with Hardy is in 'noticing such things' and caring about them. But this involves something of the plastic texture, the wiry and mobile articulation, which Georgian verse, again taking tips from Hardy, helped develop as part of the staple of modern poetry. And there is an anticipation of Lawrence in a liquidly alert and tender expressiveness which empathetically establishes the small, delicate creature and its extra-humanness:

> Apples and plums I know
> (Plums are dark weights and full of golden rain
> That wets neck-feathers when I dip and strain,
> And stickies each plumy row).
>
> But past my well-kept trees
> The quick small woman in her puffy gown,
> That flutters as if its sleeves and skirts had grown
> For flying and airy ease,
>
> Has planted little bushes
> Of large cool leaves that cover and shade and hide
> Things redder than plums and with gold dimples pied,
> Dropping on new-cut rushes.

> At first I thought with spite
> Such heady scent was only a flower's wide cup;
> But flower-scents never made my throat close up,
> And so I stood in my flight . . .[14]

This (the woman herself almost avianized by the bird's-eye view) is moving towards the kind of anti-anthropocentrism which distinguishes modern nature poetry and of which Lawrence is an originator (another matter to which I shall return in later chapters). Protesting in 1925 against 'humanizing' art, Lawrence wrote

What an apple looks like to an urchin, to a thrush, to a browsing cow, to Sir Isaac Newton, to a caterpillar, to a hornet, to a mackerel who finds one bobbing on the sea, I leave you to conjecture. But the all-seeing must have mackerel's eyes, as well as man's.[15]

Many of Lawrence's 'birds, beasts and flowers' poems present exactly this simultaneous perception of the man's consciousness and a consciousness of forms of being other than his. The active ego (so insistent in Lawrence) undergoes a kind of suspension or negation in an attempt to attain some state outside the isolated self, to escape what Lawrence described as 'each man to himself an identity, an isolated absolute, corresponding with a universe of isolated absolute' (*ibid.*, p. 173). This process of extinction as a function of renewal, this dissolution and metamorphosing of consciousness – a radically subjective process even when meant to bear on the renewal of a society, a culture, a civilization – is a crucial element of Romantic psychology; it suggests negative capability. It can, of course, be creatively fertile to the highest degree, bringing potently into play the empathetic imagination to reach across a universe of isolations. Its danger, though, is that it entails a passive lapsing and receptivity in the poet which can become, paradoxically, an incapacity to reach out and beyond the poet's own psyche, to make active choices and commitments, thus defeating its purpose (of renewal). I want to look at another poem by Bottomley which seems to have some such paralysis, at least symbolically, as its subject.

'The End of the World', in the first of the anthologies, has

weaknesses – as in much of Bottomley, a faint aura of aestheticism, some quaint phrasing, too much indebtedness to
Miltonic-Wordsworthian blank verse models. But to one
reviewer it seemed to show 'one of the most marked technical
developments of Georgian verse – the disappearance of the
adjective' (Rogers, p. 55). It is all-of-a-piece, compact in
texture, concretely realized; the lines, in movement and ono-
matopoeic effect, recreate the endless sigh and sweep of falling
snow; the relentless pentameter shuts the reader into a sense of
the cold entombment which overtakes a couple cut off by
days-long snowfall in a remote farmhouse:

> The dawn now seemed neglected in the grey
> Where mountains were unbuilt and shadowless trees
> Rootlessly paused or hung upon the air.
> There was no wind, but now and then a sigh
> Crossed that dry falling dust and rifted it
> Through crevices of slate and door and casement.
>
> (*Georgian Poetry 1911–1912*, p. 25)

Bottomley achieves an eerily drained, nerveless effect. There's
an impression of detailed actuality –

> For more than three days now the snow had thatched
> That cow-house roof where it had ever melted
> With yellow stains from the beasts' breath inside;

– and, at the same time, of unreality. Drastic reduction of
visibility, the effects of light, sound and movement – 'shapes
loom larger through a moving snow' – begin to create an
*un*natural world; mountains are 'unbuilt', trees are
'shadowless'. At first the couple, 'Watching the strangeness of
familiar things', are pleased with the respite from normal
occupations, but gradually the strangeness becomes menace,
and in imperceptible stages life ceases – the clock stops, 'A
butterfly, that hid until the Spring / Under a ceiling's shadow,
dropt, was dead.' A broken bed is burned in the grate for
warmth, but 'the coldness deepened'; the man falls asleep and
the woman seems to abandon as futile any attempt to reawaken
him. The poem would be better without her final speech,
which is insipid rhetoric, but it moves steadily through its

half-lit world to this point of paralysis. Though stylistically by and large pre-modern, it dramatizes a subjective world which seems to emerge from a characteristic limbo of consciousness in which the real and the dreamlike interchange and co-exist. No new vision, no joy of resurrected consciousness (the awakened, eager consciousness implicit in Bottomley's rendering of his willow-wren), springs here from annihilation. It seems possible to relate the poem's atmosphere of creeping psychic menace to that common malaise of Romantic and modern poets, a sense of the futility or impossibility of action for the sensitive man in a world of utilitarian values and the abstractions of scientific thought. More largely, this looks much like the impotence entailed in disconnection from 'community', from 'history'; it appears to speak the failure of that essentialism Bottomley elsewhere espouses. And in this poetry of paralysed, drained, haunted consciousness – one expression of a larger problem of *acute* consciousness – we find a connection with Robert Graves: the psychic deadness and the haunted condition against which he agonizingly built defences, and in the struggle with which, we may read the poetry as signifying, he eventually forged means of renewal.

The invalidism of much of Bottomley's life was a kind of exile from the world of action around him, with which he was at odds in a conventionally poetic way, but there isn't the fierce passion of being at odds with their world which drove both Lawrence and Graves to forms of actively chosen exile. Nevertheless, the two poems I've discussed provide a Georgian source of both the Lawrentian and Gravesian poetics, and a model of the see-saw of the Romantic imagination between energy and inertia – between a drained, oppressed, haunted consciousness and an eager, awakened openness to experience striving to reach out for knowledge of unlikeness to self.

III

'Kubla Khan', 'The Ancient Mariner', 'The Pains of Sleep' are among the most famous expressions in literature of a phantasmagoric state of consciousness, beset by psychic menace, the real and the dreamlike interchanging. Such poems also seem to express kinds of paralysis, perhaps the result of opium-taking but reflecting a general mental condition. In 'The Eolian Harp' Coleridge records a state of mind in which 'many idle flitting phantasies, / Traverse my indolent and passive brain': indolence and passivity of mind give us fertile associations with other Romantics. In a letter of 14 October 1797, to John Thelwall, Coleridge expresses a sense of consciousness as a barely tolerable burden, in the face of which a state is sought which is almost oblivion except that the subject knows he is in such a state:

I should much wish, like the Indian Vishnu, to float about along an infinite ocean cradled in the flower of the Lotos, & wake once in a million years for a few minutes – just to know that I was going to sleep a million years more.[16]

In the present century, Edward Thomas, writing to Gordon Bottomley, reveals a desire for the same kind of floating awareness stripped of the pain and difficulties of full consciousness: 'How nice it would be to be dead if only we could know we were dead. That is what I hate, the not being able to turn round in the grave & to say It is over.'[17] A complex of ideas involving life-in-death (a Coleridgean theme, after all), death as an escape from life, and dying *into* life, relates these statements not only to recurrent obsessions of Lawrence and Graves, but also, for example, to the themes of deadness and paralysis in T. S. Eliot's poetry. C. K. Stead saw Eliot's 'impersonality' as a Modernist version of negative capability, and 'negative capability' – for Keats, a form of dying into life – would seem to be an attempt to characterize aspects of the mental condition involving this complex. The two intensely subjective states which Keats set in opposition to each other, negative capability and the oceanic egotistical sublime ('to float about along an infinite ocean . . .'), can be seen, I suggest, as alternative versions of a similarly passive and yielding cast of mind. It's a Romantic cast of mind which is passed on to modern poets; Eliot's poetry, I think, remains essentially conditioned by it, as I shall discuss in the chapter devoted to him. It invites evasion of a reality felt as intractable and futile, where realization of self is endlessly frustrated, and which gives rise to an acute problem of identity: not only where does the poet belong in such a reality apparently commanded solely by the utilitarian and the 'scientific', where the pursuit of *self-interest* is felt by him as an imposition of *false* selfhood, but also, how does he define a sense of subjective coherence within its abstract and impersonal structures, let alone reach out beyond self? These dilemmas cannot be resolved since they are constituted by the pressures and in the formations of that very reality being evaded. The snows of 'The End of the World' descend.

But the tradition to which this cast of mind belongs is also an organicist one. The model of a seasonal cycle, the myth of descent into an underworld and consequent renewal, the idea of passive suffering and decay as fertile, are intrinsic to it. There is a 'deep black source' says Lawrence, writing of Thomas Hardy's *Return of the Native*, 'from whence all these little contents of lives are drawn ... Three people die and are taken back into the Heath; they mingle their strong earth again, with its powerful soil, having been broken off at their stem' (ed. Beal, pp. 172–3). In his book *River of Dissolution* Colin Clarke sees Lawrence as embodying this organicist Romantic tradition:

> Like the Romantics Lawrence is endlessly concerned with what Keats had called 'self-destroying' – the process of dying into being, the lapsing of consciousness which is yet the discovery of a deeper consciousness, the dissolution of the hard, intact, ready-defined ego...[18]

Keats himself, always seeking some 'amulet against the ennui',[19] fought the dreamy inertia which had such powerful attractions for him, and Lawrence's review of *Georgian Poetry* points to a close kinship between Keatsian energy, the eager and spontaneous impulse towards activity and life, and his own vitalism:

> I think I could say every poem in the book is romantic, tinged with a love of the marvellous, a joy of natural things, as if the poet were a child for the first time on the seashore, finding treasures ... it is all the

same, keen zest in life found wonderful. In Mr. Bottomley it is the zest
... of the utter stillness of long snows ... (p. xix)

(Some Georgian poetry is all too childlike!) That he finds 'zest'
in the creeping paralysis of 'The End of the World' is a function
of the paradox we are looking at: the Romantic phenomenon of
sensibility which mixes ennui and 'love of the marvellous',
inertia and zest, as opposite but inextricable aspects of the
same complex experience. Romantic poetry presents the two
aspects in many kinds of relationship, but a sudden access of joy
as the new is perceived arising from deadness or corruption is
characteristic.[20] Lawrence above all is spokesman for the
intensely excited grasping at life which forms one pole on an
axis, of which the other is extreme life-weariness:

For man, as for flower and beast and bird, the supreme triumph is to
be most vividly, most perfectly alive. Whatever the unborn and the
dead may know, they cannot know the beauty, the marvel of being
alive in the flesh. The dead may look after the afterwards. But the
magnificent here and now of life in the flesh is ours, and ours alone,
and ours only for a time.[21]

A statement which neatly opposes those of Coleridge and
Edward Thomas given above.

However, the terms in which Lawrence greeted *Georgian
Poetry* reflect a major predicament of modern poetry. He saw it
as a rejection of an over-intellectualized concentration in
modern writing at that date on formalism, moral didacticism
and pessimism – a rejection, really, of positivist naturalism:

The nihilists, the intellectual, hopeless people – Ibsen, Flaubert,
Thomas Hardy – represent the dream we are waking from. It was a
dream of demolition ... (p. xvii)

An arbitrary set of Aunt Sallies, but nihilists for Lawrence
because they seemed to be part of a process of destruction
('demolition') of the subjective life, the life of feeling and
spontaneity, in favour of the public and intellectual life. In
favour, that is, of what Gosse called the 'objectivity' of 'the
close of the Victorian age'; one recalls Virginia Woolf's famous

attack on fictional naturalism, on the 'materialists' as she calls them, in her essay 'Modern Fiction' (*The Common Reader* (First Series), London, Hogarth, 1925). For the kind of modern poet in question, this is where the enemy lies; in Graves, too, there is a strong anti-intellectual animus, and both he and Lawrence elevate 'unreason' into a principle. The poet feels overwhelmingly afflicted by his society's impersonal structures, the antithesis of the life of feeling and of the concretely phenomenal and sensational on which poetry depends, ways of thinking themselves having become abstract in order to fulfil industrial-technological functions, replacing a religion-structured world where thinking was done in terms of concrete images and symbols. As we have so often been told, he has lost touch with, or deliberately renounced, such frameworks for living, as 'faith', 'roots', 'tradition'. How, then, does he live with the intense subjectivity of his cast of mind, the extreme sensitivity, the 'acute consciousness' he is possessed of? What defences can he build, what amulet against the ennui can he discover, how is the waking from the dream of demolition to be achieved? The response of many Romantic and modern poets is to pursue a refuge in some psychic or imaginative other world, one which can come to seem as 'real' as the everyday world. Versions of this, whether we see it as a flight from reality or a visionary and creative reinvigoration, can be traced in Lawrence and Graves. Graves, building defences, fighting to survive, to overcome deadness and paralysis, makes a mythology. Lawrence sets out on an expedition, a penetration, further into the authenticity and vital core of self, and into the 'marvel of being alive in the flesh'.

IV

Lawrence may oppose a nihilistic Thomas Hardy to the spirit of Georgian poetry, but G. S. Fraser pointed out that 'Graves, Sassoon, Blunden all at one time or another visited Thomas Hardy at Max Gate, and received his poetic blessing ... So we can see Hardy as a brooding, presiding spirit inspiring these Georgian poets.'[22] The fourth anthology was dedicated to

Hardy. Hardy the poet, of course, has often appeared problematical. He has been seen as expressing, and his style and technique as reflecting, an emotional attachment to the fixed rhythms of a lost rural life, and at the same time to nineteenth-century determinist and mechanistic ideas. He seems excluded from the patterns of Romantic psychology and vision I've been invoking – an anti-Romantic – in the way he replaces the nebulous Romantic malaise (ennui is an *indefinable* unease) with an apparent certainty of the malign and hopeless nature of reality, a reality which regenerates only as meaningless mechanism. One kind of objection has been R. P. Blackmur's, that 'he dispensed with tradition in most of his ambitious verse ... it is damaged ... by the vanity of Hardy's adherence to his personal and crotchety obsessions'.[23] But it is just this rootlessness and personal centredness which call for attention here, and there is much to link him with poets from Edward Thomas and Gordon Bottomley to Lawrence himself. The particularity and the organicism of movement in these lines from 'On Sturminster Foot-Bridge' owe much to Romantic examples:

> On a roof stand the swallows ranged in wistful waiting rows,
>   Till they arrow off and drop like stones
> Among the eyot-withies at whose foot the river flows:
> And beneath the roof is she who in the dark world shows
>   As a lattice-gleam when midnight moans.[24]

It is hard to see in writing like this the 'Machine Age' structure Donald Davie in his *Thomas Hardy and British Poetry* claimed to find, and the gleam in the darkness and the moaning midnight are undisguisedly Romantic notations.

A substantial part of the poetry of Hardy's old age, belonging both in date and temper to the twentieth century, has come to be widely admired; its quirks of style are seen as essential to the textures of thought and feeling, in ways, I suggest, bearing some comparison with Gerard Manley Hopkins's proto-Modernist, experimental distortions. But even in many of the nineteenth-century poems one can find a three-way mixture and tension of an archaic, a Victorian and a modern Hardy. This offers a special register of expressive possibilities. The

solemn Victorian diction and perhaps rather mechanical
stanza-pattern of 'To an Unborn Pauper Child' may be taken
as vehicles of a life-negating pessimism:

> Fain would I, dear, find some shut plot
> Of earth's wide wold for thee, where not
>> One tear, one qualm,
>> Should break the calm.
> But I am weak as thou and bare;
> No man can change the common lot to rare.
>
> (p. 128)

But that is not the final effect of the poetry. The shorter lines
and the effort to rhyme are made to seem expressive in a way
which anticipates Lawrence's rhyming poems. The archaic
oddness of 'Fain' heaves at a burden of compassionate longing;
'dear' is tenderly inserted; 'find' alliteratively recovers the
surge of longing from 'fain'; 'shut plot' protectively contrasts
with the exposed effect of 'wide wold'. 'Thee' and 'thou' possess
that shade of tenderness not available to the modern or non-
dialect 'you'; the counterpointing metrical effect of 'One tear,
one qualm' (the two feet seem to me almost spondees) and the
inversion 'weak as thou and bare' carry an emotional charge
which leads to the long sigh of the final line, where the
monosyllables suggest a resignation embodying the mindless
rootedness of peasant life – but which is to be movingly
overturned in the next, culminating stanza. This is not Hardy
at his finest – there *is* a shade too much contrivance about the
poem – but it takes a hold on one. What strikes us in such
poetry is Hardy's extreme sensitivity, of which the ungainly
lunges of style, the apparent uncertainties of feeling, give us an
authentic rendering: the sense that again and again, for all his
Victorian attempt to neutralize through systematization the
damage experience can do him, it catches him on the raw. In
the close attention to and concern with the subject, the mix of
expressive means, and the vulnerable consciousness expressed,
this is the essential Georgian poetic.

That 'shut plot', the impulse for withdrawal from the pains
of consciousness, clearly echoes Coleridge's 'flower of the Lotos'
and Thomas's 'grave'. In an article which draws together

various strands in Hardy criticism, Robert McCarthy focused
on Hardy as precisely this kind of poet:

> Hardy experiences the lonely burden of consciousness as an extreme
> sensitivity to the frustrations and anguish of human existence. The
> sensitivity, in conjunction with the poet's thwarted 'pre-lapsarianism'
> – his sublimated expectation that the world would offer very much
> more than merely 'neutral-tinted haps and such' (CP 873) – makes
> Hardy peculiarly susceptible to nostalgia for unconsciousness, to the
> soothing allure of what in several poems he calls 'nescience'.[25]

The poetry is full of those subjective 'hauntings' which, I've
suggested, so often manifest the modern poet's insecure sense of
identity and of his place in the world. 'Wessex Heights' fits a
distinctive aspect of the Romantic-modern tradition, the
poetry of solitariness or loneliness (Hardy's second wife said
that it refers to actual women in his life whom he felt he had
lost), and also epitomizes a difficult self-scrutiny, the characteristic Romantic-modern exploration of consciousness itself.
Placing himself on the heights gives the poet a vantage point
from which to scrutinize – himself:

> Down there I seem to be false to myself, my simple self that was,
> And is not now, and I see him watching, wondering what crass
> 　　cause
> Can have merged him into such a strange continuator as this,
> Who yet has something in common with himself, my chrysalis.
> 　　　　　　　　. . .
> There's a ghost at Yell'ham Bottom chiding loud at the fall of
> 　　the night,
> There's a ghost in Froom-side Vale, thin-lipped and vague, in a
> 　　shroud of white,
> There is one in the railway train whenever I do not want it near,
> I see its profile against the pane, saying what I would not hear.
> 　　　　　　　　　　　　　　　　　　(pp. 319–20)

Here is indeed the 'modern poet' emerging from his 'chrysalis',
or at any rate a predominant kind of modern poet. Where in
The Prelude the self seeks to be unified, here it seems irrecoverably fragmented, disconnected even from an earlier more 'real'
self, the vainness of the attempt to focus this elusive subjective
existence being virtually admitted. Here is the sense of dis-

connection too from an earlier living community, the ghostly
presences of which still crowd about one just beyond reach; the
image of the moving railway-carriage as analogue of a life
which is always transient and which isolates one from the
world being passed by, picking up the Baudelairean *poésie des
départs* and to be picked up in its turn, as I shall discuss, by such
poets as Eliot, MacNeice and Larkin; and the bewilderment,
the helplessness in the face of this, the incapacity to see what is
at the root of the calamity ('wondering what crass cause . . .').
These lines are *metrically* haunted by ghosts: they seem to obey
no recognizable metrical precedent, hovering between various
of the standard patterns but settling into none, contributing to
the effect of something lost beyond recovery. The very difficulty Hardy has bringing each line to a close realizes a mental
state which finds experience amorphous and difficult to
manage. His famous vision of cosmic negativity, a determinist
and mechanistic view of humanity dwarfed and made sport of
by blind, implacable forces – Hardy as one of 'the nihilists, the
intellectual, hopeless people' – comes to look like an elaborate
defence erected by the acutely conscious and sensitive man. As
McCarthy puts it, 'Hardy's nostalgia for unconsciousness
reduces to a desire for invulnerability' to the sufferings of
existence. The usual Romantic versions of escape from an
intolerable reality are replaced by a meeting of that reality
head-on and a schematization of its implacability, of a kind
which falsifies the complex reality which the vulnerable Hardy
knows to exist. It's a structure, a system, to set over against the
amorphous subjective flow, occupying somewhat the same
place that Christianity came to occupy for Eliot or myth for
Robert Graves. That the many poems which directly illustrate
this system are Hardy's less successful or interesting has become
a general verdict. But the invulnerability, as in 'To an Unborn
Pauper Child', is always breaking down; it is his vulnerability
that we value Hardy for. And in his greatest poems, notably
some of those addressed to Emma Gifford after her death, he is
able in a most astonishing way to realize a sense of 'totality of
self', redeeming that experience of subjective fragmentation,
and of consequent value in existence, without the intrusion of

the falsifying system. Albeit by a most peculiar strategy, what was lost has been recovered.

For R. P. Blackmur all this counts against Hardy, as something related does against D. H. Lawrence; it shows him 'deprived of both emotional discipline and the structural support of a received imagination'. Hardy sets up 'a scaffold . . . out of the nearest congenial materials strong enough and rigid enough to support the structure imagination meant to rear'. But isn't it often proposed as a cardinal rule that the artist should make use of the materials close at hand ('immediate experience') since those are what he is likely to understand best? Isn't a criticism so much formed as Blackmur's by Eliotic principles of 'structural support' or 'tradition' entrenching the kind of falsifying system I've just described – seeking fixation of a reality more deeply engaged by imaginations like Hardy's or Lawrence's as amorphous and *poly*morphous? I shall touch on this again. In any case, as John Bayley asked in *The Romantic Survival*, 'Is there any reason why the ordered imagination should be of itself superior to the dispossessed one?'[26]

v

D. H. Lawrence's own contribution to the first Georgian anthology, 'Snap-Dragon',[27] has much, in feeling and technique, which reminds us of Hardy. The effort to keep to a rhyme-scheme imparts an awkwardness which, like Hardy's, is made to seem necessary. In fact, throughout the poem the rhyme-scheme has to be progressively revised under the pressure of the emotion – to an extent which represents a cracking of the formalist shell, that accretion of past poetic practices, which both Hardy and his admirer Graves found essential. Yet the formal restraint helps create the tension which makes this a classic poem of sexual frustration; both Lawrence and Graves struggle in their work with the afflictions of that English sexual puritanism already challenged by Hardy. Also, there are touches of cliché in the diction, but the uncertainties only add to the effect of a speaker who is undergoing the intense and awkward emotions of youth. This

speaker swoons with sexual longing but it seems his relationship with the girl in the poem is too undeveloped or the couple
are too inhibited for their longings to be gratified except in
terms of an excited kind of psycho-sexual 'battle', centring
upon the flower of the title. The rhyme-pattern is overlaid with
a delicate formality of repetition which helps give the effect of
hesitation and tense expectancy (a tension, an inability to press
forward, vastly different from Prufrock's 'Do I dare?'!):

> She bade me follow to her garden where
> The mellow sunlight stood as in a cup
> Between the old grey walls; I did not dare
> To raise my face, I did not dare look up
> Lest her bright eyes like sparrows should fly in
> My windows of discovery and shrill 'Sin'!
>
> *(Georgian Poetry 1911–12, p. 113)*

However, the formalizing processes intervene more lightly
than in Hardy or Graves between the poem and the particular
personal situation from which, like so much of Lawrence's
writing, it springs (in this case, Lawrence's relationship as a
young man with Louie Burrows). James Reeves has described
the poem as 'a sort of psychological short story in verse' (*D. H.
Lawrence: Selected Poems*, London, Heinemann, 1951, p. xiii).
Lawrence is an heir to Hardy in writing poems which are, as
here, like scenes from novels (and novels which are like
extended poems – the poems often seem to need reading in
continuous sequences like a narrative), but the autobiographical source is more overt. It is Lawrence who gives us Georgian
'direct experience' – 'a consuming interest in life' – at its most
extreme. And this requires a verse-technique which is experimental in a manner different from the Modernism of Eliot or
Pound.

The pert, searching verse-movement, disrupting metric
expectations (again like Hardy), helps activate images of
peering and enquiring. Oddities of grammar like the pedantic
'Lest her bright eyes ... should', figures which have almost the
shock of conceits ('eyes like sparrows'; 'windows of discovery')
give us the intent effort of watching and seeking-out. There is a
tense note of sexual curiosity, at once inhibited and unguarded,

but it is a poem about *discovery* in larger ways: 'Things I was out
to find.' The unrestrained way Lawrence is moving forward
the Romantic obsession with inward discovery is felt in the
state of violence which the poem repeatedly approaches: verbal
strain like the archaic 'reiver' to describe the cuckoo (a bird
itself an emblem of violation), or the barely suppressed violence in such lines as:

> my own throat in her power
> Strangled, my heart swelled up so full
> As if it would burst its wineskin in my throat ...

> A brown bee pulling apart
> The closed flesh of the clover ...

> like a weapon my hand stood white and keen,
> And I held the choked flower-serpent in its pangs
> Of mordant anguish ...

This expresses the sexual frustration, but it also marks the urge
to perceive and feel newly, in a way which is like a new life – to
undergo the 'pangs' of birth. This and the intensely *personal*
quality are interwoven aspects of the same urge, because the
intimacy and immediacy of 'direct experience' are a radical
challenge to established forms and orthodoxies of all kinds. The
Georgian image of sunlight between old stone walls comes to
life in 'stood as in a cup', is felt as personally, sensuously, *newly*
apprehended; 'cup' recurs a number of times (a kind of leitmo-
tif, Gilbert points out), suggesting something not yet quite, but
on the brink of being, possessed. This urge deepens and intensifies – repetition and rhyme not only imparting intensity but
helping create the quality of a rite – into one towards a kind of
sacrificial experience, a dark ecstasy of destruction and disintegration, implied in that violent strangling and choking and
pulling-apart, and in references to a darkness which is also rich
and fructifying:

> And in the dark I did discover
> Things I was out to find ...
> This bird, this rich
> Sumptuous central grain,
> This mutable witch ...

> This clot of light,
> This core of night.

> Till her dark deeps shook with convulsive thrills, and the dark
> Of her spirit wavered like water thrilled with light ...

This is the characteristic Lawrence see-saw, taken over from the traditional Romantic conflicts, between the dark, corruptive side of the psyche and its creative, healing side. 'Cruelty and Love' was the original title of the poem; that sex itself, the sexual struggle between male and female, might be destructive is openly allowed here. The potentially dangerous and destructive – what is psychic threat in other poets – is delved eagerly into by Lawrence; there are no embargoes, moral or other, on what the poet is 'out to find'.

'Snap-Dragon', to adapt A. Alvarez, is 'emotional realism',[28] a vivid dramatization, in which the formal procedures of the verse co-operate, of common and recognizable subjective experience – of youthful sexual enquiry and awakening (naturally accompanied by a certain half-smothered, half-admitted violence of emotion). Both Lawrence and Graves came to place the man–woman relationship at the very centre of things; it is what everything of value and importance turns upon. Its pursuit, as Ellman and Feidelson said of the pursuit of 'totality of self', amounts to an almost religious enterprise; indeed, for Lawrence and Graves it is inseparable from the pursuit of subjective wholeness. Of course, this reflects a general movement in modern life towards intensified valuing of personal relationship, and it is not to deplore this movement to note that personal relationship is thus filling the vacuum left by the discrediting of old systems of belief and value (and having to satisfy unprecedented demands and expectations). Clearly, too, such valuing tends to place primacy on intense present experience, rather than some ultimate 'fruit'. However, the subjectivism of 'Snap-Dragon' is too extreme for it to be possible to leave the poem there. What the poetry's obsessiveness, its violences and dislocations, its fervid insistence on repetition and recurrence, seem to signify is that with Lawrence the sought obliteration of self in nature or sex is only a means of sharpening the *consciousness of* self. The suspension or hovering of consciousness is suggested in lines which recall Bottomley's 'Netted Strawberries':

> Again, I saw a brown bird hover
> Over the flowers at my feet;
> I felt a brown bird hover
> Over my heart, and sweet
> Its shadow lay on my heart.

This again seems akin to negative capability. ('As if it would burst its wine-skin in my throat' looks more than a chance echo of Keats.)[29] The poem's structure works against resolution; it circles, moves in fluid loops and eddies, nothing brought fully to completion, the ecstatic swoonings almost an end in themselves. The poem see-saws between impassioned energy and this potent state of hovering, of the lapsing, passive, negated self. This latter state, though, certainly isn't Hardy's 'nostalgia for unconsciousness': the poet avows in his final line that 'death I know is better than not-to-be', he would rather be irrevocably dead than enduring any kind of half-consciousness or death-in-life. Rather, to use Clarke's terms, it's a 'dissolving of the hard, intact ready-defined ego' in the search for 'a deeper consciousness'. Nevertheless, the poem is a kind of flight from the outer and objective world; a vigorous attempt to embrace the flame and the darkness *within*.

Blackmur distinguishes between poems by Lawrence in which the self is the radial point, where there is a radiating outwards, and those in which self is the focal point, where everything moves from the outer inwards. Lawrence's nature poetry, I've said, seeks a reaching-out to unlikeness-to-self. The hovering state in 'Snap-Dragon' – both a nature poem and love poem – seems to involve some such reaching out for annihilation of self in the other. At the same time, though, there is the Lawrentian *conflict* with the other; antagonistic wills rear up against each other – 'Until her pride's flag, smitten, cleaved down to the staff'. It is a classic Lawrence situation: the self which seeks to be more triumphantly self contradicts the self which seeks to be lost in other. Of course, this *is* a problem of consciousness, peculiarly so since Descartes and as a result of the cultural and historical developments I have touched on; it is only Lawrence's vividness which is extraordinary, one might say. But as we've seen, the effect is one of extremity, reflecting the general acuteness of the problem for the modern poet. In seeking to be more fully self, Lawrence finds self ever less stable and coherent, less resolved, more polymorphous; at most, the losing in other only seems an attempt at disintegrating the old self in order to renew the self. Book after book shows that the movement outwards was important for Lawrence, but it's difficult to see that consciousnesses which are radically unlike each other are ever brought into union in his poetry, even in that where self is the 'radial point'. What a poem like 'Snake' so finely accomplishes is the experience of the beast utterly separate from and unabsorbed by the human consciousness. Lawrence feels so hyper-acutely the foreignness of what is not himself. This is a unique strength; nobody else has written poems like 'Snake' or, for that matter, like 'Snap-Dragon'. But objects outside him remain for Lawrence 'isolated absolutes' because he cannot imagine likeness or congruity with anything like the intense clarity that he can separateness, and because his unmitigated insistence on the ceaseless flux of immediate experience denies the fixed *connections* of stable structures. Though in 'Snap-Dragon' there is movement outwards, though the young man and woman commune and interact in a sense – perhaps the way the woman is brought to confront sexual feelings accomplishes at least some breaking-out of self-containment – the couple remain in a state of suspended and unstable relationship. Indeed, the speaker's sense of male triumph, though it is seen as ephemeral and part of the natural give-and-take of sexual relationship (Lawrence is far from being unsubtle or insensitive about such things), tends to put the focus back on the relentless 'I' of the poem, which remains its centre; it is poetry not of solitariness but of solipsism.

Robert Graves did not need to seek the darkness within; he was propelled willy-nilly on a short cut to it by the wretched realities of the First World War. He spent the next twenty years or so building a psychic and imaginative structure which would enable him to live with this experience; his other world, or other consciousness, had to be a 'place' in which the pain and horror could be insulated, rendered harmless. Psychic threat is penned in, not admitted and engaged in Lawrence's fashion. In 'Outlaws', from his 1920 volume *Country Sentiment* (a title which represented an attempt by Graves to escape the horrors of war but attached to a volume which, with half-conscious irony, actually announced Graves's apostasy from the rustic Georgian sentiment with which as a youthful poet he had associated himself), two distinct areas of consciousness seem to co-exist: that of daylight vision, 'the eye', the rational self; and that which is 'beyond sight', the topsy-turvy world of the outlaws or 'old gods', the suppressed irrational self. The struggle to keep the rational mind from submerging in the 'nets of murk', the 'sea of black' – the 'neurasthenia' produced by Graves's war experiences[30] – is manifested in the fierce grip of the ballad stanza and the desperately emphatic accenting of the lines. But we can already see in the

> Old gods almost dead, malign
>   Starving for unpaid dues:
> Incense and fire, salt, blood and wine
>   And a drumming muse,[31]

a preliminary appearance of the pagan iconography of the White Goddess theory, and it is *The White Goddess*, called by Daniel Hoffman 'perhaps the most extreme statement of Romantic primitivism we are likely to have' (p. viii), which must certainly be seen, for all the problems with which it confronts the reader who is a mere ordinary mortal, as the successful culmination of a series of attempts by Graves not only to cope with his war-induced neuroses but also to reconcile the conflicts more deeply embedded in his nature. Like other Georgians Graves was profoundly conditioned by his class upbringing; the nursery, the public school, the regiment, the university, all generate nostalgic affections and clan loyalties. But in his case, as he testifies in *Goodbye to All That* (the significance of this indispensable book's title needs no emphasis), this conditioning was traumatically confronted by other realities, those of war and sex. His relationship and collaboration with Laura Riding between 1926 and 1939 were both a symptom of his deeper neurosis and an attempt to address it; the distress she caused him, and the extraordinary resources it called up in him, are second in significance only to those of the war. He was only ever able to cobble together an uneasy repose in the later poetry. The effort always shows; there's often a hint of hysteria, always a sense, beneath the formal elegance and technical accomplishment, of fiercely controlling himself; something in his careful structures which defies symmetry, a limp, a healed-over wound. The dislocations of ballad metre in the quatrain above are an example, at once cunningly effective yet as if unavoidably compelled. His abruptly curtailed poems, however urbane, have the effect of being too painful to go on.

In the well-known poem 'The Cool Web' Graves sees the rationalizing structures of language, and by implication the ordered structures of poetry itself, as a defence against psychic chaos. This need to situate a filter or medium between the acutely sensitive poet and the rawness of direct experience – a need felt, it seems to me, by all those modern poets who in some sense seek 'impersonality' – is obviously a contraposition to the kind of plunging into a sensuous and psychic maelstrom we witness in 'Snap-Dragon'. While, though, there is this affinity with Modernist impersonality, Graves's 'reverence for the logic of language' (Hoffman, p. 176), his classically orthodox and lucid syntax and sequential organization of the poem, oppose Modernist fragmentation at the same time as embodying a formalist outlook which is the obverse of Lawrence's, but which answers to implacable urgencies in Graves himself. His imagination was in its own way as 'dispossessed' as Lawrence's, his inclinations as iconoclastic, but where Lawrence lets his imagination go forth, so to speak, revelling in its dispossession, Graves seeks the 'bliss of repossession' ('Down', p. 22). His colloquialism, his 'language close to common speech', is literary and class-restricted beside Lawrence's; his experimental use of an accentual line in reaction against smooth iambics is less radical than the experimental freedoms Lawrence takes; his White Goddess has much in common with traditional *femmes fatales* of literature. He constructs a formalist art of his own design out of largely traditional materials; he repossesses rather than making it new. In the aftermath of the first world war all serious poets were faced with reconstruction; Graves's labour of remaking out of such shattered materials was heroic, and (later) influential. But there is, paradoxically in view of some of the bitter experience of his life and of a stubbornly non-conformist side to his temperament, an essential *literariness* about his sensibility which includes a love of the exotic and the fantastic to link him, however distantly, with Georgians like W. J. Turner and Walter de la Mare. In his later work, in fact, he becomes the ultimate Georgian essentialist – a tougher, more intelligent and imaginatively fertile Bottomley – distilling out in classically formed concentration the timeless essences of man's relationship with the universe. This is sometimes seen as a kind of final realism, but equally, and perhaps more crucially, it's a disengagement from the modern world. Form becomes the meaning of the poem, it fixates, it denies the polymorphous historical flux. Graves constantly *acknowledges* modern life, but in a way that amounts to a kind of disdainful brushing-aside. His long, enislanded sojourn on Mallorca is symbolic of a self-exclusion from contemporaneity which is also deeply Romantic. His autobiographical account of his early years, for all its value *as* history, is a way of saying good-bye to history. That he wrote *historical* novels – for all their entertaining professionalism and ingenuity – permitted him not to take novel-writing seriously. Even *The Long Week-End*, 'A Social History of Great Britain 1918–1939', again a book of some value, documents the two decades between the wars with a dry relish which amounts to a dismissal of the frivolities of contemporary history; Laura Riding is celebrated for her recognition that 'historical Time had effectively come to an end' (p. 200).

This brings us to the important affinity between Lawrence and Graves, their attraction to a 'Romantic primitivism': both poets turn, in Hoffman's phrase, to 'archetypal, often atavistic emotion' (p. viii) as a way of disintegrating the abstractions of modern civilization, as an answer to what they see as its living death. It's a renewed form of Romantic alienation, and the old myths of death and rebirth, with their ritualist and orgiastic elements, the 'barbarous knowledge' they offer, have a luminous appeal for men who feel shaken to the roots. (I've quoted Barthes's point that myth 'organizes a world without contradictions'; he refers also to the 'major power of myth: its recurrence', p. 135.) If *The White Goddess* is a monument to this Romantic primitivist interest and feeling, so is Lawrence's *Apocalypse* (the relatedness of the two works has not, as far as I know, been much commented on). Both are indebted to Frazer, though Graves goes in for a brand of scholarship which is at once pernickety, audacious and wayward, while Lawrence's method is more intuitional; 'unlike Lawrence', says John B. Vickery, Graves 'reflects *The Golden Bough* less by a process of casual absorption and empathy than by an exhaustively detailed study of the text itself'.[32] The way the mythopoeic impulse works differently in each poet but finally amounts to the same self-isolating quest for the timeless can be plotted if we consider Lawrence's 'Medlars and Sorb-Apples' (1921), which makes use of the Orphic myth, together with Robert Graves's 'Instructions to the Orphic Adept' (1944).[33]

I agree with R. P. Blackmur that in poems like 'Medlars and Sorb-Apples' self is for Lawrence the exclusive focal point; I disagree that it is one of those lacking structure to the point of 'hysteria'.[34] All poems are stylizations, irrespective of whether the quality of emotion or experience their patternings construct be 'personal' or 'impersonal': I want to locate here a distinction precisely in that constructed quality. The very informal, slightly whimsical jottings which open the poem are not only an example, as Graham Hough puts it, of Lawrence's 'mode of vision – in rapid intuitive glimpses – ... represented on the page by the arrangement of the lines' (p. 206), but are *structured* by the declarative insistence of their own sensory peculiarity and idiosyncrasy of vision:

> I love you, rotten,
> Delicious rottenness.
>
> I love to suck you out from your skins
> So brown and soft and coming suave,
> So morbid, as the Italians say.[35]

Graves's opening, by contrast, uses a formal and literary rhetoric:

> So soon as ever your mazed spirit descends
> From daylight into darkness, Man, remember
> What you have suffered here in Samothrace,
> What you have suffered.

(p. 159)

Like Lawrence's, Graves's poem combines vivid realization with idiosyncrasy of vision, and uses structural repetition. But his repetitions have an incantatory quality (this is among what he calls his 'magical' poems), prayer-like, generalizing, removing us from the directness of intimate personal experience. The poem is 'in part translated from the *Timpone Grande* and *Compagno* Orphic tablets', and hence, in what seems a characteristically Gravesian pose, can claim a certain impersonal authority. (In the matter of what constitutes 'authority' Graves is highly original.) The Orphic Adept is being formally instructed in what to do when his 'mazed spirit' descends, after death, into Hades. Lawrence's poem, on the other hand, launches out in an erratic way from its spontaneous, acute sensation of the rotten fruit, worries away at it in a characteristically eddying and revolving way, until the mythological dimension is arrived at almost by chance:

> What is it?
> What is it, in the grape turning raisin,
> In the medlar, in the sorb-apple,
> Wineskins of brown morbidity,
> Autumnal excrementa;
> What is it that reminds us of white gods?

The notion of initiation into mysteries is presented with a similar, almost surrealist, sharpness of definition in each poem, but again Graves's lines have a more formal and 'literary' measure than Lawrence's: 'They will welcome you with fruit and flowers, / And lead you toward the ancient dripping hazel ...' In Lawrence, seemingly unpremeditated discoveries replace the foreknowledge of Graves's adept, but the device of repetition, like a winetaster rolling samples on his palate, creates our experience of these discoveries just as a more formally rhetorical repetition creates Graves's oracular voice.

The theme of rebirth pervades Graves's work; 'The Survivor', for example, perhaps recalls his experience of reading his own newspaper obituary after having been reported dead during the war. The adept being enjoined to 'remember / What you have suffered' picks up the memory theme of his *Pier-Glass* poems twenty years earlier (the ghostly woman 'Drawn by a thread of time-sunk memory'). The landscape through which the adept must pass is a Romantic country of the mind – occurring in many Graves poems (a salient example is the earlier 'The Terraced Valley'). The details here have some likeness to Baudelaire's 'artificial paradises' of which I shall speak later:

> The Halls of Judgement shall loom up before you,
> A miracle of jasper and of onyx.
> To the left hand there bubbles a black spring
> Overshadowed with a great white cypress.
> Avoid this spring, which is Forgetfulness;

Instead, at another pool, 'the pool of Memory', the adept must reply to certain riddles, the answers to which will have been supplied by the oracle:

> Then you shall answer: 'I am parched with thirst.
> Give me to drink . . .
> I also am of your thrice-blessed kin,
> Child of the three-fold Queen of Samothrace;
> Have made full quittance for my deeds of blood . . .'

This might be read as Graves's own effort to purge himself of the burden of guilt which the 'deeds of blood' he committed during the war have left him with (he said long afterwards that he felt he had been guilty of murder). He has sought absolution by dedicating himself to the true Muse ('three-fold Queen'); and the consequent escape from the bonds of Time is conveyed by imagery familiar in a similar connection in both Yeats and Eliot, imagery of the wheel – specifically, here, the Orphic wheel of birth, death and rebirth:[36]

> But they will ask you yet: 'What of your feet?'
> You shall reply: 'My feet have borne me here
> Out of the weary wheel, the circling years,
> To that still, spokeless wheel: – Persephone.
> Give me to drink!'

Not, at the still centre, Yeats's *Anima Mundi* or Eliot's Christian God, but Persephone – an aspect of the White Goddess. In this moment of visionary experience, the adept achieves immortality, to become one of the 'lords of the uninitiated / Twittering ghosts', and an oracle. The poem's final lines seem to be a metaphor for poetic inspiration; the poet, after his visionary journey beyond Time, is 'reborn' into ordinary consciousness, but may now *command* his experience – is freed of the 'twittering ghosts' which have haunted his subjective existence and helped make it unmanageable – and, taking 'serpent shapes', may speak with the voice of an oracle in formally achieved poems about that experience:

> Pronouncing oracles from tall white tombs
> By the nymphs tended. They with honey water
> Shall pour libations to your serpent shapes,
> That you may drink.

Subjectivity has been stabilized, a *transcendent* self has been fixed.

This close to which the poem is brought has a calm hieratic beauty, and like 'Snap-Dragon' it can be read as a dramatization of common experience, in this case the universal human desire to cheat death (and this aim of evading mortality is firmly in the Romantic tradition). But I have had to read in (with the help of Graves's autobiographical and other writings) the poem's 'real' source in the poet's subjective life, in his personal psychological problems, to see it as employing the mythic material to enact the drama of his own consciousness. Preserving a Georgian sense of craftsmanship, Graves called Lawrence's poems 'sketches for poems, but nothing more'.[37] But the fastidiousness of his own art, of arrangement, pruning, modulation, may lead us to suspect Graves of dodging his experience, even of what C. H. Sisson has called 'superficiality';[38] mustn't there be an element of pose in a poet who contrives to combine a stiff upper-lip with wearing his heart on his sleeve? Yes, but the Romantic pose is symptomatic of the inhibition about direct feeling, the defensiveness against his own emotionalism; it is essential to the construction of a way of *living with* his experience and the raw intensity of his own emotional life. Lawrence, by contrast, is 'peculiarly unembarrassed and open about his feelings' (Alvarez, p. 148). For him, as he says in the *Georgian Poetry* review, 'Everything that ever was thought and ever will be thought, lies in this body of mine' (p. xix), hence the only route to the sacred mysteries is through the drama of his own flesh and blood, his own urges and sensations, a reckless exposing of his subjective being.

The verse of 'Medlars and Sorb-Apples' moves slowly, lingeringly; the evocation of the peculiar, death-like flavour of the fruits slowly transmutes into a prolonged savouring of isolated selfhood, imagined as an initiation into the 'wonderful' experiences of the underworld:

> Sorb-apples, medlars with dead crowns.
> I say, wonderful are the hellish experiences,
> Orphic, delicate
> Dionysos of the Underworld.

The poem seems to express a positive lust for dark places. Harry T. Moore places it with other poems which deal with 'female secretiveness' and 'the Underworld of love',[39] but Lawrence plunges here into an even more total human underworld, the private places of decay and corruption. Attention is often drawn to Lawrence's distinction in the 1920 essay *Pornography and Obscenity* (London, Faber and Faber, 1929) between the creative and the excremental flows, but sometimes, as here, he seems to see the creative and the excremental as inextricable aspects of the same vital principle.[40] 'Parting' in the poem affirms the activity of leave-taking – 'Orphic farewell, and farewell, and farewell' – as an absolute good since it frees us from the deadness of the fixed and the stable; but it also seems closely related to the 'departure' Lawrence talks of in 'The Crown', to what he calls there 'the temporal flux of corruption'. 'In the soft and shiny voluptuousness of decay ... there is the sign of the Godhead.'[41] The encounter with the 'white gods' of this poem seems an affirmation of godhead in the excremental flow, in the rich glut of rottenness, godhead known through voluptuous surrender to the 'Autumnal excrementa ... Flux of autumn', and of this too as a source of creative regeneration. The dilating swell of the lines, the sweep of intoxication, grow richly orchestrated; repetition and rhythmic recurrence strain to fuse in an ecstatic unity (which, in this case, makes one think of the egotistical sublime) the ideas of 'parting' and of, again, new encounter or discovery:

> A kiss, and a spasm of farewell, a moment's orgasm of rupture,
> Then along the damp road alone, till the next turning.
> And there, a new partner, a new parting, a new unfusing into
>   twain,
> A new gasp of further isolation,
> A new intoxication of loneliness, among decaying, frost-cold
>   leaves.

The Gravesian rebirth has to do with a return – as, it's true, a special kind of being, an elect servant of the Muse – to ordinary social living, of which he grudgingly concedes the need. In 'Medlars and Sorb-Apples', decay and parting are a dissolution out of which the Lawrentian phoenix of self rearises, foreshadowing such famous poems as his 'The Ship of Death'. For Lawrence, modern social living has become an irrelevance, an attitude tonally conveyed by the anarchic surges and swirls, the intoxicated exclamatoriness, of the verse; the rebirth is into a greater sufficiency of self, into greater and more joyful isolation – 'The *sono io* of perfect drunkenness / Intoxication of final loneliness'. But 'rebirth' is a tricky term with Lawrence. We might notice that despite a heightened, surreal clarity giving a sense, as in the 'Instructions', of dimensions beyond everyday consciousness, detail such as the 'damp road' and 'decaying, frost-cold leaves' not only provides the physical sense of a 'gasp' caused by cold air, but also a shock of recognition in the midst of the intoxicated raptures – the vigorous, down-to-earth Lawrence continuously relocating his poem in the ordinary physical world. 'I cross into another world', says Lawrence in 'New Heaven and Earth', but he is risen, not born again, has not shed the flesh and blood – a prophetic resonance sounds in the echoes of Isaiah 65:

> risen and setting my foot on another world
> risen, accomplishing a resurrection
> risen, not born again, but risen, body the same as before,
> new beyond knowledge of newness, alive beyond life . . .
>
> (p. 256)

A related idea occurs in an essay 'The Risen Lord':

> But floated up into heaven as flesh-and-blood, and never set down again – this nothing in all our experience will ever confirm . . . Flesh and blood belong to the earth, and only to the earth. We know it.[42]

Lawrence's imagination baulks at the notion of spirit *distinct* from the bodily. Such passages, though using the Christian imagery in which Lawrence's imagination was steeped as he grew up, are, like Graves's mythology, neo-pagan in feeling – or, as Hough puts it, 'Lawrence's philosophy is basically naturalistic' (p. 223). Alvarez's way of putting it is that 'Lawrence's mysticism is merely his first-handedness' (p. 156). It's true that Lawrence heightens and intensifies physical sensation to a point where many critics reach for the term 'mysticism':

> Going down the strange lanes of hell, more and more
>   intensely alone,
> The fibres of the heart parting one after the other
> And yet the soul continuing, naked-footed, ever more
>   vividly embodied
> Like a flame blown whiter and whiter
> In a deeper and deeper darkness
> Ever more exquisite, distilled in separation.
>
> So, in the strange retorts of medlars and sorb-apples
> The distilled essence of hell.

But the 'resolve' which 'forms' is a 'state of feeling-awareness'; the soul itself is 'embodied' ('naked-footed'): the 'flame', however traditional an emblem of the spiritual, seems palpable and animate rather than flamily evanescent – the organic thrust and swell of the verse is too material, it forbids really

numinous emotion. And after all, it is the rotting *flesh* of the
fruits which is the condition on which the whole visionary
experience depends. It is what Lawrence wanted poetry to do:
'it makes a new effort of attention, and "discovers" a new
world within the known world' (ed. Beal, p. 90. Gilbert's *Acts
of Attention* aptly takes its title from this passage). Graves's
imagination, too, is bound by materiality, eschews the ineffable; his treatment of myth may even look rationalistic like
Frazer's, except that it is the atavistic emotion of myth which
excites him. 'I am no mystic', he asserted in the 1960 'Post-
script' to *The White Goddess*. The 'trick of time' which he
experiences (see 'The Terraced Valley', p. 107), translating
him into some bizarre other, seemingly extra-historical, dimension of consciousness, is a psychological peculiarity, fuelled by
painful maladjustment and unbearable memories with which
he can in some sense come to terms once he discovers the
mythological 'faith' which allows the suffering to be contemplated without intolerable distress. He wants this faith to
provide a refuge, an imaginative release from time-bound
historical existence, yet his sense of reality – it is one of the
conflicts in his nature – is relentlessly empiricist, rooted in the
concrete 'hedge-rose' and 'thrush's melody' to which he symbolically returns after death in 'The Survivor'. Despite points
of contact between these two poets and the work of Yeats, Eliot
and Pound, Yeats's occultism and Eliot's mysticism are of no
more use to them than Modernist structures. The examples of
Lawrence and Graves, I suggest, offer correctives to the mysti-
fying tendencies in those major Modernists (which I shall look
at in other chapters). Georgian poetry, after all, not only put
'interest in life' before style, but was a rejection of both Naturalist positivism and Symbolist transcendentalism in favour of a
concentration on the psychological and the life of the senses.[43]
What this leaves us with, though, is a contradiction between
the materiality of each poet's responses and perceptions, rooted
in Lawrence's 'magnificent here and now', and the longing of
each to be free of his material historical situation.

'Snap-Dragon', 'Medlars and Sorb-Apples', and Graves's
'Instructions' all have a kind of ritual or sacrificial experience,

one involving what seems appropriately called 'archetypal, atavistic emotion', at its centre. In addition, the last two enact a classic process of the Romantic sensibility, of which I think Keats's famous Moneta passage in his revised *Fall of Hyperion* provides an example. In the persona of the Orphic adept, Graves, like Keats's poet, attains through ordeal a visionary moment; the self of Lawrence's poem similarly undergoes a visionary journey. What I see the poetry doing in all three instances is enacting a heightened drama of consciousness in which the aim is to gain a foothold in the unmanageable flux of experience, to gain mastery of experience which is in some sense difficult or recalcitrant. It is what we have seen Hardy, too, trying to do. That the drama has to be engaged inwardly is inherent in the felt dissociation of inner and outer worlds. The chaos, as Lawrence called it, indubitably exists in both: 'The chaos which we have got used to we call a cosmos. The unspeakable inner chaos of which we are composed we call consciousness ...' (ed. Beal, p. 90). But that outer world is almost by definition unappropriable; the necessary transcendence and transformation can only be peformed inwardly.[44]

The emphasis on memory is significant. Romanticism crucially includes disconnection from the past in its sense of breakdown of continuities, even of the individual from his own past; much Romantic historicizing involves an effect of abrupt disjunction from an earlier phase of history, now set in contradistinction to the present; *The Prelude* will re-forge connection with the poet's own past; Hardy feels severed from an earlier self. At the still centre for Keats was Moneta, the Goddess of Memory; Lawrence's poem turns on the 'powerful reminiscent flavour' of the rotten fruits (a kind of phenomenon made famous by Proust). A 'preoccupation with memory' was what a 1930s critic, Geoffrey Bullough, found in Georgian poetry: 'a desire to investigate the half-apprehended notions, the obstinate questionings and blind misgivings of sensitive and introspective souls'.[45] One recalls that the lines in the 'Intimations of Immortality' Ode from which the phrase 'obstinate questionings' comes also speak of 'shadowy recollections'; clearly, remembrance is crucially implicated in that whole 'sensitive and introspective' enterprise of Romantic and modern poetry of which Wordsworth is an initiator. When Graves, in *The White Goddess*, comes to formulate his theory of poetic composition he connects the creative act with what he calls 'proleptic thought' and 'analeptic thought', both of which involve 'a suspension of time', and adds, 'one can have memory of the future as well as of the past'.[46] The centrality of the kind of sensibility characterized by the egotistical sublime or by negative capability again becomes evident; the creative act, renewal of the visionary gleam, involves a passive 'lapsing-out' of normal, time-imbued consciousness, and 'memory' takes on an expanded connotation – not just ordinary everyday recall, but a suspended state of rich creative ferment which may involve oracular knowledge of the future or the kind of journeying into territories beyond the here and now imagined in 'Medlars and Sorb-Apples', as well as, in Graves's words, 'recovery of lost events'. As I've suggested, I see Hardy as constructing a personal version of this expanded form of remembrance; he doesn't in any ordinary sense *remember* Emma Gifford in a poem like 'After a Journey', he *recovers* her, she becomes emotionally and psychically real, re-realized to him – even halfway to being physically re-embodied. He can then carry that realization back into his ordinary time-determined life and continue 'faltering forward'; this has been made at least bearable.

There was always, of course, the element of escapism in the Romantics' interest in the past. The effort of remembrance may have to do, like the interest in myth itself, with a yearning to recapture some supposed 'forgotten' unalienated state of the distant human past, like that 'sense-awareness, and sense-knowledge of the ancients' Lawrence speaks of in *Apocalypse* (p. 42). Yet as William Barrett, with impeccable logic, has pointed out: 'our psychological problems cannot be solved by a regression to a past state in which they had not yet been brought into being'.[47] I want to discuss shortly the implications of this as an evasion of present reality. But psychoanalytic theory in the present century has been based largely on the concept of memory as selective, constituting a truncated, incomplete self, excluding from consciousness the other. The pervasive effort in Romantic and modern poetry is to totalize memory in order to impart imaginative and psychic coherence to the poet's subjective life; remembrance helps create and sustain identity for the alienated poet, and it imbues the processes of cognition and envisioning with concreteness in a way which is fundamentally involved with poetic creation itself, the poetic creation which is what, if anything, can give the poet in a hostile society his 'meaning'. Lawrence's poetry may not be so fraught with retrospection as Hardy's or Yeats's or Edward Thomas's, or with Eliot's themes of 'memory and desire'; his famous battle with nostalgia in 'Piano' is in one sense a clearing of the decks for his concentration on the intensely lived present moment. He never imagines consciousness as other than fluid and protean. Nevertheless, 'powerful, reminiscent flavour' is a crucial phrase in the effort it indicates to place and identify some elusive echoing intuition, to make the elements of subjective consciousness cohere. 'Remembrance is like direct feeling', wrote William James, 'its object is suffused with a warmth and intimacy to which no object of mere conception ever attains.'[48] W. H. Auden, though with importantly different inferences, also saw individual consciousness as constituted by 'doings memorized and *felt*' (*New Year Letter*: my italics). At the level of empirical psychology alone, it is acute of Graves to suggest in the 'Instructions' that we become fully conscious – even, in a sense, cheat death – by memory. And direct feeling, a revolt against 'mere conception', is where Georgian poetry starts. I've noted the centrality for both Lawrence and Graves of the man–woman relationship, and the mysteries of sexual love, are of course, traditionally beyond the reach of conceptual understanding. And those mysteries are subsumed in the felt mystery of consciousness itself, its resistance, for all the attempts, to conceptualization. It is through such processes, at once concretizing and 'visionary', immediate and retrospective, that experience, for the acutely conscious poet, acquires palpable shape, becomes manageable.

VI

The example of Hardy's poetry offered a willed and defensive schematization of reality at odds with a sensitive openness to a more complex, plural reality, in particular to the flux of the inner life. From Georgian origins informed by Hardy's example it was possible for, on the one hand, the unstable openness of Lawrence's poetic, and on the other, the formalized stasis of Graves's, to develop.

Both poets seem to believe that man cannot be reborn into a new purified and vital existence without a voyage through the dark places of the psyche, which may involve some sort of Orphic-like blood-rite. In Graves's case the wretched miseries of the first world war were, perhaps, a kind of actual blood-rite; and we know that Lawrence, though not involved in active service, was also deeply affected by the war. It may be that this belief should be taken more figuratively than literally,[49] but it expresses an attitude of Romantic primitivism which stands in a problematical relationship to the actual forces and events of twentieth-century history. Since our century has seen its share of these 'dark places of the psyche', is this focus not regressive and morbid, even perverse? Or, since the history of our century has abundantly shown that such dark places really exist, can it be said that in exploring them Lawrence and Graves are situating and diagnosing its crisis – with particular effectiveness, because they are such impressive realists of the inner world? That by contesting their time poets can be of their time is a point I have made in my Introduction.

Yet, in revolt against the whole state of things which, most critically, manifested itself in the war, Lawrence and Graves opt for disengagement from *history*. Their work finally seems to me to fail in bridging the gap between inner and outer, not to bring them into dynamic relationship. It runs into that impasse which Stuart M. Sperry, in an interesting essay, calls Romantic Irony,[50] a 'kind of irresolution', a 'sense of indeterminacy'. This ultimate impotence of the Romantic imagination is what, if we wish, we can see the snows of Bottomley's 'The End of the World' as expressing. It seems that creative energy on the one hand, creative passivity (negative capability or whatever one calls it) on the other, finally become a jammed polarity. Graves retreats for virtually the latter half of his poetic career into the circularity of 'one story and one story only',[51] Lawrence, in his imaginative life at least, drives further and further into a 'final loneliness'.

Many solutions, [Graves has written] have been found to the problems of how to separate oneself from the non-poetic world without turning anti-social. The fact is, that in this carefully organized country no poet can altogether avoid the responsibilities of citizenship ... (*The Crowning Privilege*, p. 103)

The problem is intelligently acknowledged, and as a citizen Graves took honourable stands. He was resolutely opposed to Fascism (of which he saw the Franco version at first hand in Mallorca), loathed anti-semitism, was staunchly egalitarian and, of course, pro-feminist. He made clear his dislike of Yeats's, Eliot's and Pound's politics. But the attitude to the responsibilities of citizenship is undoubtedly somewhat grudging. Graves does feel that it is the poet's primary obligation to *separate* himself from the 'non-poetic world'. The 'middle terms of actual human societies ... are at best contingent or secondary'. He would much rather get away from the kind of 'carefully organized country' where such responsibilities press to one, Mallorca, where, presumably, he found them doing so less. There is a disjunction of poetic and non-poetic worlds; Graves's writings leave us in no doubt that his rapt experience of his other world is what he really lives for; it is there that meaning resides. His mythological 'faith', moreover, is not one that can place him in a community of belief, as unlikely to be widely shared as Yeats's, or as Pound's economic creed or Eliot's rarefied philosophical Christianity. There is also, as I've said, an important sense in which Graves goes beyond even 'the experience itself' to distil out too concentratedly the essence of experience, so that he becomes too removed from contemporaneity to be, after all, a 'modern'. He is too successful in writing 'timeless' poetry. On the face of it, 'passivity' may not seem a Gravesian trait, yet his stress on a necessary poetic state of trance, and his insistence on unconditional submission

to the extra-historical power of his Goddess, seem a relinquish-
ment of commitment to courses of action in the contemporary
world. One might put it that exile and the White Goddess were
active existential choices; so they were, yet one might also see
them as made in order to obviate the further need for action
and choice. Each poem can now fatalistically recycle the same
patterned adventure; the well-made poem, with its carefully
functioning form and mannered purity of style, mimes an
inviolate stasis of consciousness, becomes a substitute for the
newly discovered.

For Lawrence, by contrast, there can be no stasis:

> We should ask for no absolutes, or absolute. Once and for all and for
> ever, let us have done with the ugly imperialism of any absolute ...
> All things flow and change, and even change is not absolute. The
> whole is a strange assembly of apparently incongruous parts, slipping
> past each other.[52]

The universe, as well as consciousness, in the 'Chaos in Poetry'
piece, are 'a strange and for ever surging chaos'. Here Lawrence may seem to welcome the pluralism, the epistemological
openness, now often felt to be our inescapable condition. And
he seeks, we've seen, a new world in the known world, not a
release from, a fixity transcending, the mutability of material
existence. The problem is that this seems to go beyond pluralism to anarchy, an anarchic infinity of possibility pursued, we
see in 'Medlars and Sorb-Apples' (with its limitless succession
of Underworld meetings with 'a new partner' and of 'a new
unfusing into twain'), exclusively within the self – totality of
self becomes infinity of self. In *Apocalypse*, though, he appears
set against any 'final loneliness' or sufficiency of self:

> What man most passionately wants is ... not his own isolate salvation
> of his 'soul' ... There is nothing of me that is alone and absolute
> except my mind ... So that my individualism is really an illusion. I
> am a part of the great whole, and I can never escape. But I *can* deny
> my connections, break them, and become a fragment. Then I am
> wretched. (p. 110)

What, then, *does* Lawrence aim at? If individualism is an
illusion and what is wanted is an unfragmented 'great whole',

how can all be a strange assembly of incongruous parts, a chaos? This 'great whole', coming, as I indicated at the outset, together with an apprehension of timeless 'origin', of a history-free consciousness, must, surely, militate towards closure, against free selfhood. The 'strange assembly', on the other hand, suggests a tyranny of openness, because no resolve *is* ever finally formed – it leaves no place for active choice and shaping. Mind, we see, is in both cases the enemy, wanting the absolute, but this seems a way of excluding volitional intelligence, conscious choice (and isn't the 'great whole' anyway a kind of absolute?). Lawrence's idea of an utter authenticity of selfhood which is at the same time belongingness at a deep level of being, even enchanced by that belongingness, is a powerful and important one. But he will press to extremes, into a contradiction both terms of which, though ostensibly liberating, constitute a kind of determinism; both work against a freely collaborative pluralism of 'citizenship'. Though written at different times, the impulse of such pronouncements, I think, is always against the dynamics of life in the socio-historical domain.

Lawrence's wanderings in the latter part of his life, his vain quest for a place and a community answering to an ideal vitalism of his imagination, and finally his illness and premature death, seem a symbolic confirmation of 'final loneliness'. Public hostility and incurable illness were, of course, more than symbolic forces to contend with, but there was an ever-increasing distance from his roots and from social relatedness. It is hardly necessary to stress how extraordinary this is in view of the quite exceptionally organic and actual feeling of community he shows in his earlier writings. A story like 'Daughters of the Vicar' clearly makes the wilful severing of oneself from the living community an act of psychic self-mutilation. Yet his later writings more and more displace 'the middle terms of actual human societies'. Something that Edward Thomas wrote in 1913, with remarkable insight, suggests that the problem was implicit in the very method of Lawrence's poetry, which

... makes us rather sharers in a process than witnesses of a result ... Mr. Lawrence writes in a concentration so absolute that the poetry is less questionable than the verse.[53]

Not only does art, arguably at least, require a 'result', but the obsession with 'flow and change', with process, with the indeterminate, is taken so far that it rules out the fixed structures (however tentative) of any kind of relatedness. Everything is judged by its effect as stimulus or irritant on himself. It's difficult to see how his anarchic and utterly personal proceeding can shape the basis for the necessary patternings of 'community' or a shared culture, how his inward revolution, unless in the most indirect ways, can reshape an outward world.

The ache for vital renewal is powerfully conveyed in Lawrence's 'The Ship of Death' and other late poems such as 'Shadows':

> then I must know that still
> I am in the hands of the unknown God,
> he is breaking me down to his own oblivion
> to send me forth on a new morning, a new man.

(p. 727)

But it is an *unknown* God; Lawrence can only insistently reiterate the word 'new' – what concrete form the renewal might take he does not and cannot know. The universe remains 'a strange assembly of apparently incongruous parts'; this is what the poetry vividly creates, whatever renewed vitality of civilization may be talked about in his, as in Graves's, various writings. With Graves, it is the poetic and non-poetic worlds which remain utterly incongruous. This is not to say, and I don't think I have implied, that the poetry of either Lawrence or Graves has no bearing on 'life', but outer worlds offer them no sure foothold; it is the inner world which is real, and as Graves says in 'Through Nightmare', 'There's no way in by history's road.' (The poem admires his muse's capacity to experience as a reality 'a lost and moated land' beyond time.) For all the directness and immediacy, the Romantic poet is still inalienably 'different', cut off, in his imaginative life at least, from ordinary men.

CHAPTER 2

Strangers to nature: modern nature poetry and the rural myth

Thus D. H. Lawrence, a miner's son, having acquired enough education to be able to write, was able to write with more verve than most of his contemporaries. He had not inherited the stale thought of a class. But on the other hand, for the reason that he moved out of his class, his thought and vision faded.

(*Modern Poetry*, p. 76)

It may seem a simple point, but in making it Louis MacNeice was appreciating an important source of Lawrence's strength. Lawrence grew up in closer touch with a real England, both industrial and agricultural, than virtually any other writer of his generation, and was able to express that reality with such freshness and 'verve' because he was unencumbered (in a way resistant to 'education') by the conditioned responses of a cultural establishment. It is not so much that his vision 'faded' as he travelled away from his roots, but that it became more and more internalized. Like the Romantic poets before him, he was always conscious of a 'social' mission, and creativity on the scale of Lawrence's (his surpassing achievement, the trio of great novels, falls outside my scope here) invariably refuses to be reduced to the measure of its detractors. But he repeats, I think one can generalize, a classic Romantic profile: what begins as a challenge, with revolutionary implications, to a social condition, withdraws to an inward or 'other' world. Marilyn Butler's *Romantics, Rebels and Reactionaries* emphasizes how threatening to the middle-class reading public which maintained English literary culture any programme for a 'language really used by men' was bound to be. It seems indisputable that a class hegemony of this kind had to be broken if a *modern* poetry, attuned to changed social and economic realities, was to be written. Robert Graves's deeply ingrained class-consciousness was traumatically shaken, with the result that he felt compelled to say *Good-bye to All That*; Edward Thomas's distinctive voice, as I shall discuss in my next chapter, partly derives from his estrangement from his class background. In a different way, the capacity of the expatriate Americans – Pound, H. D., Eliot – to redirect English poetry had to do with being outsiders.

Moreover, although always on friendly terms with Edward Marsh, Lawrence could not long remain in tune with what his Georgian Poetry enterprise came to represent. As a 'movement', Georgian Poetry was of limited force because Marsh and most of his contributors, despite their concern for 'realism', didn't know enough about the realities of their world. That this can be said of a man so involved in public affairs as Marsh (at the time, secretary to Winston Churchill, First Lord of the Admiralty) is perhaps symptomatic of what made possible the disaster of the Great War, and Rupert Brooke's cavalier attitude to that war (Brooke having been Marsh's original inspirer in founding *Georgian Poetry*) reinforces the impression of a failure of realism. So, too, do so many poems' remote, semi-mythical or rural-mythical settings. The kind of Georgian poet who produced these belonged, more or less, to the tradition of English literary gentleman. He was often a cultured and sensitive man who knew that changes were affecting his world, but there was a gentlemanly innocence about him which disabled him from compelling imaginative response to those changes. Bottomley's *King Lear's Wife*, for example, is an entirely willed and literary concoction, removed from any actual world or historical context. Even W. H. Davies, with his background as a down-and-out, and who wasn't innocent but sometimes skilfully deployed a rhetoric of innocence, aspired fervently to join this class.[1] Philip Larkin's brilliant use of the word 'innocence' in his 'MCMXIV' – not meaning any *ordinary* kind of innocence – speaks volumes about the state of English culture immediately prior to that date.

The Georgian, I've said, is a craftsman, cherishing traditional forms and, while disdaining the more extreme kinds of Romantic role-playing and aestheticism, a largely unexamined Romantic notion of the nature and role of poetry as offering truths of a vaguely spiritual and 'eternal' kind: as David Perkins puts it, 'poetry that concentrates on elemental human feeling and experience . . . ' (*A History of Modern Poetry*, p. 214). (Even Lawrence tended to see poetry as specialized and visionary in a way prose fiction isn't.) The Romantic otherworldliness had become orthodoxy and got a hold as a conditioning factor. The books were elegantly produced; they help witness to the way a cultured class preserved an Arts and Crafts ideal, along with a cult of an unspoilt rural England and a taste for the pre-industrial (a love of the picturesque and the simplifyingly 'elemental'), even while aspiring to 'a new strength and beauty'. And *Georgian Poetry* sold many thousands of copies; poetry became a craft and the craft became a commodity. If the contributors were 'the last group of young poets to enjoy the esteem of the ordinary reading public',[2] that reading public determined the limitations of the verse it consumed. (In any case, the phrase as used here perhaps betrays a certain nostalgia; there was soon to be no such securely located and homogeneous entity as an 'ordinary reading public'.) The function of the marketable product was recreational; if poets sometimes took themselves more seriously, that was an acceptable gentlemanly eccentricity. True, some of the poets were confusedly in revolt. Masefield, with a show of vigour and a new naturalism of diction and subject (however quaint these may now look), tried to bring seriousness back into poetry, allowing the reader of the anthologies an impression of gritty realism. But his eventual appointment as Poet Laureate probably signifies how limitedly challenging his endeavour really was. More and more the anthologies were claimed by work of which W. J. Turner's often-quoted 'Romance' is typical, the title itself indicating a sort of final dilution of Romanticism:

> When I was but thirteen or so
> I went into a golden land,
> Chimborazo, Cotopaxi,
> Took me by the hand.
>
> (*Georgian Poetry 1916–17*, p. 3)

Lines skilfully packaged to appeal to the escapist inclinations of a busy, middle-class, largely city-dwelling audience; even the typographical arrangement seems designed to *look* shapely on the page, to give an illusion of reading 'poetry'. My concern is not to score easy points off such productions, but to underline how pervasive was the desire to be innocent of history.

Eliot, who more than anyone made Georgianism look *passé*, nevertheless seemed from the start to have 'withdrawn', and I think that his peculiar sense of reality and his limited social range – producing the notorious caricature of English common life in the final passage of 'The Burial of the Dead' and later taking the form of an avowedly conservative social philosophy – signify in him too, like the English-born Lawrence and Graves, a problematical disengagement from 'history's road'. I shall return to this in more detail; for the moment I want to notice that in the literary London of the time, Eliot could not help having dealings with Harold Monro, the publisher of *Georgian Poetry*. Monro himself offers a kind of case-study of the disaffected middle-class liberal in the early decades of our century. That he marketed poetry from his Poetry Bookshop marks perhaps a kind of compromise between his inherited commercial instincts and his disaffection from that prosperous class into which he had been born.[3] He can also be taken as representative of the busy city-dweller for whom his bookshop catered, wedded so often to a dream of rural England, what I call the rural myth. After Monro's death, Eliot wrote with marked sympathy of his work. Monro, he said,

is obviously not a 'nature poet'. The attitude towards nature which we find again and again in his poems is that of the town-dweller, of the man who, as much by the bondage of temperament and habit as by that of external necessity, must pass his life among streets.[4]

That reference to the 'bondage of temperament and habit' suggests to me a heartfelt fellow-feeling. Yet town-dweller as he was, Monro yearned incessantly for the country. As if by reflex action, he slots into the tradition initiated by the early Romantic poets when they turned to 'nature' as an expression of their sense of alienation from a newly burgeoning industrial-capitalist system, hoping to discover a new integration of the self on the pattern of the organic growth of the natural world. Problematically, this impulse could quite easily be merged (the kind of accommodation some might see as typical of the English mind) with an older tradition: the country house as the ideal order of existence, the goal of every *nouveau riche*, every city tradesman, since the breakdown of feudalism. I think one can argue that the two, though ideologically at odds, tended to reinforce each other, taking powerful hold on cultured sensibilities. Everywhere intelligent people, who usually live in cities and daily use the products of factories, have for two centuries and more felt it all but obligatory to express their repugnance to urbanization and factory production. Although life close to nature has become increasingly remote for most people, poets, especially British poets, have found it enormously hard to resist the rural myth; and the contention of this chapter is that the rural myth is a primary means of the closure which reinforces subjective isolation. We see poet after poet striving to recapture in the experience of the countryside a sense of 'organic' community and of historical continuity. But again and again these turn out to be countries of the mind. Harold Monro is the arch-poet of the country weekend. Eliot manages to make a not wholly implausible case for this as a serious poetic enterprise, but it is difficult to see how a countryside viewed only as a place of weekend refuge can sustain those profounder satisfactions. And of course, the ever-increasing dejection in Monro's poetry, on which Eliot commented, shows that it did not.

Eliot knew well that for himself, any attempt to write a country poetry would be a falsehood. Like most thoughtful modern people he deplored the desecration of nature, and the locations he used as starting points for his meditations in one of the greatest of modern poems, *Four Quartets*, are country places. But they are places visited on outings from the city and no effort is made to present them as anything else. The motif of the visit is skilfully woven into the poem's patterns of fleeting, passing intimations; the poem remains largely urban in feeling: 'the attitude towards nature ... is that of the town-dweller'. W. H. Auden is a very different poet, but his bucolics, say, or 'limestone landscape', have equally little to do with the 'rural myth'. His poetry shows deep affection for *industrialized* English landscape. One way of seeing Auden (especially the later Auden) is as a twentieth-century example of the Horatian poet, essentially urban in sensibility, a category to which his friend and follower Louis MacNeice also belongs. In a later chapter, I wish to contrast their more ready acceptance of an urban and industrial reality with the effects for the modern poet of the rural myth. Yet versions of myth, we have seen, continue to be felt by poets as having great imaginative and psychological potency. It seems widely felt, as one commentator has put it, that 'Myths which were ever true myth cannot die, for it is part of the definition of myth that it exists outside time, making intelligible the permanent realities.'[5] This use of myth to detach from history is, of course, what Barthes seeks to expose as deception: 'myth is a type of speech *chosen by* history [my italics]: it cannot possibly evolve from the "nature" of things' (*Mythologies*, p. 110). And 'the country' is found so readily to offer symbols of that timelessness. We have already seen in Lawrence and Graves how a quest for the timeless goes together with a rejection of the urban and an intensification of subjective isolation.

Not that Robert Graves, for all his emphatic denouncing of urban-industrial civilization as a fit source of poetry, can in any way be aligned with the purely escapist kinds of Georgian trivia. His 'Return' after the war, in the poem of that title, to the 'kind land' of Georgian rural poetry elicits ironically facile versification, jingling rhythms and nursery diction which mock and parody the Georgian simplicities:

> Here, Robin on a tussock sits,
> And Cuckoo with his call of hope
> Cuckoos awhile, then off he flits,
> While peals of dingle-dongle keep
> Troop discipline among the sheep
> That graze across the slope.

> (*Collected Poems 1975*, p. 43)

The cuckoo's 'call of hope' and the 'troop-discipline' of the sheep can only be recorded derisively by this war-traumatized poet. It is true that Graves sought a healing influence from nature, but he sought it in the 'wild land' of his 'Rocky Acres' rather than from a soft pastoral landscape:

> This is a wild land, country of my choice,
> With harsh craggy mountain, moor ample and bare.

> (p. 7)

However, the poets of his own time for whom he recorded approval, while dismissing with seemingly wilful perversity all the more celebrated moderns, are mostly rural poets and more or less traditionalist in manner (as well as Frost, they include Hardy and W. H. Davies, but not, interestingly, Edward Thomas.) Constantly deploring modern man's broken bond with nature, he castigated English poets for not knowing their natural history: 'Not one English poet in fifty could identify the common trees of the Beth-Luis-Nion, and distinguish roebuck from fallow deer, aconite from corn-cockle, or wryneck from woodpecker' (*The White Goddess*, pp. 458–9). His long self-exile on Mallorca, as already noted, was a chosen rejection of urban-industrial civilization, and he wrote scornfully of 'the confirmed townsman, who is informed of the passage of the seasons only by the fluctuations of his gas and electricity bills or by the weight of his underclothes' (*ibid.*, p. 481). The poet's essential material, he believed, is agricultural, involving the celebration of the recurrent seasonal cycle:

The Goddess is no townswoman ... Agricultural life is rapidly becoming industrialized and in England ... the last vestiges of the ancient pagan celebrations of the Mother and Son are being obliterated, despite a loving insistence on Green Belts and parks and private gardens. (*ibid.*)

Yet, as I said earlier, Graves repossesses rather than making it new; his 'agricultural life' seems very largely a literary construct. It is rooted in the natural imagery of the pre-industrial English poets and of their anti-industrial Romantic successors, as his White Goddess is to a large extent a synthesized feminine principle derived from the Ladies and crones of those poets. (Milton and Pope, town-bred poets, don't fit this bill, so are

castigated beyond reason.) That for which he intransigently
rejects town life and indeed everything contemporary is the
rural *myth* with a vengeance. It is all mythic essence, generated
by subjective needs, the need to shield himself, to escape
certain realities of his experience which have proved almost too
hard to bear. Graves's theory, says Seymour-Smith, 'is subjective. His "age of the Goddess" is the expression of a state of
longing in him ... ' (*Robert Graves*, p. 388). Hence, for all his
great gifts, Graves chooses a mode of self-exclusion and withdrawal; he chooses the Romantic myth of the poet as oracle,
transcending time. His celebration of 'agricultural life' takes its
place in a series of peculiar and eccentric options which compound the limiting subjectivism of his poetic.

Graves admiringly quoted Robert Frost's dictum about free
verse being like playing tennis without a net, and Frost contained and formalized his Romantic impulse in a way which
stands some comparison with Graves. Frost needs touching on
here not only because of his crucial sojourn in England from
1912 to 1915 and formative effect upon Edward Thomas, or
because his poetic is transitional between the nineteenth
century and the modern, but because his countryside appears
at first not to be the dream, the country of the mind of so many
of his British contemporaries. As in Hardy's poetry, the voices
we hear are those of working countrymen. But the New
England countryside he records, like that of Hardy's 'Wessex',
is a depopulated one (as a result of that relentless American
history of 'going west') and the lonely and haunted voice of the
poet himself insistently takes over – 'He thought he kept the
universe alone' ('The Most of It'). And despite much delicacy
of observation, he doesn't engage nature in an unreserved or
totally committed way; there is something urbane and deliberate about his relationship to it, a philosophical detachment
which is actually more in a tradition of urban poetry. It is his
way of resisting the encroachments of the subjective malaise, of
the problem of acute consciousness. In fact, as has often been
observed, the farmer-poet is a pose. Frost is really a kind of
Augustan pastoralist, and as such easily taken up by the
American Establishment. This is not to minimize the extent to

which a darker 'Romantic' consciousness is felt in the poetry, or the strength of it. But though, in one of his most famous lyrics, 'The woods are lovely, dark and deep', the poet resists their romantic lure and continues like a good workmanlike New Englander about the day's business. Thus, his rural myth finally serves a different purpose from that of the British poets under survey here, and certainly has little to do with the 'Romantic primitivism' which some of them find so attractive.

'Nature poetry', if any usefully distinct definition can be given it, is poetry which experiences nature itself as a source of some philosophical or 'protoreligious' consolation.[6] It derives from the eighteenth-century concept of Nature as an ordered system (hence accorded that capital initial) and therefore evidence of a deity or at least of some ordering and creative force or presence. Romantics like Wordsworth and Coleridge could superimpose on this eighteenth-century rationalization the sense of nature as organic and so in absolute antithesis to the mechanicism of the industrial revolution. (A good test of the point of departure is Crabbe: he has finely accurate natural description and acute renderings of country life, but he is not a nature poet because his interest is not in nature *per se*.) If nature is organic – not made by man – it bespeaks a Creative Spirit; so the contemplation of nature – even in a simple poem concerning, say, the small celandine – establishes a link between Man and a 'meaning' and is an act of moral significance. The writing of a poem, moreover, is an identification with that Creative Spirit which breathes through nature. The pathetic fallacy is the figure which pre-eminently governs nature poetry; its countries (to apply that useful phrase again) are ones of the mind, its landscapes projections of subjective states, emotional and moral. This is so, however objectively precise the descriptive detail; nature *must* be faithfully observed in order to effect that identification of poet's psyche with shaping spirit which is part of the pathetic fallacy's job.

'Pent' is a key word for denoting the Romantic imagination's response to the city. It seems to derive from *Paradise Lost*; 'As one who long in populous city pent ... ' (IX, 446). Cities, after all, are what the Fall has led to; the rural myth is a

version of the Eden myth.[7] Coleridge used it more than once;
he says in 'Frost at Midnight' that he was 'reared / In the great
city, pent 'mid cloisters dim'. Clearly, the implications are of
city life as an unnatural imprisoning; Blake's citizens of
London bear their 'mind-forg'd manacles'. Keats has the word
in this early sonnet:

> To one who has been long in city pent,
>   'Tis very sweet to look into the fair
>   And open face of heaven, – to breathe a prayer
> Full in the smile of the blue firmament.
> Who is more happy, when, with heart's content,
>   Fatigued he sinks into some pleasant lair
>   Of wavy grass and reads a debonair
> And gentle tale of love and languishment?[8]

'Heart's content', 'sinks into some pleasant lair', 'love and
languishment': in these insistent euphonies the country is
envisaged as a place of escape, a refuge from that site of
seething activity, the city, which so drains one's energies
('Fatigued'). A received antithesis of country peace, a place of
passive and reflective occupations, and city fret, informs the
lines. But in another early piece, 'I stood tip-toe upon a little
hill', nature doesn't just passively answer the young poet's
yearnings; it is enlisted as the *theatre* of his bemused and fanciful
self-inquisition, its 'gentle doings' in active collusion with his
subjective meanderings, his 'sweet desolation', his soul 'lost in
pleasant sufferings'. This is the Romantic experiencing of
opposites as locked in an irresolvable interdependence, of
which I have already spoken. Nevertheless, for the rest of his
short life Keats struggled with this dualistic 'poetical character'
(as he called it); he recognized that unalloyed happiness is
impossible, an idle dream, but refused ever finally to surrender
to the (for him) powerful lure of accidie, to mere 'languishment' in the pleasure-pain emotional complex. The continuing presence of this Keatsian-Romantic kind of 'poetical
character' in the present century is instanced, I shall argue in
my next chapter, by the poetry of Edward Thomas, a poet
whose rejection of the city for the country fails to alleviate a
profound distress.

What distinguishes so obviously rural a poet as Hardy from this Romantic line of nature poetry (for all his affinity with Thomas and influence on the Georgians) and makes him more modern is a much greater degree of detachment from nature in the observer. Tom Paulin in *Thomas Hardy. The Poetry of Perception* (London, Macmillan, 1975) discusses in detail Hardy's view that objects in nature have no 'relation to each other or to us' (p. 25). Nature in Hardy tends to dwarf man, rather than to enlarge his sense of meaning and enlarge him morally; it is more impersonal. Hence, in 'The Darkling Thrush', for example, though the natural scene is made to mirror the poet's own state of mind, it does so impersonally, just as a mirror does throw back a reflection. (M. H. Abrams's mirror and lamp scheme takes, as it were, a new turn.) Nature has no direct connection with the speaker and exerts no moral influence upon him – the 'joy' of the bird remains entirely ambiguous, may or may not have meaning for the speaker; it does not involve Hardy in the way the joy of the nightingale's song (that poem being echoed by phrases in Hardy's) does Keats. It is surprising, really, that Eliot was so antagonistic to Hardy, since he might have seen suggested in this detachment ways of moving towards 'impersonality' and the escape from Romantic emotion. Eliot's account of Hardy in *After Strange Gods* sets up the case which R. P. Blackmur was to reiterate: Hardy is 'an interesting example of a powerful personality uncurbed by any institutional attachment or by submission to any objective beliefs ... He seems to me to have written as nearly for the sake of "self-expression" as a man well can', and he is guilty of 'extreme emotionalism'.[9] What seems apparent from the bristling, not to say *emotional*, tone of this passage is that Hardy's 'full stare at the Worst' – his insistence that the worst can't be escaped – and his uncompromising treatment of the more basic passions frightened Eliot. He is therefore one of those who have to be rounded up and safely incarcerated in the despised categories of Romantic 'personality', 'self-expression' and 'emotionalism'. Hardy the provincial is removed from the Eliotic notion of centrality, of 'the classic'; but Hardy's poetry does encompass town life in its varied subjects, and I've suggested that the 'self' which is expressed is in fact problematical in a centrally modern way. It may be that Eliot's own later dissatisfaction with *After Strange Gods* indicates a degree of recantation, but his account wilfully disregards the complex ways in which indulged Romantic emotion is held at arm's length in Hardy's poetry, and, even more oddly, how much he himself has in common with Hardy in the compulsion to erect a shield against the world to protect his own vulnerability and sensitivity. His version of what Hardy does with landscape, moreover, is sadly wanting:

> ... he makes a great deal of landscape; for landscape is a passive creature which lends itself to an author's mood. Landscape is fitted too for the purposes of an author who is interested not at all in men's minds, but only their emotions ...

Yet for Lawrence, Hardy was one of the 'intellectual' people! It is nonsense, of course, to say that he was not interested in men's – and women's – minds, and there is no grasp at all of how landscape, for Hardy, is the record of human habitation. Landscape, I've said, does *not* simply offer itself to him for the purposes of pathetic fallacy. And his countryside is *not* mythic, not a place to escape *to*; people dwell there, one could almost say, by 'bondage of temperament and habit', even if, often, only ghosts remain after the progressive depopulation of the English countryside. Eliot might have seen this – enough ghosts haunt his own poetry, enough disembodied voices speak in it; Hardy strongly anticipates him in his Virgilian or Dantesque figure of life as a journey through a ghost-inhabited underworld.

Although A. E. Housman did not actually appear in the Georgian anthologies, Monro, introducing his selection *Twentieth-Century Poetry* (London, Chatto and Windus, 1929), called Housman the 'spiritual father' of the Georgian movement. I've preferred to see Hardy behind what was valuable in Georgianism; as the figure who, though a country poet, achieves the first major expression of 'modern' consciousness in British poetry, the haunting becoming an element in a modern way of experiencing and perceiving. And even less than to

Frost could one apply to Housman the term Romantic primitivism. Here it is rather a case of the *faux-naif*. It is true, though,
that a large proportion of Georgian offerings bear that *faux-naif*
stamp. They perpetuate the Victorian antiquarianism of Housman's language and feeling, and his particular vein of lyric
essentialism. Less easy to catch was the archaically Gothic
shiver which Housman combined with what at one time was
considered a 'modern' cynicism and pessimism. His lecture *The
Name and Nature of Poetry* (1933) might seem to preach the
Georgian gospel when it speaks of the need for 'truth of
emotion' in poetry; and T. S. Eliot responded to its account of
poetry finding its way 'to something in man which is obscure
and latent, something older than the present organisation of his
nature' (p. 46). These phrases might, after all, suggest Romantic primitivism, were there not so much factitiousness about the
essay, at the opposite pole to anything spontaneous and intuitive. Moreover, poetry, we are told, should be 'pure from the
least alloy of prose' (p. 11). While avoiding the problematic of
those modern poetics which seek to express the essential and
timeless in an historically constituted contemporary language,
this rejection of a 'language close to common speech' virtually
excludes any attempt at all to engage a modern reality. It
shows Housman to conceive of 'the nature of poetry' as utterly
removed from the workaday world. A Parnassian technical
polish in the verse, a cameo quality, relates Housman to the
nineties Aesthetes who were his contemporaries, as do his
'golden boys' and a mild libertinism of atmosphere. Reading
him, indeed, one thinks of Pound's Hugh Selwyn Mauberley.
The lyric skill is real, but the self-conscious nostalgia and
disillusion with which he writes of the countryside –

> Tell me not here, it needs not saying,
>   What tune the enchantress plays
> In aftermath of soft September
>   Or under blanching mays,
> For she and I were long acqainted
>   And I knew all her ways.[10]

– appear brittle and affected beside any of the comparable
qualities, what might be pointed to as antiquarian or gloomily

fatalistic, in Hardy. 'Witless nature' lacks the Hardy reso-
nances, seems morbidly indulged:

> For nature, heartless, witless nature,
>   Will neither care nor know
> What stranger's feet may find the meadow
>   And trespass there and go,
> Nor ask amid the dews of morning
>   If they are mine or no.

No doubt Housman really felt the disillusion, and certainly the
subjectivity and self-consciousness of his verse foreshadow the
modern. But any nexus between the codes of Housman's
society and the disenchantment is studiedly broken; the Professor of Classics retiring to the countryside as a refuge from the
fret of town life, there dejectedly to indulge his sophisticated
anxieties, both handles his material in too cerebral a manner,
and suffers from the split in the late-Victorian mind whereby
useful industry (in Housman's case textual scholarship, at a
time when Classics could still be regarded as a bulwark of the
established order) and art are seen as belonging in different
worlds. (The way Arnold's Scholar Gypsy withdraws from
society is an important antecedent.) The myth of a rural
England on which the *Shropshire Lad* poems feed their enervate
Romanticism is, ultimately, a decorative and barren irrelevance. Housman's *Last Poems* appeared in the same year as *The
Waste Land*. Some of Lawrence's finest verse had already been
written, radically contrasting in its naturalness of utterance
and vividly empathetic strivings to engage revitalizing sources
in nature.

The unlettered W. H. Davies – a variant of that 'peasant-' or
'worker-poet' who from time to time surfaces in literary history
(the phrases betray the class-attitudes inscribed *in* that literary
history) – obviously contrasts with Housman. His 'All in June'
is a modestly exact record of ordinary experience in a personal
idiom:

> A week ago I had a fire
>   To warm my feet, my hands and face;
> Cold winds, that never make a friend,
>   Crept in and out of every place.

Today, the fields are rich in grass,
   And buttercups in thousands grow;
I'll show the World where I have been –
   With gold-dust seen on either shoe.

Till to my garden back I come,
   Where bumble-bees, for hours and hours,
Sit on their soft, fat, velvet bums,
   To wriggle out of hollow flowers.[11]

The effect of authenticity here is supported by a letter Davies wrote to Edward Thomas on 24 January 1907:

Surely this cottage was made for cold storage purposes. I am writing this letter within two feet of a good red fire and my hands are aching with the cold. When I sit down with my eyelashes touching the fire and place my hand at the back of my head I really think I have hold of the North Pole.[12]

Value – 'rich', 'gold-dust' – is a quality of nature; and so is a kind of community – 'my garden' isn't exclusively possessed, it is a place one shares with other creatures. This speaker knows how to value leisure because he was born to a class which was not supposed entitled to any. The relished alliterative effects and succession of stresses on 'soft, fat, velvet bums' undermine, together with the first stanza, any effect of the garden as an unreal Eden. This irreverent and down-to-earth Davies in some poems rather enjoys the rebellious and mischief-making element in his own nature:

For how to manage my damned soul
Will puzzle many a flaming devil.
                (*Collected Poems*, p. 268)

The simplicity of Davies's songs of innocence and experience may lack the Blakean intensities, but it is quite free of Housman's nursed disillusion, and springs from a direct and varied involvement with life and the world which is quite other from Housman's social isolation. The simplicity does not always have this sort of validation, but in the best poems it is *un*self-conscious, proletarian, subversive. It was, of course, this kind of quality which attracted George Bernard Shaw to Davies's *Diary of a Supertramp*. 'Certainly I could prepare a lecture',

Davies wrote to Thomas on 7 August 1909, having been asked to address a 'League', 'but those people want me to speak in praise of work, and you know very well that the most pitiful sight in this world is a hard working man.' But the Shavian echo here is incidental; Davies knew well that 'pitiful' was only too often the exact word for the lot of the hard-working man. This is not the obscure alienation of a Romantic artist like Thomas himself; Davies was uncomplicatedly in touch with a social reality, and could say in direct terms what was wrong with it.

Davies's verse, then, possesses some of the elements of an example: it suggests a possible way out of the poetics of iso-lation and extreme subjectivity. But perhaps even had his talent been large enough, he lacked the intensive poetic edu-cation needed for the task. (Is it the case that a large enough talent anyway sets about procuring that education? Did Law-rence start much ahead of Davies in this respect?) What his *actual* example highlights is this: a man like his friend Thomas *did* possess what might be thought the necessary education and trained intellect, only to find that the very possession of them intensified his isolation. To echo again Lawrence's 'Snake', the voices of the education on offer appear to be alienating ones. At a lesser level than this, however, Davies found it hard not to trade on the Supertramp persona; he knew only too well how to ingratiate himself with the public by means of slim volumes of neat, accessible pastoral lyrics. He began to write to order, became obsessively anxious about how public and critics were receiving his verse since his livelihood now depended on it, and his personal art got swamped.[13]

By contrast, Andrew Young and R. S. Thomas, both rural clergymen, have in common a kind of working relationship with the countryside which seems to help free their poetry of merely decorative, literary, or self-serving elements. It is not the easy relationship a country-dweller of earlier centuries might have had, as Norman Nicholson has noted of Young: 'Like most men to-day, he is a stranger to nature. However much he may love the wild creatures he is always odd man out, spying on their private lives through field-glasses.'[14] They are, of course, in a long line of country-clergyman-poets, but there is a new tone, an edge of modernity in the way of looking and feeling. Young doesn't find nature a consoling refuge. A beech-wood is like 'a haunted house', he expresses a sense that 'even in my land of birth / I trespass on the earth', and if Nicholson's note suggests an affinity with Edward Thomas's awkward kind of rapport with nature, Young's 'A Prospect of Death' –

> There will be time enough
> To go back to the earth I love
> Some other day that week,
> Perhaps to find what all my life I seek.[15]

– strongly echoes Edward Thomas's poems of search and the final rest which he both fears and longs for: 'In hope to find whatever it is I seek' ('The Glory'). Like Edward Thomas a minute and exact observer, Young is unassertive, fresh and homely in the manner of W. H. Davies. Perhaps the more exact comparison is with George Herbert;[16] he has a remark-able knack reminiscent of Herbert, of concentrating a per-ception in a wittily unexpected finish. He lived and worked in his time and yet in part was a stranger to it; he turned to nature, and was a stranger there too, but his precise unforced use of the natural scene, poem after poem a minor epiphany, embodies his unease while at the same time conveying a direct and actual experience of the countryside. However, Philip Larkin, in a review of *The Poetical Works of Andrew Young*, has a telling conclusion:

Some years ago, Kingsley Amis wrote a poem ('Here is Where') which said in effect that while nature poetry was all very well in its way, in the end one wants humanity and human emotions. It is an apt comment on Young's work. To walk all day without meeting a soul can be refreshing and restoring. But at last one is glad to get back to humankind again.[17]

Larkin stresses the oppressive *emptiness* of Young's countryside: 'There are no people; to read him is like walking all day without meeting a soul. The silence, the absence are in the end intimidating.' Here, it seems to me, Larkin gets to the heart of the problem. Of course for some people rural life remains in our

century a reality, not a dream, not a myth. But the countryside
was already emptying in Hardy's time, and to the extent that
there has since been a recolonizing process, it has been by the
opposite of indigenous country-dwellers. However intimate the
modern poet strives to make himself with natural things he
tends to remain a stranger; his nature poetry will either be
artificial and programmatic or a matter of uneasily caught
intimations surrounded by daunting silences and absences.
The tradition began with the great Romantics seeking
wholeness, organic integration; ironically, the course the tradition has run only seems to demonstrate the impossibility of such
integration.

R. S. Thomas is of a later generation but continues the line.
He has expressly stated his sympathy with his namesake
Edward:[18] the problem of relatedness and identity, the sense of
isolation, these two Thomases share would seem for both to be
in some part entailed in their Anglo-Welshness. However, the
feeling one encounters in his poetry is altogether more abrupt
and harsh than anything in Young or Edward Thomas. His
religion gets more insistently into the poetry than is the case
with Young, a remarkably unconsolatory religion. He, too,
responds to nature in a realistic and disenchanted manner; the
landscape which situates his vision is one akin to Graves's
Welsh 'Rocky Acres'. But all those effects of acute subjectivity
– the haunted consciousness, the Romantic otherness and rootlessness – are notably less in evidence: 'R. S. Thomas is not
self-absorbed.'[19] If anything, the problem is one of an excess of
objectivity, an unremittingly diagnostic manner. The adults in
'Children's Song' who 'probe and pry / With analytic eye' in a
forlorn attempt to grasp the world of childhood could well be
taken for emblems. The object defies the poet not because it is
obscure or fugitive but because it is *there*, in a way which
proscribes that subjective appropriation so much the
Romantic-modern aim. Many of Thomas's effects have a
powerful bareness suggesting that this is all that can usefully be
said of the matter. Nevertheless, the poetry focuses a sense of
the enduringly meaningful qualities of country life, as in 'The
Village':

> Stay, then, village, for round you spins
> On slow axis a world as vast
> And meaningful as any posed
> By great Plato's solitary mind.[20]

'Nature's truth / Is primary' ('The Minister', p. 33), and Thomas's archetypal Welsh peasant Iago Prytherch is presented 'Enduring like a tree under the curious stars' (p. 11).

There is a certain impression of the poet-minister as 'odd man out', able only to observe without affecting, but his subject is the objective inscrutability of God's creation (and his own place in it), not his personal superfluity and ineffectiveness. Isolation is certainly his theme, but it is not quite the Modernist isolation; this isolation is endemic in human existence, and endures along with it. The unignorable spread of modernity is a kind of abhorrent freak: nothing has really changed since the world began, a sense of changelessness unthinkable in an urban modernist or even in Edward Thomas. His Wales has sometimes been read, I think, as an original Wales, a focus for nationalist identity, but this does look rather like myth-making. In fact, his 'untamed land west of the valleys' is worryingly emptied of history, remote from the towns and industrial valleys where more recent history has happened. The verse is modernly spare and taut, without the unassumingness of Young's style, sometimes almost brutal to match the vision of the harshness of essential existence; but if 'modern' consciousness seeps continuously in at the edges of the poetry, not least in the sense of the inaccessibility of the divine, it doesn't take a hold. And Thomas's provincialism seems not just geographical. He may assert the meaningfulness of country life, observing it with a priest's compassion and eye for the beauty of severity, but his way of placing man in the bleak Welsh landscape –

> In the hill country at the moor's edge
> There is a chapel, religion's outpost
> In the untamed land west of the valleys . . .
>
> ('The Minister')

– seems to imply that man himself is a kind of remote and barren province, and I suppose this must express a vision of man as fallen, an outcast dependent on God's Grace for any recovered sense of connection with a 'centre'. In recent years Thomas's poetry has perceived that connection, though pursuing it with a passionate resolve, as tenuous and problematic in the extreme. Nature for Thomas, then, is no source of renewal and only in niggardly moments is it one of joy; he is not at all the conventional country poet which the many deceptively brief and simple, Georgian-looking verses might initially suggest; but in his case, too, nature is the focus for a problematical tendency to disengage from history. A relatively late poem speaks of 'history's Medusa stare' ('Where', 1978); once caught by history, we are powerless to negotiate even the most limited connection with saving grace. It is, we will see, a Christian reading of history having affinities with Eliot's but at odds with W. H. Auden's.

Years ago, F. R. Leavis rightly declared of Edmund Blunden that he was 'a poet who, though he wrote about the country, drew neither upon the *Shropshire Lad* nor upon the common stock of Georgian country sentiment'.[21] Blunden's choice, on returning from the war, of rural subjects and traditional form and diction, isn't a refusal to come to grips with present reality. Like Sassoon and Graves, the marks of the psychological disturbance with which the war left Blunden remained with him for many years. (His *Undertones of War* belongs beside Graves's *Good-bye to All That* and has a similar relationship to its author's poetry.) There is none of Davies's ingenuous response to nature, and his verse seems to labour along under a burden:

> I saw the sunlit vale, and the pastoral fairy-tale;
> The sweet and bitter scent of the may drifted by;
> And never have I seen such a bright bewildering green,
>   But it looked like a lie,
>   Like a kindly meant lie.[22]

It is clear from this – directly comparable with Graves's 'Return' – that despite deep feeling for the countryside, it offers Blunden no healing rest. Its charms are acknowledged as 'merciful' but specious:

Nymph of the upland song and the sparkling leafage young,
For your merciful desires with these charms to beguile
For ever be adored: muses yield you rich reward . . .

But 'nature smile[s] and feign[s] where foul play has stabbed
and slain', unable to ameliorate the deeper malaise his experiences have induced in him. Blunden is one of the first to write
'nature poetry' containing that modern lack of ease and sense
of the malevolence of nature to which Ted Hughes was later to
give more extreme expression. Hughes's focus on the threatening *otherness* of nature, an otherness, which unlike R. S.
Thomas's 'thereness', self longs to subsume or be subsumed by,
is most centrally prefigured by Lawrence; but three poems
which strike one as closely aligned in what they evoke are
Blunden's 'Malefactors' (one notes the title), Edward Thomas's
'The Gallows' and Hughes's 'November'. Man and nature and
the relationship between them is the theme of all three poems.
Do they form a continuum, echoing each other, affecting each
other? Does consciousness, heightened by Cartesian presump-
tions, inevitably estrange us from nature and isn't the rural
myth, as a version of the Eden myth, the fundamental nostalgia, yearning for an impossible re-integration with nature?
Isn't history (man-shaped and shaping man) by definition a
disrupting of nature and the contemplation of nature necessarily a turning-away from history, an intensification of subjectivity, which can never anyway heal the intrinsic breach
between man and nature? The questions become urgent
because the emergence of modern technologies and accompanying social transformations (the individual 'informed of the
passage of the seasons only by the fluctuations of his gas and
electricity bills . . . ') mean, in a way made more acute by the
shattering experience of modern warfare, that the traditional
ways of thinking about the man and nature dichotomy won't
do. All three poets know this, with a keenness beyond the
trivial kind of Georgian. All three make use of the countryman's (in Thomas and Hughes a gamekeeper, in Blunden a
miller) custom of hanging up on trees or fences shot 'vermin' –
crows, stoats, rats and so on – as a warning to their kinds.
Thomas describes the weasel which 'swings in the wind and

rain' on the 'gallows' of his title, Blunden speaks of the 'clumsy gibbet', Hughes of the 'keeper's gibbet', and in one way or another the same system of analogy is applied – animal equals the free spirit, gamekeeper or miller equals implacable law. Each poem pursues existential issues to do with the mortal creature and remote powers which seek to limit its freedom, and with the relentless war of attrition between man and nature, each exerting its craft, cunning, and will to survive.

The gamekeeper recurs in Hughes's poetry (it is Hughes's own brother's occupation) as well as in Thomas's writing (and of course in Lawrence's too), and is essentially an ambivalent figure. He may be seen in one light as a conservationist. But then, for what purpose is he conserving? He is a man of the people but does not serve them: he persecutes the trespasser and poacher as he persecutes innocent creatures: all are vermin from the point of view of those the gamekeeper serves, who would keep the land and its fruits for themselves. However, where Thomas betrays worries about the game-keeper's function and role as oppressor even though he is drawn to him as rooted countryman, Hughes appears much more to identify with a man seen not only in close touch with nature, but *necessarily* complying with nature's harsh laws. His 'November' marks a more extreme development. It seems to tip the balance in favour of nature; the tramp in the ditch survives by dint of his almost total identification with nature, blending into it:

> I thought what strong trust
> Slept in him – as the trickling furrows slept,
> And the thorn-roots in their grip on darkness;[23]

Like the creatures on the keeper's gibbet, he is 'Patient to outwait these worst days'. There is an implication that more sophisticated human life ultimately forfeits the capacity to endure, that slowly but surely nature is reasserting its domin-ion in the face of man's depredations. These are matters I shall address later; Hughes's poetic thinking may be seen as a kind of coming out the other side of the Romantic-modern conscious-ness of breach between man and nature, a striving to reassimilate them to each other, albeit in a way which the reader schooled in urban humanist attitudes may find (perhaps rightly) hard to accept. Not only is nature not moral or benevolent, but its malevolence is merely its otherness, and must be welcomed, not fought against. Blunden and Edward Thomas – and Hardy behind them – were, of course, no less acutely aware of the fragility of the whole human enterprise. Blunden images this in 'Malefactors' by the disused mill – 'the sluices well, / Dreary as a passing-bell' (in a way closely echoing the same imagery in Thomas's poem 'The Mill-Water'). In both, the dried carcases flapping in the wind suggest emblems of the superfluity of sentient existence and both are again poems of silences and absences; and these emphases express a modern distress – in what sense does consciousness ever make free agents of us? – rather than old-fashioned feelings of the transience of earthly things. But neither quite suggests Hughes's extremist notion of nature *displacing* man.

Nevertheless, the strain and effort of Hughes's language can be seen as an intensification of a quality already present in Blunden's. The sense of some grave *disruption* which Blunden's poetry gives is all the more pronounced because one seems to be in the presence of an innately pre-modern, almost eighteenth-century sensibility (consider the verse-structure and diction of the lines quoted above: 'Nymph of the upland song ... '). It is one which, however, is too honest simply to turn away from a modern reality, even though that reality can only be contemplated and introduced into the poetry in very oblique ways. How fully Blunden experiences nature as not all charm, as imbued with very threatening kinds of power, is clear in 'The Pike', which inevitably invites comparison with Hughes's 'Pike', both now well-known poems, both making the ineradicable predatoriness of nature their focus. Blunden subtly has the lurking predatoriness emerging from pictures of the bright vivacity and soothing richness of nature, until finally nature's benevolence again appears 'a kindly meant lie'. The way the poem proceeds with something like the composed formality of the Augustan pastoralists he so much admired,

very much a *crafted* poem, seems worlds away from the directness and vitalism of Hughes, his rejection of the tyrannically
formalizing, logocentric, human-centred intelligence, yet in
Blunden's poem too there is something challenging the ordered
human perception of things: 'the miller that opens the hatch
stands amazed at the whirl in the water' (*Poems of Many Years*,
p. 34). Indeed, it is astonishing how exactly Blunden's poem, if
we substitute the miller for the boy fishing, pre-enacts
Hughes's. If Hughes more obsessively elucidates the way the
predatoriness, which can sometimes go to self-defeating lengths
as in the two pike which preyed upon and killed each other,
may strike a chord in our own darker natures, that darker note
also sounds clearly enough through the Augustan constraint of
Blunden's.

Although in point of time, in rural subject-matter and in its
careful craftsmanship, Blunden's verse belongs with the Georgians, its rich textures are not Georgian; he eschews those notes
of the affectedly simple, of the crudely realist or of lyric essentialism which can be so tiresome. Blunden's is still a very
conservative poetic, made up of a very conscious handling of
traditional materials. But it is poetry of particular sensibility,
and it does not in any way deal in falsification. The old-
fashionedness is deliberately constructed; the literary myth of a
rural England is set in a frame and celebrated for, as it were, its
intrinsic, self-reflecting values. This is an objective process, a
way not of intervening in but of co-existing with history: one
realizes, simply, that like Graves Blunden could not face the
reality he knew head on and stay sane. Edward Thomas and
Ted Hughes each develop a more radical poetic, and in doing
so each is impelled, I will argue, more deeply into the subjective impasse. Blunden's Augustan restraint is, seen relatively,
both a safeguard and a limitation.

CHAPTER 3

The 'poetical character' of Edward Thomas

I

Edward Thomas's poetry is made out of a haunted and restless temper compounded by a life that gave him no rest. R. George Thomas commented:

The sheer amount of Thomas's reviews is forbidding ... At a conservative estimate I think that these preserved [i.e. by Thomas himself] reviews represent about two-thirds of Thomas's total output ... a minimum of 1,122 reviews – just over a million words about 1,200 books. During the first four years [i.e. 1900–4] he averaged 80 reviews a year ... between the Chrstmasses of 1905 and 1912 he was contributing 100 signed (or full-length) reviews annually to the *Daily Chronicle* or the *Daily Post* ... to *The Nation*, *The Athenaeum*, or *The English Review*, besides at least 50 shorter notices to weeklies and, after 1907, a monthly article or two-column unsigned review to *The Bookman*.[1]

Financial harassment and sheer fatigue intensified his innate darkness of temper. Weariness is a recurring theme; in *The Icknield Way* he writes: 'There will never be any summer any more, and I am weary of everything. I stay because I am too weak to go, I crawl on because it is easier than to stop.'[2] Relations with his family were often strained, and, too inwardly troubled to settle to a permanent job, he travelled ceaselessly about the countryside of England and Wales, in what was really an inner quest, for the rest and fulfilment he could never find. He becomes the type of the socially estranged Romantic artist, given over to subjective intensities. His importance is now widely recognized; in this chapter I shall try to show how his case presents in particularly heightened form what I have called the problem of acute consciousness, his poetry expressing the characteristic Romantic-modern yearning for social relatedness and identity, vitiated by the lure of inaction or, at best, a disabling indeterminacy.

'Not the fruit of experience, but the experience itself': in view of the life and temperament I have just sketched, it is not surprising that Thomas felt his experience to have born little in the way of fruit, and that he turned to focussing on 'the experience itself'. One of the distinctive features of Thomas's poetry is its concern with the 'feel' of an experience, with what the mind *does* to an experience. Jon Silkin observed:

The poetry often, and perhaps at its best, conveys the impression of a mind thinking about itself, and its responses to its past experience. The prose is less conscious of itself and more concerned with the mood it evokes. This is hardly surprising, because the prose came first, and because the poetry then drew on the material of the prose ... A painful honesty subsequently corrects in the poetry the indulgence and nostalgic dislocation of some of the prose.[3]

Hackwork though much of the prose may have been, some of it demands attention in its own right, and I shall return to its important relationship with the verse. This 'mind thinking about itself' may be observed in poems such as 'Aspens', of which the final stanza runs:

> Whatever wind blows, while they and I have leaves
> We cannot other than as aspen be
> That ceaselessly, unreasonably grieves,
> Or so men think who like a different tree.[4]

'*I* was the aspen. "We" meant the trees and I with my dejected shyness', explained Thomas to Eleanor Farjeon.[5] Such poems, such a state of mind, have their origins deep in the Romantic tradition ('dejected' immediately offers a link back to so central a poem as Coleridge's 'Dejection: An Ode'), yet the extreme extent of self-consciousness here, the way the proposed identity between outer landscape and inner one is not allowed to pass unexamined – to coalesce into an inviolate Romantic image – but must be glossed and qualified, carries forward that modern distancing of the observing consciousness from the natural scene and even from itself I have noted in Hardy. And what this gloss implies is that there are modes of experiencing – 'dejected shyness' or no – which may be valued for their own sake, outside the scheme of value regarded by the general run of 'men'.

Moreover, the recording of experiential phenomena of this kind comes together with an ontological concern with the perception of essences, which, however, continually elude grasp. It might be said that a great deal of poetry attempts to convey the exact nature or essence of a thing or an experience, but Thomas delves into the mental processes attendant upon this in a peculiarly obsessive way. This is apparent in the poem called 'Parting':

> The Past is a strange land, most strange.
> Wind blows not there, nor does rain fall:
> If they do, they cannot hurt at all.
> Men of all kinds as equals range
>
> The soundless fields and streets of it.
> Pleasure and pain there have no sting,
> The perished self not suffering
> That lacks all blood and nerve and wit,
>
> And is in shadow-land a shade.
> Remembered joy and misery
> Bring joy to the joyous equally;
> Both sadden the sad. So memory made
>
> Parting to-day a double pain:
> First because it was parting; next
> Because the ill it ended vexed
> And mocked me from the Past again,
>
> Not as what had been remedied
> Had I gone on – not that, oh no!
> But as itself no longer woe;
> Sighs, angry word and look and deed
>
> Being faded: rather a kind of bliss,
> For there spiritualized it lay
> In the perpetual yesterday
> That naught can stir or strain like this.[6]

Not, obviously, an intoxicated Lawrentian departure into the visionary unknown: the implications of this ordinary experience of parting are for Thomas strangely baffling. The poem refers specifically to Thomas's parting from his son Merfyn when the latter embarked for America with Robert Frost in February 1915; father and son had not always had the best of relations, but that in itself is hardly unordinary.

This is not a simple piece of nostalgia or lament at parting, nor is it just saying that the past always appears less painful than the present. The self which 'is in shadow-land a shade' immediately recalls Hardy's ghost-inhabited underworld, the detached earlier self of 'Wessex Heights', but as with Hardy – or, later, Philip Larkin – the treatment of memory and the past is seldom in Thomas simply nostalgic. The poem exemplifies what I have said about the interconnection for the Romantic and modern poet of remembrance and the effort to achieve a sense of grasp, coherence and concreteness in the subjective processes. The essence that the poem is seeking to crystallize is always on the point of fading out altogether and keeps having to be caught up anew – the poem looks, for instance, as if it's never going to recover from that silence after the first stanza-break, and even then it can only find the '*soundless* fields and streets of it'. The fluctuations of thought and feeling and the corrugations of the verse realize for us the acute discomfort of a state of consciousness, a psychological disposition, in which more or less normal experience becomes an almost intolerable burden, to be mentally heaved and strained at in an effort to get it into some sort of manageable form. 'Parting today' is 'a double pain', while the present is a state of being in which, almost by definition for Thomas, the pressure is never taken off; the movement of the verse itself 'stirs' and 'strains' to convey this state.

What sort of a mental condition is this and what sort of 'poetical Character' – I hope to show the appropriateness of Keat's phrase – makes poetry out of it? Many affinities with earlier poets can, of course, be found in Thomas. The rhythms and diction (mostly) of ordinary speech yet the tendency towards involved and paradoxical thought – an oblique, angular play of mind involving the repetition of words and syntactical arrangements with progressive shifts of meaning – and a terse conjoining of perceptions or ideas which is almost wit were it not for the reticence, all these qualities have their parallels in poetry which goes back behind the Romantics to the Metaphysicals and Elizabethans. At the same time, they are qualities which can be put in the context of the post-Romantic effort to restore 'thought' and 'common speech' to poetry. Much, also, can be made of affinities with country poets such as Hardy and Robert Frost. But centrally behind Thomas stand the Romantics: Wordsworth, Coleridge, and Keats. Michael Kirkham (*The Imagination of Edward Thomas*, Cambridge, 1986) has examined Thomas's debt both to Wordsworth and to the Coleridgean conversation poem. If I discuss Thomas's book on Keats in some detail it is not because I think it Thomas's only important work of prose or criticism, or Keats the only important influence on his poetry (though I do think him the most central of that trio of great Romantics), but because it brings to the fore so many of the Romantic-modern traits and continuities which are of concern to this study.

What Thomas called, with characteristic self-dissatisfaction, the 'rotten little book on Keats' which he published in 1916 pinpoints the extent to which he was the possessor of that 'poetical Character' which in Keats's definition 'enjoys light and shade'.[7] When in the book (not, of course, so rotten after all) he quotes (p. 53) from the closing stanza of 'Ode to Psyche' one senses him savouring the complex of contrasts in 'bright Torch', the darkness and coolness of night, 'warm Love', and (an especially positive sympathy here) 'dark-cluster'd trees'. (I've noted Hardy's use of this kind of Romantic notation, his 'latttice-gleam' at midnight.) Thomas emphasized the interdependence for Keats of books and nature; to Keats, he says, 'The beauty of Nature immediately suggested the beauty of poetry and the translation of one into the other' (p. 38). Just how bookish Thomas himself was is apparent from any glance at his mass of prose writings. Yet in both, any tendency to take *refuge* in books was countered by an intense immediacy of experience, as well as an anxious desire for human connection:

Thomas singles out for quotation Keats's 'I like, I love England – I like its living men ...' (p. 17).

The *ways* of perceiving and experiencing are strikingly alike. Thomas admires in Keats's letters the 'direct presentation of the moment's phases of mind and moods of temperament' (p. 84), and 'Keats's fidelity to the observation or feeling of the hour' (p. 36). Thomas recognizes in Keats the kind of passive extinction of self in the experience of the moment, the same kind of giving of himself to the weather and other natural manifestations, that is present in his own poems:

So he could lie awake listening to the night rain 'with a sense of being drowned and rotted like a grain of wheat'; if a sparrow came before his window he could 'take part in its existence and pick about the gravel ...' (pp. 75–6)

Thomas's 'Rain' begins with a similar surrender to the night rain, and draws to a close with something like the Keatsian attraction to death:

> Like me who have no love which this wild rain
> Has not dissolved except the love of death ...

> (p. 87)

His 'Digging' ('To-day I think / Only with scents ...') is a compact expression of the Keatsian abdication to sense-impressions, to the moment's experience. In another poem Thomas loses himself in the life of a butterfly:

> And down upon the dome
> Of the stone the cart-horse kicks against so oft
> A butterfly alighted. From aloft
> He took the heat of the sun, and from below.
> On the hot stone he perched contented so,
> As if never a cart would pass again
> That way; as if I were the last of men
> And he the first of insects to have earth
> And sun together and to know their worth.

> ('The Brook', p. 231)

In 'Sleep and Poetry' a butterfly was one of those 'peaceful images' which helped bring Keats release from 'Despondence! miserable bane!' and its alliance with release in sleep may bring to mind such Thomas poems as 'Lights Out' where he speaks of 'sleep that is sweeter / Than tasks most noble'. But in Thomas's lines as in Keats's, even the butterfly appears to be losing itself, dissolving its being, in a moment of intense sensuous experience ('As if never a cart would pass again ...'), echoing the *poet's* abdication to such a moment; the identification of man and creature is in 'to have earth / And sun together ...'. Significantly, this is not the characterizing of life beyond the self which Thomas's friend Bottomley achieves with his willow-wren or more notably Lawrence with his animals, not that realizing of a vital otherness, though it acknowledges a world in which humanity only shares. It is a sort of fusing in shared near-oblivion, a 'merging' which Lawrence would have abhorred; provisionally at least, the problem of consciousness *separating* us from nature is side-stepped. These points of rest and self-extinction are always bounded by a sense of continuing reality: 'as if' registers that carts *do* pass this way, so that much of the poem's effect and meaning emerges from this posing of the moment against the continuing reality. It is an example of what William Cooke has called Thomas's 'psychological theme of attempted escape and necessary return'.[8] And the poem does end with a partial breaking of the spell, a breaking of a kind even more notable in, for example, 'The Lane'.

Many of Thomas's poems enact in their perplexity both an alienation from, and a reconciliation with, the actual. When Keats effects a gathering-up of sense-impressions into a concentrated flight of the imagination, to be followed by a rueful return to reality (the ending of 'Ode to a Nightingale' is the obvious example), it is the escape which makes life meaningful and tolerable, which makes possible the reconciliation with life. 'All that I could lose / I lost' says Thomas in 'The Brook', indicating by this very statement that the losing is never total. And Thomas is quick to find in Keats his own antipathy to the vaguely romantic or transcendental: 'though a lover of the moon, a most sublunary poet, earthly, substantial, and precise, a man but for his intensity, singularly like his fellow-men ...' (p. 39) Thomas's metaphysics are rooted in the physical. It is essentially the same paradox I've pointed to earlier in Lawrence and Graves. 'Meaning' resides elsewhere than in the time-bound world of 'citizenship' or history, but this is not mysticism. Only the palpable world of empirical phenomena can be trusted; numens and abstractions, whether religio-philosophical or socio-political, are totally discredited for this kind of Romantic-modern poet. But where Lawrence and Graves derive a certain gratification from being 'different', Keats and Thomas each have a frustrated yearning to be 'like his fellow-men'. Not the least of the disabling tensions in Thomas is this between his democratic identification with the ordinary man (in 'Parting', 'Men of all kinds as equals range' the strange land of the Past) and his overpowering sense ('but for his intensity') of his own 'difference' – the difference of the romantic artist.

Thomas draws attention to the closing stanza of 'Ode to Psyche', with its placing of 'a sanctuary' among dark-clustered trees (p. 53). Keats's wish to build a fane to Psyche 'In some untrodden region of my mind' is echoed in, among other poems, Thomas's 'Over the Hills':

> Often and often it came back again
> To mind, the day I passed the horizon ridge
> To a new country, the path I had to find
> By half-gaps that were stiles once in the hedge,
> The pack of scarlet clouds running across
> The harvest evening that seemed endless then
> And after, and the inn where all were kind,
> All were strangers.

(p. 77)

Despite the physicality and particularity of detail, it becomes evident – one notices, for example, the poised effect of 'horizon ridge', the enjambment suggesting some climactic passing from the known into the unknown – that this 'new country' does to all intents and purposes only have its existence in the poet's mind. Again the poet disconnects from an earlier self; the actual day of visiting that 'country' is gone beyond recovery, has no tangible reality. A similar phenomenon is symbolized in the song of 'The Unknown Bird'. The poet told 'the naturalists' about the bird, but they were at a loss to identify it. The moment of escape which the symbolism represents, further-more, cannot be reclaimed. The bird 'never came again'. 'I did not know my loss / Till one day twelve months later suddenly / I leaned upon my spade and saw it all' says the poet in 'Over the Hills', and continues:

> Recall
> Was vain: no more could the restless brook
> Ever turn back and climb the waterfall
> To the lake that rests and stirs not in its nook,
> As in the hollow of the collar-bone
> Under the mountain's head of rush and stone.

'Loss' offers a startling ambiguity, suggests the losing of the over-burdened, over-conscious everyday self in the moment of release, as well as the failure to recapture the moment. And the final lines form a secondary image of the poet's restless and impossible quest, already imaged in the difficulty of finding his way to that 'new country'. The poem ramifies in a character-istic Thomas manner; the 'rest' which was restlessly sought and found briefly (though it hallucinatorily 'seemed endless then') on that one day twelve months previously, cannot be recovered however habitually, compulsively still pursued. The people met in the inn, though 'kind', were and will forever be 'strangers'. What in the poem, by an almost hallucinatory process, have become symbolic features – the horizon, the path, an inn, the 'strangers' – are consistent with their use in other poems; they intimate the fulfilment, in a restful place with 'kind' (and equal) people, which constantly eludes Thomas. Whatever work it is the poet pauses in to experience his country of the mind is clearly unrewarding by comparison. It is a very strange, very troubling poem, not least in the way it seems, contradictorily, to accept that the recall is 'vain' and the present work must be got on with. But the contradiction, I'm suggesting, is the point. Different as this is from the escape into the imagination which is Keats's 'Untrodden region of my mind', it is like in its representation of an inward quest for fulfilment and self-extinction, for 'sanctuary' or rest, and it is like in the imaging of this quest in terms of physical scenery (the dark-clustered trees and mountain ridges of Keats's poem). Neither poet makes mystical claims for his moment of release; it remains a slightly bewildering psychological oddity:

> Surely I dreamt today, or did I see
> The winged Psyche with awaken'd eyes?

or as Thomas puts it in 'The Unknown Bird': 'As if the bird or I were in a dream'. But Keats's *cri de cœur* to Reynolds, 'lord! a man should have the fine point of his soul taken off to become fit for this world',[9] is what both poets felt acutely, and for both, I think, this paradoxical means of reconciliation with life through escape is a mode of rendering experience manageable for the ultra-sensitive man. The persistent effort in 'Over the Hills' to 'see' again the new country in the mind's eye, to recover or re-connect with the psychic experience – 'It became / Almost a habit ...' – indicates the subjective necessity involved.

The centre of his sympathy for Keats is found by Thomas early in his book:

In spite of his energy, courage, and independence, he enjoyed and suffered from what he himself called his morbidity of temperament ... His morbidity of temperament was inseparably kin to the sensitive passive qualities without which his poetry would have been nothing. I do not mean that his poetry sprang from his morbidity simply, but that both had to do with the brooding intensity of his receptiveness, that they inhabited the same enchanted treasure-caves. Eagerness and joy went with it also. (p. 11)

It is this 'brooding intensity of receptiveness' which is so alike in the two poets, in neither wholly free of an element of morbidity. Two aspects of this are linked, one represented by the phrase 'enchanted treasure-caves' and the other by the terms in which Thomas writes of the Odes and 'The Eve of St Agnes': 'Love for vanished, inaccessible, inhuman things, almost for death itself – regret – and the consolations offered by the intensity which makes pleasure and pain so much alike – are the principal moods of these poems' (p. 51). Though Thomas is far from the Gothic Revivalism of 'The Eve of St Agnes', he can talk fancifully of a 'castle in Spain' in 'Wind and Mist', or refer in 'The Path' to

the path that looks
As if it led on to some legendary
Or fancied place where men have wished to go
And stay . . .

(p. 145)

R. P. Eckert wrote of Thomas's childhood: 'He had always a
lively fancy'; he used to wander alone about the suburban
commons near his home with an imaginary companion, 'a
spiritual self', and these became 'an almost mythical land'.[10]
So the 'legendary or fancied place' and the curious *alter ego* that
sometimes figures in his poems (in 'Over the Hills', I've suggested, he *becomes* in his mind's eye that disconnected other self)
have their origin in childhood imaginings. Books and nature
are interdependent for Thomas, we've noted. Unobtrusively
the poetry taps a reservoir of reading in folklore, legend and
fairy-tale; the allusions are made discreetly to play off a touch
of mystery, of the unknown, against his solid natural physicali-
ties. The fanciful 'place' stands in both Keats and Thomas,
fairly obviously, for that region of the mind in which each
quests, the 'place where men have wished to go and stay'. The
link between such places and the 'groundwork of regret', the
'love for vanished, inaccessible, inhuman things, almost for
death itself' signifies the yearning to escape the troubling arena
of historical change and process, 'the weariness, the fever, and
the fret' of being human and humanly conscious.

In this psychological patterning[11] 'melancholy' seems
inextricably associated with 'sensitive passive qualities'. In
writing of Keats, Thomas dwells almost obsessively on passivity
and stillness. The 'Ode on Melancholy', he writes,

is one of the central poems of this period, admitting, as it does so fully,
and celebrating, the relationship between melancholy and certain
still pleasures. Nowhere is the connoisseurship of the quiet, withdrawn spectator so extremely and remorselessly put . . . (p. 53)

I have already touched upon 'The Brook' – there are many
such poems – where Thomas himself appears as something of a
'quiet, withdrawn spectator', absorbing mood and sense-
impressions, passively opening himself up to the perceptions

and experience of the moment. He, also, presents a connoisseur's delicate handling of that experience. Of his own passive
temper he wrote to Gordon Bottomley in 1907:

Why have I no energies like other men? I long for some hatred or
indignation or even sharp despair, since love is impossible, to send me
out on the road that leads over the hills & among the stars sometimes
... I was told the other day that I seemed a calm dispassionate
observer with no opinions. I hope I am more. I have no opinions, I
know. But cannot the passive temperament do something, a little?
For I have impressions of men & places & books. They often overawe
me as a tree or a crowd does the sensitized paper; & is that nothing or
as good as nothing? (p. 148)

(One sees the significance of that title 'Over the Hills'.)
Neither poet was without *energies*, but both were susceptible to
this lassitude, the condition of accidie which seems close to
endemic in Romantic psychology. 'I have this morning such a
Lethargy that I cannot write', wrote Keats on one occasion,
'... I am in that temper that if I were under Water I would
scarcely kick to come to the top'.[12] And this lack of strong
active drives not only sets the poet somewhat apart from 'other
men', but is also, it seems to me, a constituent of the famous
'negative capability'. I take it that what Thomas means by 'the
sensitized paper' is a photographic analogy: the Keats or
Thomas temperament is able to give itself up totally to 'impressions' or images of an 'overawing' kind, to receive their imprint
with minute fidelity, in the process undergoing an extinction of
self, a 'taking part in'. The 'poetical Character' which 'enjoys
light and shade' is usually linked by Keats's commentators
with the separate reference in the letters to 'negative capability'.

Thomas, too, repeatedly admits and celebrates 'the relationship between melancholy and certain still pleasures', and
records 'the consolations offered by the intensity which makes
pleasure and pain so much alike'. As we've seen, he noted in
Keats the inseparability of 'morbidity of temperament',
'brooding intensity of receptiveness' and 'eagerness and joy'.
He seems to be pointing to this intensity in himself when he
writes again to Bottomley: 'But seriously I wonder whether for
a person like myself whose most intense moments were those of

depression a cure that destroys the depression may not destroy the intensity ...' (p. 163) The 'Ode on Melancholy', writes Thomas, 'taken literally, seems to say that the bitter with the sweet is worth while – is the necessary woof of life ...' (p. 54). It is an essentially Romantic idea ('sensibility' has much to do with it), and many of his own poems turn on something very like it. We have noted the coupling of 'Pleasure and pain' in 'Parting'. His own 'Melancholy' employs throughout a Keatsian-Romantic notation (with, in addition, obvious echoes of Coleridge): the misting over, the retreating into vagueness at the end, is deeply Romantic:

> Yet naught did my despair
> But sweeten the strange sweetness, while through the wild air
> All day long I heard a distant cuckoo calling
> And, soft as dulcimers, sounds of near water falling,
> And, softer, and remote as if in history,
> Rumours of what had touched my friends, my foes, or me.
>
> (p. 193)

In part, the poem is a posing of the Keatsian question, 'Do I wake or sleep?' The poem pivots, however, on the line and a half preceding those quoted – 'What I desired I knew not, but whate'er my choice / Vain it must be' denotes Thomas's central dilemma, the crippling incapacity to define the fulfil-ment which is always sought; yet growing directly out of this – inextricably bound to it – is the melancholy which is so savoured, the strangely sweet despair (not a '*sharp*' despair'). The dilemma is voiced in 'The Glory' with a typical simplicity of paradox: 'In hope to find whatever it is I seek', while a more convoluted statement of the paradox occurs in the fourth stanza of 'The Other'. The desire is active enough, one might say, but the passivity lies in the recalcitrance towards that 'choice'; a crucial absence is felt, but of what is unknown, and irrecoverability is made a good; the longing is, in its strange sweetness, its 'pleasant pain', almost self-sufficient. Keats's version of the same psychological phenomenon is famous:

> Ay, in the very temple of Delight
> Veil'd Melancholy has her sovran shrine,
> Though seen of none save him whose strenuous tongue
> Can burst Joy's grape against his palate fine.

Keats and Thomas share the fine palate. It is in referring to this passage that Frank Kermode notes the likelihood of the Romantic artist in the modern world being 'cut off from life and action, in one way or another . . . a man who experiences it [the power of joy] will also suffer exceptionally . . .' (*Romantic Image*, p. 6). Such an artist's isolation is strongly suggested in 'Melancholy'; the poet is drawn towards and intensely conscious of the 'dear' human world, and at the same time jealous of his own *difference*. He wishes to lose contact with human voices (which, significantly, grow distant like *history*), and yet regrets doing so – joy and suffering come together: the vacillation and ambiguity of feeling are wholly typical of the kind of temper to which 'negative capability' is natural. There is no pressure towards a resolution of dilemmas and ambiguities; it *would* seem to be the case that in such poetry a cure for the depression would be a destruction of the intensity.

'Melancholy' certainly betrays traces of that temper which when under water would 'scarcely kick to come to the top'; elsewhere in the poetry there are references to a certain 'poison' at work, recalling Keats's dreamer who because he cannot keep pain and pleasure apart, 'venoms all his days' (*The Fall of Hyperion*, Canto i, l.175). There is also in 'Melancholy' something of what Thomas finds in Keats's sonnet 'Bright Star': 'a man troubled by the principal unrest of life cries out for that same calm, for the oblivion of "melting out his essence fine into the winds", for "soothest sleep that saves from curious conscience"....' (p. 72). Thomas is attracted in 'Bright Star' to 'would I were steadfast as thou art' and 'steadfast, still unchangeable'. The continually changing effects of light and weather and of the seasons on the English countryside often seem to image for him 'sublunary' alteration. Yet these changing effects are valued. Critics have long noted that Thomas is at once infinitely troubled by the burden of human consciousness, and yet celebrates its uniqueness. Some poems may suggest a Keatsian embracing of death, but at the other pole there is the statement in 'The Other': 'And yet Life stayed on within my soul'. He himself makes a point of Keats's having 'loved life too well to turn his back on anything by which men were moved' (p. 78). Both poets hover between expressions of 'joy' and 'melancholy', between love and life and vitiating apprehensions of the 'unrest of life', of death itself.

I have tried to characterize, then, a Romantic intensity, the kind of psychology which produces a poetic handling of experience like that in 'Parting'. 'Wind and Mist' dramatizes more or less overtly the 'psychological theme of attempted escape (to the house on the hill) and necessary return (to the earth below)'. (Stan Smith warns against foisting 'a crude allegorical meaning' on the poem: it seems to me its theme *is* psychological as well as to do with the very material sufferings Thomas underwent in the house.) In doing so, it records the ceaseless flux of Thomas's consciousness, in which what is 'in the mind' can become actual, the 'firm ground' can turn to cloud ('the visible earth ... like a cloud'), in which reality and 'fancy' co-exist and interchange; that haunted, hallucinated consciousness which appears in some Georgian poetry takes heightened form – in fact, Thomas's mental condition while living in the house became such as to cause his wife Helen to fear for his sanity. The 'one word' with which the poet leaves us confirms the vacillation between earth and cloud-castle (and between present and earlier self), the impossibility of 'choice' –

> 'I want to admit
> That I would try the house once more, if I could;
> As I should like to try being young again.'
>
> (p. 155)

– other than that imposed by irresistible external circumstances. The subject of 'Wind and Mist' was the house at Steep in Hampshire in which Thomas and his family lived from 1909 to 1913. As Cooke puts it: 'The house was magnificent, but they never felt at home there' (p. 58). Thomas's wavering about Frost's invitation to return with him to New Hampshire in 1914 shows itself as part of an inveterate indecision, and of a deep sense of his own capacity to 'feel at home' any more in New Hampshire, as he put it to Frost, than in old. In his book *The South Country* he spoke of 'those modern people who belong nowhere', and no less than three poems have the title 'Home'.

One of these takes stock of the poet's life (R. George Thomas thinks it may have been written after a visit to Thomas's parents).

> Not the end: but there's nothing more.
> Sweet Summer and Winter rude
> I have loved, and friendship and love,
> The crowd and solitude:
>
> But I know them: I weary not;
> But all that they mean I know.
> I would go back again home
> Now. Yet how should I go?
>
> This is my grief. That land,
> My home, I have never seen;
> No traveller tells of it,
> However far he has been.
>
> And could I discover it,
> I fear my happiness there,
> Or my pain, might be dreams of return
> Here, to these things that were.
>
> Remembering ills, though slight
> Yet Irremediable,
> Brings a worse, an impurer pang
> Than remembering what was well.
>
> No: I cannot go back,
> And would not if I could.
> Until blindness come, I must wait
> And blink at what is not good.
>
> (p. 117)

This and 'Parting' are obviously related; both were written in February 1915 under the pressure of Thomas's impending enlistment, and have similar movement and verse-form. 'Remembering ills' recalls 'Remembered joy and misery' in the other poem, where a subtly different case is put. But here the mood modulates, clearly enough, into an acceptance barely suggested in 'Parting'. The first two stanzas express the Thomas ambivalence about relatedness ('friendship and love') and 'solitude', and the longing for relief from an over-burdened consciousness ('all that they mean I know'), but then

comes the definitive self-diagnosis – 'this is my grief': it provides a point of reference for much of the rest of his poetry. Not
only does 'my home' almost certainly represent a deluded
longing, like the cloud-castle in 'Wind and Mist', but the poet
knows that he can never escape the curse of dissatisfaction. He
can never be finally certain that it is 'there' he wants more
than 'here', just as there can be no final abandonment of the
present – 'I cannot go back' – for the refuge of that 'strange
land', the past. The dilemma is complicated by the fact that he
does value the here and now, and such a poem as 'The Sign-
Post' indicates a possible preference for this over the unknown.
So, in the final quatrain of 'Home' both aspects of the Romantic solution to the dilemma – refuge in nostalgia and retrospection, or release into 'countries of the mind', 'enchanted
treasure-caves', death or 'whatever it is I seek' – are rejected. I
think it a remarkable stanza, too distinctive to be a mere echo
of Hardyesque fatalism. The powerfully pared-down ordinariness of diction itself implies an acceptance of the ordinary
human lot, and one detects ambiguity in the blinking at what
is 'not good', an admission that maybe there *is* something
about 'what is' to make it worth putting up with (this *does*
somewhat recall Hardy, 'faltering forward' at the end of 'The
Voice'). After the hesitancies and vacillations, a provisional –
though passive – decisiveness. So, repeatedly, one is struck by
an effect of Thomas's poems holding the line against the
sapping dissatisfaction, unease and weariness, refusing finally
to deny the worthwhileness of this life and this world.

A poem which objectifies this dialectic in Thomas's
consciousness, with its tensions of Romantic and counter-
romantic, is 'The Chalk-Pit'. Like 'Wind and Mist' the poem
is a dramatic dialogue between two voices, allowing the dialectic teasing convolutions. The two speakers have followed a
road which leads to an abandoned chalk-pit and one thinks
that he has visited 'the place' – these are familiar Thomas
symbols – before, looking like an 'amphitheatre', with a few
trees for actors; but these have now been cut down. There is a
certain Hamlet-like note,[13] a straining to peer into the
unknown, intertwined with that experience of emptiness and

silence I've spoken of as characteristic of the modern country poet:

> its emptiness and silence
> And stillness haunt me, as if just before
> It was not empty, silent, still, but full
> Of life of some kind, perhaps tragical ...
>
> ... better leave it like the end of a play,
> Actors and audience and lights all gone;
> For so it looks now. In my memory
> Again and again I see it, strangely dark,
> And vacant of a life but just withdrawn.
> We have not seen the woodman with the axe.
> Some ghost has left it now ...
>
> (p. 203)

That 'In my memory ... strangely dark' recalls again 'Parting' – the poem shares with 'Parting' and 'Home' a sense of the past and an earlier self being just beyond reach and yet impinging crucially on the present. Some essence has receded beyond recovery, but present action also seems inhibited. There is something of the Keatsian hovering between stillness and action; one thinks, too, of Eliot's 'Between the motion / And the act / Falls the shadow'. Both speakers seem curiously arrested, perplexed about where what they are experiencing points them. It is another poem which battles with the way the mind colours reality – the shape, the feel which consciousness gives to an experience, a curious distancing of the experiencing mind from the subject of its ruminations. In fact, if the old conundrum about appearance and reality is under debate here, the emphasis is on the way consciousness hallucinates:

> For another place,
> Real or painted, may have combined with it.

Here more clearly than ever the two speakers are the two sides of Thomas's mind – Thomas meeting himself, as he keeps doing in poems. In fact, there is a receding line-of-mirrors effect, one 'Thomas' echoing another into the distance or into the past – 'Or I myself a long way back in time', and the 'man of forty' (l.43) whom R. George Thomas points out is a self-portrait;

the girl of twenty (1.48) is 'based on' a memory of his courtship of Helen. Perhaps one might see an element of the ludic in this – there *is* a certain wry playfulness. But the slipperiness of identity, of subjectivity itself, was no game for Thomas: the hallucinatory effects to which it contributes in the poem, the way the structure and movement of the verse realize the 'feel' and intensity of the mind's operations, don't allow us to respond to it as such.

Each speaker attempts to come at some suspected 'core' of significance ('I cannot bite the day to the core', says Thomas in 'The Glory') from a different direction. But this never totally yields itself to the mind's grasp, as the last of the two to speak admits. At the same time, he rejects the 'romantic' solution; he will have nothing to do with what his companion calls 'fancies':

> 'You please yourself. I should prefer the truth
> Or nothing. Here, in fact, is nothing at all
> Except a silent place that once rang loud,
> And trees and us – imperfect friends, we men
> And trees since time began; and nevertheless
> Between us still we breed a mystery.'

Yet still there is no positive resolution of Romantic and counter-Romantic, or of the dilemma of which is more real – here and now, or 'there', the past, the 'legendary or fancied place'. The potency of the Romantic experience is still felt: the speaker cannot deny that 'mystery' existing in the relation of man to nature. Though his scepticism seems to disallow any response of a mystical or transcendental kind, the implication is, as felt by Lawrence and Graves, that there are mysteries, not least in the nature of consciousness itself, which continue in a positivist age to elude conceptual grasp, that any 'truth' which does not take account of 'mystery' will be insufficient. (R. George Thomas refers us to a prose passage in which Thomas writes of a 'community' with the trees felt 'in a way not to be spoken except by putting out his hand to touch their bark and leaves'.) At the same time, the sense of being a 'stranger to nature', at least in part, remains, and the emptiness of the scene admits a missing of social or human connectedness. Often, it is as if Thomas's poetry has its existence in the very interstice between nature and human community, unable quite to achieve contact with, to be finally at one with, either. It is what that teasing, nearly ludic, progress of the poem enacts: Thomas is, more fully than most, a poet who can never come to the point of 'final truth'; this is absolutely character-istic of the sort of temper, something very close to 'negative capability', we have seen Thomas to possess in common with Keats. His chronic restlessness and acute self-consciousness – he repeatedly complained of both in his letters – combine to eliminate from his poetry the possibility of experience being precipitated towards some definite end. Sperry's 'Romantic Irony' is present in even purer concentration here than in the cases of Lawrence and Graves. Hence we are left with the experience itself, which is pored over incessantly; valued, and despaired in, for its own sake alone.

II

In her book *Edward Thomas. A Poet for his Country* (London, 1978), Jan Marsh comments that 'Thomas's work ... does not require, nor will it bear the weight of much critical exegesis and interpretative analysis'. This implies a reductive way of seeing Thomas as if he is simply there to be admired, like the English countryside he writes about (there is 'a strange impres-sion of timelessness' about the poems). But there is no sign of the poems sinking beneath the growing weight of commentar-ry:[14] this suggests how complex a case Thomas, with his pecu-liar 'poetical character', is, neither to be excluded from 'exege-sis and interpretation' in the promotion of a mystique of enduring Englishness, nor to be scoffed at by those with inter-national horizons as old-fashioned and insular. Further, this accumulating work on Thomas consolidates our awareness that the interdependence of Thomas's prose and verse, as we have seen in considering the book on Keats, is of a specially interesting kind.

The prose and verse together impress upon us how compli-cated a man Thomas was and how acutely conscious of his own complications, and how that fact entrapped and circumscribed

him both in his historical moment and in a state of almost nar-
cissistic concentration on the operations of his own mind and
sensibility – which, however, the best poems contemplate in
that unfolding way I've noted, rich with surprise and possibility. 'Entrapped in his historical moment' is itself a paradox
if we consider his attitude to history. History was his subject at
Oxford, but 'I have no historic sense and no curiosity', he says
in *The South Country*. 'I have read a great deal of history – in
fact, a university gave me a degree out of respect for my
apparent knowledge of history – but I have forgotten it all, or
it has got into my blood and is present to me in a form which
defies evocation or analysis. But as far as I can tell I am pure
of history.'[15] Cathedrals, as historical objects, are, he says,
'incomprehensible and not restful'. There's a sort of willed
blankness in these comments, corresponding to a larger crippling of volition and blotting out of vision beyond the overwhelming present experience – how can cathedrals be incomprehensible to a man of his education and capacities? This is
from an essay 'History and the Parish':

Some day there will be a history of England written from the point
of view of one parish, or town, or great house. Not until there is such
a history will all our accumulations of information be justified. It
will begin with a geological picture, something large, clear, archi-
tectural, not a mass of insignificant names. It must be imaginative
... The peculiar combination of soil and woodland and water deter-
mines the direction and position and importance of ancient track-
ways; it will determine also the position and size of the human settle-
ments. The early marks of these – the old flint and metal
implements, the tombs, the signs of agriculture, the encampments,
the dwellings – will have to be clearly described and interpreted.
Folk-lore, legend, place-names must be learnedly, but bravely and
humanly used, so that the historian who has not the extensive sympathy and imagination of a great novelist will have no chance of
success. What endless opportunities will he have for really giving life
to past times in such matters as the line made by the edge of an old
wood with the cultivated land, the shapes of the fields, with their
borders of streams or hedge or copse or pond or wall or road, the
purpose and interweaving of the roads and footpaths that suggest the
great permanent thoughts and the lesser thoughts and dreams of the
brain ... (pp. 72–3)

As if to contradict himself ('I have no historic sense'), there is in
this passage a good deal which suggests the professional historian's eye, and an attractive concern with historiography as a
humane and cross-disciplinary activity, not mere documen-
tation. (What is suggested is not unlike the way Raymond
Williams has – for example, in his novel *Border Country* – of
reading the history of human lives in a landscape.) At the same
time, an amateur pursuit of personal whims ('What endless
opportunities . . .') is not too far from being licensed – nor,
surely, a wanting to get very quickly *away* from history. As Stan
Smith has put it (Smith is the most original and challenging of
Thomas's commentators) that sense of the land and the communities to which it gives rise 'is not ultimately historical at all
but biological'.[16] The immemorial in the countryside and
country life – even country names seem to carry with them
their own antiquity: 'What a flavour there is about the Bas-
setts, the Boughtons, the Worthys, the Tarrants, Winterbour-
nes, Deverills, Manningfords, the Suttons: what goodly names
of the South Country' (p. 73) – is a buttress Thomas needed,
like Hardy, against a psychically threatening sense of mortality
and of things passing. He seems to seek an almost religious
bond with the land, always to be looking for what Smith calls
'an irrepressible cultural essence' in his country places and
characters. The recurring figure of the rooted and acclimatized
countryman (of which his own other selves such as that 'man of
forty' in 'The Chalk-Pit' are sometimes examples) seeks to
embody this essence; he is, of course, infinitely elusive, met by
chance on lonely tracks, ultimately a construction of mind like
the longed-for countries. 'An Umbrella Man' which David
Wright sees as a prose counterpart to the poem 'Man and Dog',
presents a kind of Leech-Gatherer ('like a branch of oak . . .
never having to fit himself into human society': pp. 75, 78);
Thomas is at pains to give him a history, roots in an indigenous
culture, even, as a soldier, involvement in history, expressly, as
it seems, to emphasize his present state of being cut adrift from
history. The man is both part of nature as Thomas longed to
be, and 'pure of history' as Thomas felt himself to be – it is a
tragic irony that makes Thomas a victim of an all too historical

reality in his death near Arras in 1917. For all Thomas's 'concern with occupation of the land',[17] his 'History and the Parish' points towards the things in the poetry which work *against* the specific and the local and the communal in which it seems to be situated, and towards a way of making it look as if history is just a scribbling in the margins of 'the great permanent thoughts', or even of the perhaps unsituated privacies of 'the lesser thoughts and dreams of the brain'. Similarly with the interest in legend and folklore: ostensibly these inscribe a populist, communal experience, but in a way which stresses permanence and essence rather than historical process, and come to furnish Thomas with the symbolic goals of an inner quest, the 'fancied places' I have discussed.

What Thomas actually knew, and registered in poems like 'As the Team's Head-Brass', about the effects of the war on the English countryside, is that history disrupts, redirects those organic rhythms which are the object of his emotional attachment. To offer Thomas as a spokesman for organic community is not to be seeing quite clearly where this kind of interest takes him: his own failure to find psychic nourishment in it is repeatedly manifested in visions of himself as, for example, 'one of the helpless, superfluous ones of the earth' (p. 61). It's interesting, and disturbing, that signs of a cult of Thomas accompanied the rise of Thatcherism in England. Smith writes of Thomas's 'populist vision' and his 'ambiguous amalgam of radical and conservative sentiments': this translates only too easily into a romantic populism whether of the Left or the Right, a hankering after a kind of enduring Englishness which can somehow lift England clear of the tide of history, circumvent the blight of class divisions, and work all manner of wonders. Thomas has been championed by those who have invested in the notion of the *continuity* of Englishness. He is seen as resisting fashion and foreignness; as, in another kind of manifestation of conservatism, representing a cherished British middle way – one, for example, between Georgianism, and Modernism, on which succeeding poets can build. There are certainly ways in which Larkin, Hughes or Plath stem technically from Thomas, but his technical discoveries were

responses to the expressive demands of an extremist or radical
sense of 'abyss' – 'All lost ... in the undefiled /Abyss of what
will never be again' ('The Word') – of *discontinuity* as much as of
its opposite; and the expression of love of country in his
writings is utterly free of little Englandism or of distrust of
foreignness (the most important friendship of his life was with a
foreigner). To read Thomas as if his poetry actually confirms
the continuities it insistently contemplates is only to half-read
him.

Such essays as 'Leaving Town' from *The Heart of England*
(which can be set beside the poem 'Early One Morning'), or 'I
Travel Armed Only With Myself' and 'A Return to Nature'
from *The South Country*, give some idea of the extent of Thomas's
alienation from the town life amid which he grew up. His
refusal to enter the Civil Service, as his father wished, or to
accept the several remunerative jobs offered him during his
life, his estrangement from his father and adopting of such
surrogate father-figures as James Ashcroft Noble, father of
Helen Thomas, and the Wiltshire countryman 'Dad' Uzzell,
all add up to an almost wilful severing of roots and connections,
a rejecting of any kind of stable anchoring of his life such as his
time and class might have provided. And with this rejection
goes any means of getting a grasp on, making sense of, his
experience, his place in the scheme of things. 'These streets are
the strangest thing in the world. They have never been discovered. They cannot be classified. There is no tradition about
them ... They suggest so much that they mean nothing at all.
The eye strains at them as at Russian characters which are
known to stand for something beautiful or terrible, but there is
no translator ...' (p. 52). 'I travel armed only with myself'
(p. 58) because there is nothing else to be armed with, no
effective interpretative equipment. 'For what I have sought is
quiet and as complete a remoteness as possible from towns ...
[I am] one of whom to pursue is never to capture ... nearly
everything which the average ... and the superior and the
intelligent man is thinking of, I cannot grasp ... I expect there
are others as unfortunate, superfluous men ...' (pp. 56, 58).
Thomas's exceptional powers, in some ways yielding him so

much subtle grasp and insight, habitually fail him in the moment of final definition: there is no way of 'translating' what he intuits ('I cannot bite the day to the core').

The fact is that by background and education Thomas was equipped for the life of a sophisticated townman but that he then with painful self-consciousness *chose* a country life. What is striking is that despite the self-consciousness he never really seems to have scrutinized his rejection of the suburban and the bourgeois in ideological terms; as I've said, his mind always shied away from abstract explanations, and it's hard not to feel that this serves to feed the sense of absence, the elusiveness of the essences. But he could never fully be what he chose: for all his poems' particularity in the rendering of country things, what those poems insistently tell us is that Thomas never *belonged* to the land. 'I am not a part of nature', he writes in the passage (a kind of prose-poem in itself) from *The Icknield Way* which later became the poem 'Rain'. There was no root-edness; as I've noted, he was always on the move from one part of the countryside to another – 'This is my grief. That land, / My home, I have never seen.' This is further compli-cated by his feeling sometimes that because of his Welsh ances-try he was an outsider in the England he loved. There is a letter in which he speaks of feeling profoundly 'at home' in Wales; it's curious, then, that despite trying to live in several different places, he never attempted to establish a home there. The country characters in his essays and poems are closely and sympathetically observed, but there is always a distance between the writer and them; he could talk to country people *almost* as if he were one of them, but he remains a bookish man, not a working countryman. A review by Philip Larkin of William Cooke's book on Thomas was headed 'Grub Vale'; Larkin suggested that Thomas as the scribbler in a country cottage succumbed to a degree of romance, 'the romance of scraping a living from the printed word'.[18] While we may think this reflects a general condition of economic dis-placement suffered by the artist in an industrial society, the element of truth in it – that Thomas, so to speak, made his own bed and had to lie in it – is not altered by how agonizing a romance it became for him, how ultimately tragic its outcome.

His 'populist' sympathies are reflected in the fact that nobody wrote more perceptively than Thomas about the effects of the war on the ordinary people of Britain, concerning which *The English Review* commissioned him to write. The essays 'Tipperary' and 'It's a Long, Long Way', with their effect of the effortlessly factual and documentary, *are* in fact a kind of history-writing; yet his focus – though he reports the occasional exception who saw the war as class-inspired or who offers some other kind of 'historical' explanation – is on the myopia of the ordinary people's reactions to the war, on their lack of a sense of what the war might be said to be about, and on their almost biological patriotism. The more 'intellectual' patriotic frenzy of the middle classes Thomas found epitomized in his own father, as the poem 'This is no case of petty right or wrong' records. As usual, his father could do no right. Typically, the poem removes the war from the historical arena. 'Little I know or care if, being dull, / I shall miss something that historians / Can rake out of the ashes . . .' (*Collected Poems*, p. 257). Moreover, his writings at this time are more than usually preoccupied with the problem of what England *is*: yet again, it is something which for Thomas defies definition, defies grasp. 'This England', another in this series of reports from the home front, ranks surely, with its dignified informality, beside the famous set-pieces about love of country, but what becomes clear as one reads through to its eloquent culmination is that Thomas feels he must sacrifice himself to the land, to the English soil, before he can belong to it, or before he can possess the *meaning* of England:

it seemed that either I have never loved England, or I had loved it foolishly, aesthetically, like a slave, not having realized that it was not mine unless I were willing and prepared to die rather than leave it . . . Something I had omitted. (p. 164)

It seems to me odd to talk, as some people have done, as if Thomas's death in the trenches was some kind of inevitable destiny, the fulfilment of a death-wish. 'Home', I've said, despite the indulged Keats-like longing for a state resembling death which sometimes surfaces in the poetry, finally rejects the Romantic solution. Thomas wanted to live, hoped to return from the war, and, as another of the poems 'Home', beginning 'Fair was the morning', seems to say, could hardly bear to think of his family at home lest it should weaken his resolve somehow to earn that vital connection with the English soil. Nevertheless, that *was* his resolve, and a profound need, the only way he could see of release from 'superfluity'. What Thomas positively achieved, though, can be seen by comparing 'This England' with the poem which derived from it, 'The Sun Used to Shine'. Here a really complex state of mind replaces the rather single-note plangency of the prose essay, mapped by a much more selective particularity of detail and the kind of eddying syntax and movement which manages to make felt, without ever stating it, some more profoundly engaged conviction than the decision tentatively but consciously formed in the prose.

The prose-style itself, that of the self-conscious literary man, contributes to the distancing of Thomas from his subjects. Returning to the quoted passage from 'History and the Parish', we note how discreet yet determinative the rhetorical modelling is, a low-key elegance, seemingly unpretentious, but with a touch of artificiality – the careful modulations, the judicious pauses and expansions (his more youthful writing was, of course, blatantly artificial). The prose is never quite relaxed, always a little tense. Generally, there is a severely punctilious full-stopping which signals locally a larger inhibiting consciousness, that which prevents Thomas making connections, becoming part of, being at one with, or alternatively, finally defining, anything; the over-conscious artist sits on the sidelines, noting and analysing ('I go about the world with a worried heart and a note book', he wrote to Gordon Bottomley (p. 158). There remains both in the interest in 'folk-lore, legend, place-names' ('What a *flavour* there is' about those south country names) and in the language itself an obstructing residue of the observer from outside, the collector of beauties and curiosities. And in the final sentence quoted the writer's mind is rapidly getting away from the object and into a phantom locality: we have seen that there are many poems by Thomas in which an apparently physical locality or phenomenon – like the inter-weaving roads and footpaths here ('interweaving' suggests the characteristic way Thomas's verse takes the pressure of this kind of thought-movement) – metamorphoses into a landscape of the mind, becomes a metaphenomenon. It is one of the tensions in Thomas's poetry (at once unresolved but fruitful) that using language which appears to be virtually pure of abstraction or of metaphysical content he turns out to be a philosophical poet, a poet exploring the 'mind's morphology itself' (J. P. Ward, see below). I have tried to show something of the way he makes poetry out of a peculiar troubled 'con-noisseurship' of certain kinds of experiential phenomena; 'A kind of higher philately or connoisseurship' was what he himself diagnosed in Pater (p. 122). Thomas treats his country subjects with such delicacy, sympathy and intelligence that it is easy to be lulled into that reductive view of him as poet-countryman which even a fairly recent book (1978) such as Jan Marsh's offers. But it is his outsider's view of the country that helps give his poetry its tensions and intensities, and his incess-ant failure to belong there any more than in the city throws him back on an intense savouring of the experience itself and minute inspection of the operations of mind which attend it, as the only arena in which he can find any kind of value or satisfaction.

To see Thomas's life in the country as a version of waiting for Godot – the resolving epiphany which will make sense of things never eventuates – seems not entirely fanciful: that what con-nects Thomas with Beckett or Kafka is as significant as any sense in which he is a traditionalist is suggested by J. P. Ward in his essay on Thomas and Modernism in the Edward Thomas issue of *Poetry Wales* (Spring 1978). The anxieties of the Modernist consciousness haunt his work everywhere: he is aware of the rain 'accusing and trying me and passing judge-ment'; or one might cite the astonishing part-Dickensian, part-Kafkaesque short story 'Saved Time', with its 'old grey man with cobweb hair' who keeps the shop where time is saved and whose 'large long grey hands wriggled and twitched like two rats cleaning themselves' (p. 105). It seems quite feasible to construct a reading of this story as about a state of alienation from a nation of shopkeepers, for whom time is money, and saving both is paramount; for the Romantic-modern artist, as we have seen, time is not to be saved but transformed. 'Thomas never went completely "over the edge"', wrote Edna Longley,[19] but he often lived as near the edge as Lowell or Plath. We know from Helen Thomas that the fictionalized account of an attempt at suicide in *Light and Twilight* (1911) was Thomas's own attempt.

Thomas's kinship with the Moderns – all that which makes it difficult to see him as belonging in any real way with the confirmers of continuities and traditional pieties – extends to his preoccupation with the slipperiness of language: even there, the medium for *making* sense of things, it's hard to find a toehold. That anxious full-stopping in the prose suggests a fear that language will get away from him, but in the verse he makes most creatively original discoveries about how to let the words describe their own syntactical arcs.[20] It is not so much in diction itself as in the natural, self-determining flow and rhythm of the sentence that Thomas makes his contribution to establishing 'a language close to common speech' as the dominant language of modern poetry in English. As some critics have interestingly argued, seizing on a phrase from the poem 'I Never Saw That Land Before', he decided he must *trust* the words, that the language can't be bullied, is 'not to be betrayed'. However, he is caught in something of a cleft stick here. He conceives of language and the land as being organically related, and then of words as knitting up a seamless ahistorical community of meaning – hence, supplanting what was really an historicist understanding of language as a communal practice, he can move words out of the realm of merely utilitarian or positivistic discourse into one which, again, is essentialist and 'biological'. Plug into that and you plug into something which is meaningfully enduring: 'Will you ... / Sometimes ... / Choose me, / You English words' ('Words', p. 127). That sense of seamlessness is reflected in his striving for verse-sentences which are like organic growths, avoiding the disruptingly showy word or phrase, in their stylistic reticence apparently *not* like the Modernists. Ward interestingly suggests a distinction between Thomas's use of language, and that of the Symbolists and Imagists: 'the way to the *parole-langue* distinction opens' (p. 77). Modernism, I've suggested earlier, longs to take poetry out of the realm of linguistic signification altogether, to disrupt and transform it, whereas Thomas is content with speech as it is practised ('Make me content / With some sweetness / From Wales ...'), trusts linguistic 'competence' as a poetic resource. Yet contradictorily, the poem implies, with startling up-to-dateness, language perhaps speaks *us* as much as we speak it. Language is both essence like the land, and constructs us; is conceived of as both concrete and timeless. But the poem has no way of negotiating such a paradox – here the way opens too to that fathomlessness on top of which so many of Thomas's poems seem to float; language has not, finally, plugged into 'meaning'. He runs some way back out of this impasse by acknowledging that words are in a state of flux, constantly being remade in social use: 'Worn new / Again and again; / Young as our streams / After rain'. Words are both old and young, still rooted in nature itself, both passively worn like clothing and actively worn like tools – but here, of course, there is an edging back into the utilitarian realm and into historical process: we use and shape and choose words, they don't just choose us. They live certainly, but live in the fret of historical change, and I don't think Thomas wants to see either how crucially one has to engage with historical determinations, or how malleable the flux of language is, how firmly it has to be grasped to yield meaning. It is exactly like, indeed his *choice* of life in the country: he could then passively surrender himself to nature, waiting for its epiphanies to *choose him*, freed – somewhat as I have suggested is the case with the forms of exile *chosen* by Lawrence and Graves – of the need to contemplate more determinative actions. What Thomas actually finds is that words, like nature, perplex him, complicate and ramify his perceptions, and his verse-sentences can only pursue those windings until they arrive at a hiatus which has the *feel* of a clarification, and has to stand for one, but in which nothing is conclusively defined.

Alun Lewis wrote in his 'To Edward Thomas' of

> your striving
> To make articulate the groping voices
> Of snow and rain and dripping branches . . .[21]

In fact, language for Thomas becomes so untrustworthy that he turns very often to non-human speech in the search for a language that will tell him something:

> Some things I have forgot that I forget.
> But lesser things there are, remembered yet,
> Than all the others. One name that I have not –
> Though 'tis an empty thingless name – forgot
> Never can die because Spring after Spring
> Some thrushes learn to say it as they sing.
>
> ('The Word', p. 221).

How tentative and baffled this sort of thing is has often been remarked upon: it makes us feel that the seeming unpretentiousness of Thomas's language, its effect of ordinary speech, is actually a way of endlessly skirting the final struggle with meaning, not in the least dishonestly, but because of an existential disablement, which his poetry paradoxically realizes for us in all its savoured indeterminacy. What has been called a 'blocking out' process seems involved in the poems;[22] there's a sense in which he doesn't trust language *enough*, doesn't trust it as one does a tool to make sharp incisions in reality. 'His poetry manifests a faith that language and tradition need not be new-minted but can be "worn new"', writes Edna Longley (p. 11); the more essential fact is that his poetry manifests no faith at all, whether in language or anything else. He wants no dealings with history, yet doesn't really trust timelessness or essence – these have always a phantom quality. What he says of himself, that history 'has got into my blood and is present to me in a form which defies evocation or analysis' is truer than he will allow: he cannot speak what he knows, that the absences he is ceaselessly troubled by are entailed in the very turning-away from history. Thomas's world is full of words; he cocooned himself in them every day, yet all that the words add up to is 'empty thingless names'. Up to a point it's possible to see Thomas's poems as pondering, and to value them for being intent upon not betraying, a normative experience of how things are, that there are more things in heaven and earth than we can intellectually encompass. But the windings of his verse-sentences lead him through nameless and impalpable regions which can be made as little ultimate sense of as the labyrinthine worlds of Kafka or nameless localities of Beckett. He could not see a way out of his cocoon of words; any sense of 'future' was as elusive to his grasp as any other satisfaction – 'all that had once been alive and was memorable though dead is now dung for a future that is infinitely less than the falling dark rain' (p. 112), and in this respect, it is true, the hiatus at the end of his life is like the hiatus at the end of his poems. Past or future, memory or desire, neither yields determinations.

Nevertheless, to vary the figure in a way suggested in the prose version of 'Rain' – 'like the unborn I wait and wait' – there is a way of seeing his cocooning as a prolonged and painful process of gestation which finally issued, through the prose, in the small, indispensable body of poetry. For all its faults, the prose is constantly throwing up a poet's perceptions; and at its best, especially in the criticism and the directly autobiographical prose immediately preceding or contemporary with the poetry, it is enviably exact and lucid. Besides the importance for his own poetry of the book on Keats, and the kind of value of his *Richard Jefferies* (1909) which Q. D. Leavis indicated when she called it 'a classic in critical biography', the key critical text is *Walter Pater* (1913). This is the book in which he turned on his youthful idol and became the best critic of his own faults (but Thomas was always hyperconscious of his own faults, that was part of the disability), as well as mapping out a programme for a language close to speech before that was the received wisdom. One is pulled up again and again by the unforced rightness of what he has to say here about style. The remarkably percipient 1913 review of Lawrence's *Love Poems and Others*, quoted in an earlier chapter, gives us the means of appreciating how adept at close reading Thomas was before, again, that became an orthodoxy. He was virtually the first reviewer to recognize the qualities of Pound's *Personae*, and as for his reviews of Robert Frost's first two books, they were certainly the most important to appear at the time, and still offer some of the most valuable comments on Frost's poetry. Nobody in England was writing better criticism than Thomas in those years. Yet even in these critical writings, for all their lucidities and pre-empting of developments in twentieth-century criticism, and though one may appreciate their reticence and refusal of showiness, there is a certain withholding of decisiveness complying with the indeterminacies of the poetry.

Thomas's 'real place' is as a recorder and elegizer of 'the final passing' of the 'rural world' of England, wrote David Wright (p. 27). It would be pointless to deny that something of the kind is a brooding presence in Thomas's poetry, but that isn't what is really important about Thomas, unless we see the loss of a pre-industrial England as somehow redeemable in a late twentieth-century world, unless, that is, we invest in the rural myth, see the repossession of some sort of essential agricultural England – a heart of England, Paradise Regained – as a tenable ideal. The complex traditionalist-romantic-modern we encounter in Thomas resists categorization, has no such definitively 'real place'. Wright quotes Donald Davie's remark that nobody 'has yet made out a case for Edward Thomas that does not sound like special pleading'. Perhaps, but nobody else is like Thomas, and it is in the nature of his case that he has no designs on us. He furnishes us with a scrupulous attending (philosophical in the issues it presses) to how subtle, rich and strange subjective experience can be, an exemplary demonstration of that value of specialness which the Romantic movement apotheosized. Yet to feel himself awash in indeterminacy, helplessly 'pure of history' and yet not, either, truly 'a part of nature', and that his fellow men too often 'all were strangers', was in fact to be acutely attuned to a more impersonal consciousness, that of his place and time in history.

CHAPTER 4

'*Myself must I remake*': *W. B. Yeats*

I

The year in which Edward Thomas died at the age of 39, 1917, was the year in which W. B. Yeats, at the age of 52, married Georgie Hyde-Lees. He was a kind of elder statesman of twentieth-century poetry; it is common to say that when Pound and Eliot arrived in London and began announcing their prescriptions for a new poetic, Yeats had already made the necessary discoveries independently. He had seen the need to throw off nineteenth-century rhetoric and begun forging a poetry which could 'come to terms with immediate experience . . . in a language close to common speech'. He was getting a remarkable range of experience into his poetry, bringing it under artistic control, finding it immensely difficult, yes, but not close to unmanageable in the way I've noticed in some poets. And from roughly the period of *Georgian Poetry* onwards he was to explore with the command of a master artist a theme of particular concern here, the plurality of consciousness.

In 'The Chalk-Pit' we have seen Edward Thomas conducting a dialogue between two sides of his own consciousness; 'The Other' is a complex interrogation of his own pursuit of an *alter ego* which he never quite seems able – as with all his experience – to grasp or define:

> I travelled fast, in hopes I should
> Outrun that other. What to do
> When caught, I planned not. I pursued
> To prove the likeness, and, if true,
> To watch until myself I knew.

(p. 27)

Yeats appears to conduct a similar quest, with a more decisive energy:

> I call to the mysterious one who yet
> Shall walk the wet sands by the edge of the stream
> And look most like me, being indeed my double,
> And prove of all imaginable things
> The most unlike, being my anti-self,
> And, standing by these characters, disclose
> All that I seek ...[1]

But the modern poet's problem in fixing identity, so very troublesome for Thomas, is here taking on a peculiar dimension. It is as if Yeats wilfully *dismantles* self. And this seems entirely logical: since 'identity' is indeed so problematical, why not take it apart and start again? Auden, we shall see, did something of the kind even more radically. Yeats's is really an opposite move to that we see in Thomas, away from the idea that there is a 'myself' to know, even though it won't be known, an 'other' who, for Thomas, though an aspect of his own consciousness, seems to stand inaccessibly *outside* him. It is towards, in a sense more challengingly (among other things, there isn't that same frustrated, baffled note), an unlikeness to self within likeness.

Nor is it the same movement we have been looking at in other modern poets. Lawrence, we have seen, seeks to be reborn into a state more fully self; the inner quest is for 'totality', or perhaps more precisely a solipsistic anarchy of self – and Yeats abhorred 'mere anarchy'. Graves has survived such unbearable experiences and suffers such difficult inner conflicts that he must always be on the defensive; consciousness is such a fragile affair, why should anybody want to play games with it? He could not comprehend anybody wanting to adopt the sorts of 'obviously false' parts Yeats did, scornfully referring to 'Yeats's posturings', to 'the Brocken Spectre Yeats' (see Seymour-Smith, *Robert Graves*, p. 469). Both Graves and Hardy strive to create a state of personal consciousness in which it is bearable to live, a self which will hold, however provisionally, together; something, as I will inevitably touch on in my next chapter, serving a similar function to the state of *impersonal* identity T. S. Eliot sought to construct. It is true that Hardy is unable to invest in the vision of organic wholeness at which the Romantics had aimed, scrutinizing himself in 'Wessex Heights' as if, in an almost hallucinatory way, more than singular. In 'The Darkling Thrush' he sees his own state of mind reflected in nature as in a mirror. This is breaking some of the ground for Yeats, but there remains the sense of being divided from nature as well as split off from another (former) self, and therefore incomplete. Yeats, unable like Thomas to be content with mere indeterminacy, reaches past such obstacles; admits, and indeed cultivates, the plurality of self, his goal being a totality not only of self, but of inner and outer consciousness. In 'Coole Park and Ballylee' he *says* nature is a mirror, confronts the division of self from nature head-on, almost exults in it:

> Upon the border of that lake's a wood
> Now all dry sticks under a wintry sun,
> And in a copse of beeches there I stood,
> For Nature's pulled her tragic buskin on
> And all the rant's a mirror of my mood[.]

(p. 275)

It is a measure of how far Yeats has travelled from 'nature poetry'; he is calculatedly standing apart both from nature and himself, mocking his own and nature's melodramatics. This *invited* plurality enables him, I suggest, not only to interinvolve self and unlikeliness-to-self, but to engage history and at the same time stand aloof from it. It is he who most fully explores the antitheses of isolation – the Romantic otherworld beyond time-bound existence – and the material here and now, the historical world of an actual human society. It is one which is indeed local and actual, Ireland in the decades on each side of the turn of the century, peopled by historical personalities who inextricably enter the weave of the poetry. The objective and subjective consciousness are in his poetry constantly in a state of dialectic; his poetry comes nearer to realizing them as necessarily involved with each other than virtually any other in our century.

There is no need to draw attention as I shall in the cases of Eliot and Hughes to how much Yeats's poetry is about his own life and mind, since the poetry publishes this fact so openly. Unequivocally on the Wordsworthian pattern, Yeats made the study of his own mind as an inspiration for poetry a lifetime's object. 'One goes on year after year getting the disorder of one's own mind in order, and this is the real impulse to create', he wrote to his father;[2] the need to get his mind in order arose in part from its extraordinary capaciousness, its bent for a far-flung eclecticism. But I think there are two factors which put Yeats at an advantage in avoiding 'final isolation'. One is that the 'actual human society' to which he could relate – Ireland with its struggle for *national* identity – was so much more definite and unitary than the vague and shifting notions of 'England' with which English poets had to deal. An excellent account of this and its accompanying sense of a culture being made, of dreams being turned into realities, can be found in John Lucas's *Modern English Poetry: From Hardy to Hughes*. What matters is that Yeats was provided with a 'public' realm which could be felt as 'real'. Perhaps also it is difficult in a city like Dublin and a country like Ireland to live an anonymous life, or perhaps the Irish temper is particularly given to self-revelation. Whether or not this is to stereotype Irishness, the fact is that Yeats lived much of his private life in a fairly public arena, in front of an audience he could address, so that public and private in his poetry appear aspects of the same thing: in speaking of his own life and mind, he is *ipso facto* speaking of public affairs. Late in his life he finds 'my friends' portraits' hanging in the Municipal Gallery and notes that the visitor can 'Ireland's history in their lineaments trace' (p. 370). His poetry's public voice is achieved with an ease which British poets find hard to emulate: Auden comes closest to it.

The other advantage is that while he observed and was certainly touched by the calamities of his time, he escaped the actual experiences of combat which were so disabling for some of his greatly gifted younger contemporaries. The Easter Rising and the Civil War took place on his doorstep and yet he was not directly a participant. Sometimes this is a problem: he could imagine his friend Major Robert Gregory facing death with an equanimity which, so far as one can tell, hardly existed among combatants. Yet the way *Meditations in Time of Civil War* confronts the impinging of history –

> Last night they trundled down the road
> That dead young soldier in his blood:

– is paralleled only by the War Poets and the thirties poets in England, and by and large they either died, or turned away because the reality was too hard to bear, or because the effort to warn was so obviously fruitless. In poem V of the magnificent *Meditations* the speaker turns away from those participants in history not in any attempt to extinguish their reality but as a conscious act of seeking an antithetical reality. These famous lines are unavoidable, since they are at the heart of what I need to say about Yeats:

> A brown Lieutenant and his men,
> Half dressed in national uniform,
> Stand at my door, and I complain
> Of the foul weather, hail and rain,
> A pear-tree broken by the storm.
>
> I count those feathered balls of soot
> The moor-hen guides upon the stream,
> To silence the envy in my thought;
> And turn towards my chamber, caught
> In the cold snows of a dream.

(p. 230)

The self which envies these men of action seeks its anti-self: dream seeks reality, reality seeks dream. But the very terms 'antithesis' and 'anti-self' assume the reality of the thesis and the self. This ambiguous relationship to what is happening immediately around him is directly the subject of the poem, the title itself miming the precarious balancing act between isolation and involvement, dream and reality. Admittedly there is an attempt to neutralize the material, historical reality, 'to silence the envy', so that the other reality can be envisioned. But what the poetry here and in so many Yeats poems does is to insist on both realities, to manifest each as inescapable, inextricably involved, as I said, with each other. There are problems, of course. An advantage of the plural vision is that all selves and all 'realities' can be seen as true ones, but against this, an intractable difficulty emerges concerning choice and commitment.

If, then, the case is as I have stated it, how could Frank Kermode come to say of Yeats that he

is the poet in whose work Romantic isolation achieves its full quality as a theme for poetry, being no longer a pose, a complaint, or a programme; and his treatment of it is very closely related to his belief in what Pater called 'vision' and the French called Symbol. (*Romantic Image*, p. 29)

The answer is that the life-in-history Yeats's poetry dramatized was at every point experienced as imperfect, craving its antithetical state, life-out-of-history. His vision of an Ireland where a future was being forged co-existed with another, fatalistic, vision of civilization coming to an end. Here he is as fully committed to an otherworld as any poet in the Romantic tradition. There can be no doubt that what Yeats longed for was 'the artifice of eternity'; that the poetry does not in fact endorse that ideality, the inviolate stasis of consciousness with which Graves's poetry seeks to rest, but rather realizes the value of a plural consciousness, was, in a sense, despite himself. In the early volumes this sense of the imperfect was wrapped in the misty *ennui* that was instantly available for the *fin-de-siècle* poets:

> And, ever pacing on the verge of things,
> The phantom, Beauty, in a mist of tears;
>
> (pp. 12–13)

Baudelaire had defined beauty as 'quelque chose d'ardent et de triste, quelque chose d'un peu vague'. It is sad because it *has to be* vague and elusive, since once grasped it becomes mundane, ordinarily imperfect, subsumed by a positivist bourgeois world, though lesser poets than Yeats indulged and rather enjoyed this for the easy let-out from action it provided. These evocations in Yeats's youthful verses, and his interest in the occult and in the supernatural figures of Irish mythology, are early expressions of a desire to believe that the elements of a non-

material world are 'real', are 'facts', just as much as the flawed
material reality of the everyday. He is attracted to a mystical
idealism in a way Lawrence, Graves and Thomas are not. He
could find a sympathetic friend in Arthur Symons, interpreting
French Symbolism as a revolt against the outer world and the
language of utilitarian discourse, and another in William
Morris with his cult of a medieval Golden Age. In this, of
course, he was very much of his poetic generation, one seeking
to identify with an older Ireland, that of a Celtic Twilight,
affiliating with the Aesthetic movement in repudiation of a
materialist Victorian society. That repudiation took a different, but trenchant, form in another Irishman, invoked in my
Introduction and one of those known personally to Yeats,
Oscar Wilde. In the question of identity, it was as if Yeats knew
too well what he was, where he fitted as a member of the
Protestant Ascendancy: he felt himself too identified with a
materialist Victorian Anglo-Ireland, and wanted none of it.
Referring to Villon and Dante, he said that in their work 'we
gaze not at a work of art, but at the re-creation of the man
through that art, the birth of a new species of man ...'[3] He
must remake himself.

'The Lake Isle of Innisfree' is an exemplary case of the
poetry of flight, involving versions both of the rural myth and
the self-exile, the isolation, of the Romantic artist. In *The
Wanderings of Oisin* Yeats's hero leaves the world of action, itself
not the world of present action but the heroic pagan world of
ancient Ireland, to spend three hundred years in the world of
dreams, in the island of dancing, the island of victory, and the
island of forgetfulness. But – Graves's adept, we might recall,
was instructed to 'Avoid this spring, which is Forgetfulness' –
Yeats didn't in fact flee to a lake isle, and Oisin finally returns
to the world of action. In an actual Ireland, Yeats's practical
and organizational abilities, his threefold involvement with
Irish Nationalism, Maud Gonne and the Abbey Theatre
venture, as well as such public affairs as the Hugh Lane
controversy, kept him face to face with a worldly reality,
maintained the complex play of antitheses in his life and his
art. 'The fascination of what's difficult' is what one notices

throughout Yeats's life both as man and poet; once free of the Nineties pose, there is little trace of the Romantic accidie. He may complain in the poem of that title that 'theatre business, management of men'

> Has dried the sap out of my veins, and rent
> Spontaneous joy and natural content
> Out of my heart
>
> (p. 104)

—has robbed him of the capacity for Romantic 'joy'. He may feel he lives in a squalid, ungracious, non-heroic age where 'No Second Troy' is possible, and that poem along with so many others contemplates the estranging and isolating effect upon Yeats of his famous passion for Maud Gonne. She herself became for him an image of a complete perfection disastrously fallen from having given itself over to 'the world'. But what we actually observe is his capacity to be many things at once. He is a manager of men at the same time as a dreamer and a rider of that Pegasus which 'on Olympus leaped from cloud to cloud'. He is able to acknowledge and celebrate his own Romantic inheritance while accepting its inapplicability in a changed world:

> We were the last romantics – chose for theme
> Traditional sanctity and loveliness;
>
> ('Coole Park and Ballylee')

He is able to stand outside and objectify his subjective predicament, to see it as one among many possible selves, one of which may live in the here and now, while another undertakes voyages to Byzantium.

Then marriage and the birth of children combined with theatre business and management of men to bring the poet integration into 'ordinary' life, the life of a man with both domestic and public affairs. Yet the repeated operation of the principles of plurality and antithesis is remarkable in Yeats's life; simultaneously there comes, by means of what Yeats took to be his wife's spirit-mediumship, a newly enlarged access to the occult world. And making a family home at Thoor Ballylee contradictorily provided him with a concrete symbol, the

Tower, actualizing the situation of the isolated artist.[4] He now literally had, not a lake isle, but a refuge into which he could turn away from the outer world to pore, in the light from his lamp, over inner and occult mysteries. It is also at the time of his marriage, in *Per Amica Silentia Lunae*, that his doctrine of the self and the anti-self, the idea that in the course of 'the quarrel with ourselves' we pursue an opposing, reversed self, surfaces explicitly ('Ego Dominus Tuus' forms a prologue to the essay). 'I think that all happiness depends', he once wrote in a diary note, 'on the energy to assume the mask of some other self ... a rebirth as something not oneself, something ... created in a moment and perpetually renewed ...' (Jeffares, p. 197). *All happiness depends* on it: life is intolerable without the capacity for momentarily discovered but constantly renewable self-embodiments in the antithetical. Here are the beginnings of the system expounded in *A Vision*, another of those systems compiled by modern poets out of a need to impose on the ruins of the old objective beliefs a subjective order of the imagination, a coherent mythology which can provide, as Yeats famously said of *A Vision*, 'metaphors for poetry'.[5] Robert Graves subtitled *The White Goddess* 'A historical grammar of poetic myth', Yeats first called *Per Amica Silentia Lunae* 'An Alphabet', both implicitly acknowledging that in order to produce its meanings poetry necessarily draws upon and manipulates a formal system. But that system is not felt to be already in place; it has to be put there.

Yeats's 'thought' has been discussed in a great number of books and this is not the place to cover that ground again. Moreover, as he himself admitted, he tended to over-elaborate in what could become a sterile way; he felt, A. N. Jeffares points out, 'that once he had formed the idea of the mask he became over-allegorical and his imagination became sterile, for nearly five years' (p. 197). *A Vision* is certainly nowhere near so readable as *The White Goddess*, but if by comparison, as Seymour-Smith has said, it is unsophisticated in its eclecticism, Yeats's thinking has a sweep which is in the end the opposite of Graves's need to close the story off, to have things tidy and final. It is marked by that unwillingness ever to rest content, not to entertain further possibilities, that characterizes his whole life's endeavour. Like Graves's, however, the system may be seen as a strategy for resolving antithetical possibilities, 'conflicts between the poets and their society as well as conflict within the poets themselves'. It removes those conflicts into a subjectively objective realm (the anti-self is to be discovered *within* the self) where the problems of consciousness can be ritualized by the imagination, wrought into poems. The precise status claimed for that realm is, as Graham Hough has written, obscure:

Yeats's Anima Mundi from which the images of the poet are derived is Jung's collective unconscious, from which come the archetypes of myth and legend. Yeats's mask is the unconscious, in Jung's sense, not in Freud's – not the waste-paper basket for discarded experiences and desires, but the vehicle of the buried faculties, those which are unused in the conscious life ... We find in both the same fertility and the same obscurity about the exact status of the myth. When Jung explains ecstatic and mystical experience in terms of the unconscious we feel the same uncertainty as we do when Yeats talks about 'the condition of fire'. Into what country are we being led? Are Byzantium and the collective unconscious psychological or meta-physical entities?[6]

Hough's 'vehicle of the buried faculties' brings us back to Lawrence's 'plumbing of a depth', Eliot's 'sinking to the most primitive and forgotten'. But certainly our experience of the poetry must be that while Yeats constantly talks of the supernatural as a reality, he is not wholly given over to a supra-psychological view of what that speaker in Thomas's 'The Chalk-Pit' calls 'mysteries'. What both Graves and he *do* experience as intense realities are change, mortality, social estrangement and a violent, threatening world where the collapse of civilization appears an imminent possibility. It is precisely because of this that the recourse to the other realm, and a faith in the power of the poem to recover its truths, becomes so urgently necessary.

II

Hic, the first of the two speakers in 'Ego Dominus Tuus', is the spokesman for the modern 'objectivity' and materialism. Like the comparable speaker in Thomas's 'The Chalk-Pit' who sees only actualities and will not 'mix my fancies up with them', as against the speaker who is conscious of 'a mystery' between man and nature, *Hic* reproaches *Ille* for being 'Enthralled by the unconquerable delusion, / Magical shapes'. He in turn is reproached by *Ille* for seeking the 'modern hope' of an objective self, one fit for the social and political affairs of the world, since those who 'love the world'

> serve it in action,
> Grow rich, popular and full of influence,
> And should they paint or write, still it is action:
> The struggle of the fly in marmalade.

(p. 181)

For *Ille* the pursuit of worldly things can only bring the artist misery:

> What portion in the world can the artist have
> Who has awakened from the common dream
> But dissipation and despair?

(p. 182)

When *Hic* offers Keats as a repudiation of this, *Ille* turns his argument on its head, surmising that Keats's 'luxuriant song' brought him no satisfaction because it was *only* of the world. Keats's dreaming is no more than childish longing: 'I see a schoolboy when I think of him, / With face and nose pressed to a sweet-shop window.' But this 'coarse-bred son of a livery-stable keeper' must surely have longed for refinements, for an unworldliness, which were always to be beyond him. It is evident how reluctant Yeats is to relinquish the dream or image of 'otherworld', and I want to argue that the effect of this is that he holds world and otherworld in what I called in an earlier chapter a jammed polarity. He cannot commit himself to the world, it belongs too much to 'practical men who believe in money, in position, in a marriage bell, and whose understanding of happiness is to be so busy whether at work or at play, that all is forgotten but the momentary aim'.[7] The touch of aristocratic disdain in the view of Keats reflects Yeats's sense of the everyday world of the common man, especially when it is tainted by any form of trade or commerce (the livery-stable keeper), as inevitably corrupt and materialist, so that the romantic dream, the sense of the difference of the romantic artist, is involved with Yeats's nostalgia for an aristocratic social order: that and his anti-materialism are bound up together. His distaste for those who see no other need than to 'fumble in a greasy till' ('September 1913') and anxiety to establish his own descent through no 'huckster's loin' ('Pardon, old fathers'), although as George Moore mischievously remarked, he came from 'millers and shipowners on one side',[8] might itself be seen as rather vulgarly bourgeois. But it is a response, really, to a widespread modern experience of the disorientating effects of democratic forces, a tendency to experience this as a falling apart, and to be distrustful of the politics which are bringing it about. (In particular – and Lawrence, for all his iconoclasm, shares in this – the mass is feared, a fear long rooted in the minds of cultured people and throughout our own century producing a difficult and in some ways understandable ambivalence about democracy on the one hand, and 'mass-production' and 'mass culture' on the other.) Indeed, the objective self, *Hic*, is preferably to be discarded altogether, so that the subjective self may devote itself to seeking the image, its own opposite, which will lift it clear of the world of action, of the struggle of the fly in marmalade:

> By the help of an image
> I call to my own opposite, summon all
> That I have handled least, least looked upon.

As envisaged here, the undertaking is not unlike Lawrence's goal, journeying into 'final loneliness', of a reborn phoenix of self: 'a direct connection is forged between intense subjectivity and a timeless reality'; 'actual human societies', with their unideal and worldly commitments, their 'responsibilities of citizenship', are omitted.[9] 'Those men that in their writings are most wise / Own nothing but their blind, stupefied hearts.' Then why the need for the *dialogue* at all? As in poem after poem, what actually seems to produce the poetry is the intensity of the struggle with 'the world'. Again and again the poem reverts to a kind of seduction by the 'sweet-shop window' of the human and natural world, to the pull of its demand for 'action' and for the exercise, to invoke the title Yeats gave his 1914 volume, of 'responsibilities'. (In that volume the poet renounces the Celtic Twilight, with the exception of its notion of an Ireland made up of an almost mystic unity of peasant and master, its 'Dream of the noble and the beggar-man' ('The Municipal Gallery Revisited'), a notion which he carries with him as he then enters passionately into the controversies of his actual contemporary Ireland. The Irish middle classes become the enemy, castigated for avoiding their responsibilities as patrons of culture.) And clearly this must be so: the ceaseless pursuit of what is opposite, of what is hitherto 'least looked upon', *must* entail the leaving open of all possibilities. Responsibility itself offers antithetical possibilities, to life, or to art, and I don't think Yeats ever saw the choice between 'perfection of the life or of the work' as cut-and-dried in the way some critics have suggested. Characteristically, he hovered ambivalently, as does the poem 'The Choice' (p. 278) itself in stating the dilemma.

Some such detachment as that envisaged by *Ille*, which includes detachment from the fear of death, is what Yeats imagines his friend Robert Gregory to have achieved as an airman in World War I:

> I know that I shall meet my fate
> Somewhere among the clouds above;
> Those that I fight I do not hate,
> Those that I guard I do not love ...
>
> (p. 152)

This is certainly not the spirit in which Edward Thomas went to the war, and the disinterested aloofness from actual human societies ('Kiltarten's poor') is made explicit. Those measured octosyllabics, forming up into precise pairs ('Those that I fight ... Those that I guard ...'), hovering as if in mid-air like the airman himself, contemplate a kind of ultimate exempting from worldly fears and imperfections, a rapt defiance of mortality and change. The poetry of Yeats's old age, finding

a means for the imagination to transcend mortality, is anticipated. But the delight imagined is indeed a 'final loneliness':

> A lonely impulse of delight
> Drove to this tumult in the clouds;
> I balanced all, brought all to mind ...

And the poem goes nowhere, simply, if one may put it so, hangs
in the balance. This was *too* simple, Yeats couldn't escape the
fascination of what's difficult. 'In Memory of Major Robert
Gregory' admits in the very amplitude of its architecture the
impossibility of any such rapt immunity from worldly human
attachments, fears, desires, regrets. It acknowledges too the
impossibility in the imperfect actual world of that Sidney-like
self-completeness which Gregory is seen to have embodied:
such might have existed at some past peak of civilization, some
phase of perfect 'Unity of Being' such as was initiated 'somewhere about 1450' (*Autobiographies*), but can no longer, according to the Yeatsian nostalgia, be looked for – 'What made us
dream that he could comb grey hair?'. And in any case,
Gregory as apotheosized in the poem is a kind of *Hic* and *Ille* all
in one, 'all life's epitome' – 'all things the delighted eye now
sees / Were loved by him', and the stanzas go on to enact that
delight in the multiplicity of things, characteristically crowd-
ing example on example, demonstrating the necessary inter-
involvement of the various Yeatsian antitheses, of action, for
example, and the 'secret discipline' of intellect and
imagination.

Moreover, contemplating combat from this distance is not at
all the same thing as violence close at hand. A year or two
earlier, the resources of the kind of short line used in 'An Irish
Airman' (but more freely varied), its capacity to balance all,
bring all to mind, had been put to work with stunningly
greater range and subtlety. 'The Easter Rising', wrote Louis
MacNeice, 'gave Yeats a shock at once enlivening and horrifying. He had built an Ireland out of words and now he saw
them translated into action.'[10] The shock elicited one of the
great poems of the century. The line is here more distinctively a
rocking trimeter, rhyming uneasily, coming in short breaths,

catching the poet's mixed and troubled feelings, his turning of the meaning of these events over and over in his mind. The phrase 'Polite meaningless words' is repeated as the meaningless exchanges of words are repeated in the Dublin streets, but exchanging is to become a problematical unavoidable nub in the poem. The mediocrity and clownishness of Dublin life, the lack of serious purpose in Ireland, is to be 'changed utterly', these clowns are to attain their heroic anti-selves. Women Yeats had known in his youth exchange their 'young and beautiful' selves for the shrillness of political activism, only to be changed again by participation in the Rising. So, too, Yeats's view of 'the drunken vainglorious lout' MacBride does not change yet does: the state of consciousness the poem expresses is one in which selves and anti-selves, indeed all possible opposites, can be contemplated simultaneously. The singular consciousness – political single-mindedness – changes the human heart to stone:

> Hearts with one purpose alone
> Through summer and winter seem
> Enchanted to a stone
> To trouble the living stream.

(p. 204)

Sterile fanaticism opposes the ever-changingness, the variety, the plurality, of the living; the unstable trimeters tumbling around this antagonistic still centre. 'Minute by minute' the living world undergoes momentary experience, the concrete *experience itself*, unhindered by that teleology, that abstract idea of eventual fruit which dehumanizes the rebels. 'The political class in Ireland ... have suffered through the cultivation of hatred as the one energy of their movement', wrote Yeats in the 1909 *Autobiographies*. The poem's final paragraph hangs all in the balance, at once deeply troubled and exultant:

> O when may it suffice?
> That is Heaven's part, our part
> To murmur name upon name ...
>   ...
> Was it needless death after all?

...
> And what if excess of love
> Bewildered them till they died?

The obsessive effect with which the names of the rebels are chanted over joins the revolving metrics, the reiterations of phrase, and the pregnant oxymoron 'a terrible beauty', to effect the poem's vacillation between antitheses, which in turn reflects the poet's own bewilderment – the refusal to 'make a stone of the heart' which is also a standing aloof from the expression of 'love' in terms of politics, the appalled reaction to the use of violence and yet the endorsement of heroic action. The plural consciousness is both enabling and disabling. The revolving both celebrates the rebels, creating a martyrology, and enacts the unwillingness to come down decisively on one side or the other.

The sense of daily Dublin life, the historical actuality given by the use of those names, the preparedness to focus so intently on an event of such a nature, the homage paid to men and women of 'action', all add up to an acknowledgement of 'the world' as 'reality', and to a refusal to write off intervention in history as of no avail. Indeed, the changing of the rebels into martyrs, murmuring name upon name with the tenderness of a mother for her child, is itself a political act. At the same time, 'the full horrors of entering history' (John Lucas, p. 120) are revealed to Yeats. And the dilemma about 'responsibilities' – how does one choose between, on the one hand, the horrors which often succeed upon political 'action', and on the other, acquiescence in political ills? – is likely to be met by the twentieth-century reader with manifest recognition. The poem is indeed a tackling of difficulties, the probability that there is no complete solution to that dilemma will no doubt be felt by many people as a reality of their own experience. 'Easter 1916' continues to matter greatly to us because its formal procedures so adequately realize that power of fanaticism to trouble the living stream which is still so much, and probably likely to remain, part of our world. This, I suggest, helps account for the hold the poem takes on us, in accordance with my contention that for a poem to work depends upon some 'recognition' in the reader, and that hence purely formalist accounts of poems are insufficient. As I said in my Introduction, this is not a question of merely affirming given perceptions, and the kind of critique which places Yeats in a mode of poetry which 'performs . . . the work of [capitalist] ideology'[11] by constructing the 'I' as a kind of 'super-subject' which is unitary and 'non-contradictory' won't wholly suffice either. Such poems as this and the *Meditations*, surely, bring the contradictions of self into the open, 'foreground' precisely the fragility, the changings, of subjectivity, the dangers of imposed or accepted roles, the extreme difficulty of exercising freedom; processes which uncover the suppressions of consciousness, enable for the reader recognitions within recognitions. In the actual poetry, the transcendent 'super-self' is only one of the selves at issue. But for all this, the poem never wholly lets go of the hovering aloofness to which 'An Irish Airman' was to be given over. Louis MacNeice did not like the illiberal elements of Yeats's politics, yet it is quite easy to read 'Easter 1916' as an expression of the liberal imagination and of its 'bewilderment' and inefficacy in the face of twentieth-century history, the very problem I will later find embedded in MacNeice's own poetry. 'A terrible beauty': a self and its anti-self revolve and interchange throughout the poem, locked, to repeat the phrase, in a jammed polarity. One self deplores change, wants to keep things as they *were* (betrays nostalgia for the country-house culture and the roles it assigned to women: 'When, young and beautiful, / She rode to harriers . . .'); its anti-self is seduced by the catastrophic finality of change, sees in it the potential for a kind of sacrificial purging which recalls Graves's and Lawrence's Romantic primitivism. And that Yeats should then have moved in the direction of 'An Irish Airman' and 'The Second Coming', with their apparent fatalism in the face of the 'blood-dimmed tide' of modern war and revolution, has often been found disturbing.

'The Second Coming' (1919) has always struck me as close to panic. No wonder, one might say: the 'mere anarchy' Yeats perceived being loosed upon the world was something to panic about, and it is a pity that 'the best' were not more widely moved by the same depth of response. And it could again be read, especially in the 1920s and 1930s, with a shock of recognition: the tide might be that of Marxist revolution, or that of Fascism – whichever the individual reader feared most. But if the poet's sight is 'troubled', this doesn't here seem the troubled liberal imagination; the poem is too ready to prophesy inescapable doom. Yeats appears to lose nerve, to abandon plurality and go for the kind of single unqualified vision which 'Easter 1916' is so appalled by. It is almost as if written by the anti-self of that poem. The governing oxymoron has gone: what here 'Slouches towards Bethlehem to be born' is terrible without the beauty. But the 'changing' strategy is still in operation: we experience the poem as compelled into being by terror which it then attempts to change into an antithetical marvelling at the supernatural, impersonal, extra-historical functioning of *Spiritus Mundi*. That this manœuvre seems imperfectly under control, as well as an inappropriate 'change' to make, is part of the poem's problematical case. 'Leda and the Swan' (1923), by contrast, is prodigously controlled and concentrated in its handling of similarly apocalyptic material (a framed moment enforcing the victim's powerlessness and crisis), and commands its antitheses – male, female; mortal, divine; tender, violent – with dazzling aplomb. The rape of Leda might be the rape of the poet himself by his fascination for overmastering 'brute blood', his own surrender to the glory of a violent god. In any act of violence, are there gains to set against the terrors? It is another version of the case put in poem I of the *Meditations in Time of Civil War* – are 'sweetness' and 'gentleness' necessarily consequent only upon the desires of 'bitter and violent men'? The god comes from the air and returns to it, aloof and indifferent like the Irish Airman: can the mere mortal share any of that transcendent impassivity by acquiescing in the inevitable ravagings and cataclysms of history? Should we let things happen how they must, trying only to school ourselves in the nature of that 'how', rather than attempting actively to intervene in and shape history? The poem's concluding rhetorical question – that device for which Yeats had such a fondness but which must mean he cannot decide on an answer – leaves all unresolved (it is not, after all, *merely* rhetorical). Yeats said that he meant the poem to be about annunciation; as with Graves the poet is servant of powers beyond himself, a medium of oracular speech. Yet, in a further extension of plurality, it is susceptible of a quite different reading: violent acts lead inevitably to greater, more catastrophic violence:

> A shudder in the loins engenders there
> The broken wall, the burning roof and tower
> And Agamemnon dead.
>
> (p. 241)

This 'liberal' position is undeniably in the poem, but it isn't affirmed, is left to hang in the balance, all the poem's antitheses and pluralism still in play. But then one has to set against this extraordinary passionate ambivalence the way the *Meditations* (1922) may readily be experienced by the reader as a statement of the predicament of the ordinary individual in a world of war and disorder, violence and uncertainty. It is another case of violence close at hand eliciting a less heady response; the reality of civil war taking place on the poet's own doorstep is not easily transposable into the romantic, mythic realm of 'Leda and the Swan'. However particular to Yeats the symbols used – 'The road at my door', 'The stare's nest by my window', 'Sato's gift, a changeless sword', even the 'magical unicorns' and 'brazen hawks' (recalling the desert birds of 'The Second Coming') – there is an effect, to which the linking personal 'my' actually contributes, of a kind of Everyman speaking. And if, as discussed earlier, the poet turns away from 'the world' to the 'cold snows' of his private dream, into the Tower of his isolation, towards the land of Imagination, the transcendent 'Heart's fullness' –

> The abstract joy,
> The half-read wisdom of daemonic images,
> Suffice the ageing man as once the growing boy
>
> (p. 232)

– this may strike us as the natural reaction of the individual who finds he is powerless to intervene in history. And this, for my purposes, is the salient point about Yeats. His poetry expresses with a greater eloquence and immediacy than almost any other in our century the sense of a real history sweeping us up in its movement and yet of our powerlessness to affect it. Auden, too, was to make much of this, of the 'crowd of ordinary decent folk' obliged to stand helplessly by while atrocities are committed ('The Shield of Achilles'), but I shall return to his case as one which proposes alternative options to Yeats's. Yeats does offer a strategy by which to make oneself a possessor of power, but it is finally a strategy entirely *within* oneself, a kind of subjective consecration of the very powerlessness.

After all, Yeats, the manager of men and theatre business, the Irish Senator, the 'sixty-year-old smiling public man' in 'Among School Children', did try out the masks of public life. But this 'comfortable sort of old scarecrow' again has his anti-self. While he accepts the reality of ageing and of human limitation, the private inward man is troubled as ever by a yearning for images of the immortal and unchanging, for 'cold art', for the 'self-born mockers of man's enterprise'. The poem's final stanza is an extraordinary effort to fuse the material and the ideal, an achievement of the 'heart's fullness' without excesses of asceticism or arid intellect – without, one might say, fanaticism. The whole poem's strenuous meditation represents an attempt to blend opposites – 'it seemed that our two natures blent ... Into the yolk and white of the one shell' – to give everything, every thesis and its antithesis, its due. The ecstatic surge of these final rhetorical questions sweeps us into a blossoming or dancing which enacts an assimilation of the human with the perfect, of the subjective with the objective, a 'unity of being' like that of the tree and its parts, or the dancer and the dance: citizenship fused with inner vision, human limitation fused with the enduring abstract perfection, world fused with otherworld. But if this is the unitary super-subject, it is all too aware of the precariousness of its balancing act. The contrary-pulling impulses play out their drama with less total fusion in 'Byzantium' and 'Sailing to Byzantium'. The need to accept human nature and life as they are, in all their sensual grossness and confusion, is set against the desire for invulnerability, for the artifice of eternity, in a manner again having things both ways, declining to come down finally on one side or the other. The poems fully realize the inescapable power of nature and time and beside it the insubstantiality of the vision, the 'miracle' envisaged in 'Byzantium', yet wrest a victory from nature and history through the power of the mind and imagination to envisage that which is beyond their depredations, to undertake the subjective journey to Byzantium, a power which robs nature of its omnipotence. Consciousness *does* set us apart from nature even while we are governed by nature, its endlessly changing shapes enabling a kind of defeat of nature.

The poetry of Yeats's old age has always been, with its harsh (at times forced?) vigour and sensuality, its effect of coming down at last to the bare rock, a source of wonder and perhaps discomfort for readers. One self, indeed, grasps the traditional calm of old age; 'My temptation is quiet', says the poet in 'An Acre of Grass' (p. 346). But an antithetical self refuses to be content with this: 'Grant me an old man's frenzy, / Myself must I remake . . . ' The 'Crazy Jane' songs echo Feste at the end of *Twelfth Night* or Lear's fool on the heath and construct a world which prefigures that of Yeats's fellow-Irishman Samuel Beckett. If Yeats, as Richard Ellman has said, 'is more the poet of the sea torn by sexuality and tormented by time than the poet of the perfect moment',[12] this final world is one in which sexuality and mortality are in a strangely defiant way celebrated. The timeless is conceived, as it was by Shakespeare, as not 'out there' but immanent in the materiality of things (a notion I shall come back to in discussing Ted Hughes). 'The Circus Animals' Desertion', probably written within a year of his death, appears at last to acknowledge the failure of creative energy, yet snatches another triumphant poem from that very subject; appears to confess that whatever splendid images the artist may create, in the end they are eloquent blarney and he must come to terms with bare material reality, yet won't disown the 'masterful images' which 'Grew in pure mind'.

The wonderful 'Lapis Lazuli' (1936), however, renews the

attack on political fanaticism; only art, only the power of the imagination, offer renewal, a means of remaking. The politicized women may well be right that 'poetry makes nothing happen':

> I have heard that hysterical women say
> They are sick of the palette and fiddle-bow,
> Of poets that are always gay,
> For everybody knows or else should know
> That if nothing drastic is done
> Aeroplane and Zeppelin will come out,
> Pitch like King Billy bomb-balls in
> Until the town lie beaten flat.

(p. 338)

But this is not to have grasped the Shakespearean insight that we are all merely players in a great, extra-historical drama, and that our task is to perform our plural roles for all we are worth but not to try to rewrite the lines: the drama will play itself out whatever we do. We must seek behind our limited roles the impersonal archetype, 'more type than man, more passion than type'.[13] Yeats had commented in *Per Amica Silentia Lunae* in connection with 'Ego Dominus Tuus':

If we cannot imagine ourselves as different from what we are, and try to assume that second self, we cannot impose a discipline upon ourselves though we may accept one from others. Active virtue, as distinguished from the passive acceptance of a code, is therefore theatrical, consciously dramatic, the wearing of a mask ... (*Mythologies*, p. 334)

Civilizations come and go but this task, this need of imposing a discipline upon ourselves, forever remaking ourselves, does not alter. Scrutinizing the lapis lazuli medallion given him by Harry Clifton, Yeats sees the effects of change inscribed on the stone itself, 'Every discoloration of the stone ...', yet the Chinamen carved upon it appear to have achieved final impersonal discipline, a full understanding of one's powerlessness to make things happen or prevent them happening. Aloof on their mountain, they have been remade, able, with a gay impassivity which defies ever-changing nature, to balance all, bring all to mind:

I
Delight to imagine them seated there;
There, on the mountain and the sky,
On all the tragic scene they stare.
One asks for mournful melodies;
Accomplished fingers begin to play.
Their eyes mid many wrinkles, their eyes,
Their ancient, glittering eyes, are gay.

The gnomic mode requires of the reader the very equanimity
read by the poet in the medallion; it is open and intertextual;
the provocative stances and apparently unrelated parts must
be calmly interrogated and permitted to settle in the reader's
imagination, forming the whole new thing which is the poem.
If in the years immediately before his death Yeats insists on the
reality of Crazy Jane's bare material universe, it is in order to
grasp more wholly a plural consciousness. The artist, Yeats
said, sheds the deceptions entertained by those hysterical
women: 'The other self, the anti-self or the antithetical self, as
one may choose to name it, comes but to those who are no
longer deceived, whose passion is reality.'[14] In face of our
objective powerlessness, we may, like the Chinamen, achieve a
subjective power, the ever-remaking power of the mind or the
imagination, where time and history have no sway. To see
consciousness as empowering in *this* way may be to acquiesce in
that objective powerlessness, and I think this a real problem.
But through all his mature and late work subjectivity itself is
opened up and interrogated in a way which seems to me also a
form of dissent, not at all confirming the 'freedom' of the
subject such as can be readily assimilated by ideology.

CHAPTER 5

'Here and now cease to matter': T. S. Eliot

I

My reasons for choosing to discuss T. S. Eliot at some length don't only have to do with his unavoidability on the map of modern poetry. He strikes me as the central case; to express in its acutest form a 'problem of consciousness' at the heart of the modern experience, a perception of consciousness as utterly amorphous and disordered, powerless to yield meaning. My theme in this chapter is the peculiar interdependence in Eliot between what I take to be the intensely personal sources of his poetry and the way he has appeared to speak for his time – a kind of oracle indeed. Like Yeats he is always seeking the *inclusive* consciousness, to wear the mask of the man who has 'known it all', but without the Yeatsian readiness to balance world and otherworld; rather, with the effect of a kind of cancelling-out, so that 'here and now cease to matter'. Perhaps more than any poet he presents a case of loss of trust in the fruits of experience, a sense of the futility of action, of intervention in history; a turning elsewhere in quest of meanings – elsewhere being both 'inward' and 'beyond'. In his biography of Eliot Peter Ackroyd writes, in sentences which suggest the *necessity* of biographical study of Eliot:

His own need for order reflected that which existed among his generation; his own fears of fragmentation and meaninglessness ('the Void') were also theirs. He had, I believe, a clairvoyant sense of his time – clairvoyant because he found its preoccupations within himself.[1]

It has long been a commonplace that Eliot's use of a fragmentary method expresses the fragmented modern consciousness;
but only gradually, and only recently with fullness, have the
documents become available to clarify that what these devices,
techniques, strategies of 'fragmentation' most urgently and
directly embody are the stresses of Eliot's personal life. Of
course, Eliot had views about culture and civilization and it is
not only by chance that they get into the poetry. But Eliot's
subtle awareness of history and the poetry's effect of repre-
sentatively addressing a modern crisis of being occur simultaneously with a peculiarly intense seeking to be 'pure of
history'. As I've said about Edward Thomas, the subjective
condition may be seen as coincident with an historical reality.
Because 'his time' felt itself, as Eliot personally did, in an
historical limbo, the very subjective impasse the poetry
embodies functions to make what could be taken for a general
or 'impersonal' statement.

Eliot's 'Critical Note' which prefaced the *Collected Poems* of
Harold Monro when it first appeared in 1933 (a year after
Monro's untimely death), is of exceptional interest in foregrounding this matter of 'personal' and 'impersonal', subjectivity and history. Eliot concluded with what Stephen Spender,
in his review of the book, called a 'bitter reflection':

There was no way out. There never is. The compensations for being a
poet are grossly exaggerated; and they dwindle as one becomes older,
and the shadows lengthen and the solitude becomes harder to endure.

'This may well be true,' commented Spender, adding of
Monro:

One has the impression of a blind, erring and suffering man, but the
enormous reward his valid suffering has to offer is that his very
incoherence should acquire significance . . .[2]

I've said (chapter 2) that Eliot's essay on Monro seems to
express heartfelt fellow feeling, and that Eliot makes out a case
for Monro as the writer of a valuable kind of minor verse.
Geoffrey Bullough may have had Monro in mind when he
wrote, as I quoted earlier, of Georgian poetry's 'preoccupation

with memory' and 'desire to investigate the half-apprehended notions, the obstinate questionings and blind misgivings of sensitive and introspective souls'. This seems to me usefully to summarize that whole strain of subjective realism, with its hauntings and disjunctions, one finds in Hardy and in some Georgian verse; but wouldn't, in fact, Bullough's phrases also fit Eliot's *Prufrock* poems readily enough? And what Spender calls Monro's 'very incoherence' acquiring significance – could that not describe the effect of the apparent 'fragmentation and meaninglessness' of *The Waste Land*? Moreover, reading Monro, Eliot seems, while not dispensing with the idea of an impersonal tradition, to endorse more fully than before the value of the personal. 'The historical point of view', he wrote in the Critical Note, 'tends to emphasise what a man has in common with others', but this was bound to be unfair to Monro because 'the vision is the personal vision of Harold Monro', who 'does not express the spirit of an age; he expresses the spirit of one man'. But he does this 'so faithfully that his poetry will remain as one variety of the infinite number of possible expressions of tortured human consciousness'.[3] 'Tradition and the Individual Talent' is very much of a particular moment in Eliot's strategy for creating a climate for his own verse. But it seems to me not to date markedly. It represents a very subtle negotiation between the concept of an author's individuality and one of a text as 'impersonal', as part of an historical continuum, a gathering-point of historical pressures – of a kind, in fact, that already goes some way in the directions undertaken by more recent critical theory. In the Monro 'Critical Note' of some fourteen years later, however, Eliot is much more prepared to lay stress on 'the spirit of one man', on the 'personal expression' of 'tortured human consciousness', on (in Spender's phrase) the 'valid suffering' of an individual. What has happened in those fourteen years, we may ask, to 'the escape from personal emotion' so insisted on in the earlier essay? And why should Monro's very minor achievement have provoked the kind of interest it did in Eliot?

'Gerontion' may provide some clues. Monro's 'centre of interest', wrote Eliot, is 'in the spectres and the "bad dreams"

which live inside the skull, in the ceaseless question and answer
of the tortured mind ... '. Gerontion has 'no ghosts' yet his
brain seems haunted by its very vacancies. This old man in
whose 'dry brain' the drama of despair is played out, the
variety of image and allusion giving an effect of a vast 'weariness of knowledge',[4] who has lived long only to feel an absolute
spiritual vacancy and impotence, speaks with a voice which
does not *appear* to be that of the poet himself. Full of echoes of
the Jacobean drama Eliot had been reading at its time of
composition (very close in time too to the writing of 'Tradition
and the Individual Talent'), the voice establishes an 'objective
correlative', being shut up in a house, for the sense of there
being 'no way out' that Eliot later noted in Monro. For
Gerontion, there are only questions to which no answers are
returned: 'After such knowledge, what forgiveness?' His neuro-
tically anxious 'Think now' gets him nowhere; it leads him only
into a rhetorical impasse, an implacably revolving unanswer-
ingness. The language itself at certain points dissolves in
enigma, borders on meaninglessness. That obsessive 'Think
now' about history's 'cunning passages, contrived corridors'
makes us feel that the limbo-like nightmare and impotence are
states into which, somehow, history has manœuvred the
speaker. The impotence is in the 'Gull against the wind', the
'old man driven by the trades', in Gerontion's relentlessly
fruitless examination of his predicament. This seems pursued
for its own sake, almost as a substitute for the positive action
and involvement from which Gerontion has all his life been
excluded, and I think what we note is that Gerontion fails to
interpret history, comes up against a blankness, retreats into a
private nullity:

> I that was near your heart was removed therefrom
> To lose beauty in terror, terror in inquisition.
> I have lost my passion: why should I need to keep it
> Since what is kept must be adulterated?
> I have lost my sight, smell, hearing, taste and touch:
> How should I use them for your closer contact?
>   . . .
>   Tenants of the house
> Thoughts of a dry brain in a dry season.[5]

History has somehow got him cornered in his subjective purgatory, and his torture is that he cannot let go, cannot achieve the oblivion of unconsciousness (despite loss of sight, smell, etc.), but continues obsessively preoccupied with his 'thousand small deliberations'. It is again an instance of the overburdened consciousness together with a blankness about the capacity of history to offer meanings.

The apparent allusion to the corridor between Germany and Poland 'contrived' at Versailles certainly gives objective grounds for a feeling akin to Yeats's of powerlessness in the face of history. But the problem, I suggest, goes deeper. The poem marks the first point in a *personal* poetic progress (which it would not be entirely inappropriate to call a pilgrim's progress) at which it becomes evident that the Prufrockian condition of isolation and impotence is not ahistorical but represents a reaction *against* the processes of history. The 'jew' who 'squats on the window sill ... Spawned in some estaminet of Antwerp, / Blistered in Brussels, patched and peeled in London' *is* an agent of history, but in the form of a rootless and spiritually devoid commercialism which now seems to have become the civilization's directing principle. The tone of revulsion signals the unwillingness to see involvement in history, if that is what is entailed, as meaningful. It has been held against Eliot that those lines, with the demeaning lower case 'j' (though in more recent printings this has become upper case), have an anti-semitic ring. But there is no evidence that Eliot condoned persecution of the Jews; rather, in Eliot's thinking and that of others like him at the time, there are unexamined assumptions about what Jews are and do. They are identified in particular with commerce. Hence they have been instrumental in that triumph of a democratizing commercial spirit which is interdependent with the growth of an impoverished mass-culture, fertile ground for commercial exploitation. (Here, of course, Lawrence, Yeats and Eliot share similar antipathies.) That is a major symptom of the sickness afflicting our civilization, for which – it is a theme of *The Waste Land* – we need a cure. But this equation of Jewishness with commercialism and its attendant ills, and in turn of those with the growth of democracy, reflects, surely, a reading of history which is blatantly reductive and tendentious. For all the subtlety of Eliot's mind, there seems, as with Graves and Edward Thomas, something disabling and inhibited about the way in which history is approached, an unwillingness to consider it as in any way productive. There appears to be a process of willed *self-exclusion* from history.

The distrust of history and of the temporal goes together with a distrust of 'the visible world'. I will give at more length the passage on Monro from which I have already quoted, since it betrays, I think, such interesting self-recognitions:

I feel always that the centre of his interest is never in the visible world at all, but in the spectres and the 'bad dreams' which live inside the skull, in the ceaseless question and answer of the tortured mind, or the unspoken question and answer between two human beings. To get inside his world takes some trouble, and it is not a happy or sunny world to stay in, but it is a world which we ought to visit. The external world, as it appears in his poetry, is manifestly but the mirror of a darker world within ... Under the influence of this sincere and tormented introspection, the warm reality dissolves: both that for which we hold out our arms, and that at which we strike vain blows. (pp. xv–xvi)

This suggests a way of experiencing material, historical, time-bound existence, daily life, as never wholly real. The resulting state of isolation, procrastination, inertia, crippling introspection – the apparent unreality or 'nothingness' of things sapping the will for action and involvement – finds expression in all those devices we think of as Eliotic innovations: the imagery of closed rooms, the hesitant and groping verse-movement, the anaphoric phrasings, the fractured lines and inconsequential rhyming, the cinematic elisions and ellipses, the disembodied consciousness or depersonalized bodily fragments (eyes, arms, fingers), the painfully self-examining monologue, the nervous snatches of dialogue ('the ceaseless question and answer'): 'What shall we ever do?', 'Nothing again nothing' ('A Game of Chess'), 'That's nothing to me and nothing to you' and 'Nothing at all but three things' (*Sweeney Agonistes*). The effect of a 'coming-and-going of many lives across fixed points of

loneliness and boredom',[6] of a closed-in or closed-off world, is
crystallized in lines which form a touchstone of modern isolation:

> We think of the key, each in his prison
> Thinking of the key, each confirms a prison ...
>
> *(The Waste Land*, ll. 413–14)

The claustrophobic flat in which the action of *Sweeney Agonistes*
– that dramatic *fragment* – takes place, and the aimlessness of
the inhabitants' lives, echo Gerontion's sterile incarceration.
All these fragmentary characters, lacking whole personality,
live on the edge of nothing, which they fear above all but
cannot escape. Dusty and Doris preparing for the party, like
the woman preparing herself for an assignation in 'A Game of
Chess', are, obviously, frantically keeping at bay the 'darker
world within', only to find that the guests who knock for
admission are emissaries *from* that darker world.

Eliot, despite the sense which pervades the poetry's strategies
of an insecure hold and of the unreliability of the ordinary
'visible world', did not deny that in certain senses that world is
real and important. He believed that 'even the most exalted
mystic must return to the world, and use his reason to employ the
results of his experience in daily life'[7] and that the Christian has
a duty to apply himself to practical matters. Once established as
a poet, he put a good deal of energy into an effort to become a
force in public life. *The Criterion* always sought to be more than
just a literary forum, and the biographies document how fully
Eliot packed his life with public lecturing, membership of
committees, and so on. It is one of the paradoxes of this
withdrawn man, but perpetuates one of the larger paradoxes of
the Romantic tradition – we have seen that intense subjectivity
and otherworldliness are *products* of a commitment, often, to
redressing 'false' social values. Concomitantly, the strong pull
back in Eliot's poetry towards the visible and the sensory, the
attractiveness of these for him, have always been noted:

> Now the light falls
> Across the open field, leaving the deep lane
> Shuttered with branches, dark in the afternoon,
> Where you lean against a bank while a van passes,
> And the deep lane insists on the direction

Into the village, in the electric heat
Hypnotised. In a warm haze the sultry light
Is absorbed, not refracted, by grey stone.
The dahlias sleep in the empty silence.

(p. 177)

We recognize familiar experience, can identify the impressions
and sensations, are prepared to credit the record of an actual
event in an actual landscape. In these lines at least, a concrete
physical world is honoured; there is no sense of revulsion. So
memorable are such passages that they tend always to run in
one's mind. Yet we gradually notice how much of this is mere
suggestion, *using* the concrete and the local, but scrupulously
avoiding commitment to, investment in, them.

The rhythmic insistence, the way the extremely skilful
deployment of stress sustains a lulling movement, the static,
hypnotized quality of those impressions and sensations, have
an extraordinary effect of suspending us ambiguously between
two worlds. The passage is largely impressionistic in method –
the open field and *the* deep lane are only partially particular-
ized, and 'you' need not be, after all, the poet himself on a
specific occasion leaning against an actual bank. This
impersonalizing and generalizing use of the definite article and
of *we* and *you*, rather than *I* (suggesting a subject not fully
centred, still distrustful of itself twenty years after *The Waste
Land*), recurs throughout *Four Quartets*; it also helps convey the
poem's anti-individualist statement, its concern with the idea
of a Christian *community*. A certain timelessness as well as
blurring of locality attach to the scene, the lines do not define a
wholly specific moment in the here and now. This impressionism is in fact a development of Imagism: the 'thing' is
concretely there, but intimating an indefinite and timeless
hinterland (more of this in a moment). But 'building his
imagery upon an objective structure', Eliot achieves 'defi-
niteness of statement and indefiniteness of suggestion'.[8] In lines
like these, in fact, we experience the physical world with an
almost metaphysical intensity (an even more notable example
– wonderfully fine as poetry whether or not one accepts its view
of reality – is the opening section of 'Little Gidding'). There is

an effect of the time which helps define the everyday outer world having been suspended, and of something *super*natural about the natural scene – 'light', 'hypnotised', 'the silence', 'electric' – an almost hallucinatory effect. 'Light' hints inevitably at the mystic, and, as A. D. Moody has noted, the 'modern' diction – 'van', 'electric', 'Hypnotised', 'refracted' – interjects disorientatingly upon this scene of dreaming rusticity.[9] The 'warm reality dissolves'. Phrase after phrase in those comments on Monro has, one sees, the pressure of self-reflection. Though one can't deny the presence of 'impersonal' religious feeling in *Four Quartets*, the dominant effect of the poetry is to lead us into a world where the sense of reality is very peculiar and personal, to take us more completely 'inside the skull' of the poet – away from 'objective structures'.

II

I have suggested that Harold Monro might serve as in certain respects a representative case – the disaffected bourgeois and hopeful liberal intellectual of the early decades of the century, whose vision darkened as the years wore on. When young, Monro belonged to that liberal intellectual movement represented by figures like the Schlegel sisters in E. M. Forster's *Howards End*, to what Leonard Woolf called the 'wonderfully hopeful and exciting' ambience of the early years of the century.[10] Optimistically, he wanted poetry to herald a new age, and to bring poetry to the people. He flirted with most of the current philosophical fads, including Nietzscheanism and the sorts of pseudo-religion Eliot satirized in references to the Russian theosophist Madame Blavatsky and to invented figures like Madame Sosostris, Mr Silvero and Madame de Tournquist. Rejecting Christianity, he tried to nurse religious feeling in the form of the vague pantheism fashionable in those years, experimenting with meditative exercises as a result of his acquaintance with Edward Carpenter. To this end, as we've seen, the rural fantasy of Georgian poetry, what Stephen Spender called Monro's 'weekend landscape', is often enlisted, but, as Spender says, 'the country is never observed'; Monro,

Eliot pointed out, was in fact an inveterate 'town-dweller'. In 1913 Monro wrote in a review of a book of poems called *Streets*, by Douglas Goldring, that no poet had yet succeeded in writing 'a London poetry', despite the fact of the town 'being the one all-commanding reality of our present existence'. Henley and Binyon, he said, 'can neither of them satisfy us, because the city has not forced them to write'.[11] For poetry of the city which seemed written out of necessity the English poetry public had to wait, of course, for Eliot – his 'Streets that follow like a tedious argument', his 'thousand lost golf-balls' of suburban Sundays, his city-dwellers who 'Droop in a hundred A.B.C.s', his 'If it rains, a closed car at four', his 'Birth, copulation, and death'. Here indeed, one might say, is a poet forced 'by the bondage of temperament and habit' into writing of the Baudelairean *ennui* of modern city life, of a place where life, as Monro translated from a poem called 'Townsman' by the French poet Charles Vildrac, 'is consumed in unfulfilment'.

Some brief attention at this point to the work done by another townsman, F. S. Flint, a friend and associate of Monro, will allow me to complement what I have said of the Georgians with some remarks, necessary to what I have to say about Eliot, on Imagism and related developments. Flint joined Eliot in contributing a note to Monro's *Collected Poems* and wrote in Eliot's *Criterion*. Like Monro, he is a minor poet who, however, voiced with a certain authenticity the experience of passing 'his life among streets'; he's been called 'an interpreter of London'.[12] For a few years he was an indefatigable participator in literary affairs, aligning himself with Pound's Imagism rather than Georgianism, the self-appointed historian and explicator of the Imagist programme (which eventually brought him into conflict with Pound). An extraordinarily accomplished linguist and probably more widely read than Pound and Eliot (despite a working-class, self-taught background), he was important as a translator of and commentator upon Continental poetry. Conrad Aiken is reported to have said that Flint's translation of Jean de Bosschère's *The Closed Door* in 1917 'influenced Eliot directly – "a cadenced, highly colloquial verse, the unacknowledged fountain of a lot of that period"'.[13] His interest for us here is his role as a mediator of the Symbolist aesthetic to Anglo-American Modernism, and in the way he expressed crucial antitheses of this Romantic-Symbolist-modern tradition. Combining the lives of Civil Servant and poet-critic, he lived daily the post-Industrial-Revolution dissociation of art and life, the conflict between acceptance and escape, world and otherworld.

In Monro's magazine *Poetry and Drama*, Flint wrote: 'Poetry is a quality of words put together at the behest of the emotions and the imagination, irrespective of forms ...' (1, 4 (December 1913), 479–80). And in the Preface to his own significantly titled *Otherworld* (1920):

Clarity and sincerity of speech and purpose are the perennial qualities of all good poetry, and those who will strive after these qualities ... and who will disburden themselves of the lumber bequeathed to them from the past, are the men who will be heard ... (p. xi)

Behind this, I suggest, is a long liberating sweep which passed from the English Romantics to the French Symbolists and back to the Anglo-American Modernists. Arthur Symons in *The Symbolist Movement in Literature*, such an influential book for Yeats, had said of Verlaine:

It was partly from his study of English models that he learnt the secret of liberty in verse, but it was much more a secret found by the way, in the mere endeavour to be absolutely sincere, to express exactly what he saw, to give voice to his own temperament, in which intensity of feeling seemed to find its own expression, as if by accident.[14]

The line of descent is clear if we look at essential Romantic theory such as that of John Stuart Mill:

Poetry is feeling, confessing itself to itself in moments of solitude, and embodying itself in symbols, which are the nearest possible representations of the feeling in the exact shape in which it exists in the poet's mind.

What *is* poetry, but the thoughts and words in which emotion spontaneously embodies itself?[15]

We can see here the characteristic Romantic osmosis between Impressionism (recording impressions spontaneously received through the senses) and Expressionism (giving direct and immediate voice to the emotion.) We also see how both may relate to a primitivist antipathy to 'thought' or conscious artifice – 'intensity of feeling seemed to find its own expression, *as if by accident*'. The quest is for Herbert Read's 'true voice of feeling'. Pound's *Credo*: 'I believe in technique as the test of a man's sincerity',[16] or his statement in a letter to Harriet Monroe that 'Every literaryism, every book word, fritters away a scrap of the reader's patience, a scrap of his sense of your sincerity',[17] fit the same pattern. The case for liberty in verse is the Romantic case against the restrictive rules and artifice which remove poetry from 'life'; but the Romantic tradition is itself perceived by such as Pound, T. E. Hulme and Eliot as having become dead literaryism. Hence the Imagist manifesto.

Flint concentrated on the question of free verse or what he preferred to call 'unrhymed cadence' – 'There is no difference between prose and verse ... "Free verse" has no measure and it cannot, therefore, properly be called "verse". "Cadence" would be a better word for it.'[18] The French influence is again paramount, just as it is so important for Eliot: Mallarmé treated prose and poetry as interchangeable; Rimbaud turned to prose-poetry. Pound's declaration that 'Poetry must be *as well written as prose*' is well known; Ford Madox Hueffer remarked in *The English Review* for March 1921 that 'I had to make for myself the discovery that verse must be at least as well written as prose if it is to be poetry ... ' (p. 221). A kind of recycling of Wordsworth's recommendation of 'a selection of the language really used by men' implicates both Georgians and Imagists. Flint's 'liberty in verse' is another manifestation of the attempt to get 'a consuming interest in life' into poetry; it suggests a renewed development of the 'organic' or 'expressive' form which Wordsworth and Coleridge had espoused as a means of achieving a truer report of experience than seemed possible using Augustan conventions. Wordsworth's footnote to the effect that 'much confusion has been introduced into criticism by this contradistinction of poetry and prose, instead of the more philosophical one of poetry and matter of fact, or science'[19] is an insistence on the power of poetry to assert the

value of subjective (non-factual) experience. What Wordsworth and Coleridge wanted (at least initially, whatever their
later differences) was to break out of an art which over-
formalized experience and excluded various elements of it. Yet
there was always in this insistence a trap waiting to be sprung:
matter of fact and science are, after all, part of *life*.

And as they grew older, they settled into a conservatism
against which Shelley felt impelled to revolt. With statements
like 'nothing can be equally well expressed in prose that is not
tedious and supererogatory in verse' (Preface to *Prometheus
Unbound*), he helped set the divorce of prose and verse on its
heady course again. The contradiction incipient in Wordsworth's programme – the danger that 'liberty in verse' means
breaking free of all connection with the ordinary world
(matter-of-fact) – becomes glaring in Shelley's. His intention is
to reject those elder poets' subjectivism, to oppose otherworldliness and embrace historical process; one ought to be
able to turn back to Shelley and say, *this* is the positive lead
poetry in the modern world needed. But the movement to
which he gives such a powerful onward impulse is precisely in
the opposite direction. Fine as Shelley's intellect was and
indispensable as the *Defence of Poetry* is, his mind and imagination were always drawn to an unworldliness, an ideality,
which are in opposition to the ordinary world and the processes
of history. His libertarian politics are ultimately a freedom *from*
politics: hence, despite their opposed overt politics, his importance for Yeats. I am not wishing to disallow that poetry may
perhaps express certain unchanging – 'eternal' to use the
Shelleyan word – aspects of the human condition, or to claim
that such an idea is wholly mystification. I have alluded to
Kermode's *The Classic*, which is a valuable discussion of the
difficult relationship between permanent 'essence' and historically variable 'disposition', and my argument is about the
danger of seeing these as detachable from each other, or of
eliding 'permanent' and 'otherworldly'. That direction, taken
by these poets' late-Romantic and Symbolist successors, is
reflected in, for example, J. S. Mill's belief that poetry is only
possible if the poet 'can succeed in excluding from his work

every vestige of such lookings-forth into the outward and
every-day world' (p. 57). Once Victorian values well and truly
got a hold, with their emphasis on 'duty to society', any radical
programme *had* to oppose active social involvement. So once
again poetry excludes certain areas of 'life', the Symbolist
movement carrying even further this direction away from the
outward and social world and towards the inward and the
'timeless'; moving, while still seeking 'the true voice of feeling',
further into a numinous and esoteric world of 'art', further
entrenching the estrangement of art from life.

The Imagist manifesto, like the Georgian anthologies but in
more trenchant style, appeared to propose a remarriage. Flint
himself remained closer to Verlaine's insistence on personal
feeling: 'L'art, mes enfants, c'est d'être absolument soi-même.'
He opposed not only the late-Romantic 'lumber' but also the
art which 'can cut ... too curiously and produce enigma,
which was the fate of Mallarmé'. Though he wrote verse in the
Imagist manner, he succumbed pretty thoroughly to the subjective impasse – and in fact gave up writing poetry altogether.
But perhaps not altogether amiss was his lack of sympathy for
the depersonalized techniques, akin to abstraction in painting
and first promulgated for English poetry by T. E. Hulme, at
which the contemporary movements in the arts aimed in their
crusade against Romantic emotion. Imagism, and its brief
refinement Vorticism, if less extreme than Continental Futur-
ism, were manifestations of art for the Machine Age (a
favourite phrase of the time). Among other things, there was a
kind of logic by which this kind of movement, whether crudely
manifested as a love affair with the elegance and power of
machinery (as by the Italian Futurists) or more subtly as an
Eliotic quest for the nurture and discipline of imposed order,
could lead to reactionary and authoritarian attitudes. And it is
my contention that Imagism, notwithstanding appeals to the
Classical virtues, didn't really break that Romantic nexus of
'true' poetry and the timeless. On the contrary, the 'image' as
Pound found it exemplified, in particular, in H. D.'s work, and
as developed and adapted by T. S. Eliot, represented, in effect,
a distilling out of timeless essences. Pound's own model Imagist

poem, 'In a Station of the Metro',[20] works, I think, to fix a conflation of fleeting, momentary impressions in a permanent and universal image. Though themselves ephemeral, the blossoms on the bough force upon us a reminder of ineluctable recurrence, shift us into the realm of the eternal. The once-only quality of faces glimpsed in the underworld dimness of a metro station and inviting a teasing momentary hint of the notion of rebirth, which Lawrence might have sought to realize in all its liquid immediacy – 'the experience itself' – is suppressed. This may be, in the Imagist prescription, 'direct treatment of the thing', with no diffusive explication, but the 'thing' strives to stand for an epiphany, a window through to some imagined domain of pure meaning, unsullied by the insufficiencies of temporal linguistic practice. It is an aestheticizing method, platonist in its implications; the image is itself a structuring device, the ideality of its form removing it from the unideal flux of life, reducing the material 'faces in the crowd' to figures in a pattern. Eliot was pursuing a logical development of Imagism in his later poetry: such images were, while ostensibly a combining of the temporal and the timeless, ultimately a means of divining an extra-material and extra-temporal 'reality'.

However much poetry may depend on a psychic hinterland words carry with them, 'ordinary speech' both resists leaving symbols and images unexplained, and is dependent upon the contingent and non-essential – language as a socially determined practice and the ideological baggage words bring with them also. This is the problem of Symbolist poetry, a problem Eliot inherits. In their efforts to render subjective life accurately, writers have come to be much concerned with something like the 'stream of consciousness' which William James thought habitual to human experience, and which he asserted ordinary language, because it seeks to select and rationalize, falsifies (see *The Principles of Psychology*, chapter 9). But just as organized utterance involves explanatory discourse, so this unorganized stream involves, surely, a large amount of discursive rumination; neither is adequately represented by images or symbols alone. And poetry must, after all, be a product of conscious thought: if it's a question of the *sub*conscious, it can do no more than *suggest* things about it. Pure Idea, or unsullied Meaning, or the inward forms of our psyche – Shelley's 'eternal music' or Eliot's 'dark embryo' of consciousness – in order to become intelligible at all to us, must be given an embodiment which is both mimetic of *things we know* and organized into structures which *make sense* to us in one way or another – of which the relationships between parts are graspable, which *construct* meaning. 'Pure' or 'essential' meaning exists only beyond meaning, is meaninglessness; the notion of variable 'dispositions' conferred by a particular material time and place in history, and of the 'competence' applied in the life-situations in which language is used, seem unavoidable; intelligibility, in other words, depends upon recognition and 'competence' in the reader, which means at the same time an inescapable struggle with the closures built into language itself. Poetry forfeits some of its claim upon us, art and life begin to disengage, whenever a process of this kind is not central to it. Edward Thomas's poetry is stylistically more innovative and sophisticated than it has sometimes been given credit for because it does most resourcefully adapt into verse the natural movement of discursive speech and make this instrumental in exploring the concrete 'stream' of consciousness.

T. S. Eliot was more subtle than Flint in his discriminations about prose and verse, and alert to the danger of too much 'liberty in verse' – the stricture is famous: '*Vers libre* has not even the excuse of a polemic . . . there is no freedom in art . . . as the so-called *vers libre* which is good is anything but "free", it can better be defended under some other label.' And he not only distinguished between prose and verse, but between *poetry* and verse, poetry being only that verse which emerges from the 'dark embryo' which, he said in the essay on Monro, 'gradually takes on the form and speech of a poem'. (Kipling is simply 'a great verse-writer' because nothing in his work seems to tap those more obscure lodes of consciousness.)[21] Eliot is implicitly rejecting (his immediate target in the 'prose-poem') the idea that prose can be poetry if it is the right sort of Shelleyan 'echo of the eternal music'. (Insisting indeed on the distinction between prose and poetry *as well as* the Wordsworthian one between poetry and matter-of-fact.) But Eliot remained committed, basically, to the Imagist poem, to the poem as instantaneous complex (Pound's word) of content and form: the image serves a simultaneous, idealizing double function, it both communicates and structures, is both epiphany and order. As I shall try to show, despite notable modifications in *Four Quartets* in the direction of the discursive, he never freed himself from the Symbolist tradition of which Imagism is a renovation: the everyday world and ordinary, prosaic speech are only distant echoes of a timeless ideality and are never, finally, to be trusted – for Eliot, 'a language not to be betrayed' exists only beyond language since language itself *always* betrays.

III

Let me recapitulate what Eliot said at various times about imagery, symbol and the 'auditory imagination'. Early in his career he admired that 'telescoping of images and multiple associations' which he found in the Metaphysical poets and then connected with Laforgue and Corbière, and prescribed as desirable in the modern poet: 'When a poet's mind is perfectly equipped for its work, it is constantly amalgamating disparate experience ... in the mind of the poet these experiences are always forming new wholes' (*The Metaphysical Poets*, 1921). Later he asked: 'Why, for all of us, out of all that we have heard, seen, felt, in a lifetime, do certain images recur, charged with emotion rather than others?' and went on to list some of the 'memories' which form the imagery of his 'Journey of the Magi', commenting: 'such memories may have symbolic value, but of what we cannot tell, for they come to represent the depths of feeling into which we cannot peer' (Conclusion to *The Use of Poetry and the Use of Criticism*, London, 1933). In Paris in 1911 Eliot heard Bergson lecture, and his sense of a fragmented and discontinuous surface consciousness as a mere echo of a deeper impersonal flow is much indebted to Bergson; Lyndall Gordon quotes from Bergson's *An Introduction to Metaphysics*:

'I perceive at first ... all the perceptions which come ... from the material world ... Next, I notice memories ... These memories have been detached, as it were, from the depth of my personality ... they rest on the surface of my mind without being absolutely myself.'[22]

The reference to the auditory imagination comes in an essay on Matthew Arnold:

What I call the 'auditory imagination' is the feeling for syllable and rhythm, penetrating far below the conscious levels of thought and feeling, invigorating every word; sinking to the most primitive and forgotten, returning to the origin and bringing something back, seeking the beginning and the end.[23]

Such statements recognizably develop out of the Romantic-Symbolist positions mediated by Arthur Symons and F. S. Flint: the meaning of a poem is not 'logical', images and symbols emerge from the 'dark depths' of our being, from 'the place below sleep', and have a life and significance of their own, more compelling than the significances constructed by the rational consciousness. I have already in my Introduction connected this with Lawrence's 'sense-awareness, and sense-knowledge' by which he imagined the earliest civilizations to have lived: 'A completed thought was the plumbing of a depth, like a whirlpool, of emotional awareness, and at a depth of the whirlpool of emotion the resolve formed ... There was no logical chain to be dragged further.' The Romantics made the pathetic fallacy a structure of vision, a means by which 'the resolve formed'; they projected themselves into the surrounding world, used the natural landscape to map an interior landscape, to give definition to unseen and intangible 'depths'. As Modernism evolves, though Eliot still wants the mind of the poet to be 'always forming new wholes' (indeed, he wants it *because* of this), there is less confidence about the possibility of wholeness; fragments and symbols come to belong together: what we can know of the depths necessarily only comes to us in fragmentary form. (Keats seems more centrally to anticipate the modern than Coleridge in being more willing to accept the indeterminate.) The leaving out of links in the narrative chain, and the telescoping together of disparate images, however startlingly new these may have looked in Eliot, were, then, part of a continuous process; but not only this, happening when it did, this was consonant with Freudian and Jungian psychology. 'Connecting links are left out', hazarded Matthiessen in 1935, 'in an effort to utilize our recent closer knowledge of the working of the brain' (p. 15). The connections are to be made, the implication is, 'far below the conscious levels of thought and feeling'. So when Eliot says, in his note on Monro, that

It is a poet's business to be original, in all that is comprehended by 'technique' ... only so far as is dictated, not by the idea – for there is no idea – but by the nature of that dark embryo within him which gradually takes on the form and speech of a poem (p. xiii)

and that 'The external world, as it appears in his poetry, is manifestly but the mirror of a darker world within', he is formulating a view of the necessary structure of the modern poem – but it is a view coinciding exactly with his own needs.

The intensity and excitement generated by the 'telescoping of images' in Eliot's work does not, I think, grow less as the work recedes from us, as it loses the shock of newness, but worries of one kind or another have always been voiced about the poetry 'forming new wholes'. An obvious problem with this fragments-and-symbols poetic is that anything can be put together with anything else and offered as 'incoherence acquiring significance', nothing which can be conceived of as emanating from that deep source can be dictated *to*. Eliot's mind is so disciplined and subtle and his sensibility so extraordinarily developed that *ipso facto* a high degree of control is exercised. But it won't finally do to see those inchoate materials of poetry as belonging to some territory where rational consciousness and life-in-history exercise no rights. This is applying closure when the poem is really open, making it mystically 'symbolic' when it is really intertextual. The auditory imagination and the related functionings of emotion-charged images and 'memories' having the power of symbol ('but of what we cannot tell') are what for Eliot unify the poem. His hypersensitivity to relationships of rhythm, syllable and image is comparable to a sculptor's sense of spatial or a musician's of auditory relationships, and analogies with musical organization, with modern painting and cinema, have their uses in discussing how a poem like *The Waste Land* affects us and signifies. But, though we may speak semiologically of the 'languages' of the other arts, a poem's medium is *language*, which, as I've suggested, is primarily rational and cognitive, has grammar, syntax and for practical purposes 'meanings'. Language *is* shaped by the fact that it has to be used, put into practice, in every kind of daily human transaction. Then again, when we elide Cleopatra and Dido with the modern woman in 'A Game of Chess' we are depending upon our competence in a *cultural* language: the signs don't come from nowhere. Poetry *is* a kind of linguistic and cultural 'practice', its effects in some part depend upon the resonant manipulation of these functions, which ideally the poet seeks to bring into potent co-operation with the sensitivities of his 'auditory imagination'.

Among the complaints which have been brought against the method of *The Waste Land* is that it is a means by which the poet avoids responsibility, balks the implication of the 'scenes' he creates.[24] Eliot's accounts of the source of poetry and its processes of composition have been interpreted in terms of giving birth or 'evacuation'. C. K. Stead speaks of 'This image of the writing of poetry as a birth in which the role of the conscious mind is that of midwife' (p. 136); Peter Ackroyd of

his belief that poetic composition was not an activity that could be consciously controlled, that it had its roots far down in the unconscious. The metaphors which he employs to describe this process are curiously disagreeable ... his description of poetry as a 'secretion' ... an 'evacuation' and even a 'defecation'. The impression given is of some sticky, viscous, unpleasant material which has to do with the satisfaction of obscure and uncontrollable personal needs. (pp. 261–2)

The midwife's responsibility and authority are no more than contingent; if poetic composition is 'not an activity which could be consciously controlled', one has a justification for the apparent balking of responsibility. What is clear is that for Eliot bringing poetry into being involves pain, involves the handling of threatening matter, impelled by its own force, likely to get out of control, to fragment unmanageably. The threatening, disagreeable matter must be got into some sort of cage where it can be left to speak for itself or, at best, be negotiated with in safety. I earlier spoke of the need to situate a filter or medium between the acutely sensitive poet and the rawness of direct experience which is felt by a succession of modern poets. 'Impersonality' and 'the mythic method' were for the earlier Eliot the means of meeting this need; Anglo-Catholicism is the later. Eliot's theory of poetry no less than his practice have to be seen for what they are: the product of a particular subjective condition, of the horrors which Eliot experienced in his personal life, so intense that they could not find expression in a connected manner at the 'conscious levels of thought and feeling'. I think this explains Eliot's pronounced interest in 'personal vision', 'personal colouring', 'the expression of a tortured human consciousness' in Harold Monro.

In the first issue of his *Poetry Review* (January 1912) Monro wrote that the goal of the modern poet

is nothing less than the final re-welding of metre to meaning; and it cannot, in the nature of things, be achieved until man has attained a second innocence, a self-obliviousness beyond self-consciousness, a super-consciousness; that condition, in fact, produced by a complete knowledge of his own meaning. (pp. 11–12)

This fits with Lawrence's calls for a recovery of a more authentic consciousness ('a second innocence') and is influenced by the same fashionable Nietzscheanism.[25] If Eliot's poetic theory and practice were in tune with recent 'knowledge of the workings of the brain', they also complied with this view of modern man's predicament having to do with his tortured over-consciousness. Recovery means memory, and over-consciousness, psychoanalysis seemed to suggest, blocks recovery, reifies the falsifications, rejections, which perversely memory itself operates; D. H. Lawrence was of course foremost in the attack on that function of over-consciousness. Yet it is easy to associate memory in Lawrence's own poetry with acute consciousness, as D. W. Harding (see my chapter 3, note 11) does in his discussion of 'Piano', and it is noteworthy that while discussing 'Piano' in his *Practical Criticism*, I. A. Richards also drew attention to how Lawrence's poem struggles with a pervading modern *self*-consciousness: 'A widespread general inhibition of all the simpler expansive developments of emotion (not only of its expression) has to be recognised among our educated population.'[26] Paradoxically, the wracking of memory to furnish meanings and connections is itself a function of the over-consciousness; our excessive self-consciousness estranges us from the Other, from *each* other, the perception went, yet the attempt to recover any shared existence is itself, of its nature, an act of crippling self-consciousness. And the speaking personae of virtually all Eliot's poems from J. Alfred Prufrock to the authorial voice of *Four Quartets* have in some sense or another to deal with difficulties of extreme self-consciousness.

In these lines from 'Burnt Norton':

> There they were, dignified, invisible,
> Moving without pressure, over the dead leaves,
> In the autumn heat, through the vibrant air,
> And the bird called, in response to
> The unheard music in the shrubbery ...

> (pp. 171–2)

the images reach after elusive hints of some 'other reality', suggest a trance-like state in which something beyond or below 'connected' consciousness can be grasped at. In effect, the rational connectiveness which serves our utilitarian civilization is felt to be a falsification; it is actually an alienating and disintegrating agent, cutting us off from the more essential if frightening sources of our being. They are frightening because they challenge the complacencies of the *inauthentic* consciousness to which modern civilization has brought us. We are haunted by memories or remote intimations of such deeper realities, of some original unified consciousness or community. Monro's 'old houses', wrote Eliot, 'are not so much haunted by ghosts as they are ghosts themselves haunting the folk who briefly visit them'. In his own 'East Coker':

> In succession
> Houses rise and fall, crumble, are extended,
> Are removed, destroyed, restored ...

> (p. 177)

Ancestral houses are motifs in his meditation on his own origins, the original community from which he derives, on the theme of 'In my beginning is my end.' Eliot talked, as we've seen, of 'seeking the beginning and the end', of 'memories' which may have 'symbolic value' and 'come to represent the depths of feeling into which we cannot peer'. He had always been pre-occupied with the paradoxes of the way things change yet recur; and with the idea of the vulnerable and transient individual's necessary context in what in his case he formulated as 'tradition', a whole, stable and continuing structure of 'memories' which that individual might tap. In *Four Quartets* this structure becomes 'The Idea of a Christian Society'; the work is in part a poetic advocacy of the critique and schema advanced in the prose essay (1939) of that title. The memory theme relates to a searching of the unconscious or semi-conscious mind for compulsively significant imagery or symbol, for a submerged real connectiveness. The Christian 'community' which Eliot proposes is, of course, only a provisional worldly arrangement, a sort of marking time before the Reality which exists *beyond* the world and its histories.

The excessively self-preoccupied inauthentic consciousness is always trying to stave off these hauntings by the deeper or other reality. It is attacked, in fact, from two sides. As the speaker in 'Journey of the Magi' finds, the journey to salvation is gruelling and one would gladly forego it. On the other side, however, lies the abyss, the void, the 'horror'. The perilous balance between the two is sustained only at the cost of neurosis and barely suppressed violence. (W. H. Auden, as we shall see, has a fine image of this in his ironically 'free one' who is 'poised between shocking falls on razor-edge'.) There is a radical tension in the subject between a surface wish to conceive of itself as free, autonomous and coherent and its deeper apprehension of the opposite. The state of nightmare or extreme nervous tension is reflected in the 'bad night' motif which recurs in Eliot's poetry – in 'Rhapsody on a Windy Night', for instance, or the opening passages of *The Waste Land*, or *Sweeney Agonistes* – 'When you're alone in the middle of the night ... '. D. E. S. Maxwell commented of the Sweeney poems:

The relation between Eliot's poetry and Jacobean drama is that each has as its background a violent world, peopled by creatures unsure of their relations with each other, and with spiritual forces above them ... The background of the Sweeney poems is a 'cavernous waste shore', the sound of an epileptic's shriek, the plotting – in 'Sweeney Among the Nightingales' – of Rachael and 'the lady in the cape' against 'the man with heavy eyes'.

Of *Sweeney Agonistes* he adds:

It is partly the unthinking violence of modern life that this play portrays –

> Any man might do a girl in
> Any man has to, needs to, wants to,
> Once in a lifetime, do a girl in.[27]

(The estranging gender-role enforcements implied here are, of course, an aspect of the problem.) Like Maxwell, William V. Spanos, in an interesting but as far as I know little-noted essay, sees *Sweeney Agonistes* as looking back to the Jacobeans, to the 'existential' apprehensions of death in Donne and Webster, to 'the metaphysical shudder in Jacobean poetry', and at the same time compares it with the modern Existentialist writing of Kafka, Sartre, Camus, and to 'the "ontological insecurity" of the absurdists' anti-heroes'. ('Ontological insecurity' might be a passable term for what I've discussed in Edward Thomas's poetry, in Hardy, and in the Georgian poetry of haunting.) It seems to me a uniquely original work, as well as to provide further evidence of how directly out of his personal alienation Eliot's poetry springs, and of how much, while this *is* personal – 'not like other men' – it nevertheless takes its place in a whole body of writing about the *Angst* and alienation of the modern individual.

As Peter Ackroyd points out, Eliot knew, from his life with his first wife Vivien, all about the world of furnished flats; he wanted to write a drama, but one dealing with that 'modern life' of which he had gained close knowledge. Here then, one might suppose, one would find a depiction of ordinary life, material reality. But the action, like so much in the poems, falls in a space suggestively *between* the ordinary and the metaphysical. The mode (obviously) is not that of realist drama, which Eliot had decried in his essay 'Four Elizabethan Drama-tists' written at the same time (1924). Yet the rhythms of the dialogue and the evolving structure of the action have drama-tic coherence, they hold together in a stylized way which remarkably anticipates the drama of Beckett. Despite its desig-nation as 'fragments' and inclusion with the 'Unfinished Poems', the piece works as a whole. Here Eliot doesn't need the strategy of building a poem out of very obliquely related sections, a method which betrays what one feels is the immense effort for him of holding things together. This is a new dramatic *kind*, projecting a vision of the Void – 'Nothing at all but three things . . . Birth, and copulation, and death', unconcerned with 'character', neither tragedy nor comedy. True, Eliot's hope that a more popular audience might be reached through dramatic writing was to lead to the brittleness of his later plays. These now seem so dated, where the *Agonistes*, though of its time in coinciding with a revival of interest in 'verse drama', hints at an almost post-modern pastiche and indeterminacy. However, the pastiche draws on his love of music hall, a love which here and elsewhere reflects, surely, a limiting notion of popular entertainment. The music hall seems to have meant for him (see his 1923 piece on Marie Lloyd) 'the working class man' keeping his place like Yeats's peasantry, uncorrupted as yet by the democratic dreams catered for in more commercia-lized and mechanical media such as cinema and radio. Never-theless, the pastiche and stylization of *Sweeney Agonistes* repre-sent a discovery of an alternative technique to that of *The Waste Land* for achieving detachment, for bringing to the surface darker elements of consciousness in a form in which they may be ritually and bearably contemplated.

Spanos's reading runs thus:

It is Sweeney's function as a Fury figure . . . to drive the denizens of the postwar Jazz Age wasteland into awareness of their bad faith in thinking that entertainments in their flat will provide security from death (Pereira) and thus into consciousness of their radical alien-ation, or, in Heidegger's terms, of the non-relational nature of and the impossibility of outstripping death.[28]

As so often, Eliot's protagonists are caught in a web of talk – 'I've gotta use words when I talk to you' – without communication; the 'jazz-age' rhythms and refrains (crossed with those of the music hall, but both jazz and music hall influences divorced from their sources in shared popular experience) function to weave this intransitive, contentless linguistic web. We feel the imminence of an absurd world, the impulse to flee confrontation with the void (Sartre's 'la fuite'). Yet once again, I would suggest, the intensities generated, the compulsive quality, take us beyond the impersonalizing stylization – they refer us back to that direct personal experience of the world of furnished flats, mundane in itself but endured as a series of nightmarish reiterations, in which the work has its origins. *Sweeney Agonistes* comes to appear the kind of expression of personal 'valid suffering' Eliot was to dwell on in the Monro essay written a few years later. But here, hindsight allows us to say, is Eliot on the brink of the leap of faith – the perception of the absurdity of the created material universe is the opening of a door. This is not realized in the 'melodrama' (as Eliot subtitled it) itself, and presumably that failure is part of the explanation of his continuing to regard it as unfinished. But the epigraphs he attached point us to such a conclusion, particularly that from St John of the Cross – 'Hence the soul cannot be possessed of the divine union, until it has divested itself of the love of created beings.' Meaning does not reside in the world of created beings.

IV

To read Eliot's poetry as about the desire to escape the world of created beings, to escape ordinary reality, may seem unfair. There is so much reality *in* the poetry. The personal crisis Eliot was undergoing at the time that he wrote explicitly of poetry as an 'escape' was such that escape in some form was perhaps the only practical option:

Poetry is not a turning loose of emotion, but an escape from emotion; it is not the expression of personality, but an escape from personality. But, of course, only those who have personality and emotions know what it means to want to escape these things.[29]

Poems are formal constructions, they don't 'express personality', they are an ordered refuge from the problematical unreality of personality. But as Harry discovers in *The Family Reunion*, there is no final escape from the hauntings of acute consciousness, from the shadows inside the skull, or from time and personal emotion:

> It seems I shall get rid of nothing,
> Of none of the shadows that I wanted to escape;
> And at the same time, other memories,
> Earlier, forgotten, begin to return
> Out of my childhood. I can't explain.
> But I thought I might escape from one life to another,
> And it might be all one life, with no escape.
>
> (p. 306)

Eliot weaves together the memory theme and something akin to the crisis theology of Christian Existentialism. Harry, to echo Spanos's reading of *Sweeney Agonistes*, is driven by the Furies to a point of 'authentic' recognition – which at the same time resembles the traditional *contemptu mundi*, a desire for release from a mere worldly state ('one life') into being at one with the spiritual ('all one life': unitary, uncontradictory). (The other epigraph attached to *Sweeney Agonistes* alludes to the Furies.) This *contemptu mundi* had been expressed with uncharacteristic directness and simplicity in the 'Death by Water' section of *The Waste Land*; Harry's wife had drowned; death by water signifies a dying into a new life free of, or at any rate reconciled with, the afflictions of the old. The feelings of guilt and fear – the 'memories' relating to his wife – which haunt Harry can hardly be unconnected with Eliot's personal experiences (as the 'other memories ... Out of my childhood' must echo the memories of America which increasingly came to affect Eliot). 'Escape' need not have pejorative implications if one says that Eliot found his escape, his death by water, in embracing Anglo-Catholic religious beliefs, in the ideal of a Christian devotion, a devotion having both aesthetic and ascetic aspects, which may reveal glimpses, hints, of a greater spiritual reality, from within the necessary confinements of *this* world. In an effort to resolve his personal alienation, Eliot the sceptic made the leap of faith.

Eliot thought that in Monro's work the state of mind of the much denigrated 'Georgian week-ender' acquired a special significance:

Monro's poetry, so far as it is concerned with the countryside, is ... that of the perpetual week-ender, oscillating between departure and return; his city is that of the man who would flee to the country, his country that of the man who must tomorrow return to town. Now, this is not only a state of mind important enough to deserve recording in poetry, but it also becomes, in some of Monro's poems, representative of something larger and less easily apprehensible, a *poésie des brefs départs*. (p. xv)

His essay on Baudelaire was written about three years before that on Monro, and in it Eliot describes Baudelaire as having sought a means of 'salvation from the *ennui* of modern life', even if that salvation should be, paradoxically, damnation. Involved in this quest is his 'poetry of flight', which is reaching out towards something, dimly apprehended, beyond the 'romantic idea':

Baudelaire has all the romantic sorrow, but invents a new kind of romantic nostalgia – a derivative of his nostalgia being the *poésie des départs*, the *poésie des salles d'attente*. In a beautiful paragraph of *Mon Cœur mis à nu*, he imagines the vessels lying in harbour as saying: 'Quand partons-nous vers le bonheur?' and his minor successor Laforgue exclaims: 'Comme ils sont beaux, les trains manqués.'[30]

Thus Eliot contrives a positive significance out of that 'romantic nostalgia' which is part of his own sensibility and inheritance from the Symbolist temper and aesthetic. Maxwell usefully described *poésie des départs* as 'a specific aspect of French symbolist poetry, the vague nostalgic regret associated with voyages and departures, a regret that is at the same time exhilarating.' For Eliot, he said, it has a 'deeper meaning', it implies 'Eliot's departure from the beliefs of his earlier poetry to full acceptance of the Christian faith' (p. 136). I think also that Eliot seizes on this phrase *poésie des départs*, this state of 'oscillating between departure and return', this condition of the *salle d'attente*, as an expression of the directionless condition of modern man, of a state of mind which *is* a state of oscillation, of not knowing where one belongs or where one is going. It is nostalgic, moreover, because somewhere in the emotional complex is a vague sense that some unflawed, unfallen state – in Edward Thomas's words, 'some ... place where men have wished to go / And stay' – exists as an attainable bourn. But, if each return means coming back to an absurd existence ('Even the most exalted mystic must return to the world ... '), each departure – or to put it another way, each 'escape' – means the possibility of transcendence. Eliot may not mean that Monro's *poésie des départs* is what he says it is in Baudelaire, a 'dim recognition of the direction of beatitude'. But he feels that it at least implies a thirst for the ineffable, a religious impulse, and that where there is a choice of departures, the route towards beatitude is a possibility. As he makes clear in the essay on Baudelaire, a knowledge of the choice between God and the Devil is, for him, almost as important as making the *right* choice.

A departure is made, a journey or quest is begun, at the very outset of Eliot's *Collected Poems* – 'Let us go then, you and I ... ' Indeed, there is an atmosphere of *salles d'attente*, of *trains manqués* – of suspended action, 'vague nostalgic regret', and missed opportunities – about the whole of the 'Love Song' and 'Portrait of a Lady':

> 'And so you are going abroad; and when do you return?
> But that's a useless question.
> You can hardly know when you are coming back,
> You will find so much to learn'.
> My smile falls heavily among the bric-à-brac.
>
> (p. 20)

Incomplete, non-volitional selves seem to address each other; the phrase 'bric-à-brac' itself deftly evokes a haphazard coming-and-going which accumulates meaningless objects. In the 1920 poems, Eliot's assortment of '*déraciné* cosmopolitans' – the Jew squatting on Gerontion's window sill, Burbank ('Chicago Semite Viennese'), Grishkin, Rachael *née* Rabinovitch, as well as their counterparts in *The Waste Land* – suggest another kind of 'coming-and-going'. The suggestively devised names, often with a ring of the assumed or composite, of *illusory*

identity or personality, convey a shiver of distaste and apprehension: something fearful is overtaking European civilization.
The reference to Conrad's 'Mistah Kurtz' in the epigraph to
'The Hollow Men' reminds us, among other things, that 'His
mother was half-English, his father was half-French. All
Europe contributed to [his] making.' The poems in French,
'*Mélange adultère de tout*' and '*Lune de miel*', are comic versions of
poésie des départs. The journey in quest of the Grail is supposedly
a unifying metaphor in *The Waste Land*, while it has often been
pointed out that journeys are in some way involved in each
section of the poem. The opening paragraph introduces
another homeless refugee – 'Bin gar keine Russin, stamm' aus
Litauen, echt deutsch.' To take just one example from *The
Waste Land*: the line quoted, in 'The Fire Sermon', from Verlaine's *Parsifal*, connects both with the Grail legend and the
nostalgic regret of the French Symbolists. In 'Ash-Wednesday',
VI, we have the 'brief transit where dreams cross', followed by
the image of a journey out to sea which seems to prefigure the
later 'Dry Salvages':

> The white sails still fly seaward, seaward flying
> Unbroken wings.
>
> (p. 98)

Here the *poésie des départs* is assuming its movement in the
'direction of beatitude'. In both 'Journey of the Magi' and
'Marina', in Maxwell's words, there are 'glimpses of the
world's affairs seen during a journey which, when ended, will
mean that the world can never again be seen in the same way,
and that its interests must be set aside' (p. 151). It is in this
'direction of beatitude' that Baudelaire's ships in the harbour
asking when they will set out for happiness are ultimately, for
Eliot, pointing; and the line is echoed again in 'Marina':

> ... let me
> Resign my life for this life, my speech for that unspoken,
> The awakened, lips parted, the hope, the new ships.
>
> (p. 110)

I think the sense of serenity which the beautiful 'Marina'
conveys suggests a reconciliation with life after the torments of

the earlier poetry, but a reconciliation which is possible only because a *spiritual* rebirth has been perceived as a reality, one which one can 'make' or recover for oneself – 'I made this ... ' (It was written very close in time to the almost morose 'Journey of the Magi', where the 'reconciliation' has none of that radiance, seems almost grudging.) So, finally, the injunction of *Four Quartets* is to 'fare forward, voyagers', seeking to divest themselves of all delusive thoughts of past and future, the voyage imaging an intent devotional concentration on the goal of beatitude. It is a solution to the problem of consciousness: the amorphous self has become resolved, impersonal, free of illusory 'personality', in its self-abnegation.

For a poet of a later generation, Philip Larkin, we deceive ourselves with all such questings after the transcendental, all such journeyings into the unknown.[31] His peculiar talent emerged in 1940s Britain precisely at a moment of widespread reaction against the imaginative attractions of romantic flight; his 'Poetry of Departures' contains a devastating deflation of *poésie des départs*. His own consummate use of the journey metaphor in 'The Whitsun Weddings' (the train journey is a recurrent motif in modern poetry and I shall say more about this in discussing Louis MacNeice) enacts his vision of life as a random affair, not heading anywhere for certain, except – as so many of his poems insist – death. What evidence have we, his poems ask, that anywhere we 'escape' to will be any different from where we are? He is capable of perceiving that brink to which so many other poets have come – the edge of that madness (as he seems to think it) which is the crossing of the boundary between ordinary consciousness and the consciousness beyond, which is the poet shut forever in his 'final loneliness', his paradisal Tower – but he chose to return to the absurdity of the world we know. For Larkin, it was not without its compensations. When Eliot, plainly speaking out of what had seemed to him his own experience, and as he made Harry echo in those lines from *The Family Reunion*, said of Monro, 'There was no way out. There never is', he was affirming his conviction that *this* world offers no way out: the journey towards beatitude is the only one that counts.

v

For Eliot, then, Baudelaire suggested the departure in the direction of beatitude, and his importance for modern poetry has long been a commonplace. In this section I make something of a detour, but its purpose is to consolidate the context in which I am seeing Eliot, and in particular a fundamental connection: for both Eliot and Baudelaire, the practice and profession of poetry are a discipline, imposing order on a life otherwise felt as meaninglessly chaotic, lived always on the edge of the abyss, the horror. Such a state, however, means that active involvement in the world's affairs appears futile, vitiated by the monster *Ennui*:

> C'est l'Ennui! – l'œil chargé d'un pleur involontaire,
> Il rêve d'échafauds en fumant son houka.
> Tu le connais, lecteur, ce monstre délicat,
> – Hypocrite lecteur, – mon semblable – mon frère!

Long before Eliot, Baudelaire imagined relief from *ennui* through release into another world. The unknown, the new might be found, for example, through embarking on a voyage on the ship of death:

> O Mort, vieux capitaine, il est temps! levons l'ancre!
> Ce pays nous ennuie, ô Mort! Appareillons!
> Si le ciel et la mer sont noirs comme de l'encre,
> Nos cœurs que tu connais sont remplis de rayons!
>
> Verse-nous ton poison pour qu'il nous réconforte!
> Nous voulons, tant ce feu nous brûle le cerveau,
> Plonger au fond du gouffre, Enfer ou Ciel, qu'importe?
> Au fond de l'Inconnu pour trouver du *nouveau*![32]

Not only does this bring Eliot's journey motif to mind, but also Lawrence's 'The Ship of Death', his insistent use of the dying to be born again myth as an expression of a relentless quest for the unknown, the *new*.

It does not matter for Baudelaire whether one chooses heaven or hell: like all opposites for him, even heaven and hell (a characteristically extreme position), are the *same*. This leads to almost endlessly contradictory statements in his writings, and as Michael Hamburger has said in *The Truth of Poetry*, there is not a lot of point in trying to make sense of these in the ordinary way. Sartre's book on Baudelaire, however, suggests a way of seeing the contradictions: everything appeared the same to Baudelaire because his massive egotism merely projected *himself* into everything he observed. Whatever he found outside himself he also found inside himself, he was 'victim and executioner' at the same time. Perhaps this is the ultimate significance of 'Hypocrite lecteur, – mon semblable – mon frère!' It is an extreme of the Romantic orientating of the universe around the self; but it helps us to see solipsism, the experiencing of versions of *ennui*, and a certain tendency to self-destructiveness or at least will to suffer, as connected elements of Romantic psychology.

'Verse-nous ton poison ... ' – the imagery of poison is used generally by Baudelaire to denote an insidious desire, like that bred by alcohol or opium or even by evil itself, which destroys in being embraced. In 'Le Balcon' the breath of the loved-one is itself poison; the self-inflicted nature of his suffering is explicit in 'L'Héautontimorouménos' ('The Self-Torturer'), the poem in which he calls himself both victim and executioner, exclaiming: 'C'est tout mon sang, ce poison noir!' He *chooses* to suffer – as Sartre's analysis would have it – and the self-pity which this allows, again like opium, is desperately indulged. There are some grounds, of course, for Mario Praz's view of this in terms of sado-masochism: '*Ennui* is only the most generic aspect of the *mal de siècle*; its specific aspect is – sadism.'[33] But however pathological Praz's *Romantic Agony* may show Romantic obsession and its images to be, the sado-masochism in Baudelaire, along with the 'decadence' and 'dandyism', are best seen, it seems to me, as just such a source of imagery as that provided by the 'systems' of modern poets: Yeats's *A Vision*, Graves's *The White Goddess*. The constant equivalence of crime or evil with 'volupté' is given us with such exhibitionistic insistence that it is the exhibitionism rather than the specific sado-masochistic paraphernalia that seems to demand interpretation. The notorious Satanism may be seen as a necessary projection of Baudelaire's egotism: even while feeling that everything was the same, he had to try to prove that he was different from others, and a way of doing this was to carry perverse postures to extremes. These extreme states of mind are one of the precedents Baudelaire sets for modern poetry.

A sapping of energy and will which makes existence appear futile is, I've said, common in Romantic psychology; I have instanced Keats's struggle with it, his writing to his sister Fanny that 'there is nothing like ... an amulet against the ennui'. 'Le Démon' in Baudelaire's 'La Destruction' – the common case of the addict seeing his addiction as a seducing demon – leads the poet onto 'Des plaines de l'Ennui, profondes et désertes'. This *ennui* is not only 'un monstre délicat', but also 'l'obscur ennemi' which, like an illness of which the cause cannot be discovered, saps the poet's life – and Time, of course, is the enemy's ally:

> O douleur! ô douleur! Le Temps mange la vie,
> Et l'obscur Ennemi qui nous ronge le cœur
> Du sang que nous perdons croît et se fortifie!
>
> ('L'Ennemi', p. 16)

The Romantic sickness is often 'obscure'; the poet is unable to rationalize his sufferings, unable to assign them to a definite source. Moreover, if fulfilment is not found in one situation, and yet everywhere there is sameness, no fulfilment can be found anywhere. As Sartre suggested, the theory of 'Correspondances' is itself, in one light, a device to make everything seem an echo of himself, and if everything echoes everything else, of course the result is a desolating sense of sameness.[34] Baudelaire initiated that modern poetry which attempts to *explain* feelings of *ennui* in terms of the oppressive monotony of modern city life. If the modern poet is a stranger to nature, he also feels a stranger in the city; wherever he is, he is a victim of displacement, dispossession. Baudelaire the *flâneur* has no *economic* relation to the streets; in any case, if everything is the same, there is no other to relate to. Typically, however, this urban milieu exercises a fascination, a hold over the poet, as we see in Eliot's romantic embracing of the urban scene even while evoking its squalor and disorder. Urban complaint and cele-

bration of what Sartre refers to as 'le mythe de la grande ville' –
the antithesis, one might say, of the rural myth – occur simultaneously. As Sartre says of the city in Baudelaire's poetry,
'Tout y est *poésie* au sens strict du terme' (p. 53); he welcomed
its oppressions as an opportunity for poetry. 'Vrai Parisien' as
he called himself, born in the heart of Paris and leaving it only
when doing so was unavoidable, he created the image of the
foggy unreal city upon which Eliot capitalized,[35] where the
inhabitants pursue a death-in-life existence, not communicating with each other, hardly to be distinguished from the
corpses in the cemeteries:

> Pluviôse ... verse un froid ténébreux
> Aux pâles habitants du voisin cimetière
> Et la mortalité sur les faubourgs brumeux.
>
> ('Le Spleen', p. 68)

In his book *From Baudelaire to Surrealism*, a paean to the
Symbolist aesthetic, Marcel Raymond wrote that 'With the
help of the disordered material supplied by his perception or
memory, [Baudelaire] creates an order that is the infallible
expression of his soul.'[36] 'La servante au grand cœur' uses
memories of a childhood servant to localize, as it were, the
larger remorse of the poet's own soul. Frequently associated in
his poetry with memory, so often regretful, are perfumes. This
is pre-eminently Proustian territory, but the same phenomenon occurs in Edward Thomas's 'Old Man' when the poet
sniffs the sprig from a bush and is unable to remember its
precise significance, reminding us, in its turn, of Eliot's 'such
memories may have symbolic value, but of what we cannot
tell'. In this kind of Romantic-Symbolist poetry sense-impressions generally are felt to suggest mysterious kinds of memory.
The famous 'Correspondances' has it:

> L'homme y passe à travers des forêts de symboles
> Qui l'observent avec des regards familiers.
>
> (p. 11)

As Walter Benjamin discusses, these obscure correspondences
are to be forged in subjective consciousness because in the city,
in the outer world, one never meets a familiar gaze, everything

is unrelated to everything else. Here is the tradition to which Eliot's theories of imagery belong. That phrase 'memory and desire' which echoes through Eliot's poetry, and its association with odours ('aromatisé'), might derive directly from Baudelaire's prose-poem 'La Chambre Double', where the poet dreams of a room in which 'L'âme y prend un bain de paresse, aromatisé par le regret et le désir.'

This 'bath of idleness', with its mingling of opposites in a suspended dream-state, fits with the common reluctance in Romantic psychology towards action. 'Il devient *flottant*', says Sartre of Baudelaire, 'il se laisse ballotter par ces vagues monotones ... Personne n'est plus éloigné de l'action que Baudelaire' (pp. 37, 52). This is the condition of oscillation, of the waiting-room, and it is all part of the sense of *difference*; he is not going anywhere as men of action are. His poems 'Le Cygne' or 'L'Albatros' not only illustrate the insistent self-pity, but are classic statements of the notion of poet as exile, a special being not fitted for the society of ordinary men; and exile, of course, is a key signification of the journey motif. The otherness is a bid to escape *ennui*, the *ennui* of being like others, a bid which 'poésie des départs' repeatedly figures. 'L'Invitation au Voyage' fantasizes of some other realm of existence where all is superior to the reality we know (and again a kind of bath of idleness):

> Là, tout n'est qu'ordre et beauté,
> Luxe, calme et volupté.

(p. 51)

In 'La Chambre Double' he speaks of 'ce parfum d'un autre monde, dont je m'enivrais avec une sensibilité perfectionnée'; this 'perfume of another world' is what poetry of departures means for Baudelaire. 'Comme vous êtes loin, paradis parfumé' proclaims the poet in the appropriately title 'Moesta et Errabunda' ('The Dreamer and the Vagabond'). The destinations are necessarily artificial worlds, the 'artificial paradises' of Baudelaire's poetry, attained through whatever means of intoxication offers itself (sometimes perhaps induced simply by imagination: one thinks inevitably of Yeats's 'artifice of eternity'), releasing the poet from the terrible burden of time-bound consciousness. Another prose-poem, 'Enivrez-vous', asserts:

Il faut être toujours ivre. Tout est là: c'est l'unique question. Pour ne pas sentir l'horrible fardeau du Temps qui brise vos épaules et vous penche vers la terre, il faut vous enivrer sans trêve.
Mais de quoi? De vin, de poésie ou de vertu, à votre guise. Mais enivrez-vous. (p. 286)

It is important that the destination, the other world, should remain undefined, for to localize it immediately infects it with the *ennui* of ordinary sober consciousness, eliminates otherness, newness. 'Le Voyage' asserts that 'les vrais voyageurs sont ceux-là seuls qui partent / Pour partir' – the travellers do not know where they depart *for*. It has always been noted that this poet who wrote endlessly of voyages and distant places never himself made a journey if he could avoid it (another point of affinity with Proust, undertaking, from the confines of the famous cork-lined room, a vast journey in search of lost time). The fantasy paradise evoked in 'A Une Malabaraise' reminds us that Baudelaire, when in fact bound, at the instigation of his mother and stepfather, for India, cut short his journey and returned to Paris.[37] To have allowed himself a glimpse of the reality of India would surely have disallowed its high-Romantic idyll. The phial of laudanum (the prevalent use of laudanum by the Romantic poets has been studied by Alethea Hayter in her *Opium and the Romantic Imagination* (London, 1968)) offered a surer release: 'Dans ce monde étroit, mais si plein de dégoût, un seul objet connu me sourit: la fiole de laudanum; une vieille et terrible amie ... ' (p. 235). It is characteristic that he should embrace a *terrible* friend. Baudelaire praises Poe for his artificial landscapes, and compares these to the effects created by opium: 'L'espace est approfondi par l'opium; l'opium y donne un sens magique à toutes les teintes ... '[38]

The necessary indefinition, the 'vague nostalgic regret', belong, according to Baudelaire's definitions of 'Beauty' in the *Journaux intimes*, to its feminine type; the deliberate pursuit of evil to its masculine type:

J'ai trouvé la définition du Beau, – de mon Beau. C'est quelque chose d'ardent et de triste, quelque chose d'un peu vague ... Le mystère, le regret sont aussi des caractères de Beau ... et enfin (pour que j'aie le courage d'avouer jusqu'à quel point je me sens moderne en esthé-tique, *le malheur* ... le plus parfait type de Beauté virile est Satan ... (p. 1255)

But whatever the appearances here and in 'Hymne à la Beauté' –

> De Satan ou de Dieu, qu'importe? Ange ou Sirène,
> Qu'importe, si tu rends, – fée aux yeux de velours,
> Rhythme, parfum, lueur, – ô mon unique reine! –
> L'univers moins hideux et les instants moins lourds?

(p. 24)

– Baudelaire was not an advocate of 'l'art pour l'art' (which he attacked), of good and evil being irrelevant in the realm of art. On the contrary, the perception of a moral antinomy is crucial to the force and inspiration of his own art. As Sartre said, Baudelaire had an intense moral life (p. 54), and I think Eliot is right that Baudelaire's choice of evil was an affirmation of the existence of good. The whole point – every anxious rhetorical cadence and every exaggerated posture betrays this – is in the consciousness, the deliberateness of the moral enormity of what he is saying; at a level working obscurely beneath the surface exhibitionism, Baudelaire intends us to know that he does not mean what he appears to say. The Satanism, says Eliot, 'is redeemed by *meaning something else*'; actually Baudelaire is con-cerned 'with the real problem of good and evil'. It is true that near the end of his life he famously declared that he *did* mean what he said in *Les Fleurs du Mal*. 'Dans ce livre *atroce* j'ai mis tout *mon cœur*.' Baudelaire, to adapt his own useful description of his soul in the so-titled poem, is a *cloche fêlée*, and the only way he can express his highly developed moral sensibility is through these hugely impersonal gestures of perversity – the gestures of a wholly created and artificial persona, a projection of Baudelaire's own person, but writ large and extreme. His and Eliot's cases exemplify, indeed, those complicated intersec-tions of 'personal' and 'impersonal' which I have suggested particularly characterize the domain of poetry.

This impersonality is achieved in extraordinary formal control and richness of language. Baudelaire *shapes* language, he does not let it take its own direction as the creed of 'liberty in verse' would seem to permit. Michael Hamburger asserts, in fact, that 'Baudelaire's practice was more classical than is generally granted' (p. 17). One is reminded that Eliot, in his revolt against Romantic emotion in poetry, made great play with his claim to be 'classical' and connected this with 'impersonality'. But nobody would seriously claim that the great Romantic poetry is undisciplined; I have said of Eliot that his fineness of intellect, of sensibility, to which one might add, of *ear* (not always understood to be an essential quali- fication for a poet), *ipso facto* imposed control. Middleton Murry said suggestively of Baudelaire that 'His affinities were with the disciplined and contemptuous romanticism of Stend- hal and Mérimée.'[39] Disciplined Romanticism: some such defining phrase is what we need in talking of both Baudelaire and Eliot. But also as with Eliot the impersonal pose is the only means of containing the appalling nature of the poetry's mater- ial, ritualizing, as Benjamin has it, a 'defence' against 'the shock experience at the very centre of his artistic work' (p. 165). Lawrence, we have seen, copes with similar material by sublimating it in a dialectical scheme of corruption and creativity. Baudelaire 'was an allegorical poet, rather than a Symbolist', says Hamburger (p. 17), but the line between allegory and symbol is at best a fine one, and in poems like 'L'Albatros', or in that famous picture of the delicate monster *Ennui* (where Baudelaire's extraordinary visual sense joins his aural one), it is perhaps a line impossible to draw: the function served by such elaborate figurations is to externalize, ritualize, intolerably painful states.

The curious thing is Baudelaire's detachment, his objecti- vity; he does not talk about vice like a man blindly obsessed. Both Sartre and Eliot refer, indeed, to his 'lucidity'. Much as he may have admired the writings of 'the divine Marquis' de Sade, the Satanic pursuit in his own work is anxiously deliber- ate, the feelings cultivated – not only in his poetry but in his life – with controlled artifice. And if we see this as a planned strategy, it serves further ends. It gratifies his ego, enables him to feel he is avenging himself on society, but perhaps most important, allows him to confess and be absolved, by a similar principle as in religious psychology may make greater the ecstatic sense of the all-merciful love of God the greater the sin to be forgiven. He sought to achieve finally a cathartic experience of re-found innocence and truly Victorian feelings of moral rectitude. 'Il ne doute pas de la rédemption finale', says Sartre (p. 91), and depicts him as voluntarily *giving in* to his judges and censors. He cites the bizarre episode of Baudelaire's attempt, having challenged the Second Empire establishment at its very roots, to get himself elected to the Académie Française; an attempt which may be interpreted as an act of pleading to be taken back into the protecting womb of society.

It is well known that the affectionate life Baudelaire as a child shared with his mother after the death of his father and always afterwards remembered with profound nostalgia was to be followed by a shattering sense of rejection when his mother remarried and he was sent to boarding schools. If love can be withdrawn with such drastic suddenness, one must be guilty in some way; the masochistic desire to be punished, and the wish to be forgiven and welcomed back, result. Debilitating feelings of guilt are expressed in both Baudelaire's and Eliot's poetry; Eliot, the biographies suggest, was afflicted by a sense of not living up to his parents' expectations – *he*, so to speak, abandoned his parents, because he could not fulfil what he took to be their demands.[40] Baudelaire the subject of deep psychological wounding, the *cloche fêlée*, had to carry his emotional responses to extremes; to retreat self-pityingly into the 'bath of idleness'; to embrace Satanism ostentatiously; in his relationships with other people, to veer between worship and disgust. His relationships with his mother, with Jeanne Duval, his other women-friends, and stepfather, are saturated with this duality. A poem such as 'Chant d'Automne', where he asks Marie Daubrun to be mother, mistress *or* sister, seems to confirm a lack of mature capacity ever quite to sort out these kinds of feminine love from each other. He may not technically have been a virgin (I refer to Nadar's notorious contention, but how do we account for his syphilis?), but there can be little doubt that he chose forms of relationship with women which could not be satisfyingly consummated (such as women of the street for sexual partners) in order to preserve a symbolic virginity. It was an expression of the sense of intactness his egotism demanded. He could not *give* any part of himself, something which Eliot too seems to have found to be inordinately difficult and to prejudice his attitude to sexuality. A lack of spontaneity and an ascetic temper are shared by Eliot and Baudelaire; the repulsiveness of sex is a persistent and life-long theme in the poetry of both (Eliot's attitude only seeming to change somewhat after his second marriage at the age of sixty-eight).

Baudelaire praises the Victorian black frockcoat as expressing the 'heroism of modern life', as a refinement of 'dandyism': 'N'est il pas l'habit nécessaire de notre époque, souffrante et portant jusque sur ses épaules noires et maigres le symbole d'un deuil perpétuel?' (p. 950). '"Le Dandy"', noted Middleton Murry, 'is an imperturbable being above the law, inscrutable, contemptuous of the world, silent under the torments which it inflicts on his sensitive soul ... exercising a drastic discipline upon himself ... ' (p. 118). But underlying this attraction and need of the heroic discipline which the frockcoat symbolizes, is the desire to be accepted back into a state of total dependence, where society, a surrogate parent, will take full responsibility for one. This is the nostalgia of one who was in fact unable responsibly to shape and direct his own life, who continued as an adult to behave like an egocentric and wayward child, feeling desperately dispossessed, prevented from finding the satisfactions which might offset *ennui*. The situation in which he found himself was for him literally a kind of hallucination, a state of vertigo, so that the here and now could never seem real. His poverty and his persecutions in later life, if brought upon his own head, were real sufferings, against which he built the best defences he could. As a true Romantic – I shall return to this – he built them in his poetry rather than in his life.

The condition of the traveller in the waiting room, the veering between extreme states, and indeed the co-existence of

the opposites – celebration and disgust, rebellion and submission, the states of victim and executioner – provide for the
characteristic indisposition towards action and choice. As with
the apprehension of good and evil, the dualism is not at all the
same thing as the pluralistic Yeatsian striving to 'balance all',
all possibilities; it is a disordering of the senses, and a compulsion to revolt, to seize on oppositional attitudes to neutralize
the source of pain by fleeing to its negation. But the 'bath of
idleness' means never opting for one opposed state or the other,
any more than for a commonsense middle course (can we really
call Baudelaire classical when he so studiedly avoids any
'mean'?). It does not matter, I noted above, whether one
chooses Heaven and Hell, whether art is inspired by Satan or
God, and in *Mon cœur mis à nu* he speaks of a sense of the
co-presence of contradictory feelings which afflicted his entire
childhood: 'l'horreur de la vie et l'extase de la vie' (p. 1296).
Laziness and procrastination were his real defects, wrote Sartre
(p. 97), and he treated them with complete seriousness – his
real defects, that is, as against his artificial ones, the flowers of
evil cultivated in his algolagnic hothouse. Passages to which I
have referred in letters by Keats, Coleridge or Edward Thomas
correspond with this from Baudelaire's much-quoted letter to
his mother written on 9 July 1857:

Quant à mon silence, n'en cherchez pas la raison ailleurs que dans
une de ces langueurs qui, à mon grand déshonneur, s'emparent
quelquefois de moi et m'empêchent non seulement de me livrer à
aucun travail, mais même de remplir les plus simples des devoirs.[41]

Such confessions emerge from a conflict between indulged
self-pity, and self-censure genuinely directed towards reform or
at least the sought-after forgiveness. But they nonetheless
express the accidie of one who cannot rouse the energy to free
himself from his isolation. Eliot interpreted this as 'a true form
of *acedia*, arising from the unsuccessful struggle towards the
spiritual life'. It is a condition obviously related to the
'aboulie', 'a withdrawal into negative coldness, with an attendant loss of mental vigour and physical energy', which Eliot
diagnosed in himself (Ackroyd, p. 115). True, in 1848, as a

young man, Baudelaire attempted to involve himself in revolutionary activity, but he could not 'bear too much reality' and
from then on he turned more and more towards anti-democratic attitudes interconnecting with the familiar nostalgia for the
'timeless'. Revolution is only *within*. It is hard not to see the
revolt which was always Baudelaire's immediate impulse as a
pleading to be taken notice of, to be re-accepted into the
security of bourgeois society and Catholic religion (getting into
Christianity by the back door, Eliot called it). His longing for
order, expressed in the discipline of his prosody, was as pronounced and ultimately as anti-democratic in its implications
as Eliot's own.

Baudelaire's view of the poet's necessary apartness, an élite
figure, from humanity in general, amply fuelled in his case by
the egotism, the desire to feel special, is given expression in
'Bénédiction', a poem which certainly supports Kermode's
remarks in *Romantic Image* about the Romantic artist's sense
that he is made different by his suffering but is uniquely
compensated: 'Je sais que la douleur est la noblesse unique'
(p. 9). The poet is depicted as gaining through suffering a
'mystic crown' of which the splendours of the human and
physical worlds are but dim reflections – a standard Symbolist
notion. Baudelaire feels he has passed the stage at which any
meaningful amelioration of suffering can be attempted. He
feels himself 'moderne en esthétique' in embracing 'le
malheur'. The anxieties of the modern writer amid what are
felt as the depersonalizing structures of his world (technologi-
cal, bureaucratic, even democratic) are anticipated in one of
Baudelaire's favourite words, 'gouffre' – the abyss. The poem
'Le Gouffre', and Baudelaire's entry in the *Journaux* which is a
kind of gloss upon the poem, where he says 'j'ai toujours le
vertige', proclaim the tortured modern consciousness – Kaf-
kaesque, Eliotic. It is vertiginous because, perilously clinging
to the edge of the abyss, it can gain no firm hold; but also
because it is constituted of a disarrangement of the senses
(Rimbaud's famous 'dérèglement de tous les sens'), a
continuous stream of rarefied, heightened sensation which
intensifies the individual's conviction that he is 'different',

'abnormal'. In retrospect, there seems a continuous development from here to the sense of vertigo, of luridly heightened
consciousness, balanced on the edge of sanity, in such poetry as
that of Robert Lowell and Sylvia Plath.

These last-mentioned two poets, one might say, do indeed
feel 'different' from ordinary human beings, but the difference
defines itself only as a willingness to *admit and confess* to the pain,
guilt and sense of victimization which others inauthentically
suppress. It is a kind of specialness, but also of solidarity with a
common state of oppression. Lowell and Plath are engaged in a
passionate struggle with despair, protesting against the
oppressive systems imposed from without, but refusing wholly
to let go the chance of establishing a sense of order independent
of those systems. M. L. Rosenthal, who seems to have initiated
the application of the term 'confessional' to modern poetry,
writes of 'one implication of what writers like Robert Lowell
are doing: that their individual lives have profound meaning
and worth, and that therapeutic confession will lead to the realization of these values'.[42] Baudelaire deliberately sought a comprehensive knowledge of evil and suffering, and sought it
within himself – he *studied his suffering*, as Eliot well put it. *Jour-
neaux intimes, Mon cœur mis à nu* – the titles given these incidental
writings might serve as inscriptions for Baudelaire's whole
work. The lapsed and re-sought Catholicism which commentaries have made much of certainly suggests a desire for absolution, and no doubt some such desire lies behind all 'confessional' poetry; there is little point in confessing unless it brings
some relief, exorcising or setting aside in some way the pain and
guilt which has haunted one. Hence the likenesses between
psychoanalysis and confession. As Rousseau explained:

The most that I could do was to confess that I had a terrible deed on
my conscience, but I have never said in what it consisted. The
burden, therefore, has rested till this day on my conscience without
any relief; and I can affirm that the desire to some extent to rid myself
of it has greatly contributed to my resolution of writing these *Confessions*.[43]

But Baudelaire seems to have been too much a *poète maudit*, a
cloche fêlée; his will damaged too irreparably to shed the burden,

to discover any effective 'meaning and worth' – one notices already here the modern situation of the poet confronted by an *unanswering* universe, one with which no 'correspondence' can be held. He flaunts his suffering and sinfulness but cannot summon the self-abasing energy of repentance. Critics have remarked upon his total lack of reference to Christ; no divine intermediary must share in his absolution. It was to be forgiveness which recognized his utter 'otherness', for the unique enormity of *his* sins (significantly, the word 'unique' recurs constantly in his poetry). But if this is a unique form of the egotistical sublime, Baudelaire's poetry witnesses to a correlation between radically disorientated and unstable consciousness and 'confession', calculated exhibition of personal pain and weakness. Baudelaire rubs his own face in the 'irony', as he calls it, of his existence, in a way that was to be imitated by many later nineteenth-century poets; the atmosphere of Eliot's earlier poems derives most immediately from Laforgue and Corbière, but they themselves were descendants of Baudelaire. Unlike the neo-classical satirists, the 'decadent', proto-modern Romantics do not mock the world; they mock themselves. Baudelaire has a poem actually titled 'Confession', where, in a languorously moonlit setting, the poet's mistress speaks of 'cette confidence horrible chuchotée / Au confessional du cœur' (p. 44). The atmosphere in this poem of indulged dissipation, debilitation of the moral will, reflects that larger condition which makes action an unavailable option, and hence *confession* the only alternative. Indeed, the confession often has to be made because the monster *Ennui* saps the very will to resist, so that the only way to slip from its clutches is by the passively submitting act of ritual absolution – by faith, by the right form of words, or some oracular or mystic realization, rather than by taking *action* to frustrate the enemy, because of this the victim is incapable.

I have referred in my first chapter to Donald Davie's remark in his book on Hardy's poetry about poems

of a sort that is nowadays called 'confessional', and often esteemed very highly. Indeed, we sometimes hear it said that such poetry, which seems to have been written immediately out of the jangle of agonized nerves, is the only poetry that nowadays we can afford to attend to. (p. 54)

'Nowadays' was 1973 and confessional poetry is no longer so much the thing, but Davie cites the Introduction to Kenneth Rexroth's *Selected Poems of D. H. Lawrence* as an example of the misplaced valuing of poetry such as Lawrence's for its 'confess-ional' qualities:

Lawrence is sincere by virtue of the fact that the 'I' in his poems is always directly and immediately himself ... Confessional poetry, of its nature and necessarily, is superior to dramatic or histrionic poetry; a poem in which the 'I' stands immediately and unequivocally for the author is ... superior to a poem in which the 'I' stands not for the author but for a persona of the author's – this is what Rexroth asks us to believe. (p. 135)

The 'I' in a poem, I have said, is always a stylization, compli-catedly related to the empirical individual who wrote the poem. But Baudelaire's example seems to show that poetry which, unlike Lawrence's, is highly formalist and which elab-orately constructs a persona – himself, as I said, writ large and extreme – can be just as much 'confessional'. The formal struc-tures and the creating of the persona are, indeed, means to a whole artifice of confession. Nor should another kind of echoing between Lawrence and Baudelaire escape notice. I have argued that Lawrence's poetry does not finally escape solipsism, but he clearly saw in himself that solipsism which makes everything seem a *repetition* of self, and imagined dying out of that self and being born anew: 'it was all tainted with myself ... everything was me' ('New Heaven and Earth'). And being born anew figures, of course, absolution. Perhaps it is not surprising, then, that Lawrence, in 1911, could give endorse-ment to Baudelaire: 'With Baudelaire, Verlaine, and Ver-haeren, poetry seems to have broken out afresh, like a new crater. These men take life welling out hot and primitive, molten fire, or mud, or smoke, or strange vapour.'[44] This suggests that Lawrence saw those hothouse flowers of evil, however painstakingly cultivated, as germinating in the same 'original consciousness', amid the same 'strange vapours' emitted by the primitive energies of life, which preoccupied himself. In a poetry where memorable imagery, and a music as haunting as Eliot's own, tap primitive sources of that kind, the 'auditory imagination' would appear to be functioning at high intensity.

VI

J. Alfred Prufrock's love song is, one might say, a kind of confession. But where is T. S. Eliot in that poem? The 'I' of the poem is emphatically not the poet. The answer, surely, is that Eliot *is* there in the poem, but has taken great pains to make himself invisible behind an invented self-mocking persona. 'From Laforgue Eliot learnt to broadcast secrets, to confess through the defeatist persona his own despair ... ' (Lyndall Gordon, p. 29). Baudelaire (his influence mediated in the Prufrock poems through Laforgue) had adopted elaborate poses as a way, I have proposed, of studying his suffering, of holding some sort of semblance of self in place. But the poses are not to be taken seriously, they are a way of signalling the desire for forgiveness and affection which he 'really' feels. Eliot will not play those games. His theory of impersonality in poetry is a strategy of avoiding confession *in his own person*. I think we have a parallel here with what Robert MacCarthy, in the article quoted in chapter 1, speaks of as Hardy's 'extreme sensitivity to the frustrations and anguish of human existence' which produces 'a desire for invulnerability'. But we have seen that Hardy in what are perhaps his greatest poems – for the most part, that is, the poems written after her death about his first wife – moderates this desire for invulnerability, does in a manner of speaking *confess*, voices his innermost needs and regrets. I think that in Eliot's case to confess would have seemed a crack in the armour-plating, giving something away that the enemy might use against him. Invulnerability was exactly what he was after.

If the poetry produced by Eliot's arrays of generalizing and distancing devices creates the effect of embodying 'a clairvoyant sense of his time' – for at least two or three decades of the present century readers felt that he spoke with exceptional aptness to their condition – it has always been possible to read Eliot's *œuvre* as forming a 'spiritual autobiography' of a very personal nature. This reading was confirmed when Valerie Eliot, after her husband's death, included in her edition of the drafts of *The Waste Land* biographical material not publicly available before. I will quote in a moment from an example of the use that could be made of that material, George Whiteside's 1973 article 'The Psychobiographical Approach to Eliot'. Since then, Eliot's centenary year in 1988 especially acting as a catalyst, our detailed knowledge of Eliot's life has greatly increased: plays and television programmes, Peter Ackroyd's biography, Lyndall Gordon's two volumes (Gordon mentions Eliot's own reference in a letter to wanting to write in the form of 'the spiritual autobiography'), Valerie Eliot's edition of the letters. The psychobiographical approach, to borrow that unwieldy but useful term, consolidates the view that Eliot's poetry is deeply rooted in his personal problems – not least his sexual ones – and embodies certain highly peculiar ways of experiencing.

'Readers now began to see the poem', writes Whiteside of *The Waste Land*, 'as what it plainly is: an outburst of anguish (about his life, wife, sexual urges, schizoid feelings) from a man in the midst of a nervous breakdown, an emotional "aboulie"'; he goes on to diagnose a 'relatively stabilized schizoid personality'.[45] I have thought it reasonable to talk about poets in the Romantic-modern tradition as often afflicted by a kind of psychopathology, however 'relatively stabilized' for the purposes of ordinary living. I have pointed to a sense felt by the poets of difficulty in *managing their lives*. Baudelaire can hardly have said to have managed his at all. In Eliot's case the condition was stabilized enough for him to be able to pursue his public life with some success, though in his personal life people always found it hard to get 'close' to him, and he could not bear to feel intruded upon.[46] The fact remains that the wounding went very deep. This is, I believe, the only way to account for the relentless emphasis on 'the horror' in his work, and I see no interpretative approach except the 'psychobiographical' which will sufficiently give us that account. Moreover, to construct this account is to go to the heart of Eliot's poetry.

It was inevitable that the view of *The Waste Land* as expressing 'the condition of our time' should come to seem not to say everything about the poem. It was probably equally inevitable that the psychobiographical means of supplementing that view should in its turn be called into question. A. D. Moody warned against 'the error of reading the poem as a document of the early years of Eliot's first marriage – an error as extreme as to read it as a document of European culture'. Quoting this in an article 'Rereading *The Waste Land*', F. H. Langman comments that in practice 'the two errors have proved not incompatible'. He adds:

The objection to this sort of biographical reading as to the standard interpretation it accompanies is that both substitute ready-made impressions and ideas for the more difficult, complex, and significant realization of the poetry: how much more certain, how much more definite, both approaches make the details of the poem than they would otherwise appear.[47]

But *are* the two approaches incompatible? Aren't these only 'errors' when *one* of them is offered as a definitive reading? And is either approach necessarily 'ready-made'? Both seem to me made out of a struggle with the at first impermeable complexities, the unreadability, of the poem, and only by making a sensible use of whatever hypotheses and whatever data may shed light on the 'details of the poem', only through supplementing and comparing different approaches with each other, are we likely, one would think, to get that 'more difficult, complex, and significant realization of the poetry'.

It is precisely in attempting to realize that full complexity that one feels the pressing need to account for some unimaginable psychic 'horror' of which the voices in Eliot's poems insistently speak, yet for which nothing concretely realized in the poetry gives an adequate warrant. When, in his essay on *Hamlet*, he speaks of emotions in excess of any represented object of them, he seems, as usual in his prose, to be describing a poetic problem of his own. The impersonal mask, that which made it difficult to get close to Eliot either as poet or man, is explained by Whiteside in these terms:

The reason for his evasiveness is already implied by him here [in a passage from a broadcast by Eliot]: as a poet he felt impelled to express his private experience honestly; but as a man of extreme reserve he was compelled to express 'without giving himself away.' The phrasing is significant: he had the schizoid's feeling that he literally would be giving himself away if he should exercise complete openness. (p. 5)

Eliot may refuse to confess in his own person, but *The Waste Land* is certainly, what we know of his life now shows us, 'written immediately out of the jangle of agonized nerves', out of the shattering of any sense of subjective coherence, and one can perceive in the subsequent poetry something like the pattern I have noted in Graves's – a labour of remaking and healing (though the remaking is not the Yeatsian games-playing of which Graves so disapproved), a toiling to discover, as it were, an effective amulet against the *ennui*, to forge a workable *modus vivendi*. And it is this that his poems are 'about', it is this which requires their obliqueness of construction, their fragmentation, the Symbolist techniques. Even in *Four Quartets*, with its more strongly marked-out patterning and development, widely different modes are used in the various sections, with abrupt transitions between them. If his poems are constructed out of fragments he has shored against his ruin, there is always, I have suggested, the sense that the whole edifice is only just staying shored up. He stressed the *difficulty* of writing poetry in the modern world. We are likely to agree that writing poetry is never easy, and modern conditions may have been especially 'unpropitious', but as with Lawrence and Graves we may wonder whether such deeply subjective poetry doesn't compound the difficulty by declining to come to terms with various aspects of the life of our time. After all, so much of Eliot's poetry is about renunciation. And perhaps this renunciation only really makes sense if we *do* read it as a *personal* solution to a personal problem, forced upon Eliot by a peculiar individual state of alienation.

Yet there is a kind of heroism, if I may call it that, about the whole enterprise. *The Waste Land*, together with the subsequent poetry, seems to present a persistent struggle with, a refusal to capitulate to, the adverse circumstances of his life and his peculiar psychology. It has been said of 'his theory of the impersonal nature of art' that it is 'obviously the aesthetic of a suffering man'.[48] The discipline that he had to have if he was to remain a useful member of society – the influence upon him in his student days of, first, Irving Babbit and then Charles Maurras seems to have shaped for the rest of his life this disposition – was sought in tradition and orthodoxy; in, finally, 'The Idea of a Christian Society'. When he wrote the following of Matthew Arnold he might also have been speaking of his own struggle:

> It is not to say that Arnold's work was in vain if we say that it is to be done again; for we must know in advance, if we are prepared for that conflict, that the combat may have truces but never a peace. If we take the widest and wisest view of a Cause, there is no such thing as a Lost Cause because there is no such thing as a Gained Cause. We fight for lost causes because we know that our defeat and dismay may be the preface to our successors' victory, though that victory itself will be temporary; we fight rather to keep something alive than in the expectation that anything will triumph.[49]

The same resolution is voiced in *Four Quartets*:

> There is only the fight to recover what has been lost
> And found and lost again and again: and now, under conditions
> That seem unpropitious. But perhaps neither gain nor loss.
> For us, there is only the trying. The rest is not our business.[50]

The unpropitious conditions are specifically those of wartime, and this helps to explain the language of combat in these quotations. But for Eliot change is always recurrence, history an illusion; what he is saying is that the war he is living through is only symptomatic of a permanent condition of human existence. Romantic optimism or the materialist notion of progress are repudiated, but we should also not mistake such statements as expressions of a Senecan or an Augustan worldly stoicism. Despite the impersonal pronouns 'we' and 'us', there is no real sense here of solidarity, a common cause. What is being voiced is a Christian subjectivism, which (I will expand the point shortly) does not contradict 'The Idea of a Christian Society' because that society, while imposing, yes, communal and impersonal structures, aims at the relinquishing of human bonds, the resolving of the *self* in Christ, which can only be done on an individual basis; and it has its roots in the Romantic subjectivism, the Romantic realizing of self. The pessimism lurking in the sense of the 'unpropitious', in the disinclination towards any stronger affirmation than 'there is only the trying', still has clinging to it the old Romantic *ennui* and had been part of Eliot's nature from the start. Yet he gives the pessimism a peculiar kind of affirmative twist: 'The rest is not our business' because (such had become Eliot's conviction by the time of writing 'East Coker') it is God's business. The Christian quietism at which he had now arrived perfectly answered to his temperamental needs. The resolution (in both senses of the term) is creative, but would a writer before the modern period have shown the same kind of consciousness, implied in that terminology of combat, of the odds being stacked against him, of forlorn hope, of the *heroism* of his own creative undertaking?

I don't mean, of course, that Eliot consciously tried to project himself in the role of hero; but he inherited, and felt strongly to impinge upon him, a situation which over a century earlier the Romantic poets had felt themselves compelled to address. For convenience, I borrow Cleanth Brooks's formulation of this. Designating Wordsworth and Coleridge 'the first poets to bring into distinct focus the predicament of modern man', he sees their sense of the predicament as leading to an obsession with the creative act, the poem, itself.

A poet like Wordsworth found himself cut off from the world of human values and imprisoned in a 'Newtonian' universe in which the great machine of the world moved in terms of inexorable mathematical laws and therefore had no concern for, or relation to, the hopes, fears, and ardors of the individual human being. The problem was essentially a moral and philosophical problem; but the personal and cultural situation of poets like Wordsworth and Coleridge compelled them to describe it as a problem of poetic composition. For the problem addressed itself to them in this way: was it any longer possible to write poetry ... To be able to produce a poem thus became in itself a kind of moral achievement and way of bringing man back into meaningful relation with his universe ... Hence the basic reason for the fact that Wordsworth's masterpiece should be *The Prelude* – a poem about the growth and development of a poet's mind – rather than the poem it was originally designed to introduce.[51]

Before the Industrial Revolution it would have appeared, one imagines, a bizarre notion that the act of poetic composition could be self-sufficient: writing a poem was a function of something else – the desire to commemorate an occasion, describe an event or scene, to 'please and instruct', to affirm one's love of man or of God, to uphold a social ideal, in some cases simply to impress a patron. But under the conditions of industrial capitalism it becomes a kind of heroic act: in the early decades of the nineteenth century, as Marilyn Butler has put it, 'a taste was beginning to emerge to see the artist *as a hero*' (p. 2). The Romantic concern with the processes of the poet's mind, M. H. Abrams implied, leads on to a distinctively 'modern' concern with the poem itself. Coleridge, 'the innovative English critic of his time', through his insistence on the organic imagination allied to 'principles of writing', already foreshadowed this movement: he 'was enabled to maintain his double view, capable alternately of dwelling on a poem as a poem, and a poem as a process of mind'.[52] The moderns, we have seen, tend to focus upon the operations of consciousness, 'the mind's morphology itself', as the subject-matter of poetry. But now the poem, beyond even this looking by the poet at his own mind writing the poem, this self-sufficing act about the poet's own mind, has come to be seen as a structure reflecting upon its own structure, written by and about the linguistic conventions and codes which constitute it (and which are inescapably a product of history). From being a romantic hero, the author of himself, the poet becomes an inscriber of a text, authored by impersonal pressures.

Eliot certainly conceived of a kind of heroism of the text, but with his need for 'impersonality' was also in a sense already part of this later movement. As I have suggested, his commentaries *on* poetry can be read as a continuous wrestling with his own problems of composition, his own expressive needs. They formulate a poetic which will satisfy his peculiar needs as a poet; and are recurringly occupied with 'the processes of the poet's mind' – 'When a poet's mind is perfectly equipped for its work ...'. It is in *Four Quartets*, at certain points where, in a certain way, impersonality *avowedly* breaks down, that this concern becomes explicit in the actual poetry. I am thinking in particular of those passages where the voice *is* clearly Eliot's 'own' and in which he turns to his reader and speaks candidly about his own life, work and feelings (if this is not exactly 'confessional', it is taking the reader a good deal more into his confidence than he had ever done before: here a defined personality or subject appears to speak personally to another such, the reader, about, paradoxically, how difficult it is to frame speech impersonally as poetry – language *always* betrays). *Four Quartets* belongs in part to that peculiarly modern genre, the poem about writing a poem, the poem about itself, parody and pastiche its unavoidable means:

> That was a way of putting it – not very satisfactory:
> A periphrastic study in a worn-out poetical fashion,
> Leaving one still with the intolerable wrestle
> With words and meanings. The poetry does not matter.
>
> ('East Coker', 68–71)

And what Eliot is confessing here is his sense that words, meanings, are always slipping from his grasp. 'The poetry does not matter', he says, because, first, writing poems is made impossible by our very logocentricity, and, second, there is something more important, there is a meaning somewhere beyond the range of mere words, of the materials which constitute poetry, and more reliable and enduring than those can ever be: in short, the Word. Yet – this is the implication – continuing to write in the face of this is an heroic undertaking.

So there is a paradox, paradox being the principle embedded in this whole work. There is a premise, indeed, which carries over to much 'post-modern' writing, that we are driven to attempt meaning even where none is apparent; the absurd does not necessarily entail despair; writing itself is a commitment around which life can organize itself. This, I think, is often implicit in post-Eliot writing as a kind of value in itself in a world where no absolutes are acknowledged and which has disavowed any transcendental teleology, any absolute beyond it. Eliot would not have put it so, but what he is saying is that poems do not signify, are merely 'sites' for arbitrary words which do not offer any dependable view through to worlds, whether material or metaphysical, beyond themselves. Yet for Eliot, somewhere beyond the non-signification, that mere site where pre-conditioned words congregate and contend, existing in the face of his own scepticism about the power of language and the human mind to shape meaning, there *is* meaning – here once more is the pressure of the Baudelairean and Symbolist tradition. And this meaning is the barely attainable object of the poetry which is presently, in *Four Quartets*, being written. Moreover, art itself is the most closely approximating analogy that can be found for that transcendent meaning and for how it is known; the experiencing of works of art and the labour to create them (as for Yeats, art is supreme labour) are like the experience of spirituality and the effort to achieve it.

> Words, after speech, reach
> Into the silence. Only by the form, the pattern,
> Can words or music reach
> The stillness, as a Chinese jar still
> Moves perpetually in its stillness.
> Not the stillness of the violin, while the note lasts,
> Not that only, but the co-existence ...
>
> ('Burnt Norton, 139–45)

Although material in its elements, art may create the effect (the *illusion*, one might say) of 'stillness', a timeless moment, which is like spirituality, and free of ordinary emotion. But immense labour is required to achieve this among the ephemeral distractions, the 'Shrieking voices' (l. 153), of the world, and words themselves, being *of* the world, are fragile and untrustworthy: 'Words strain,/Crack and sometimes break, under the burden,/... Will not stay still' (149–53). Nor do words signify an essential reality, merely one which is an intersection of all sorts of historical and phenomenal accidents. The poem's own words *have* strained ('Or say that ...' (l. 146)), have found it difficult to say. It is only the Word, the Logos, which has meaning and reality, but as far as we are concerned, *that* is ineffable Silence or Stillness. The concluding passage of 'Burnt Norton' suggests, however, that the transcendental moment is always present, like the work of art ('all is always now'), is exempt from the corroding effects of memory and desire.

In the corresponding section of 'East Coker' – in each of the Quartets it is Section v in particular which deals with this analogy between art and spirituality – Eliot offers, in plain prosaic language which gives that almot confessional effect of candour, his own lifelong struggle with his art as an example of the common struggle against worldly distractions and the imperfections of the flesh. One notes again the language of war, and how the war has crystallized in Eliot's imagination a correspondence of war, art and spiritual discipline, the latter two viewed, like the war effort, as common endeavours. There is a further analogy, the reader begins to see, between the operations of the work of art itself, and Eliot's own life and artistic enterprise: his whole life and endeavour have been aimed at attaining this silence, this stillness, this state of quiescent waiting for the Word to reveal itself, like the epiphany achieved in the resolution of a work of art. This section, as I've already suggested, manifests something close to a contradiction, one latent in the whole *Quartets*. It seems to speak of a common spiritual quest (and we might remember Eliot's striking phrase about the 'common pursuit of true judgement' in criticism). The stress is on 'we', 'us', 'our', on a depersonalizing activity, on art which is not individualist, in the sense that it is concerned to recover meanings which have already been 'found and lost' by others; on the extinction of the sharply individual experience in total historical experience (the image derives from indecipherable stones in the graveyard at East Coker):

> And not the lifetime of one man only
> But of old stones that cannot be deciphered.
>
> (195–6)

and the extinction of individual love in spiritual love:

> Love is most nearly itself
> When here and now cease to matter.
>
> (200–1)

It suggests a freeing of the individual from the anguish of personal emotion, a communal discipline which can offset the personal experience of chaos and alienation. It is this avowed rejection of Romantic emotionalism and individualism which, of course, allowed Eliot to see himself as a classicist. How, then, can A. D. Moody say of the passage that 'the personal and private meaning dominates' (p. 221)? Such a comment implicitly recognizes that the section is most preoccupied with an attempt to grasp and interpret 'the growth of the poet's mind', with the Romantic 'totality of self', with discerning a meaning in a lifetime's experience (there is even an echo of Wordsworth in 'Home is where one starts from'). Once again we seem to confront the paradox of a longing for community which can only be negotiated, in Raymond Williams's terms, 'in and through the intense subjectivities'.

It is true, of course, that the 'knowledge derived from experience' which 'imposes a pattern, and falsifies' has been rejected earlier in 'East Coker', because that is worldly knowledge, and what is excitedly anticipated in the closing lines of the poem is 'another intensity ... a further union, a deeper communion'. My point is that the essential act of sensibility here is of the same order as that releasing fusion of subjective experience, the epiphanic moment, in which a 'meaning' is suddenly intuited after a lifetime's labour of self-interrogation that I have noted in Hardy, Lawrence, Graves or (in his minimal terms) Edward Thomas, or in the sixty-year-old poet, ever remaking himself, striving to balance and fuse world and otherworld in 'Among School Children' – or which, for that matter, one finds in Proust. Eliot's poetic sensibility, that is to say, has the same deep Romantic springs; the difference, and apparent contradiction, in his case is that he manages to recover 'meaning' in the tradition, orthodoxy and faith which for other modern poets (even those who re-cycle myth) are barren. And there is a further point to be noted, bringing me back to one of my original points. 'East Coker' insists that

the pattern is new in every moment
And every moment is a new and shocking
Valuation of all we have been.

(85–7)

It seems that Eliot, in a peculiar way, shares the Paterian view
that 'Not the fruit of experience, but the experience itself, is the
end.' The fruit of experience can only be worldly and worthless, whereas the experience itself allows a moment-by-moment
revaluation of one's being which may make possible intuitions
of the eternal.[53] The experience itself – paradox again – is
teleological; the 'end' which is latent in it is the glimpse of a
pattern beyond all worldly pattern, as it is latent in the seemingly timeless present manifested by works of art. The new is
the eternal; to make it new is to revalue tradition ('all we have
been'); poems – works of art – do *not* merely reflect their own
structures, they reflect (in some mysterious way) the structure
of eternity.

The fifth section of 'The Dry Salvages', in its turn, begins
with an evocation of 'false arts', of false attempts to communicate with the supernatural, but goes on to intimate the saint-
like asceticism which is needed in order to apprehend the
impersonally timeless. And 'Little Gidding' suggests that the
perfectly formed work of art is like the Christian Society or
community: everything in its place, dedicated to the common
spiritual quest:

> And every phrase
> And sentence that is right (where every word is at home,
> Taking its place to support the others,
> The word neither diffident nor ostentatious,
> An easy commerce of the old and the new,
> The common word exact without vulgarity,
> The formal word precise but not pedantic,
> The complete consort dancing together)
> Every phrase and every sentence is an end and a beginning,
> Every poem an epitaph[.]

(216–25)

There is, of course, something classical about this desired
balance, harmony, moderation, about the ideal that is adum-

brated. One might note, too, in passing, that it involves a kind of plea for 'a language close to common speech'; in the essay 'The Music of Poetry' (*On Poetry and Poets*, London, 1957) written (1942) at the same time that Eliot was at work on the *Quartets*, he speaks of poetry needing 'a music latent in the common speech of its time'. The paradox here is that nobody can say that *Four Quartets* is not a difficult work, dealing with matters which are hardly those of common discourse; just as its notion of a common spiritual quest turns out, in the end, to mean something very specialized, personal and private. But what the passages I have been quoting suggest so interestingly is that for Eliot it *is* poetry that matters, that in some way which Eliot himself with his infinitely subtle mind never quite pinned down (perhaps could not afford to pin down), to write the formally perfect poem, if it *could* be written, would be to achieve transcendence. Every poem that is right is an epitaph, because it is immobile, stays still, has won release from the flux of time. Of the other reality, the mystical reality beyond, the poetry of *Four Quartets* can only give us hints and echoes; it cannot persuade us that the reality is actually *there*. What it can persuade us is that the writing of the poetry itself is an heroic and indeed redeeming act.

It is striking that Eliot should, in his various writings, even while he is consciously aiming to address much larger issues than purely aesthetic ones, put so much stress on the importance of art, or culture – high art is seen as central to his 'Idea of a Christian Society'. One sees of course that the harmony of perfect art – 'the complete consort dancing together' – corresponds, in an almost medieval way, to the harmony of the Christian community, but this is analogic. Eliot may have transposed his quest for order into Christian terms, but, whatever private practices and public functions he may have adopted in the context of the church, it was in art that he compulsively worked out his salvation. I don't think that is too much to claim when one considers the spiritual autobiography I have described his art as representing, or the way *The Cocktail Party*, for example, pursues in terms of *dramatic art* the theme of 'salvation' (whatever one thinks of the success of that drama).

And such an identification of the meaning of one's life with one's art has impeccably Romantic pedigree.

Four Quartets, then, completes a spiritual autobiography which progresses from the agnostic disorientation of the *Prufrock* poems and *The Waste Land*, through the *Angst*-filled, absurdist vision of *The Hollow Men* and *Sweeney Agonistes*, to the difficult leap of faith meditated in *Ash-Wednesday* and the *Ariel* poems. The *Quartets* represent a culminating assertion of faith in the teeth of all the evidence, in the teeth of Eliot's own scepticism. In fact, there are some grounds for seeing, as in A. D. Moody's reading of the *Quartets*, 'Burnt Norton' as the culmination of that full sweep of Eliot's poetic work, with the other three poems forming a kind of codicil inspired by the conditions of wartime life. I feel, however, that it is more important, and more in tune with how we read the poetry, to observe the cohesion of the *four* poems; they form a philosophical Christian poem which seems to aim at realizing, while acknowledging that experience of the Word is impossible to represent in words, a psychic or spiritual state in which one is awake, present in one's human consciousness (because, being human, one cannot be otherwise), but uncontained by it and unaware of Time. This state appears to have direct psychological affinities (whatever a Christian might think the qualitative difference) with the states of suspended consciousness I have noted in Romantic poetry. But it is a kind of experience, the poem argues, that only the re-establishment of a community expressly ordered along Christian lines can make accessible. From the outset, the poetry conveys to us a feeling of the unreality of the world we inhabit, governed by time. We can't manipulate time in the way that we can wind forward or back an audio or video cassette, there is only ever *now*:

> If all time is eternally present
> All time is unredeemable.[54]

We can never recapture the past nor secure the future:

> What might have been is an abstraction
> Remaining a perpetual possibility
> Only in a world of speculation.

What might have been and what has been
Point to one end, which is always present.

(6–10)

We are left, therefore, with a sense of the unreality and
pointlessness of action in the world in which we live. The
poetry conveys this in its circling, repetitive, indeterminate
movement: one statement, one phrase, continuously cancelling
out another, the negative constructions giving a sense of
vacancy and indirection. I began by comparing D. H. Lawrence's notion of 'rotary image-thought', of a state of consciousness in which there was 'nowhere to get to', with the Modernist
aesthetic. Here, certainly, the poetry doesn't seem to be going
anywhere – the indefiniteness of 'perhaps' in line 2, the hypo-
thetical 'if' in line 4, '*un*redeemable' in line 5 – the condition of
our existence is a sort of stagnant present. The subjunctive
mood – 'What *might have been* ... possibility' – evokes potential
unachieved and unachievable; 'abstraction' is by definition
that which cannot be concretely grasped; 'only' adds to the
effect of diminished or cancelled expectation.

Footfalls echo in the memory
Down the passage which we did not take
Towards the door we never opened
Into the rose-garden. My words echo
Thus, in your mind.

(11–15)

Experience is represented as a matter of echoes only, in the
insubstantial world of the mind, like dreams or fantasies;
nothing is quite actual or tangible. The accretive succession of
fugitive effects (footfalls are bodiless) builds an overwhelming
effect of unfulfilment. (Philip Larkin is always confronting us
with a similar elusiveness, the way we like to deceive ourselves
that we are on the brink of some fulfilment, which, however,
never materializes; but for Larkin the situation does not
provide an epiphanic window onto another world as it will seek
to do here; our efforts to peer beyond what we have are met
only with an impermeable mirror, in which only our falsehoods
are reflected.)

> But to what purpose
> Disturbing the dust on a bowl of rose-leaves
> I do not know.
>
> (15–17)

The bowl of rose-leaves would seem to symbolize the sensory fabric of our world, the world of material phenomena. In *this* world we cannot perceive – 'I do not know' – any point in doing things. However, as the complex configurations of *Four Quartets* unfold, it becomes apparent that what Eliot seeks is to convert our lack of control over time into our means of salvation. If we resign ourselves to that lack of control, let go the *effort* to mould time into meaningful and 'humanly' rewarding patterns, then there is a 'possibility' that we might achieve transcendence. Only through always trying to recapture the past or secure the future, through our mistaken allegiance to the laws of a material and time-bound universe, do we condemn ourselves to this fruitless stagnation. It is part of the poem's dominating system of paradox that our subservience to time is seen as imposing upon us this stagnant present, which neither past nor future has the power to alleviate; and yet the redeeming opposite conceived of is equally a state of *stillness* – though an ineffable stillness absolved utterly of past, present and future; and moreover, the only possibility of experiencing that transcendent stillness is through disciplining ourselves to an abnegating stillness in our mortal lives, an absence of memory and desire. This opening passage of 'Burnt Norton' creates another of those haunted modern poetic expressions of dream-like consciousness, everything half-realized and insubstantial, but what the poem proceeds to do is to translate the sense of stagnation, of the pointlessness of action, into a passive and quiescent waiting which is paradoxically filled with positive force and potential.

The idea of co-existence – 'Not that only, but the co-existence' (145) – is at the heart of the poem: the co-existence of the temporal and the timeless; of past, present and future; of particular locality and of the oceanically infinite (sea-imagery recurring in the poem); of the personal (Eliot himself in the poem, with his personal preoccupations) and the communal or impersonal; of the material and the numinous. Past, future; body, spirit; from, towards; end, beginning; movement, stillness; the moment, eternity – all these (and other) conceptual and imagistic plays which throng the poem effect the cancelling out. At times this does convincingly suggest the ineffable stillness, the unmoving, the silence – 'I am here / Or there, or elsewhere' ('East Coker', 49–50) – the rhythmic spasms slip from our grasp, won't be pinned down in the world of here and now, urge us to surrender our fealty to historical and material limitations. Paradox, of course, is again a favourite device for achieving this kind of effect – 'So the darkness shall be the light, and the stillness the dancing ...' ('East Coker', 128). But it is also sitting on the fence, a mode of extreme scepticism; this co-existence is the negation of a pluralist vision of multiple possibility, and different, I think, from the balancing of antitheses in Yeats's poetry insofar as Yeats is more radically ambivalent about world and otherworld, never permitting one to invalidate the other. (The eagerness of Yeats's mind, the way it devours incongruous and even, to echo Auden, 'silly' ideas, is a long way from Eliot's scepticism.) In the end, Eliot's problem is that of making poetry out of what has become remote from a shared common experience of the age – or to put it another way, of too far a voyage into subjectivity. When he speaks of communality, what Eliot has in mind is rather different from anything having currency in an actual, democratized mid-twentieth-century western country. (At most it might exist among cells of High Anglican churchgoers.) And what he offers as an escape from isolation – that particular package of classicism, royalism and Anglo-Catholicism – is hardly likely to have wide appeal.

The poetry seems necessarily to involve a kind of scrupulous avoidance of commitment to the historical and the material, to the here and now, to ordinary living, to the phenomenal world from which poetry necessarily draws its materials. That in Eliot's poetry there are many and much-noted passages of a lyrical beauty which is rooted in the physical world is an essential aspect of the *struggle* the poetry communicates. But the longing to transcend time, locality and personality is always

coming up against the empirical facts, that time never *does* 'stay
still', that we always are located *somewhere*, that we are necessarily driven by our physical and emotional appetites; similarly, that the possession of personal consciousness is after all an
unalterable and determinative condition and can never
entirely be escaped by any one of us in the interests of an
impersonal community or communion. 'Eliot is attracted
above all', Father William F. Lynch has written, 'by the image
and the goal of immobility, and ... in everything he seeks for
approximations to this goal in the human order.'[55] It is the
opposite of the Lawrentian dynamism. Father Lynch's criticism of Eliot from a Christian point of view for not grasping, or
not being able to imagine, the importance of time and flux
('mobility'), and of action, as media of Christian living would
seem to have much force. It is striking that the opposing
immobilities in the poem are not counterpoised by opposing
mobilities or modes of action (action is only ever fruitless,
cannot be directed towards transcendence, though I shall
comment further on this in a moment). 'And do not think of
the fruit of action' ('The Dry Salvages', 161) – it would seem,
as I've said, that Eliot's vision is but another variety of perceiving, in the modern world, the *fruit* of experience as discredited.

> Let me disclose the gifts reserved for age
>   To set a crown upon your lifetime's effort.
>   First, the cold friction of expiring sense
> Without enchantment, offering no promise
>   But bitter tastelessness of shadow fruit ...
>   ('Little Gidding', 129–34)

But, says Father Lynch, 'jumping out of our human facts will
not help'. I take him to mean that God is in history, and in the
physical world, not merely having existence in a transcendent
realm, and requires us to live and act in the world's theatre,
and moreover to love the world as part of his creation. I've
noted, of course, that Eliot as a Christian worked hard at
adopting roles in public life, but one feels that he did so
burdensomely, as a duty, not out of 'love' for the world: Section
III of each *Quartet* in particular expresses revulsion from the
world. Seeing the poem in this perspective, we become aware

of it not as philosophically impersonal, not as uttering general and immutable truths, but as subjective wrestling with the poet's own spiritual problems. How theologically tenable it is to envisage God only as a momentary *intersection* in human life ('the intersection of the timeless moment': 'Little Gidding', 52), for whose grace we can only quiescently wait, I am not qualified to say. But whatever doctrinal view Eliot would have expressed, the poetry does not seem able to imagine God as always and actively present, and present in the past and in the future, and requiring our active and unreserved participation in his creation.

It is Time that makes life seem meaningless, dashing its possibilities, making it seem endlessly repetitious; it is this that makes life not only boring but *ennuyante*, filled with the pain of futility. Benjamin relates the motif of time in Baudelaire to the oppressive regulatory mechanisms of bourgeois capitalism, especially the repetitions of industrial labour (but one also thinks inevitably of Prufrock and his coffee-spoons), which by 'measuring out' a life rob it of a history – that history which Romantic 'memory' is perplexedly unable to re-establish – and render it a mere succession of fragments. History becomes meaningless, hence Baudelaire (though the time of Eliot, points out Lynch, is more subtle than that of Baudelaire) wished to stop time passing.[56] 'History may be servitude, / History may be freedom' ('Little Gidding', 162–3): all that a proper understanding of history can teach us, suggests *Four Quartets*, is how to liberate ourselves from this tyranny of time, from the investment in personality and emotion which trust in time permits, or from the sterile indifference and stoicism which we may adopt as a defence against such an investment:

> There are three conditions which often look alike
> Yet differ completely, flourish in the same hedgerow:
> Attachment to self and to things and to persons, detachment
> From self and from things and from persons; and, growing
>   between them, indifference
> Which resembles the others as death resembles life,
> Being between two lives – unflowering, between
> The live and the dead nettle. This is the use of memory:

> For liberation – not less of love but expanding
> Of love beyond desire, and so liberation
> From the future as well as the past . . .
>
> ('Little Gidding', 150–9)

How elegantly the lines move here, in their subtle ploy to forestall some of the very objections I have raised; how disarmingly they take us into the poet's confidence; how suavely they enact a sense of a consciousness which has known it all, of a mind which has weighed it all – 'balanced all, brought all to mind'! It is not a question of a negative asceticism or a barren stoicism, the poem will have us believe, not a freeing of ourselves from the demands of love, but of an expanding *beyond* ordinary human love. And thus we are directly back with 'Tradition and the Individual Talent', written more than twenty years earlier:

> . . . the historical sense involves a perception, not only of the pastness of the past, but of its presence . . . This historical sense, which is a sense of the timeless as well as of the temporal and of the timeless and of the temporal together, is what makes a writer traditional.[57]

The structure of the prose – 'not only . . . but', 'a sense of . . . as well as . . . and of . . . together' – is already, with a kind of elegant tortuousness, straining to encompass every subtlety, to tie up every possibility. What happened over the twenty years, *l'entre deux guerres*, we see, is that an aesthetic doctrine became assimilated to a religious one: 'a sense of the timeless as well as of the temporal and of the timeless and of the temporal together' – that kind of 'historical sense' – is precisely what *Four Quartets* is about, and Eliot himself comments on the twenty years it has taken him to arrive back at the same point. Peter Ackroyd notes that Eliot 'did not develop as a "thinker": he merely elaborated on the implications of his previous convictions' (p. 75). That essay's highly influential critical insights concerning the relationship of a work of art to the tradition in which it stands, and the essential criterion of value in a work of art being 'the intensity of the artistic process', have an objective authority which tended, for a time, to mask the extent to which the theory of 'impersonal art' of which they formed cornerstones was a defensively personal one. Eliot was in 1919 already deeply concerned with the problems of time and time-lessness, of the interactions of past, present and future; and 'the expression of personality' seemed to him – his own emotions were painful enough for it to be necessary to 'escape' them – to represent an over-investment in the temporal and particular. In his personal psychology, the need for 'expanding / Of love beyond desire, and so liberation / From the future as well as the past' was already pressing.[58]

The imagery of poetry grows, Eliot has it, from that 'dark embryo within', evolves at some deeply submerged level of consciousness, and detachment, impersonality, are essential in the poet if he is going to be 'liberated' enough from the temporal and the local to apprehend and to bear contemplating these images, these hints or intimations of 'another intensity'. His impersonality, as C. K. Stead put it, 'is a direction inward, not outward, in order to discover what is eternal' (p. 143). We see that the dazzling panoply of techniques in Eliot's poetry is designed to take out the narrative or personal 'I', to avoid locali-zation and particularization, to convey a sense of the timeless as well as of the timeless and of the temporal together. We see, too, why the 'together' is a necessary qualification: Section III of 'The Dry Salvages', for example, with its medley of material, com-monplace images – 'a Royal Rose or a lavender spray', 'fruit, periodicals and business letters' – insists that we have no alter-native but to 'fare forward' in this mundane life, since, chained in flesh and time as we are, the only way we may 'know' any-thing is in terms of its embodiment in the fabric of our temporal and physical consciousness. Indeed, the imagery of poetry may emerge from some mysterious dark embryo, yet, as Eliot knew very well, it is inevitably formulated in terms of the known, con-crete world. The Symbolist poetic from which *Four Quartets* derives is an attempt at divining the unknown in the tangible, its only possible means of expression being the tangible (and audible) itself. Nevertheless, for the poet who drew our attention to the unreality of the city and its church clock counting the hours, the local and the temporal are always unreal, and he experiences, moreover, a concomitant 'deep sense of unreality,

or equivocal reality, in personal emotions'.[59] Even Eliot's
young men seem afflicted by a sort of remoteness from vital
physical and emotional response – 'I grow old ... I grow old ...'
– are weighed down by some life-sapping weariness. According
to Gordon, Eliot said that Prufrock was 'in part a man about
forty and in part himself' (p. 45), but I think the effect of those
lines as they come in the poem is to convey the ironic point that
he is *not*, in fact, yet old. He suffers an agonizing emotional
paralysis, an 'aboulia'; the life lived by others is for him largely
unreal. Measuring out one's life with coffee spoons, that devastating image, evokes an astonishing lack of commitment, of
participation and active drives.

Of course, one cannot disagree with Eliot that life, seen in
certain lights, is an insubstantial thing:

> See, now they vanish,
> The faces and places, with the self which, as it could, loved
> them ...
>
> ('Little Gidding', 163–4)

'Self' is utterly provisional, consciousness, our only way of
knowing (and loving), is unstable, fragmented, amorphous: the
insubstantiality is so deftly caught in that hollowly echoing
internal rhyme (a repeated device of Eliot's), in the resistlessly
dissolving rhythms and syntax, that our assent is caught too.
Yes, we say: to love, to be attached, invariably entails pain of
some kind and always invites the suffering of loss. The Christian Auden, however, as I shall note in my next chapter,
refused any such ploy for invulnerability; acknowledged that
the *human* course is to *accept* the corollary as a price which must
be paid; we cannot even as Christians 'escape' the necessary
conditions of our humanity. But the goal of the spiritual autobiography which Eliot's *œuvre* forms is the mystical breaking
through into timelessness: 'To become renewed, transfigured,
in another pattern' (166). Such a breakthrough, by its very
nature, can only be hinted at:

> These are only hints and guesses,
> Hints followed by guesses; and the rest
> Is prayer, observance, discipline, thought and action.
>
> ('The Dry Salvages', 212–14)

Somewhat surprisingly, 'action' crops up after all in this
closing passage of 'The Dry Salvages'; Eliot, as always, striving
for the inclusive statement. But it is in these lines, to say the
least, a curiously static, not to say theoretic, notion of action –
almost a kind of counter-action. It is action in the service of
Christ, since all other action is

> Driven by daemonic, chthonic
> Powers. And right action is freedom
> From past and future also.
>
> (223–5)

The poetry doesn't establish this 'action' in a way that suggests
anything other than the quietism I have referred to. The state
of mind of this speaker in *Four Quartets* who has reduced
experience to its fundamentals is that of one for whom there is
nothing left but a continued disciplined wrestling with the
same problems – 'You say I am repeating ...' A sense of the
repetitive tedium of things had always been at the heart of his
perception of experience. Employing its shaping strategy of
paradox, *Four Quartets* turns this into a statement of unassaila-
ble closure: there is only one truth, or all truth is the same
(compare Graves's 'One story and one story only'). But as
Auden points out in his *New Year Letter*, written close in time,
the monist position requires only passivity: 'if the monist view
be right, / How is it possible to fight?'

Consider the medley of different verse forms used in the four
poems. A dazzling variety, one might say. Yet the effect is not
to endorse (as – see my next chapter – Louis MacNeice's poetry
does) the rich variousness of experience; rather, it is to show
that all ways of saying things amount to the *same* thing. And the
hovering throughout Eliot's work between fixed forms and free
verse, the marvellous if fastidious sensitivity with which he
handles his irregular verse vehicles, may be seen as formal
means of holding aloof from final choice and commitment. The
aged eagle (*Ash-Wednesday*) seems to wheel endlessly without
ever quite dropping to strike. Of course this paradox, this
appearance of getting nowhere – 'in my beginning is my end' –
is at the root of the poem's statement; its ultimate audacity – an

audacity so elegantly carried off that it is impossible not to admire it – is to claim the negative way as the positive one, the Baudelairean recognition of the sameness of things as the means of release into utter otherness. Thus the poem achieves its guarded, extraordinary, almost perverse affirmation. But though Eliot makes his point often enough – 'You say I am repeating' – for it to be crude in us to mistake its affirmative intention, though the patterns revolve and revolve with an entrancing cunning, and though Eliot undoubtedly committed himself to his writing and made the 'choice' of faith, I find it impossible to come away from the work without a sense that an evasion has been perpetrated. Momentous and dramatic as the poetic realization of journey, quest and struggle are in Eliot's work, the Romantic accidie, and Eliot's own endemic condition of aboulia, are being palmed off on us as principles of right conduct. We are brought to a position where, despite, or partly because of, Eliot's own kinds of expressed concern about 'culture' and 'society', Raymond Williams's strictures on the pursuit of the 'timeless' as an evasion of essential social consciousness tell heavily against him. Subtly and 'clairvoyantly' attuned to what lay 'below the conscious levels' of the time, Eliot charted the modern problem of consciousness with extraordinary intelligence and power. But in the end he spoke *for* himself, expressed a limitingly subjective vision.

CHAPTER 6

The work of Man: Louis MacNeice and W. H. Auden

I

The notion of the modern city as a fit subject for poetry was a long time taking a hold among poets writing in English, though the Americans were quicker at it than the British. In England, James Thompson's *The City of Dreadful Night* (1874) is an early but abortive attempt, and I have referred to others, but always that seductive rural myth lures the poet, making it hard for him to accept the city as a poetic habitat. Even Eliot's poetry, for all the urbanness of his sensibility, draws much on its force from being at odds with the modern urban experience. It is not till the thirties that certain young poets come to terms with it. In doing so, they tentatively point to possibilities for moderating the more extreme kinds of modern subjectivity, for writing a more 'public' poetry, founded in historical time and place. In the cases of Baudelaire and Eliot this had failed, because while they found in the streets, in Eliot's words, their 'centre of intensity', the city was for them, as G. M. Hyde, quoting Baudelaire, points out, the place where multitude is solitude ('The Poetry of the City', p. 337), still the theatre of a journey within. Yet time, history and 'objective' pressures more immediately and dramatically shape life in the city than in the country (for the poet, I mean, the user of reflective language: for the rural labourer life is no doubt objective enough); there is a certain inevitability in the 'mythe de la grande ville', with its embracing, however ambiguously, of a swarming, fallen humanity, coming to represent a symbolic antithesis to the ahistorical rural myth, with its implied retrieval of a unitary, inward Eden. Like Baudelaire and Eliot, Philip Larkin always gives in his poetry an impression of 'the town-dweller ... by bondage of temperament and habit', but his wanting 'to get back to humankind again', his interest in 'humanity and human emotion', expressed in the comment on Andrew Young I quoted in chapter 2, implies a kind of objective attention to the lives of others, to the life of a community, not a wholly obsessive concern with one's own subjective reality. And Larkin seems to me a direct and significant successor of those thirties poets, carrying on, in certain respects, where they left off.

Other poets associated with the so-called Movement of the fifties show similar traits. The indifference and disorder of Thom Gunn's city,

> the wharf of circumstance,
> Rejected sidestreet, formal monument ...[1]

remind us of the aimless coming-and-going of urban life in Eliot's earlier poetry, and behind Eliot, the transient relations, the experience of unconnectedness, in Baudelaire's city. But there is none of the finical distaste that attaches to Eliot's 'Streets that follow like a tedious argument'. Gunn's poem is 'In Praise of Cities', and the experience of meaningless tedium is stood on its head. The poem speaks of tribute to the urban 'wharf of circumstance', praises cities for their inexhaustible variety, their capacity to absorb both failure and aspiration, and, in a striking line, for being 'Extreme, material and the work of man'. Gunn is interested in the way cities, with their bewildering intricacies, embody the inscrutability of human motive, and his acceptance of the haphazard, imperfect, yet endlessly intriguing and humanly expressive actuality of cities reflects an acceptance of life for what it is, including its failures and incompleteness. The factual, non-idealist but nonetheless humanist view of the random nature of things is again like Larkin's.

In this poem, Gunn sees the modern city as man's own fullest expression of himself, as an emblem and necessary manifestation of man's hidden hungers as well as overtly conscious choices. Of course, this is to generalize what begins as a personal quality of feeling: there is a certain romanticism in this love-affair with the city, a mildly Baudelairean thrill in embracing the city's squalor and untidiness as well as its colourful and purposeful activity, and in the pleasure taken in pointedly contradicting traditional distaste for cities. Poems can only hatch in subjective consciousness, but though here the city's apparent lack of design may in part echo the poet's feelings about his own life, the poem's view is not confined by pathetic fallacy – the city possesses autonomous reality. Nor is it a justification for withdrawal, rather a source of opportunity, and if a certain emphasis on man forging his own existential destiny – 'the work of man' – was a fifties fashion, it is a refreshing contrast to the Romantic passivism. The turning of the back on nature, the espousing of what is 'extreme, material and the work of man', announces that a whole phase of sensibility is felt to have come to an end, or at least to be due for modification: the urban-industrial is no longer the primary emblem of alienation. Along with this goes a certain feeling that the random and unresolved are not incompatible with psychic well-being; that consciousness is being conscious of many things, even about the self, which will not necessarily fall into intelligible order. By the sixties it had come to be accepted that the poet's natural habitat is as much, or more, the city, as the countryside: 'Tout y est *poésie* au sens strict du terme.' Starting as 'the metaphor ... through which relational problems can be expressed' (Hyde, p. 341), the city as metaphor is transformed: as Edward Timms has put it: 'The metropolis ultimately becomes a metaphor – a dynamic configuration of the conflicting hopes and fears of the twentieth century.'[2]

How difficult such an accommodation was, and how long it has taken poets to make it actual in their work, may be seen in the case of Louis MacNeice, only a generation older than Gunn and Larkin. MacNeice had seemed in the thirties at home in the city and had expressed it with zest and energy. Yet by the fifties he seemed to have lost direction; the attempt to write poetry more public, more explicitly engaging 'history', had foundered. He was not alone in this; in the post-war period, his friend and mentor Auden, the greater poet, had also been tempted to turn his back on the endeavour. But what the comparison with MacNeice reveals, as I will try to show in the second part of this chapter, is that in certain respects *despite* himself Auden went on extending himself creatively in the writing of an open and public poetry, focussing upon a world in which 'the work of man' is paramount.

'At one time I was content if things would image / Themselves in their own dazzle', wrote MacNeice in 'To Hedli' (Hedli Andersen, his second wife), the dedicatory poem of his 1948 *Collected Poems*. 'But now I am not content'; yet when 'I lay my ear to the ground ... no one answers'. From the start, MacNeice had experienced the world as teeming with multifarious phenomena amongst which no clear answers were to be discerned, but as he grew older he became less able to make creative use of this. Robyn Marsack has it that 'he eventually learnt, through a period of deep discouragement and effort, to temper the kind of writing that came easily to him with the demanding art of opening his poems to imponderable forces, tapping reserves of dream, parable, and myth ...' and that '[a]fter appreciating in his early verse qualities of spontaneity and casual brilliance, the late measured passion takes us by surprise'.[3] My case, however, is that the attempts to 'open' his poems to 'dream, myth and parable', and to achieve a 'measured passion', ran against his natural gifts as well as against his original sense of what a modern poem should be – in this instance, first thoughts were best thoughts.[4] His natural gifts were great, as was his dedication to the writer's craft, and all his life he wrote compulsively. He strove after the thirties (influenced, I think, by Empson) to give his poems greater tightness: 'I like to think that my latest short poems are on the whole more concentrated and better organised than my earlier ones, relying more on syntax and bony features than on bloom or frill or floating image.'[5] He ransacked his dream-life for 'poetic' material, and talked of wishing to write 'parable'. But the problem was, neither tight organization nor 'imponderable forces', the sort of primitivist or extra-rational experience explored by other poets I've considered, were his real creative sources. There is much to admire in the final, bulky *Collected Poems*,[6] but reading through it, an impression of laboured determination grows oppressive. All the anxious activity, carefully signposted in various works of self-commentary and autobiography, is itself a symptom of the problem.

Perhaps just because he often felt lonely and apart, MacNeice had a compelling need to talk, to communicate. Much of his verse, like Auden's, is distinguished by an Horatian quality of heightened talk, and when, early in the war, the opportunity arose to work in broadcasting, the need to communicate found a ready outlet. Perhaps a too congenial one – John Press remarks, for example, that the use of music and radiophonic devices could cover up structural weaknesses in the writing. During the thirties, fuelled by a real excitement about the evanescent busyness of the world's things and events, that talkativeness could be made to seem apt. Imagist verse, pared down to timeless clarities, could not mirror the spawning meretriciousness of that decade, or the stylish artifice with which it was lived through. MacNeice was a man for the time; he liked making journeys, driving fast, physical discomfort and even danger (the fears he recorded were not physical ones), and liked also to apply the term 'speed' to the effects sought by modern poets. Auden and he developed the old forms ingeniously to give them the right feel and accent of newness, providing also a contemporary decor. It was a most skilful takeover, and my use of the term decor is considered, for it was a period which very much dealt in a constructed contemporaneity. 'I meet you in an evil time' opens 'An Eclogue for Christmas' (1933), memorably voicing a sensationalized, topicalized, yet not at all bogus sense of doom:

> The jaded calendar revolves,
> Its nuts need oil, carbon chokes the valves,
> The excess sugar of a diabetic culture . . .
>
> (p. 33)

Ballad, dialogue and journal forms were turned to advantage. It is fitting that the Penguin *Poetry of the Thirties* should open with Section III of MacNeice's *Autumn Journal*; this verse journal is, in John Press's words, 'the most intelligent record of what it was like to be young, sceptical, radical and pleasure-loving in England just before the Second World War'.[7] This peculiar blend of taking *pleasure* in things with *fears* about the state of things is a source of the poetry's strength; imponderable forces, in the form of hinted-at mystery or threat, are in fact more hauntingly at work in the earlier verse than in the later more 'measured' writing. Loose and discursive, the *Journal* is not all equally good. In Section IV, for example, where a love affair is remembered, one worries about a certain shallowness of feeling. Yet the inventive lightness of the verse dances almost cheekily on the edge of the sentimental, turns the ephemerality of the affair into something to celebrate. The hurrying superficial busyness of contacts and relationships in the city is deftly caught, and we are arrested by images which evoke that symbiosis of style and cheap sentiment which was a hallmark of the thirties cinema:

> I shall remember you in bed with bright
>   Eyes, or in a café stirring coffee
> Abstractedly and on your plate the white
>   Smoking stub your lips had touched with crimson.
>
> (p. 108)

A thread of irony helps keep the journal from disintegrating, a sense of the moods and pleasures as artificial and fleeting yet not worthless for all that; while the loose quatrain form, syncopated rhythms, easy run of the enjambments, and almost improvisatory flow of images and reflections, echo, too, the period's swing music.

MacNeice's talent was at ease in a province which is also particular to the cinema, the immediate moment and the 'surface gloss' of things, celebrated in the dance of sound and rhythm here:

> Sharp sun-strop, surface gloss, and momentary caprice
> These are what we cherish
> Caring not if the bridges and the embankments
> Of past and future perish and cease . . .
>
> (p. 25)

The poem is 'An April Manifesto', audaciously imparting a lyrical glamour to the decade's vogue for manifestoes promising instant action and sure remedy. The structure of that trope, 'the bridges and the embankments / Of past and future', is typical. Another railway image, suggesting life as a journey, or the precarious continuities of past, present and future, but without the Romantic mournfulness about things passing, it is no less apt for its casual feel, for not being condensed or recondite. It isn't a Symbolist or Imagist figure, the thing itself left to spread some ineffable resonance; instead, the topographical feature (here, as often in both MacNeice and Auden, man-made or industrial) is made to stand for specified concepts ('past and future'), underlining a deliberate act of communication, like a signal-light flashing insistently. Pound's injunction to avoid images like 'dim lands *of peace*' (*Literary Essays*, p. 5) is expressly contradicted. (The technique is closely allied to allegory and to the *paysages moralisés* or psychic geographies of which Auden was so fond.) This helps give the poetry its idiosyncratic blend of immediacy and didacticism; it is peculiar, but striking, that 'momentary caprice' should be formulated as a programme – a 'manifesto'.

Michael Roberts's 1936 Introduction to *The Faber Book of Modern Verse* (still a most valuable essay on modern poetry) noted that

For the moment all that the poet could do was to concentrate upon surfaces; in a world in which moral, intellectual and aesthetic values were all uncertain, only sense impressions were certain and could be described exactly.[8]

Though referring in particular to the Imagists, this could easily describe MacNeice's kind of verse impressionism. While still at school, MacNeice had been introduced by his friend Anthony Blunt to the post-Impressionist painters, and he translates their manner into verse in the way he renders, with virtuoso aplomb, profusions of shapes and colours in what gives the illusion of spontaneously achieved form (but still form – not free verse). His verse has as its most distinctive quality an effect of surfaces and of the moment being excitedly valued, with a sort of existential zest, as ends in themselves. It seems another, and refreshing, version of 'the experience itself', and as Auden was to say in 'Good-bye to the Mezzogiorno', 'surfaces need not be superficial'. However, MacNeice's empirical, anti-transcendentalist but at the same time rational-ethical temper gives rise not only to a hedonistic valuing of the here and now but to an impulse to elucidate and admonish; the example of his father's sermons, to which he listened as a child, seems to have bitten deep. 'To Hedli' regrets 'having lived, and too much, in the present', but the special poetic equation needed that excited feeling for the present, needed the way it could include warnings of doom and the atmosphere of the manifesto. The knowledge that 'the good days vanish' lurks all through 'An April Manifesto' but makes the seizing of what the moment offers all the more urgent.

Early poems like 'Belfast' and 'Birmingham' embody that interest in place which, like the topographical trope, expresses the thirties sense of being in transit, of cities and landscapes awaiting imminent doom. They have been taken as evidence of an antipathy in MacNeice to mechanization, the man-made, the artificial.[9] But here is the urban sensibility irrepressibly expressing itself. Pastoral in MacNeice, when it intrudes, is precisely that: a construct of the urban consciousness. He might hanker after the rural, but like Eliot or Baudelaire could never stay out of the city for long. In his 1938 book *Modern Poetry* he praised artifice in poetry, and noted, memorably (quoting from a paper written in his youth), that 'The dwellers in Xanadu never saw a van going down the street and piled with petrol tins in beautiful reds and yellow and greens ...'[10] That note demonstrates nicely how the interest in the non-natural, the artificial, could coincide with the hymning of spontaneous impressions. Even a late poem like 'In Lieu' (1961) – 'Roses with the scent bred out, / In lieu of which is a long name on a label' (p. 522) – is not an attack on artificiality *per se*, though by that time MacNeice was only tenuously in touch with the vision of his earlier poetry; it is a condemnation of things in the mass, which he had always distrusted – quite logically, for mass uniformity threatened the variousness he valued. Baudelaire valued 'artificial paradises' because they required unique ingenuity to construct, and stood in opposition to the sameness, the *ennui*, of the everyday. Yeats's artifice of eternity, however, *is* sameness, or stasis, which opposes the variousness and spontaneity of nature. For Mac-Neice, by contrast, artifice can actually invigorate and diversify everyday experience. The middle and later work sometimes indulged in artifice in the different sense of unproductive verbal contrivance, but MacNeice conceived of artifice as a means of infinitely extending variety, not as a threat to it.

With things in the mass belongs the spirit of bigotry, of which a lifelong hatred was bred in MacNeice by the country of his childhood. Its harrowed features are delineated in 'Belfast':

> Over which country of cowled and haunted faces
> The sun goes down with a banging of Orange drums
> While the male kind murders each its woman
> To whose prayer for oblivion answers no Madonna.
>
> (p. 17)

More recent Ulster poets have hardly said it better. The poem envisages the Ulster industrialist's puritanism as causally related to the ravaged condition of an often Catholic proletariat, incidentally anticipating Larkin poems such as 'Here' or 'The Large Cool Store':

> And in the marble stores rubber gloves like polyps
> Cluster; celluloid, painted ware, glaring
> Metal patents, parchment lampshades, harsh
> Attempts at buyable beauty.

But in 'Birmingham' similar catalogues of 'buyable beauty' lose their harshness; what the poetry strongly conveys is Mac-Neice's *pleasure* in the artificial variety and glamour, the 'buyable beauty', that floods his urban world. He is only too aware of the banality of this world and how much is missing from it, but like Larkin, and more excitedly, relishes its humanized non-ideality. The poem suggests that the pursuit of anything beyond this – 'In these houses men as in a dream pursue the Platonic Forms' (p. 18) – may anyway be a delusion; lack is a condition of things; the moment as it happens, the surfaces, the ephemeral manifestations of beauty, are really all there is. Also remarkably like Larkin is the uncensorious attitude towards the man-in-the-street and his circumscribed aspirations; hatred of things in the mass does not mean contempt for things of the masses. That exact phrase 'buyable beauty' and the ironic reference to 'Platonic Forms' convey at once the intellectual's consciousness of the mediocre and venal – how the Platonic Form has fallen and how it has become a tool of commercial interests for consumer manipulation – yet a sense that the plain man or woman are just as entitled as their 'betters' to seek fulfilment of their dreams.

Walter Allen, in an introduction to *Modern Poetry*, has written of MacNeice's 'identification', despite a certain aloofness, 'with the lives ... of what, for want of a better word, one can only call ordinary people or perhaps suburban man' (p. viii). That book offers an alternative assessment to Eliot's of the poet's situation in the twentieth century and uses both Yeats and Eliot to bounce off; MacNeice is much concerned with demolishing the Romantic view of the poet's difference from other men; his hatred of things in the mass has none of their anti-democratic animus. The poet cannot claim to be more than 'a specialist in something which everyone practices ... every one without exception puts together words poetically every day of his life' (p. 31). What 'Birmingham' expresses is the democratic urban sensibility, in which MacNeice is a direct forerunner of Larkin. Lightly satirical ironies play over the poem much as they do over the vulgarity Larkin observes in 'The Whitsun Weddings', but with the same absence of contempt or distaste; pleasure wins out over indignation. Some poems at the end of the decade – notably, 'Bagpipe Music' and 'Les Sylphides' – are more satirically incisive. The former, a unique poem, speeds through a startling series of ideas and images with a nearly surreal effect actually more like the illogic of dream than most of the later, more deliberate attempts to get dream-material into the poetry. The effect is that in this decade people live 'as in a dream' from which, imminently, they are to awaken to a terrible reality:

The glass is falling hour by hour, the glass will fall for ever,
But if you break the bloody glass you won't hold up the weather.

                                                    (p. 97)

Certainly in this poem there is an account of the debased lives
of the masses, but it is not the Eliotish account; the exuberance
realizes (i.e. does not propagandize) a protest against the
exploitative forces which are confining them to a death-in-life
existence. These two poems record a society's state of health
with admirable poise, show what Ian Hamilton called Mac-
Neice's 'lively grasp of the frenetic bored excess of a threatened
social order',[11] but there is still much pleasure taken in the
impressions struck off and the patterns contrived. And this is
just the problem: if satire presumes corrigibility, the ultimate
logic of MacNeice's vision seems to be to assert the incorrigible
plurality of things. Ian Hamilton noted in MacNeice's earliest
volume a '*submissive*' manner, a '*passive* liveliness' (my italics):

> The quietude of a soft wind ...
>
> I lull myself
> In quiet in diet in riot of dreams ...

                                                    (p. 3)

This quietude, persisting in the more mature work, means that
the plurality of things *is* incorrigible; increasingly, MacNeice
felt himself confronted with a meaninglessly, *unansweringly*
plural universe.

The playful artifice of MacNeice's thirties style, even when
protesting or warning, was the necessary expression of that
distinctive vision of the delights of an 'incorrigibly plural'
universe embodied in his most elegant lyric, 'Snow'. Such a
vision made him unable to embrace anything so single-minded
as Communism (see the deft little 1933 poem 'To a Communist', almost tender in its mockery). I want to avoid talking of
'despair', which, after all, might be thought of as a state of
singleness since it tends to blot out all but its own obsessive
action. MacNeice never betrays either that degree of obsessiveness or the closeness to despair that I've noted in Baudelaire
and Eliot, as well as, in different forms, in Graves and Edward
Thomas. But the dejection which more and more sets in seems

to arise from the fact that this vision, while it excites momentarily, *is* fugitive (imaged precisely in snow and roses); and perhaps because a certain singleness of intent *is* needed if one is positively to shape and direct one's experience. In his 1941 *The Poetry of W. B. Yeats* MacNeice argues, as I have done, that poetry necessarily uses things of the known, ordinary world and properly occupies territory which is neither mystical nor utilitarian. It may serve, that is, a kind of social function – again, the poet is not 'different' – but without being reduced to functionalism. But he questions 'whether any activity can be pursued merely as a means and not to some extent as an end in itself' (p. 23). I think, in fact, that MacNeice was exposing a larger difficulty for himself than he quite realized: his own incapacity to envisage any more ultimate end than the existential savouring of moments and surfaces. The sort of teleological no-through-road in which he found himself was to become debilitating. MacNeice's book is ambivalent towards his great compatriot, both idolizing and iconoclastic, but he himself was unable to emulate Yeats's unyielding sense of purpose, his impulse always to be remaking.

Exhilarating as it is for MacNeice, the world of 'Birmingham' is living 'in a dream' which can't quite get a grip on itself – the jerry-built houses have 'only a six-inch grip on the racing earth'. When the poem opens with 'Smoke from the train-gulf hid by hoardings blunders upward', 'blunders' seems not just the *mot juste* for the smoke but for the decade's whole conduct of its affairs, and this image of train-smoke, which recurs in his thirties poetry – 'The smoke makes broken queries in the air' ('Train to Dublin') – exactly catches the way the poet, like his time, cannot get a grip:

> I give you the incidental things which pass . . .

> I would like to give you more but I cannot hold
> This stuff within my hands and the train goes on . . .
>
> (p. 28)

MacNeice's critics have noted his frequent use of train images,[12] and Larkin, when writing 'The Whitsun Weddings', may well have recalled the train journey in the enthralling first section of *Autumn Journal*; there are direct echoes.[13] It is a metaphor well suited to a decade of rapid movement, when so many writers travelled restlessly, when events always seemed just beyond one's control. *Poésie des brefs départs* seems a necessary poetic expression of the time, and that effect in thirties poetry of inevitable coincidence between subjective state and public condition attains a sort of apotheosis in *Autumn Journal*. In a decade which was to produce the Mass Observation movement, simply *observing*, noting 'the incidental things which pass', had the force of a political programme. In her recent study of MacNeice Edna Longley quotes Geoffrey Grigson: 'The world of objects is our constant discipline. Desert it, and you become the mouth under the short moustache on the last night of Nuremberg.'[14] MacNeice's sensibility chimed with that objectivist prescription, and clearly the journalistic tendency in thirties verse is a necessary means of notation; nowhere is journalism more fully raised to the level of art than in *Autumn Journal*. What the poem marvellously conveys (the journal form most aptly applied to the journey metaphor) is an experience of the individual, and of Europe as a whole, being carried helplessly along by history – and, of course, trying to ignore the fact:

> We paid in cash and took no notice
> Of how the train ran down the line
> Into the sun against the signal.
>
> (p. 115)

It is *the* poem of the Munich autumn. It constantly debates the issue of choice, setting the enjoyment of life now against the suppression of private pleasure for the public good, exemplifying in its state of oscillation, its atmosphere of the (ominous and apprehensive) *salle d'attente*, Eliot's definition of poetry of departures, and concluding inconclusively:

> There will be time to audit
> The accounts later, there will be sunlight later
> And the equation will come out at last.
>
> (p. 153)

One is conscious of the habitual passivity, of a certain lack of rigour in the analysis; and MacNeice found, of course, that the

equation did *not* come out later. The journal-like ebb and flow
of reportage and reflection, the poet's irresolute conscience-
searching conversations with himself, achieve what seems an
inevitable and exact representation of the crisis of the liberal
mind in the face of the crisis of the time. But such is the unique
achievement of this work – conflicting personal inclinations,
self-indulgent pursuit of pleasure yet at the same time a feeling
that self should be effaced for the larger good, and all the
unresolved anxieties of the Munich autumn, contained in its
makeshift hold-all form (structural looseness made into a
virtue) – that one cannot avoid an impression of unrepeatabi-
lity. Hence the longueurs and overall failure of the post-war
Autumn Sequel, despite such things as the lovely passage lament-
ing the death of Dylan Thomas (about the first two-thirds of
Canto xx, again involving a train journey). The 'sequel' lacks
scheme and direction, disastrous in so lengthy a composition;
the positive effect which could be wrung from that irresolution
and indeterminacy in the *Journal* had its limits. (Not for the
first time, it may be noted, I am posing an enabling sense of
'indeterminacy' – refusing closure of a plural reality – against
a disabling sense, baulking the determinations of shaping and
choice.)

'London Rain', from MacNeice's last volume of sustained
good work *Plant and Phantom* (1941), seeks a way of resolving
the dilemma that 'The world is what was given, / The world is
what we make.' It starts wonderfully with 'impressions' of
night in rainy London, but then enlists 'fancy' in the service of
what is really a Protestant debate about conscience, and finally
subsides into characteristic quietism:

> My wishes now come homeward,
> Their gallopings in vain,
> Logic and lust are quiet,
> Once more it starts to rain.
> Falling asleep I listen
> To the falling London rain.

(p. 163)

It is a beautifully managed let-out, haunting, satisfying, but a
let-out it is: the poem ends where it began, and the effect is of a

'given' world of which the poet *cannot* 'make' anything. The patterned interweavings, cunning as they are, suggest an imagination indeed confined to a 'cave of making' in which the maker's voice returns always upon itself. MacNeice could only impotently admire Eliot's *Four Quartets*, with its apparent capacity to shadow forth a scheme of things; such a scheme was never evident to him. It's when he stops being able to revel in incidentalness and plurality as ends in themselves, excitedly responding to 'what was given' for its own sake, that the problems for his writing start. The experience of 'more than glass between the snow and the huge roses' converts into a depressed and impotent 'betweenness' ('oscillation between departure and return') which bogs down the poetry. He found post-war Labour Britain more dispiriting than thirties hopes might have promised, and his visits to India and Africa impressed upon him a sense of the world endlessly spawning problems inaccessible to liberal solutions, of *that* kind of plurality:

> Where smiling, sidling, cuddling hookahs
> They breed and broil, breed and brawl,
> Their name being legend while their lifewish
> Verging on deathwise founders all
> This colour in one pool, one pall,
> Granting no incense and no lotus.
>
> ('Letter from India', 1947, p. 268)

The sharp sense of the present goes, the writing silts up, the verbal play is moribund.

The diagnosis is complicated by the way MacNeice calculatedly laid out a self-analysis in his auto-commentaries on his life and work, one that makes us feel he is holding off from really intimate revelation, perhaps because he himself cannot unearth a profound core to his being. The tenor of MacNeice's work is in opposition to confessional poetry, to the anguished concentration on totality of self. It is clear, however, that the early death of his mother and the somewhat awesome presence of his father left him, though always kindly treated by those around him, in a kind of emotional and moral no-man's-land not unlike the situation of other poets I have discussed. He rejected his father's beliefs yet could not be free of his father's Protestant conscience; adding to this was a feeling of ambivalent national identity. Terence Brown cites an example of the 'typical Anglo-Irishman' who feels that 'all my life I have been spiritually hyphenated ...'[15] Here the comparison with Yeats is most instructive, the older poet still drawing such incalculable strengths from his ability to identify with 'Ireland'. Born before partition, MacNeice found in his adult life that the Ireland which might have been his – the Ireland of his father, an Anglican Nationalist – no longer existed. His English education exacerbated the effect of hyphenation, the lack of fixed attachments; indeed, it did more. Marlborough and Oxford, though his own background was modestly middle-class, elevated him to a position of privilege, which, combining with the prodigality of his talents, gave him the freedom to ponder the multifariousness of his world freely without having to make any too hard choices. In his autobiographical *The Strings are False* he says:

... I have never steered myself much. An American friend once said to me rebukingly: 'You never seem to make any positive choice; you just let things happen to you.' But the things that happen to one often seem better than the things one chooses. Even in writing poetry, which is something I did early choose to do, the few poems or passages which I find wear well have something of accident about them ... or, to put it more pretentiously, seem 'given'.[16]

Would someone less privileged be likely to feel that preference, echoed in 'London Rain', for the 'given'? And in poetry, doesn't a 'demanding art' involve something more positive than this?

One can't help observing how much came to MacNeice more or less effortlessly: his first at Oxford ('I will lounge my way in like Petronius Arbiter', he decided), his lectureship in Classics at Birmingham, even the position he occupied with such distinction at the BBC. His friend Margaret Gardiner could not understand why 'someone with so many urgent uses for his time' should so deliberately waste time, noting what might very appropriately be called an habitual 'state of oscillation': 'Louis was a great drifter, always wanting to stay on or to move on, and this restlessness, this reluctance to be pinned down in any way, was difficult to reconcile with the extreme discipline of his writings.'[17] But the fact is, I think, that the 'discipline' of the later writing is often a subterfuge, an act of anxiety doing service for the real creative thing, and as such only the alternative aspect of the lack of direction manifested in pub-crawls and other forms of time-wasting. The BBC offered a similar element of refuge. As Tom Paulin suggested in a review of *Louis MacNeice in the BBC*, his work there brought him the partial comfort of being able to enact the kind of programme for the writer he had taken part in formulating in the thirties, an artist with a social function and identity, communicating with a large public.[18] Moreover, it gave him duties which imposed at least a measure of shape and direction on his life. Terence Brown sees a 'sceptical vision' informing all MacNeice's work; one does sometimes gain the impression that he was born disenchanted. His cleverness not only made it easy for him to drift, but enabled him, in a sense, to see through things too quickly: he was disappointed with Oxford almost as soon as he arrived. This meant that once the initial zest for life's variousness began to fade, nothing could surprise him, nothing could take possession of him. The quest theme (quest being an obvious connotation of *poésie des départs*) has been much noted in his work, but it seems a vain and doomed quest from the start. So the case we observe is of a quietism and agnosticism which at first allow a positive kind of receptiveness to experience, but then more and more damagingly rob the poetry of direction; and at the same time a Protestant conscience inherited from Bishop MacNeice driving him to embrace a doctrine of the poet's social responsibility and overlaying the lyric impulse with a compulsion to elaborate, to sermonize, to soul-search.

As I've said, these conflicting impulses can achieve a peculiar blend of immediacy and didactism, celebration and foreboding, but as times changed MacNeice couldn't hold the equation together. Nor can I discover that kind of directing metaphysic, the sceptical vision, the scepticism in continuous dialectic with a sense of value, for which Terence Brown makes claims. The striving in both prose works and verse to achieve clarifications, to pursue and fix defining perceptions, results only in a variety of incidental, unresolved sharpnesses. His intellectual grasp was always enviably quick and sure, and the wide-ranging open-mindedness, as well as the refusal to countenance vaporous idealist notions, blow like fresh air through the work. But when Brown quotes (p. 176) from the verse 'a host . . . of phrases that concentrate a paradox' – 'tops of topless towers', 'the nearness of remoteness', 'the last way out that leads not out but in', 'Conditioned to think freely' – I detect evidence of a world whose plurality has now become for Mac-Neice inexplicable randomness and confusing contradictoriness. These do not seem to me to represent creative complexities, do not 'concentrate' at all. Only sporadically after the thirties are the burdening involutions of sense dispensed with, to leave a sure and evocative crystallization. As one reads through the *Collected Poems* and comes across such poems as 'The Strand', 'House on the Cliff', 'The Rest House', 'Beni Hasan', it is like a blurred picture suddenly jumping into focus. Among the last work he did before his death were the 1963 Clark Lectures, *Varieties of Parable*, and it is notable that the preoccupation with 'varieties', with an unresolved pluralism, should re-occur; but it is notable, too, that 'parable' should now take such a hold on him. Bunyan figures prominently, and it is hard not to feel the Protestant conscience nagging more insistently than ever. MacNeice now seems determined to resist a materialist view of things (he is dismissive of Brecht), and Kafka, Beckett and Golding are applauded for their capacity to raise unbelief to the level of a religious quest. Beckett's characters 'may not be concerned with God but they are concerned with spiritual meaning, even if all they know about this – or almost all – is its absence'.[19] 'What I myself would now like to write, if I could', he says, 'would be double-level poetry, of the type of Wordsworth's "Resolution and Independence", and, secondly, more overt parable poems in a line of descent both from folk ballads such as "True Thomas" and some of George Herbert's allegories in miniature such as "Redemption"' (p. 8). Did he hope that the other level of the double level might somehow, almost magically, reveal that scheme of things which had always so eluded him? In any case, this is steering riskily towards a break with the Modernist wisdom about the indivisibility of what a poem 'is' and 'says', and perhaps expresses nostalgia for a kind of poem in which at one level the 'meaning' of the poem is explicitly relatable to a world which has meaning. But isn't modern parable, as in Kafka, invariably the parable of alienation?

Auden wrote of MacNeice in 1939 that 'He is perhaps the only poet today whose work is directly in the classical tradition ... the first writer of whom one is reminded is Horace ...' Translating Horace he could indeed achieve a quality of 'measured passion'; the refusal here either to hope excessively or despair wholly is like his own:

> The little sum of life forbids the ravelling of lengthy
>   Hopes. Night and the fabled dead are near
>
> And the narrow house of nothing, past whose lintel
>   You will meet no wine like this ...
>
> (p. 549)

There is nothing Keatsian, or Lawrentian, or Eliotic, about such intimations of the underworld, no appropriation of the classical to embody subjective intensities or figure a mythic otherworld. The classical world and outlook exist objectively, in their own right. One shares John Press's regret that in view of 'his brilliance and sureness of touch when translating a congenial poet' (p. 22) he did not devote more of his energies to translating the Roman poets, but I think this kind of discipline, of steady working towards an end, was precisely what his psychology resisted. The 'classicism' is nonetheless evident in his careful craftsmanship; his adapting of classical forms – the ode, the eclogue, the verse letter; his manner both urban and urbane, reflective rather than meditative; his tone of the concerned, reasonable *homme moyen sensuel*. 'I tend to think', he wrote, 'that it is a mistake to assess poetry primarily in terms of emotion' (*Modern Poetry*, p. 40). Surely D. B. Moore was mistaken to compare *Autumn Journal* with *The Prelude*; it quite lacks that arch-Romantic cast, that kind of egotistical obsession.[20]

One thinks of Ben Jonson rather than Wordsworth: the Horatian sociableness, a love of the profuse and various, moments of lyric purity, interaction of personal and public concerns, and an artfully playful rhetoric stopping short, generally, of the dramatic dynamics of 'Metaphysical' wit. In 'Snow' peculiar grammatical tricks collapse subject and object into each other:

> The room was suddenly rich and the great bay-window was
> Spawning snow and pink roses against it
> Soundlessly collateral and incompatible[.]

> (p. 30)

The syntax almost becomes paratactic, miming the incompatibility of items. What is acting upon what and where the standpoint of perception is are so cunningly shuffled that outer and inner worlds are fused in a single experience of rich plurality. Such poetry, one might say, overcomes the subject–object dichotomy of the Romantic-modern tradition, as in more discursive form does the ebb-and-flow between personal and public in *Autumn Journal*. Though he himself often becomes his own subject, it is not a process which takes down the shutters on a shadowy private world, and despite the unsettling Anglo-Irish hyphenation, and the tension between hedonistic and ethical consciousnesses, MacNeice doesn't seem troubled by the division in self, or the difficulty in controlling subjective life, we've noted elsewhere. Not a confessional poet, he takes elements of self and constructs from them an 'amalgam', a kind of publicly personal voice – *not* the same thing as the personae or masks by means of which the tortured Romantic 'studies' his suffering. 'The poet does not give you a full and accurate picture of the world nor a full and accurate picture of himself, but he gives you an amalgam which, if successful, represents truthfully his own relation to the world' (*Modern Poetry*, p. 197). That sort of modesty and moderation is hardly in the Romantic mould; the poet, he insists, can have no claim to be legislator or prophet.

His feet are so much on the ground that it is odd that some critics, even while stressing his scepticism, should want to present him as an irrationalist, an explorer of the dark. *The*

Dark Tower, the best-known of his radio plays, is often cited, but it is a highly rationalist little allegory dealing with the presence of evil in the world and the need to confront it, based on Browning's poem, but never approaching its Gothic energies and intimations. True, he himself commented on his use of 'the dream picture' in poems like 'The Springboard' – 'This will be lost on those who have no dream logic'[21] – but this kind of detail in his work always seems to me much on the surface of consciousness, lacking the anarchic feeling of 'dream logic'. Even in the craziness of 'Bagpipe Music', or in the poems which do possess a certain haunting or eerie effect (though he is apt, too, to disperse such effects with embellishing or didactic rhetoric), I think one sees at work a quality akin to Coleridge's 'fancy' rather than something emerging, to use Eliot's terms, from 'far below the conscious levels of thought and feeling'. How urbane the trope is, the casual play with a sort of exploded or demystified synecdoche, when he celebrates a good meal in *Autumn Journal*:

> The sea in fish, the field in a salad of endive,
>   A sacramental feast.
>
> (p. 135)

How *un*sacramental this sounds, how unlike Hughes or Lawrence!

Why should his emphasis on the value of idiosyncrasy, his hatred of mass conformity and abstract system – 'Dr. Johnson had said that the poet is not concerned with the minute particulars, with "the streaks on the tulip". This, I thought, was just where he was wrong ...' (*The Strings Are False*, p. 127) – be construed as romantic irrationalism? Doesn't it, in the context of twentieth-century totalitarianisms, come to look eminently sensible? It is actually a distrust of that Romantic-modern Platonism which seeks escape from the incorrigible plurality of present place and time into a timeless, unitary otherworld. We've seen his scepticism of the 'Platonic Forms' and in Section xii of *Autumn Journal* there is a direct disavowal of Platonism. It is a concentration on the incidentality, the unavoidable contingency, the concreteness of the here and

now. He always wanted to believe that the promised land lay
somewhere up ahead, but if he could never see where, he was
sure that it wasn't the Baudelairean unknown. If Baudelaire
and Eliot were disciplined Romantics, perhaps MacNeice
might be thought of as a partly lapsed classicist, one living in
an age which could not accommodate the classicist's need for
harmony and reason. Hence the recourse to a hedged self-
expression, to quiescent indulgence in the experience itself, to a
certain dissipation of energies which might look at times like
the Romantic indiscipline. His later work couldn't 'hold the
equation together', as I put it above. Nevertheless, the pluralism of things is felt not as fragmentation, not as anarchic
disintegration, but as a limitless process of interaction ('interaction of personal and public concerns', for example). And it
follows from this, as it were, withholding from the extreme
that, despite his thirties style of contemporaneity – 'I still clung
to the importance of being modern' (*The Strings Are False*,
p. 127) – he could never, either, quite be a Modernist, and
would, one imagines, have thought *post*-modern positions
misconceived. He could not accept the Modernist theory of
difficulty, and insofar as his scepticism extends to a distrust of
the power of reason and of the capacity of language itself to
provide us with meaningful discourses, it is not anything more
than the empirical acknowledgement that rationalism has its
limitations and that language can never do all that we would
wish of it; he jibs at Esslin's reference to 'the *disintegration* of
language' in Beckett (*Varieties of Parable*, p. 120). It is not a
striking at the foundations; the element of self-conscious playfulness and artifice is not what might post-modernistically be
termed 'ludic', assuming as it does the conventions and logic of
empirical language practice. For all the self-directing structure
of much of his writing and the self-reflexiveness of his cave of
making, what issues from it is always moderated by the
requirements of communicability and often of the broadcast
time-slot.

In 1961, his second marriage foundering, MacNeice moved
out of London and tried living in the Hertfordshire countryside, where two years later his sister was to discover him alone

in his cottage suffering from the pneumonia which led to his death. One wonders whether he could have made a permanent home in the country. Certainly, despite what might be seen as this symbolic withdrawal from its affairs, he could never stop bothering himself about the plight of the century in which he had once felt so at home. From beginning to end of his writing career, the effort was to avoid reductive or totalizing doctrine and embrace plural phenomena: the immediate moment, the experience itself, the valued subjective state, and at the same time the public condition and the sweep of history. But as I've suggested, the concomitant of this is a certain drifting, a failure to fix quite what world might be 'made' out of the limitless variety of a world that is 'given'. And that particular locus of the thirties, which made the 'amalgam' of the world and the poet himself seem easy and necessary, evaporated. It is as if history has slipped through his fingers like the train-smoke. In the final analysis, the submission to the 'given', while it does not directly reiterate (it lacks the obscure intensities of the Romantic accidie), echoes in effect the irresolution of Edward Thomas, the Gravesian psychic wounding, the Eliotic aboulia. MacNeice seems to exemplify a disablement of the liberal mind in the face of the realities of twentieth-century history. In 'Didymus' (1951), the story of Doubting Thomas visiting India seems to have struck a chord; Thomas can be made to echo his own Forsterish kind of sceptical liberalism confronting the incomprehensibleness of India. MacNeice's own passage to India was a passage of doubt. The punning internal rhymes in Part III have some of the old verve and work to create the thickets of doubt through which Thomas's mind moves. But in the end the writing is over-burdened and over-prolonged; the poet does not seem to know what shape to make of his material.

It is true that the later poetry witnesses to an effort at concision and clarity, but the effort itself tends to be what we notice – that peculiar power of poems like 'Snow' to render 'the sense of perceiving in a fresh, unhabitual way'[22] is never quite recovered. One of MacNeice's last poems, 'Budgie' is sometimes offered as evidence of a regained skill and inventiveness. The diminutive budgerigar attitudinizing with utter self-

satisfaction on its *burning* perch does manage to suggest something of our time's Cartesian complacency, 'Its voice a small I
Am' (p. 539). The bobbing rhythms and flow of conceits
almost carry it off, but the 'parable' (if that is what MacNeice
intended) is a shade too forced in its contrivance, and the level
of observation fails to lift above the thoughtfully commonplace.
It does not belong with the best of MacNeice's work, so far as
that is from being commonplace, possessing such a wonderfully
easy impression of stylish yet urgent topicality, or, sometimes,
peculiarly dignified in its voicing of disenchantment. Given
this, it is to Auden one must turn for the most exemplary
demonstration that poetry of our time does not have to be
agonized and confessional, let alone turn away from 'the work
of man', to strike us as playing in a rich and essential way over
our contemporary experience. It is Auden's poetry which most
fully takes on the problematic antithesis in MacNeice's
couplet, 'The world is what was given. / The world is what we
make'; the necessity of choice, I wish to argue, is Auden's
abiding theme, both in the thirties and after.

II

Auden's 1930 *Poems* concluded with a prayer-like poem (later
given the title 'Petition') in which the force that is to cure the
sickness of modern civilization – Eliot's Waste Land, Mac-
Neice's 'diabetic culture' – is asked to 'Prohibit sharply the
rehearsed response', to 'Publish each healer' and to 'look
shining at / New styles of architecture, a change of heart'.
Much commented-on despite being dropped from the *Collected
Poems*, it has customarily been regarded as a seminal poem, and
this holds good, I would claim, not only for the thirties poetry,
but reaching across the change of heart the poet himself underwent around 1940, though the tense, portentous rhetoric was to
relax as Auden grew older.

That Auden was public school, Oxford and homosexual
might suggest a rather limiting specialness in his experience.
Yet what I have called the effect in thirties poetry of inevitable
coincidence between subjective state and public condition is

even more marked in Auden's case than MacNeice's. One of Auden's biographers, Humphrey Carpenter, quotes Philip Toynbee: 'It was not only that they [Auden and his friends] were conscious of international fascism, and had looked quite hard at some of the less cosy sides of contemporary England. . . . They shared my own intimate anxieties and hopes: they knew what it was to be a young, highly self-conscious middle-class Englishman at that particular time in history.'[23] This is, I suggest, crucially different from Eliot's 'clairvoyant' sense of his time: in *New Year Letter* Auden was to write that 'we are conscripts to our age / Simply by being born'.[24] Even as a Christian he could not experience Time as the Enemy and hence immobility as the goal in Eliot's way – 'The crime of life is not time' ('Memorial for the City'). The oppressions which reify in the poetry are not metaphysical. Carpenter records that as a boy Auden took the role of Caliban in a school play; much later, in *The Sea and the Mirror*, he was to deconstruct *The Tempest* to give Caliban ('the begged question') rather than Prospero the last, definitive word. He left school, says Carpenter, in his own words, 'a confirmed anarchist individualist'; from his schooldays on he expressed and endorsed fallible, vulnerable humanness in all its unideal manifestations. His homosexuality in particular allowed him to stand radically outside the establishments he could easily have become part of and to identify with those made to feel powerless and guilty by the authoritarian manipulations of Prospero-father-figures, those who would play at being gods on earth, or by a faceless conformism.

One way of rationalizing his homosexuality was to see it as an expression of equal comradeship superior to the exploitative inequalities of heterosexual love. I have heard a certain male and class clubbishness in his poetry complained of and a good deal of fuss has been made about the private joking and allusion. I don't myself think that this works to exclude the reader who is not a member of the club. That there were things which in the social climate of his youth it was prudent not to publicize does account for certain quirks and obscurities. Carpenter also suggests that some of the earliest poems are obscure because they attempt to express painful private emotional states which the poet himself is struggling to understand: 'The obscurity itself is the whole point of the poem' (p. 73). But we are *all* likely to feel the desire for circumspection in some personal matters, and we all experience a small-group consciousness (I have touched on this in earlier chapters) as immediate and warm where larger social aggregations are cold and 'abstract'. The effect of this, it seems to me, is to confirm the commonness of the experience Auden has to express; he is more positively impersonal, in the sense of being the poet of common rather than solipsistically individual experience, than Eliot. For some readers the lack of intensely personal emotion is a loss. Yet, to repeat a phrase I have applied to MacNeice, it enabled him to develop a manner of 'publicly personal' speech, as if he speaks on terms of personal acquaintance with large numbers of people. Sometimes the tone is even intimate, yet because Auden seems in the end to feel that the 'secrets' of private life are actually always held in common and nothing to be ashamed of the effect is of an 'impersonal' openness. And this speech, despite elements of stylized diction in the earlier and a formidable range of reference in the later poetry, and always admitting the capacity for dizzying verbal performance, is intrinsically colloquial, involves indeed the language really used by men – and women. He was on friendly terms with many women and addressed poems to several of them; his manner of address assumes a generous and egalitarian inclusiveness irrespective of gender which was perhaps easier because of a lack of heterosexual aggression. A certain quality, especially in the last couple of decades of his life, of brilliant chat, of top-end-of-the-market verse-journalism, has sometimes been held against him, but it is essentially a voice putting itself on the same level as those it is addressing, as any good journalist knows he must. Indeed, the sense of a 'club' which he can address (at Oxford he used to refer to 'The Gang') evolves, in a way bearing some comparison with Yeats, into an enabling sense of audience; unlike so many moderns, he does not seem to speak in a void.

Like MacNeice, Auden repudiated the Eliotic principle that

poetry in our time must be difficult – his *Oxford Book of Light Verse* was part of a campaign for the reinstatement of *popular* poetry – but he didn't deny that in practice it often couldn't help being so. Community has broken down, he argued, and clearly that makes poetic communication difficult: 'The problem for the modern poet, as for everyone else today, is how to find or form a genuine community ...'[25] The case to be made about both the difficulty and the unevenness of which his earlier poetry has often been indicted – those bewildering shifts of voice, clever lines and phrases strung carelessly together, the too automatic 'shifting around the required properties',[26] the private jokes and allusions, the enigmatic imagery of enemies, borders, journeys and so on – is that in using these means Auden makes a virtue of his vices. Such is his gift for the sharp observation and for giving startling animation and concreteness to the abstract concept, that one can't help attending:

> Nights come bringing the snow, and the dead howl
> Under the headlands in their windy dwelling
> Because the Adversary put too easy questions
> On lonely roads.

> *(Collected Poems, p. 39)*

The poetry survives, it seems to me, compellingly. Certainly a precocious, undergraduate kind of self-assurance papers over muddled ideas and attitudes, but the feeling is sure, an atmosphere of menace and urgency is brilliantly created, and it is exactly right for the time. More so than MacNeice, even more agile, more of a magpie, he uses the traditional-looking forms and seemingly predictable, sometimes even monotonous, metrics to 'lull the reader' (G. S. Fraser), then shifting his ground in a disorientating way. The 'evasive and elliptical' (Stan Smith, *W. H. Auden*) shifts in the early poems – there is often no coherent 'I' or speaker – are unsettling, revolutionary in their implications: we are not allowed to settle into any established notion of what constitutes legitimate identity or a legitimate system of social relationships or roles. The slipperiness of identity, of personal consciousness, for the modern poet is converted into a positive. The Romantic ideal of subjective coherence, of an organic totality of self, the feeling that 'there is no whole but the self' (see below), has to be disintegrated since it alienates us from one another, from history, and from the responsibilities of citizenship. Moreover, he invents his own grammar, resists the authorized versions: if not wholly anarchic, his grammar is certainly individualist, one might say deconstructivist, undermining the authoritarian 'lie' which received language usages sustain, which keeps the Prosperos in their places.

The poetry's anti-romantic centring in the fallible human clay and the fact that Auden is the opposite of a 'nature poet' are advertised in a suitably mock-heroic couplet from the *Letter to Lord Byron*:

> To me Art's subject is the human clay,
> And landscape but a background to a torso;

The theme of man's aesthetic nature existing in necessary conjunction with his animal nature, of Ariel and Caliban as inseparable, was to come to full fruition in *The Sea and the Mirror*. Non-human nature in Auden's poetry is invariably inert, not animistically enlivened or mystically pervaded by a shaping spirit, and he was never able to submit to nature in the negative capability way; his *paysages moralisés* (see *Collected Poems*, p. 104 for the poem of this title) are a quite different kind of figure. His landscapes are invariably imprinted with the work of man: 'Tramlines and slagheaps, pieces of machinery, / That was, and still is, my ideal scenery' (*Letter to Lord Byron*). Hardy and Edward Thomas were early enthusiasms, but his country of the mind was a very different one from Thomas's:

'I spent a great many of my waking hours in the construction and elaboration of a private sacred world, the basic elements of which were a landscape, northern and limestone, and an industry, lead mining' . . . whose features also included narrow-gauge tramways and overshot waterwheels. (Carpenter, p. 14)

True, this industrial landscape involves similar absences, those of a working community now dissolved, but the myth-making has an entirely different thrust: there is no incapacitation by

irretrievable loss, rather the effect of a territory humming with
the covert activities of guerilla warfare, where subversive cells
lead a fugitive existence among abandoned workings and communicate with each other in code (an effect actually enhanced
by some of the 'obscurity' in the poetry). There may be a
romanticizing element here as there is a certain romanticizing
of the city by Gunn, but it is on the surface only, and despite
the insistent theme of healing, such landscapes have nothing to
do with nature as a source of cure. For Auden, man is *inevitably*
a stranger to nature, his human consciousness makes him so:
'The progress of man seems to be in a direction away from
nature. The development of consciousness may be compared
with the breaking away of the child from the Oedipus relation
...' (*The English Auden*, p 298). Auden does not deny that this
simultaneously gave rise to the alienation of the individual:

At some time or other in human history, when and how we don't
know, man became self-conscious; he began to feel, I am I, and you
are not I; we are shut inside ourselves and apart from each other.
There is no whole but the self.

The more this feeling grew, the more man felt the need to bridge
over the gulf ... (*The English Auden*, p. 303)

But the opening of the gulf is not the matter for regret that it is
for Lawrence or, even more fiercely (as we shall see), for Ted
Hughes; bridging it (by means, specifically, of speech) brings
into being the city and its civic virtues. 'Homage to Clio' (1955)
presents human consciousnesses as uniquely individual and
uniquely aware of time and events, unlike 'birds who chirp /
Not for effect but because chirping / Is the thing to do'.
Consistent with his interest in industrial landscapes and the
civitas was his involvement for several months in 1935–6 in
documentary film, with its tendency at that time to focus on
the working lives of ordinary people. He chose to address his
1936 verse-letter to Byron because 'he was a townee ... and
disliked Wordsworth and all that kind of approach to nature'
(Carpenter, p. 199). 'Give me', he wrote on another occasion,
'a good hotel and a petrol pump or city streets in a fog', (*ibid.*,
p. 169). From the 1940 *New Year Letter* on, the 'Just City' is
the goal of the poetry; the city had always meant for him

'civilization' and it now becomes his dominant symbol, elaborately explored in 'Memorial for the City' (1949). The Romantics, in Part II of the poem, had 'died, unfinished, alone ... they died for the Conscious City'. *That* 'city' is ironic: abandoning citizenship and membership of the working community, voyaging into consciousness for its own sake, they had achieved ultimate, heroic isolation.

Hence, despite the profound early influence of Lawrence and a lasting admiration for Graves's poetry (emphatically not reciprocated), anything approaching Romantic primitivism is firmly resisted. 'The danger of Lawrence's writing', he decided in 1935,

is the ease with which his teaching about the unconscious ... may be read as meaning, 'let your personal unconscious have its fling' ... In personal relations this itself may have a liberating effect for the individual. But ... a piece of advice like 'Anger is just. Justice is never just', which in private life is a plea for emotional honesty, is rotten political advice, where it means 'beat up those who disagree with you'. (*The English Auden*, p. 340)

The Orators, he said, is about the failure of the Lawrentian concept of personality, for 'Lawrence did not appreciate that our real enemies are our own weaknesses' (Carpenter, p. 126). He anticipated, during his 'political' period, that socialists when they gained power would have to beware that they didn't turn into social-fascists, merely giving vent to those irrational human 'weaknesses'. What Marx and Freud importantly have in common is that 'Both desire a world where rational choice and self-determination are possible' (*The English Auden*, p. 341). The Preface he wrote with Day Lewis in 1927 to *Oxford Poetry* echoes the Imagist manifesto's rejection of Romantic emotion: 'Emotion is no longer necessarily to be analysed by "recollection in tranquility": it is to be prehended emotionally and intellectually at once.' At Oxford he was more interested in Old and Middle English poetry than in the Romantics. An element in the anti-Romanticism is an interest in science: 'In my father's library scientific books stood side by side with works of poetry and fiction, and it never occurred to me to think of one as being more or less "humane" than the other' (Carpenter, p. 8). Contrast Robert Graves's clear disjunction of the poetic and the scientific: '*The White Goddess* is about how poets think: it's not a scientific book ...' (Seymour-Smith, p. 405). If he later appeared to reject a secular scientific civilization, what he objected to was the making of Science into a god; it is actually a consistent position, still subjecting knowledge of reality to the test of empirical experience, which only shows us that science can be as fallible and chancy as all human undertakings (see e.g. the companion poems 'The History of Science' and 'The History of Truth'). It has often been pointed out that Auden's work is not without its romantic and mythologizing elements (notably by John Bayley in *The Romantic Survival*). But if Auden observed that there had 'always been two views of the poetic process, as an inspiration and as a craft, of the poet as the Possessed and as the Maker', he extended further than Graves the roles of reason and conscious craftsmanship in balancing romantic 'inspiration'; psychoanalysis, he said, had increased the artist's interest in the non-rational, but 'the interest is a *conscious* one' (*The English Auden*, p. 337) 'Only once in my life have I had a dream', he said, 'which ... seemed interesting enough to write down' (Carpenter, fn p. 77). The crafted poetic medium permits 'deliberate phantasy directed towards understanding' (*The English Auden*, p. 337). He was, then, well armed against the Romantic seduction; among British poets of the present century none (though Larkin follows him in this) offers a weightier repudiation to the pursuit of the otherworldly, or to the idea of the poet as oracle or hero. That way a terrible danger lies, the kind of manic singleness of purpose which in Auden's view does all the harm in the world. But if getting to grips with the non-utopian plurality of things, the 'world we know / Of war and wastefulness and woe' (*New Year Letter*, p. 191) becomes living as a Christian in the here and now –

> Just Now is what it might be every day,
> Right Here is absolute and needs no crown ...
>
> (*The Sea and the Mirror*, p. 324)

– it is necessary to see that this doesn't entail a simple off-loading of its earlier political implications.

Human suffering always seemed to Auden the essential fact to be addressed.

> About suffering they were never wrong,
> The Old Masters: how well they understood
> Its human position ...

The manner of this opening to the celebrated 'Musée des Beaux Arts', refusing to make a fuss, uninterested in the big rhetorical gesture, strikes an important keynote. This is not the connoisseur of fine arts patronizingly conducting the uninitiated round an art gallery; rather, a person drawing the attention of others in non-technical terms to certain things he has noticed about the paintings but assuming an equality of understanding. The very paintings he chooses to talk about possess a democratic tenor; everybody counts equally in Breughel's 'Numbering at Bethlehem' or 'Massacre of the Innocents'. The paintings, the speaker points out, are packed with incongruities all of which are given equal and co-incidental emphasis:

> how it takes place
> While someone else is eating or opening a window or
> just walking dully along;
> How, when the aged are reverently, passionately waiting
> For the miraculous birth, there always must be
> Children who did not specially want it to happen, skating
> On a pond at the edge of the wood ...

> (pp. 146–7)

The effect of this is to break down customary distinctions of worth: there is no longer any difference between the everyday and the miraculous or horrendous, or between the responses and attitudes of the different classes of society (the ploughman and those on the 'expensive delicate ship'). The 'easy-going, understressed lines ... play down and absorb the horror – thereby making it subtly more horrible ...'[27] Yes, and that playing down and absorbing device, that collapsing into each other and equalizing of different orders of things, calls into question our assumptions about what matters: it is critical, consciousness-raising, subversive. Always Auden is a poet who is weighing-up and calling into question in some such way; in much of the later poetry especially, there is the insinuation that we nearly always take ourselves too seriously, and that that is just *why* the world suffers so much. We might draw a number of conclusions from what the poem asks us to look at in the paintings (and always Auden's poems *do* ask us to look and consider, not just exercise 'rehearsed responses'):

> In Breughel's *Icarus*, for instance: how everything turns away
> Quite leisurely from the disaster; the ploughman may
> Have heard the splash, the forsaken cry,
> But for him it was not an important failure; the sun shone
> As it had to on the white legs disappearing into the green
> Water; and the expensive delicate ship that must have seen
> Something amazing, a boy falling out of the sky,
> Had somewhere to get to and sailed calmly on.

Auden is writing in December 1938: perhaps it is important when confronted with extraordinary events not to be distracted from our ordinary tasks and responsibilities (the sun, after all, gets on with its job). The stanza's unperturbed onward movement ('leisurely', 'calmly'), the two enjambments at 'shone' and 'green' spinning out the image over two line-endings till it fades undramatically at 'Water', give a sense of necessarily carrying on whatever disasters or atrocities may be occurring in the world. Perhaps our propensity for getting worked up over spectacular events is just what permits the mass-manipulators to get a hold on us. Perhaps it is as wrong to fall into disablingly emotional states about suffering as callously to disregard it: both options are pictured, and both amount to forms of passivity, inaction. If the sun gets on with its job, it is also inert, unconscious nature, as are the dogs which 'go on with their doggy life' and the torturer's horse which 'Scratches its innocent behind on a tree', and for us to be likewise is to abdicate the responsibilities involved in human consciousness – the ambiguity (obliviousness to / carrying on despite) of these details in the poem perfectly encapsulates its meaning. The relaxed verse-movement plays down what MacNeice would have experienced as the excitement of everything going on at once in a plural way, because although Auden like MacNeice fully endorses the world's variety, he always sees the need to hold it in place and step back from it as one can from the pictures in their frames, and as the poem does its subject by means of its deceptively casual rhyming form. And thus considered, the plurality suggests the idea of simultaneity, contemporaneity. Coming out of the museum, we look about us and note the suffering taking place *now*. Thus the poem becomes a pondering of the issue which was much to occupy Auden: what does art *do*, what is art *for*? 'Poetry is not concerned with telling people what to do', he wrote in 1935, 'but with extending our knowledge of good and evil, perhaps making the necessity for action more urgent and its nature more clear, but only leading us to the point where it is possible for us to make a rational and moral choice' (*The English Auden*, p. 329). In 1939 he was to decide, famously, that 'poetry makes nothing happen', but that was far from being the end of the matter, as the context of that assertion makes evident. The mirror of art and the sea of reality, the mirror which effects a certain mastery over the ungovernable sea, were to form a continuing dialectic in his imagination. In his personal image-system or symbolism the sea is a sort of shorthand for all that Romanticism entails: 'I loathe the *sea*. The sea is formless ...' (Carpenter, p. 61). 'The sea is no place to be if you can help it, and to try to cross it betrays a rashness bordering on hubris.'[28]

'Musée des Beaux Arts' stands at a watershed (watersheds: essential Auden images), belongs to a group of poems, of middle style, relaxedly formal, standing between the portentousness of the early work and the frequent playfulness of the later, between the 'political' and 'religious' periods. Yet it exemplifies the point, often made, that any appearance of discontinuity in Auden's *œuvre* is deceptive. In whatever terms and however ingeniously they may be imaged or debated, the issues first and last are suffering, and the condition that 'we do have to choose, every one of us'. In the thirties this was because 'the whole structure of our society and its cultural and metaphysical values are undergoing a radical change' (*The English*

Auden, p. 379). This involves a commitment to 'citizenship' and
to democracy: 'A democracy in which each citizen is as fully
conscious and capable of making a rational choice, as in the
past has been possible only for the wealthier few, is the only
kind of society which in the future is likely to survive for long'
(*ibid.*, p. 368). 'It was Easter as I walked in the public gardens'
commemorates 1929 as the year in which the young poet's
experiences caused him to realize that one cannot drift like the
'colony of duck' which 'Sit, preen and doze on buttresses',
cannot be inertly neutral 'Making choice seem a necessary
error' – that is, in a state in which it always seems an error to
make choices. As Stan Smith has said, that year (Auden later
gave the four-part sequence the title '1929') was the year in
which everything changed, 'a turning-point in modern history,
standing at the beginning of that "low dishonest decade"
whose obituary Auden was to write in September 1939'.[29] The
two years and two poems mark the boundaries of Auden's first
important phase, a phase of personal development which
accords so extraordinarily with a phase in history. In many
poems the prosperous classes are anatomized as disingenuously
trying to perpetuate a 'subterfuge' of possessing freedom of
action: '"There is a free one," many say, but err.' He is in fact
'poised between shocking falls on razor-edge'; one touch, and
he will fall. His fall would represent defeat of personal neurosis,
revolution in the state, but that requires action, taking into our
own hands that freedom to act which his subterfuge denies us,
and we, being human, are weak and vulnerable, prone to take
the longest way to salvation:

> Travelling by daylight on from house to house
> The longest way to an intrinsic peace,
> With love's fidelity and with love's weakness.

(p. 47)

Who or what is doing the travelling? The sick psyche/society,
presumably, seeking cure. In Auden's poetry of departures, the
journey is towards health. (The *actual* journeys Auden made
throughout the thirties were clearly part of a quest which ended
with America and Christianity.) Love is the healer, but will not

ineffably work its own ends: our intervention is vital. For Auden, hanging about in the *salle d'attente* was never good enough: if we are to be free of our oppressions, whether psychological or social – the two merge or metamorphose into each other and finally into the religious – active choices are imperative.

The ships referred to in 'Look, Stranger, at This Island Now' as having 'urgent voluntary errands', perhaps anticipating the 'expensive delicate ship' in 'Musée des Beaux Arts', seem to represent an impossible ideal, a convergence of choice and desire which the real world disallows or which only exists in fantasies of a Golden Age. There is a typically ominous subtext: a very few years later ships were to have anything but voluntary errands. 'A Summer Night' is another of these poems concerned with a moment in the poet's own life and simultaneously in European history when a life of ease and private pleasures lapsed irrecoverably into the past and active choice became unavoidable. Love 'except at our proposal / Will do no trick at his disposal', can do nothing without the intervention of our wills, and, such is human weakness, can be made to serve the wickedest of ends:

> Trees are shaken, mountains darken,
> But the heart repeats, though we would not hearken:
> 'Yours the choice to whom the gods awarded
> The language of learning, the language of love,
> Crooked to move as a money-bug, as a cancer,
> Or straight as a dove.
>
> ('A Bride in the 30s', p. 112)

In these years Auden saw art and psychology as having similar 'tasks': 'not to tell people how to behave, but ... to render them better able to choose, to become increasingly morally responsible for their destiny' (*The English Auden*, p. 341). He wrote of T. E. Lawrence that 'no-one ... better demonstrated the truth that ... it is only in action that reason can realise itself, and only through reason that action can become free' (*ibid.*, p. 321).

That decade over, *New Year Letter*, debating the relation of art to life, insists that

> ... each life must itself decide
> To what and how it be applied.
>
> (p. 162)

Because machines now dominate our lives

> No longer can we learn our good
> From chances or a neighbourhood
> Or class or party, or refuse
> As individuals to choose
> Our loves, authorities, and friends,
> To judge our means and plan our ends[.]
>
> (p. 190)

We are not, of course – it is the point of 'Watch Any Day' – as free to choose as we often think we are. Our behaviour is governed by socially constituted rules laid down in consciousness itself. 'A choice was killed by each childish illness' ('A Bride in the 30s'): the illness, as always in early Auden, is psychosomatic, induced by both psychological and socio-ideological conditioning. A whole series of early poems, Carpenter points out, is 'concerned with describing a psychological landscape severely limited by frontiers and watersheds' (p. 89). It is these repressive powers, blocking off choice, which are the adversary: the idea originates in Auden's reading of Lawrence but survives his rejection of 'the Lawrentian concept of personality'. And the effects on personality and identity of this involuntariness reify, as they must, in the poems' speaking voices themselves; the 'free one' is not at all the independent agent he simulates, but who is making that observation is also problematical. The 'I' in the poems is not a centred subject; rather, fluid in the Lacanian way. This is most marked in the earliest poems, where sometimes, as Stan Smith puts it, 'the subject seems no more than the shifting linkage of a succession of sentences, passively suffered perceptions, images, metonymies, feelings, that pass across the poem like clouds in a mirror' (p. 38). A very youthful, precocious poet, one might say, is trying to define himself; but this won't do when we see that versions of the deconstructed, decentred subject persist in the poetry. Auden doesn't confront the amorphous subjective flow with the bafflement of some of the other poets I have discussed. If he undertakes something comparable to Lawrence's 'dissolving of the hard, intact, ready-defined ego', it is because his sense of the subject is not at all as the 'free one' we usually like to perceive ourselves, but rather as a construct of inner and outer 'involuntary powers', a site at which conditionings and rehearsed responses gather. The absence of sharply localized personality is not a matter of Eliot's succession of 'voices' fastidiously shielding the poet, distancing him from 'involvement', nor is it the Yeatsian case of the poet remaking himself, striving for all-inclusive subjective totality; the poems plot a situation in which what is required is an *act* of consciousness, not just *being* but *becoming*, an existential act to break free of imposed constructions, an insertion of the will into natural and historical reality. But this is not at all an elimination of randomness and plurality, which are seen as intrinsic and necessary; it is a freeing of options, out of which meaning waits to be created. In so far as Auden finally 'finds himself', it is with the Kierkegaardian leap, his re-adoption of faith, but this is the opposite of a closing-off; it is a 'consciousness of differences' (see below), an affirmation of free play in a created universe of which difference is the essential principle. 'The Prolific and the Devourer' (unpublished in his lifetime) attacks the closures of right-and-wrong dualisms which falsify the open actuality of differences; this makes sense of that way 'Musée des Beaux Arts' disintegrates fixtures of worth and kind.

However, Eliot and Auden, antithetical poets, converge at two points: in the idea of a diseased waste land which needs healing or redeeming, and in the notion that a choice is available between, to use Auden's terms, the secular city and the godly city. Pre-1940 it is psychology and art which share, as I've noted, the 'task' of redemption: 'Cure consists in taking away the guilt feeling, in the forgiveness of sins, by confession, the re-living of the experience, and by absolution, understanding its significance' (*The English Auden*, p. 340). This adaptation of Christian terms to the psycho-socio-political reveals clearly how close to the brink of the religious Auden had always stood. Replogle notes the logic of Auden's movement through Freud, Marx and Kierkegaard, in that they 'all belong to the same ... tradition of post-Hegelian Germanic thought',[30] a tradition of dialectical thought, within which all Auden's intellectual development took place. If 'confession', that Romantic-modern constant, again crops up, with Auden it isn't the means of achieving 'totality of self'. It points the route to health, to the Just City, helping to shape a continuum which reaches across the 1940 'change of heart' to link psychoanalysis, art, democracy, and the fallen state of man.

The *Letter to Lord Byron* has it that

> ... since the British Isles went Protestant
> A church confession is too high for most
> But still confession is a human want ...

(p. 77)

In 1940 the nature of that human want is more fully spelled out:

> true democracy begins
> With free confession of our sins.
> In this alone are all the same,
> All are so weak that none dare claim
> 'I have the right to govern,' or
> 'Behold in me the Moral Law,'
> And all real unity commences
> In consciousness of differences,
> That all have wants to satisfy
> And each a power to supply.

(*New Year Letter*, p. 192)

Writing about Voltaire, Auden remarked: 'The first principle of democracy ... is that no one knows the final truth about anything' (*The English Auden*, p. 388); the argument about democracy in the lines I've quoted contrives to synthesize Freud, Marx and Christianity. The constant in this continuum from the 'anarchist individualism' of Auden's youth through the socialism of the thirties to a Christian lapsarianism and existentialism is a democratic pluralism, the notion of a world of plural options amongst which choices have to be made, but in which we must never be arrogant enough to think we have made the only right one – the effects of human weakness are humbling and levelling. And in the 1940 *Letter* the idea appears (see *Collected Poems*, p. 169) that the devil is necessary in order to sophisticate us and raise consciousness, to enable us to resist the Prosperos who think they do have possession of a final truth which is right for all of us, that they do have the right to play god in their own enchanted island empires of however small or large a scale. Caliban is the living refutation of this error, the unruly human reality which the only God who counts has created. In his address to the audience in *The Sea and the Mirror*, a dazzling mock-heroic rhetoric mimes his argument: our fallen natures entail that even our visions of the perfect life, our Edens and Utopias, are flawed, and when pursued, attempted to be made real, result in 'abruptly dreadful end[s]' (p. 171). For Yeats in 'Lapis Lazuli' the Shakespearean metaphor of the stage as the world meant that when the curtain comes down on our own little performances a great cosmic drama continues oblivious to our personal fates. *The Sea and the Mirror* deconstructs such mystifications, returns us to the obvious, that after the magic of the play we re-enter everyday life, the world of ordinary human imperfection. Here and elsewhere Auden puts the paradox that the world is 'plural' *because* it is fallen but that this is a benefit in that it enables us to achieve redemption through active choice.

This version of the Fortunate Fall is reiterated in 'Memorial for the City' with its thanksgiving that our human weakness constitutes our *'felix culpa'*; or 'Homage to Clio' where 'forgiveness would be no use' if we were not unique human individuals with our faults and sufferings. Confession and love are the keys to the whole healing or redemptive process, both pre- and post-1940. 'What can be loved can be cured. The two chief barriers are ignorance and fear. Ignorance must be overcome by confession – i.e. drawing attention to unnoticed parts of the field of experience; fear by the exercise of *caritas* or *eros paidogogos*' (*The English Auden*, p. 346). This is a clue to the poem 'Oxford' (1937), in which natural existence is opposed to 'Knowledge' and 'Wisdom'. Natural existence is a state of 'accidie' and 'Nature / Can only love herself'. The process of human consciousness wresting itself away from that state is a violent one – a Yeatsian and, as we shall see, Hughesian idea. In the gaining of knowledge and wisdom natural feeling is sacrificed. In that 'talkative city' and the country around it (one is reminded of MacNeice's 'Birmingham'), 'a cigarette comforts the guilty and a kiss the weak' who live in a 'thoughtless almost natural world', while 'Eros Paidagogos / Weeps on his virginal bed.' Something – presumably the lack of Agape, unselfish educative love – prevents the two embracing, and until they do there will be no healing. This is far from being, we note, advocacy of a reversion to nature, which is always for Auden insufficient in itself.

Because 'Lullaby' (1937) is now so well-known its extraordinary opening collision of the subversively anti-Romantic with the tender and grave (itself a word the poem plays with) is perhaps taken for granted: 'Lay your sleeping head, my love, / Human on my faithless arm . . .' But any reader of conventional love poetry coming to this for the first time will be nonplussed (though that applies to 'The Love-song of J. Alfred Prufrock' too). For the speaker in the poem who confesses his own faithlessness, the loved-one's mutability and fallibility, to which all mortal and human creatures are after all subject, do not in the least detract from his being 'entirely beautiful'. This 'philosophic love-lyric' (Rodway) offers a materialist and empirical interpretation of what are customarily regarded as mysteries. Again different orders and valuations of things are collapsed into each other – soul and body, the erotic and the ascetic, the ideal-ethical and the empirical-rationalist. It is nothing out-of-the-ordinary for lovers to swoon ecstatically, experiencing visions from Venus, and their visionary experience is not different from the 'abstract insight' supposedly achieved by mystics, which is actually just as 'carnal' in its inspiration. 'Soul and body have no bounds' – I think the mildly teasing, inflated phrases in this stanza intimate that while there is nothing to be ashamed of in the enchantments of love, visions of 'supernatural sympathy, / Universal love and hope' as well as 'abstract insight' are to be treated, according to Auden's 'empirical epistemology' (Replogle), as the purely subjective phenomena they are, though the language seems to signal that the poet prefers lovers' subjective enchantments to those of saints. (One might compare the disenchantment with which Graves, also an empiricist in one side of his nature, often wrote of love in the twenties and thirties, and there appears to be some direct stylistic influence; but the difference is that

Graves *did* seem to feel at that time that sexual love was shameful as well as foolish.) Nor is there any Eliotish equivocating here about the price to be paid for human attachments. The moralists, the 'fashionable madmen' are right about the cost that lovers will have to pay, but we must not heed them, for they are (one might say) 'stones in the midst of all', denying all that is imperfectly but valuably human, which is sufficient in itself:

> Let the winds of dawn that blow . . .
> Such a day of sweetness show
> Eye and knocking heart may bless,
> Find our mortal world enough.

'Noons of dryness' and 'nights of insult' aren't perhaps anything specific, but metonomies generalizing times of feeling unloved and unhappy, of discord and hostility. 'Involuntary powers' – a typically cryptic Auden phrase – are presumably the instinctual, subconscious drives (and conditioned social responses?) which may help us to cope with and survive the unhappy times, but which are the 'natural' existence which is insufficient in itself, for the active human expression of love is necessary as well. The repetition of 'human' and 'mortal' insists on the poem's informing idea, that our fallibility and ordinariness are far from something to regret or censure, rather, they make possible the redeeming acts of human will-to-love.

While the measured, unexpansive rhythm and stanza-form suggest being content with human limitations, the verbal music conveys tenderness and gratification. The spirit is not really too far from 'My mistris eyes are nothing like the sun' in celebrating a reality rather than an impossible romantic ideal. The impulse to see love as lifting us beyond time into an otherworldly dimension, immune to the limitations of time and place, is reversed. But the element of code in the poem, the effect of something withheld, cryptic, a little inhibited – the skilful use of catalectic trochaics, first and final syllables both stressed, is itself a kind of holding-in, of tight containment – clearly derives in the context of its time and society from this being a homosexual love-poem. Why *should* the lover feel the need to dwell so on fallibility and guilt, why is there such a charge in 'pedantic, boring cry'? Yet, as I have suggested, this imparts to the poem a crucial, subversive and emancipating effect of solidarity with the common condition. This is at once even more veiled yet less deniable in 'Our hunting fathers' where the ambition of a 'love by nature suited to / The intricate ways of guilt' is 'To hunger, work illegally, / And be anonymous' (p. 106), the paraphrase of Lenin identifying illegal love with political subversion.

'September 1, 1939' – the day Hitler marched into Poland – marks a watershed in European history and in Auden's own life. He had just arrived in New York, putting the darkened skies of Europe behind him; one suspects that his suppression of this important poem relates to uneasiness at having fled to relative safety. But this is at least understandable. All that he had striven for in Europe had been set at nought, and he needed to escape the temptation of, perhaps, despair, or certainly of 'if you can't beat them, join them'. He said in 1963 that he had feared becoming part of the British Establishment (Carpenter p. 195). To correspondents during the war he argued that since he could never have been a soldier (in fact he was assessed unfit for service by the US army), he could be of more use free to continue his work as a writer. The poem adapts the rocking trimetric line which Yeats had used to such effect in 'Easter 1916': the poet finds himself similarly perplexed about his role and identity in relation to large events – 'Uncertain and afraid'. Earlier in the same year Auden had explored in another important poem, 'In Memory of W. B. Yeats', the idea of identity as material, contingent and temporary, the cessation of which can be survived by the poet's *voice* ('The death of the poet was kept from his poems'). Here the poet takes refuge with other 'average' men in the womb-like bar in which the unstable self will be re-assembled to meet the new contingency, life in the USA, life after the thirties debacle. As I have suggested, the subjective self is never for Auden a fixed entity, is always open, flexible, in a sense impersonal. Thus the poem opens with the deconstructed subject, nicely

suggested by the feeling of being a bit lost in a strange city.
'Faces along the bar / Cling to the average day': Yeats had
encountered similar people in the Dublin streets, and there is a
similar foreboding subtext, that 'the average day' must be
relinquished – though Auden's mistrust of heroism and trust in
the ordinary is much more absolute than Yeats's and he will
not change his clowns into heroes. The mystifications, the lies,
which produce heroes are, indeed, just what his poem is dedicated to undoing. Unlike Yeats, Auden does not need occult
knowledge to explain his rough beast; 'accurate scholarship'
(one means of neutralizing fear, fear and ignorance being
interdependent) will be able to trace the wounding which has
made of Hitler a 'psychopathic god', now worshipped as the
ultimate sadistic father-figure. It logically follows, the poem is
to imply, that 'cure' can only be effected if such chain-reactions
– the woundings which madden men to become gods, the
worship of whom in turn permits them to inflict boundless pain
– are broken. Long ago Thucydides knew this, but we do not
learn from history (being all too eager to evade it).

The 'blind skyscrapers' rising 'Into this neutral air' proclaim
several things, though not, I think, while the United States'
neutrality is certainly alluded to, in any direct way that it
should intervene in the war. The city would have us believe it is
neutral, welcoming all comers – 'each language' – and allowing unhindered freedom of action and expression, but this
appearance of turning a blind eye is in fact a blind: actually,
the system is blind, totally insensitive, to the needs and desires
of the 'sensual man-in-the-street'. The ideology which supports
Authority always dresses itself in the guise of neutrality. It
would give the appearance of endorsing the democratic collective – 'Collective Man' – but in fact stands for those abiding
perversions of the collective to afflict Europe for the rest of the
century, conformist capitalism and the totalitarian state. That
it will encourage the free play of differences, that those from
many lands, fleeing the oppressions there, can here fulfil the
euphoric American dream, is refuted when the citizens find
only, if they look, that 'Imperialism's face' stares back at them
out of the mirror just as it might have done in the old world,

and that, as a later stanza confirms, the skyscrapers are 'the lie of Authority / Whose buildings grope the sky'. (Mirror-reflections in Auden, like art, always cause us to reflect.) Authority wields its power over the individual at every turn. Yet that power is unreal, only a game played by 'helpless governors' with average persons who are driven by the 'involuntary powers' within themselves – one thinks inevitably of Blake's 'mind-forged manacles' – to conform too willingly to the rules. If we 'love one another', stand together in unselfish solidarity, we can reveal the game for the sham it is; but again our capacity for love is mostly inseparable from our weakness, our fallen natures. The 'error bred in the bone / Of each woman and each man' is to place Eros – selfish love – above Agape, selfless love. As always in the thirties' poetry, all the poet can do is warn – against the lie both within and without, against both selfish individualism and the authoritarian state:

> All I have is a voice
> To undo the folded lie,
> The romantic lie in the brain
> Of the sensual man-in-the-street
> And the lie of Authority
> Whose buildings grope the sky:
> There is no such thing as the State
> And no one exists alone;
> Hunger allows no choice
> To the citizen or the police;
> We must love one another or die.[31]

But as Auden had affirmed in the Yeats elegy, for the poet, to speak is to act. Power resides in signifiers, and the lie can only be undone, unfolded, by demystifying Authority's speech, exposing its dissociation from the signified, for which a voice is the necessary instrument. The consciousness of differences with which democracy begins is also a consciousness of Derrida's *différence*, the misrepresentations or deferments which always characterize officialdom's language. The lie has it that we must obey both the state and the error bred in the individual psyche, but the subversive voice murmurs that 'There is no such thing as the State / And no one exists alone', there is only the

interdependence of individual and community. (If good were
easy, *New Year Letter* was shortly to say, we should live in a
tolerant confederation where this identity of 'men' and 'Man'
were recognized:

> Its pluralist interstices
> The homes of happiness and peace,
> Where in a unity of praise
> The largest *publicum*'s a *res*,
> And the least *res* a *publicum*[.]

(p. 191)

Because it controls the economic sanction, hunger, the system
has us think we have no choice but to obey it. But we do: we
can elect solidarity in opposition to it, to 'love one another or
die'. '[I]t is only by removing the obvious causes of misery,
poverty and social injustice', Auden had written a little earlier,
'that a democracy like the United States can protect itself
against the specious appeals of the enemies of freedom' (*The
English Auden*, p. 389). Much as he may have ceased to believe
in the efficacy of social or political means, it is hard to see why
he should afterwards have found this call unacceptable; it
seems fully consistent with his emphasis first and last on solidarity of the ordinarily human against the authoritarian lie.
Would he not accept that we die morally – or 'spiritually' –
without love? (Commentators have noted that the older Auden
seems sometimes wilfully to misunderstand his own earlier
poems.) The 'Ironic points of light' with which the Just signal
to each other across the darkness directs us to E. M. Forster's
signalling 'little lights' in his 'What I Believe': 'Hero-worship is
a dangerous vice ... a hero is an integral part of the authoritarian stock-in-trade to-day.' Freud, dying in this same year,
had perhaps been one such point of light, one of 'those who
were doing us some good'; an earlier rationalist, Voltaire, had
similarly maintained his lonely vigil, the dignity of which is
honoured in measured lines:

> So, like a sentinel, he could not sleep. The night was full of
>   wrong,
> Earthquakes and executions. Soon he would be dead,
> And still all over Europe stood the horrible nurses

Itching to boil their children. Only his verses
Perhaps could stop them: He must go on working. Overhead
The uncomplaining stars composed their lucid song.

(p. 199)

Like Freud in England and Voltaire at Ferney, Auden in
America, no oracle with access to transcendent truths, no hero,
still could go on working, could make his verses. The poet ends
by reconstructing an 'I' – 'May I, composed like them' – in
solidarity with the average person and his 'Negation and
despair', yet praying to be able through his special possession of
a 'voice' to 'Show an affirming flame'. Perhaps such a hazy
hope could only form amid the alcoholic 'stupor' of the bar as
night deepens. But the prayer-like note is struck by a poet on
the verge of the leap of faith, and Auden's Christianity is not to
be the *via negativa* of Eliot: the affirming flame it opposes to
Negation is very much *of this world*, composed 'Of Eros and of
dust'.

The 'nude young male' in the superb 'In Praise of Limestone' never doubts that 'for all his faults he is loved'. Affection
is the basis of psychological health: 'Those to whom evil is done
/ Do evil in return.' The poetry is now, in 1948, free of the
strains and tensions, the 'fear and uncertainty', of 1939: but
Auden's preoccupations have not changed. These informal,
easy-running unrhymed syllabics, alternating 13/11, represent
a quite brilliant formal discovery, effortlessly taking in many
things at once. They maintain an even and 'impersonal' stance
avoiding emotional extravagance while allowing an affec-
tionately intimate note not unlike that in 'Lay your sleeping
head' – the poem appears to be addressed to a loved-one ('my
dear') and to be sharing secrets ('secret system of caves and
conduits') at the same time as speaking publicly. Indeed, it is
now the distinction between public and private categories
which is disintegrated, the poem intimating that once private
foibles are shared they become innocent and unshameful:
'... knowing each other too well to think / There are any important secrets'. The monitory public voice of the thirties poems
now becomes a gentle expositoriness – 'Mark', 'examine' –
which finds nothing incompatible about interjections of the

lightly camp and quirky ('the nude young male'). The modesty, one might say, is the message: this acceptance of the human and worldly, a bordering on the frivolous, seems possible because the whole is rooted in the confidence provided by faith; the syllabic line sustains a manner at once lively and unassuming, subversive, mocking, levelling, combining 'worldly duty' with Christian humility. The effect of speaking as one among equals reaches its apogee in this poem; the poet includes himself among the ordinary fallible mortals – 'the inconstant ones' – who feel most at home in the tolerant, easy-going habitat symbolized by the limestone landscape. Neither the landscape evoked, nor the sophisticated Horatian voice which evokes it, are those of nature poetry:

> hear the springs
> That spurt out everywhere with a chuckle,
> Each filling a private pool for its fish and carving
> Its own little ravine whose cliffs entertain
> The butterfly and the lizard ...

(p. 414)

The pathetic fallacy and the introspective intensities are replaced by lightly allegorized scenery, the Audenesque psychic geography, the extended topographical trope, evoking a country of the mind where privacy and idiosyncrasy flourish but where solitary communing with nature is unnecessary because there is no crippling alienation. It is a landscape humanized in such a way that man and nature are in harmonious relationship.

A community dwells here without violent competition or destructive ambition, in a spirit of friendly rivalry, of pluralist tolerance:

> Watch, then, the band of rivals as they climb up and down
> Their steep stone gennels in twos and threes, at times
> Arm in arm, but never, thank God, in step ...

The citizens do not suffer extremes of despair or desire or the guilt induced by belief in 'a god whose temper-tantrums are moral', no 'huge imago' has wounded them into psychopathic crime. Here is no place for the secular saviours, the bureaucrats and social engineers, the heroes and zealots. It is 'immoderate soils' which breed 'Saints-to-be' and 'Intendant Caesars', as well as the life-deniers. Echoing Yeats's 'The best lack all conviction / The worst are full of passionate intensity', these are the best and the worst of us, the polarizations of our soul-and-body, Caliban–Ariel duality. They are certainly right to feel that this backward and dilapidated province of the mind where limited goals are settled for is 'not the home that it looks' (nowhere is, is the implication). But that is just its virtue, it is a challenge to those who would cruelly co-erce us in the name of secular Utopias:

> It has a worldly duty which in spite of itself
> It does not neglect, but calls into question
> All the Great Powers assume; it disturbs our rights.

These lines might well describe Auden's later poetry – seemingly light and occasional, even at times frivolous, it in fact never neglects 'a worldly duty', never ceases to call our assumptions into question. The drift of the poem so far has appeared to reverse the younger Auden's position that renunciation of private pleasures for the public good is imperative, to suggest instead that our rights to be private individuals are paramount: suddenly we find this easy position cut from under us. We do *not* have unqualified private rights, we have duties which disturb them, an obligation not to acquiesce in the authoritarian lie. Of course, a lively, subversive irresponsibility is often the best antidote to that lie: even poets and scientists tend to take themselves too seriously and need sometimes to be cut down to size.

Since death is a fact, the poem continues, our Common Prayer is to participate while we can in the common life. This is not wrong; indeed, there is a further point to make, which is that the pleasures of this life are not at all incompatible with salvation – their pursuit is preferable to trying to be little gods on earth. That is precisely the dangerous temptation which the immoderate soils breed. 'Agape is the fulfilment and correction of eros, not its contradiction', he wrote in 1950; the view of 'love as eros or desire for getting and ... love as agape or free-giving as incompatible opposites' is 'a revival of the Manichean heresy which denies the goodness of the natural order'.[32] This is certainly a Christian poem, but it is clear that despite his opposition to the secularization of our society Auden still has no sympathy for the life-deniers. Auden's Christian poetry never really concerns itself with envisioning eternity; its interest is in the existential situation which a belief in God allows. 'So far as the central impulses of existential thought are concerned', it has been said, 'it does not altogether matter ... in what religious sect a man finally finds his home.'[33] It is striking that when the poet in the closing lines tries 'to imagine a faultless love / Or the life to come', his imagination can only return to the earthly Eden of that limestone landscape he had known as a boy in England and rediscovered in Italy in middle age. The goal may be the godly city, but while we are in the earthly city, it is our worldly loves and duties that matter.

The sea and the mirror are once more counterposed in 'The Shield of Achilles' (1952). The ode-like form carries echoes of Keats's 'Grecian Urn' and, in the way intricate structure frames an interplay of artifice and nature (enacted in the oxymoron 'An artificial wilderness'), of 'Sailing to Byzantium'; it confers a dignity and overt seriousness unusual for later Auden. The poem in part rewrites 'Musée des Beaux Arts' in a Christian context: its subject is again the habit of art to reflect truthfully upon suffering, starkly so in this case. It is also a trenchant commentary on the limitations of subjective consciousness. Thetis, mother of Achilles, looks in the mirror of art, the images on the shield forged by Hephaestos, to confirm her subjective, arcadian-heroic, view of reality but, like Auden's own art, the shield disrupts expectations. It presents another, more horrifying, version of reality, but that also turns out to be subjectively distorted. Hephaestos is in one sense the truth-teller, Thetis the deluded romantic who is shown a truth she cannot bear, that her son's heroism will only lead to endless destruction including his own, that violence breeds violence – 'the strong / Iron-hearted man-slaying Achilles / Who would not live long' – that heroism multiplies suffering and serves totalitarian ideologies. But if Thetis represents the principle of arcadian sentiment, Hephaestos's stark realism is shown also to be insufficient. He cynically 'hobbles away' at the end because he is morally disabled: he forges weapons of destruction and then absolves himself of responsibility. The poem is sometimes read as if written to confirm Hephaestos's realism, but one would have thought the alternating points of view would make its dialectical structure obvious. Indeed, it is a version of the debate, if in much altered terms, of Edward Thomas's 'The Chalk-Pit' or Yeats's 'Ego Dominus Tuus' between the romantic and the realistic sides of consciousness.[34] Moreover, Hephaestos's provision of the shield, as Fuller points out, is like God's provision of free will (p. 229). It does not signify an unchangeable reality; the existence of evil in the world is a fortunate opportunity for us to exercise choice. Unlike Hephaestos, Thetis can at least imagine a world in which compassion and human solidarity are exercised; she *has* heard of a 'world where promises are kept / Or one could weep because another wept'. The options, in a fallen world, are not closed-off as Hephaestos's images imply: that the military execution in stanza four parodies the Crucifixion and that 'A crowd of ordinary decent folk' is cowed into watching it (Auden's recurring idea that atrocities happen casually, every day) shows that wickedness knows no bounds, but simultaneously reminds us that redemption is possible and that human decency is a reality. As these allusions signify, it is indubitably a Christian poem, but once again it also implicates a politics of this world. Its affective power lies in its representation of the totalitarian lie: its perversion of community ('neighbourhood', 'congregation'), its disempowering and dehumanizing of its victims ('The mass and majesty of this world ... Lay in the hands of others'), its brutalizing of the individual ('A ragged urchin'). In the shield we see only too vividly our century's history mirrored, but the mirror which is the *poem* performs the plurality of consciousness, disallows that singleness of consciousness of which despair is a type. 'Memorial for the City', if in places over-didactic, clarifies the point:

Whoever the searchlights catch, whatever the loudspeakers
   blare,
We are not to despair.

(p. 451)

Such events of recent history as the fall of the Berlin Wall in
1989 impart a renewed immediacy and vividness to these lines
from 1949. The lines epitomize the manner in which Auden's
poetry so effectively does mirror 'our century's history': they
metonymically evoke a lived and shared modern reality, in a
way which is in turn metonymic of the whole human experience of history (the ordinary individual harrassed and persecu-
ted by those in power). Seymour-Smith suggests that Auden's
'Spain', though 'a moving and sincere effort to express indignation and pity', lacks the 'personal reality' of a poem such as
Graves's 'The Fallen Tower of Siloam', which is 'quite as
political' (p. 285). The poem, written like 'Spain' in 1937, does
deal with the imminent collapse of a rotten civilization; in
contrast to 'Spain' it asserts that it is not the role of poets to
warn: 'It behoved us, indeed, as poets / To be silent in Siloam,
to foretell / No visible calamity.' It appears, closer to Yeats
than Auden, to see the collapse as freeing 'the poet' from the
bonds of history – 'And suddenly we were free ...' A certain
dry, disenchanted view of public affairs is succinctly conveyed,
but it seems wrong to call this 'political'; Graves, surely, is
dramatizing a *personal* freeing (from post-war neurosis, from
Laura Riding). The poem has the customary effect of curtail-
ment, of holding itself at a distance, and its language has that
characteristic distilled, slightly archaic quality ('behoved')
which removes it from localized reference. It fits with the
Gravesian striving for a pure, essentialist, timeless poetry, and
stands in opposition to Auden. Even post-1939 it is impossible
to see Auden as apolitical. Auden's travelling amongst the
babble of current discourses and his magpie-like appropriations of them, the journalistic effect, like his actual travelling (in the age of the jet-plane) between countries of the
world, are, as with MacNeice, precisely the point. It is not, as
various commentators would have it, an indication of superficiality; it is the exact 'form and pressure' of the time. I think it

not wrong to say that Auden and MacNeice *did* experience contemporary history as 'personal reality'.

In Auden's thirties poetry, 'all sway forward on the dangerous flood / Of history, that never sleeps or dies' ('August for the People'). This flood makes 'action urgent and its nature clear'. History is where the human, having separated itself from nature, realizes itself, where human will is exerted, requiring the individual to exercise responsibility. In 'Spain', another important suppressed poem, that country is both the actual and metaphorical ground of 'your choice, your decision', and such choice is imperative because 'History to the defeated / May say Alas but cannot help nor pardon'. The lines, later so much regretted by Auden, are defensible in a similar way to 'We must love one another or die': their thrust is that taking stands is the responsibility imposed upon us by consciousness, an act of solidarity without which we abdicate our humanity. Nevertheless, by 1939 Auden had come to feel that history was not making sense. The *In Time of War* sonnets concern the failure of history to achieve the Just City. But this does not mean for Auden that we have the option of escaping history; only that the dimension that would make sense of it was missing. This, of course, is the leap of faith; 'Leap Before You Look' (1941) insists on the inescapability of the existential risk: 'The sense of danger must not disappear' (p. 244). From a politics of history to a theology of history is again a continuum: in both, history is the arena of choice and decision. As Fuller puts it while discussing 'Memorial for the City', 'the realms of nature (necessity) and of history (man's freedom) are distinct. The epitaph from Juliana of Norwich underlines this point by showing that the kingdom of God is not something wholly removed from the real world' (p. 226). 'The Old Man's Road' in the 1955 poem of that title is the road of prelapsarian, prehistorical innocence; to follow it would be 'Assuming a freedom its [history's] Powers deny' (p. 462); the point seems to be that such freedom, freedom from history, is not possible for fallen man. History begins with the original sin but it is also the realm in which we are free to work our salvations. Clio, the Muse of Time, is paid homage to because her 'merciful silence' allows us the freedom of human acts, of experiencing 'the unique / Historical fact', in blessed contradistinction to the meaningless 'noise' of unredeemable nature.

Those who think they can rise above history have always been deluded; the real 'Makers of History' are, in that poem (1955), not the great, but the ordinary people who perform the common work of man and make life possible for the great. Similarly, 'Sext' (1954) celebrates that common work of man: 'How beautiful it is, / that eye-on-the-object look' of someone who is performing a vocation (p. 477). In 'Moon Landing', 'Our apparatniks will continue making / the usual squalid mess called History', but their pretentious capital 'H' notion of making history is a false one; it is those who provide for the common needs of body and soul – 'artists, / chefs and saints' – who fulfil the real meaning of history. This (1969) is a late poem, and the late poetry may at times appear self-indulgent, inconsequential: why should we be interested in a tour of Auden's house or in listening to him 'Talking to Myself'? But whether or not we are prepared to value for their own sake the unfailing fluency, play of mind and resourcefulness of a great talker and great craftsman, the refusal to take himself or anything else too seriously, to remake himself as Timon, Lear or William Blake, remains a form of democratic solidarity with the ordinarily human. The libretto for the Auden and Britten operetta *Paul Bunyan* may have simplified optimistically with its declaration that 'America is what you choose to make it',[35] but that 'the world is what we make', even though we often make a 'squalid mess' of it, is a shaping conviction of Auden's work from first to last.

CHAPTER 7

'Nothing of our light': Ted Hughes

Ted Hughes's poetry is quite at odds with Auden's kind of de-romanticizing humanism, with its import that the Redeemer works in very worldly ways. Hughes gives the salient expression in the latter part of the century, among British poets anyway, to the Romantic primitivism I have examined in Lawrence and Graves. 'Like most men today, he is a stranger to nature': that estrangement is Ted Hughes's obsessive theme. Early on much affected by Yeats, he is not like Yeats an occult poet because for Hughes the *super*natural is simply the natural. True, the oracular experience, the cycle of death and rebirth, the journey through a spirit world, these traditional motifs inspire Hughes's mythographies as they do Yeats's and those of other modern poetic mythmakers. There is a direct link with such poems as 'Instructions to the Orphic Adept' and 'Medlars and Sorb-Apples', while his poetry's account of the sickness of modern civilization and of a necessary quest for renewal places it in a large 'modern' context. 'How can a poet become a medicine man and fly to the source and come back and heal or pronounce oracles?' Hughes has asked, echoing the close of Graves's 'Instructions'.[1] In *Gaudete* the Reverend Lumb returns from the other world possessing oracular power. Hughes notably conceives of the passage through the under-world as an Orphic-like process of dismemberment followed by renewal. Indeed, we meet many of our old friends in Hughes's work: the Frazerian dying god, the Grail quest, the Oedipus figure, the *alter ego* or warring halves of the same self, the White Goddess or Jungian *Anima*.[2] And distant as Hughes may be from the Christian quietism of Eliot's *Four Quartets*, he too has

come to stress the importance of passive suffering, of patient
waiting for the 'spirit' to do its work. His poetry often records
a tense state of waiting or anticipation, a striving, like that of
the religious adept (one thinks again of Graves's 'Instructions'), to put aside the cluttering of civilized consciousness in
order to be receptive to something 'Beneath' or 'beyond' that
consciousness.

Of such poems, 'The Thought-Fox' is one of the earliest and
best known:

> I imagine this midnight moment's forest:
> Something else is alive
> Beside the clock's loneliness
> And this blank page where my fingers move.
>
> Through the window I see no star:
> Something more near
> Though deeper within darkness
> Is entering the loneliness:[3]

The concentration, in the silent midnight, is upon 'something
else', something other than the ordinary social things (the
clock) which make up so much, for example, of Philip Larkin's
world. It is into the *darkness* that we must look for this 'something else' which will heal and give meaning. There is 'no star';
we are better without the Apollonian light of secular rational
humanism, which will not guide where we need to go. Neither
will the transcendental starlight of the Symbolist poets: Hughes
is far enough on from Symbolism, detached enough from it, to
view the transcendental as a construct of man's arrogant
intelligence, a misdirection of the legitimate desire to explode
mere social being. 'Blackness is depth / Beyond star', says
Hughes in creating his bull in 'The Bull Moses': 'nothing of our
light / Found any reflection in him' (p. 45). Penetrating the
physical darkness in which the bull lives, the boy in the poem
apprehends the dark unconsciousness of the creature's being,
intuits something of that ultimate from which our petty, dead-
ening, delusive human rationalism shuts us off, identification
with which may well make the bull's kind better fitted than us
for survival on the planet. This is Hughes's poetry at its best:

the verse creates a sheer density of physical sensation which excludes 'mind' and allows the symbolic use of the darkness to emerge without strident emphasis.

In the effort to express his obsessional interest in dynamic physical energies, Hughes freely extends a device much developed by modern verse, the sentence winding on past line-breaks and stanza-breaks. (Edward Thomas is an important model, the device in his case pursuing the bewildering folds of consciousness itself.) The configurations of the verse are anything but loose and random. The poetry is full of meticulously arranged expressive coups, and Hughes's readiness for the inflated flourish often converts into a means of exact mimetic enactment. But the wittily titled 'Egg-Head' strains too didactically and melodramatically to make its comment on the way man refuses to relate to the elemental forces of nature, stumbles (because it is *not* directly re-creating animal being?) into awkward rhetoric:

> Long the eggshell head's
> Fragility rounds and resists receiving the flash
> Of the sun, the bolt of the earth: and feeds
> On the yolk's dark and hush
>
> Of a helplessness coming
> By feats of torpor, by circumventing sleights
> Of stupefaction, juggleries of benumbing,
> By lucid sophistries of sight
>
> To a staturing "I am",
> To the upthrust affirmative head of a man.
> Braggart-browed complacency in most calm
> Collusion with his own
>
> Dewdrop frailty . . .
>
> (*Selected Poems*, p. 23)

The 'flash' and 'bolt' are crude terms in which to evoke elemental energies. Still, the tenuous grammar and verbal incontinence do function to create a feeling of the ludicrousness of man's self-exaltation, of the way he deceives himself with his own sophistries: the endeavours of the eggshell-frail human skull to poise itself above the energies which fuel the universe are mocked with cruel effectiveness. The attack on Cartesian rationalism and the anthropocentric arrogance it involves is basic to Hughes's vision. Only if we forgo our 'braggart-browed complacency', put ourselves in the right frame of mind, one of quasi-religious awe, may the forces from deep within creep, like the thought-fox, stealthily into consciousness: 'with a sudden sharp hot stink of fox / It enters the dark hole of the head'.

Here, the monosyllables and consonants giving the sense of sudden presence, is Hughes's remarkable gift for creating the physical reality yet abrupt otherness of the animal world. Hughes's own comment on 'The Thought-Fox' seems entirely appropriate: 'every time anyone reads it the fox will get up somewhere out in the darkness and come walking towards them . . .'.[4] What is essential is that for Hughes the 'other' and the material are one and the same.[5] The 'Horrible Religious Error' of advanced civilization (to adapt a title from *Crow*) is to have tried to dematerialize the sources of religious emotion: matter is mysterious, the mysterious is material. The mistake is compounded by the worship of the intellect: both movements attempt to deny the sacred materiality of the universe. Such are the limitations of language that this sacred source and energy must sometimes be denoted as 'spirit' (especially in the mythic poetry), but it is spirit in the sense of an animating principle, not of an ethereal essence. Hughes's verse reminds us of the sometimes violent dynamics of Gerard Manley Hopkins's, created by the organization of great freedom within set forms, and emphasizing the thisness, the 'inscape', of the elements of the natural world. But Hopkins saw the variety and thisness of nature as evidence of a transcendent deity, the Creator; for Hughes the Deity, as the myth of *Crow* ironically sets out to dramatize, is an imperfect, fallible, even stupid creator, certainly not omniscient or all-powerful. Crow, Hughes has said, is God's nightmare's attempt to *improve on* creation, which is depicted as a thoroughly botched, messy affair. The God which human consciousness created is an incomplete representation of the ultimate reality; nature is larger and older than human consciousness, reigns over man, not man over it. Hopkins expressed the nineteenth-century crisis of faith, but Hughes's attempt is to work right through the modern impasse about belief, to come out the other side. True, we can no longer believe in a transcendent deity; God, in that sense, *is* dead. But if we perceive existence as absurd, it is because our mistake has always been to look for a governing Intelligence on the model of our own. What we must do is to return to matter, to nature, to 'a feral energy at the heart of the cosmos' (Hirschberg), and re-affirm our faith in *those*. The arcane *Cave Birds* sequence of 1978, with its ironic 'festival of all the religions'[6] – all of them illusions – seems seeking to enact a dismissal of all the established religions in order to clear the way for the reinstatement of this single original faith.

This primitivistic interest particularly links Hughes with Lawrence and Graves, but an affiliation with Eliot may appear unlikely. It is amusing to think of a character like Prufrock straying into Hughes's world; Hughes's driving emphases seem far removed from Modernist subjectivism and passivism. Hughes has put on record his repudiation of the 'absurd' vision of Beckett, and of those moderns who appear to him 'the spoiled brats of civilization disappointed of impossible and unreal expectations and deprived of the revelations of necessity'.[7] Kafka is a stunned owl with a broken wing (see *Selected Poems*, p. 71), the dead-end of the rationalist enterprise, unable to soar like Hughes's masterful hawks. Nor will Hughes have any truck with the idealist metaphysics to which Yeats, Graves and Eliot are in their various ways in thrall; his poetry is wholly a celebration of the manifested material universe. And where Eliot's sensibility is steeped in the literary, the poet only able to write at all under the stimulus of other powerful literary voices, Hughes insists in a Lawrentian way on the primacy of life itself. However, Hughes has aligned his interest in 'Shamanism' with the essential impulse of Romantic poetry: both involve 'the basic experience of the poetic temperament we call "romantic" ... The shamans seem to undergo ... one of the main regenerating dramas of the human psyche: the fundamental poetic event.'[8] It is clear enough that Yeats and Eliot give Modernist expression to that same Romantic concern with 'regeneration'.

And especially in Hughes's more recent work, there is an effect perhaps as close to 'mystical' as in *Four Quartets*, a feeling fundamentally at odds with valuing the social and the historical, seeking to wrench its very frame. Any poetry must in some sense be 'literary', and obviously Hughes's does echo with voices from the past and depend extensively on traditional, even archaic, verse-structures. The formal constraints of Yeats and Hopkins make themselves felt at the same time as the free-running accented and consonantal line of Anglo-Saxon alliterative verse. The kind of break with the poetic past for which William Carlos Williams and others have striven would mean for Hughes a severing of vital connections, a removal from the archetypal experience which interests him.[9] It is in its power to embody just that rooted and archetypal quality that 'poetry' itself is for Hughes of a 'mystic' nature. He affiliates with Eliot in the way he sees poetry as tapping psychic sources perhaps otherwise inaccessible, and in seeing the writing of the poem itself as akin to a sacramental act.

'The Thought-Fox' is about, ultimately, the poem's own coming into being. It initiates Hughes's preoccupation with the actual processes of writing, with the creating of the poem as in itself an act of recovery and regeneration. ('Almost all the poems in *Lupercal* were written as invocations to writing', he has said (Faas, p. 209).) 'I *imagine* this midnight moment's forest': how does Hughes see the poetic imagination as working, to what does he turn for his Muse, his poetic inspiration? Not, I have suggested, to Apollo the god of poetry and light. He shares, in fact, Eliot's view that the music and images of poetry come from 'below the conscious levels of thought and feeling', hence, that they are echoes of something more deeply embedded in the nature of things, more permanent, than the surface life we live most of the time. I quote again Eliot's crucial formulation:

What I call the 'auditory imagination' is the feeling for syllable and rhythm, penetrating far below the conscious levels of thought and feeling, invigorating every word; sinking to the most primitive and forgotten, returning to the origin and bringing something back, seeking the beginning and the end.

Here is what Hughes has said:

Certain memories, images, sounds, feelings, thoughts, and relationships between these, have for some reason become luminous at the core of his [the poet's] mind: it is in his attempt to bring them out, without impairment, into a comparatively dark world that he makes poems. (Faas, p. 39)

That the values of 'dark' and 'luminosity' appear to have been transposed reinforces the Eliotish paradox that the dark is really the light and vice versa. Sylvia Plath, says Hughes, 'had free and controlled access to depths formerly reserved to the primitive ecstatic priests, shamans and Holy men ...' (Faas, p. 181). Here the image of 'depths' certainly corresponds to Eliot's, and is in effect reiterated in Hughes's endorsement of Dylan Thomas: 'Poetry, he said, was to drag into "the clean nakedness of the light more even of the hidden causes than Freud could realize"' (Faas, p. 182). For Hughes too, then, it seems that poems emerge from some 'dark embryo within', and in 'The Thought-Fox', 'The Bull Moses', 'Pike' and other such poems we experience that 'dark embryo' taking form.[10] In a different but analogous way Hughes's spirit-creature 'Wodwo' is inchoate and embryonic, ambiguously gripped between nature and human consciousness: it is at this point, separating *from* nature, that the problems for man begin. As he himself has put it, for Hughes, to write a poem is to capture a wild animal.[11] Imagery of hunting and capturing recurs, and it often involves a sudden coming into possession which suggests parturition. As I've said, poem after poem has a quality of stealth, tense waiting, a sense of something sinisterly lurking or achingly imminent, a gestational quality. The fox creeping up on its prey, the hawk waiting on the wing ('The Hawk in the Rain'), the boy fishing in 'Pike' dimly apprehensive of 'Darkness beneath night's darkness', the tense anticipation and sudden epiphany in the marvellous 'Full Moon and Little Frieda', the revelatory explosion of light in the midst of stillness in 'The Horses', all enact a process of capturing what is obscure or fugitive – what is, it seems suggested, most irreducibly real.

But in these poems nature seems to be hunting man as much as man hunting nature. A force in nature waits to ambush man, crouches and then pounces, to destroy him in an act which is also an ecstasy of rewaking, of new knowledge, foreshadowing the pattern of the later mythic poems. What seems to be implied is that a bond has been broken which blindly, violently, ineluctably is always trying to re-establish itself; man is part of nature, man and nature belong together; it is man himself who has severed the bond and brought spiralling violence and destruction into the world. Nature the great reclaimer will always try to regain man and perhaps eventually devour him. Only if man himself, Hughes seems to believe, makes every effort (after all, it is man not nature who is out of step) to bring human and natural being into a closer, more directly experienced relationship can a healing of his sickness and alienation, of the incompleteness which separation from nature's otherness entails, take place. So this power of the poem to encode messages from 'below the conscious levels of thought and feeling' is a power to re-engage over-conscious man with the more permanent and original springs of his nature. Hughes falls into place with those moderns who wish to repudiate an over-conscious, rational-scientific and utilitarian civilization and who seem to affirm the writing of the poem itself as a kind of heroic ritual testifying to the contrary non-rational, non-utilitarian values. 'Full Moon and Little Frieda' –

> The moon has stepped back like an artist gazing amazed at a
> work
> That points at him amazed.

– asserts with something like the awe of miracle-witness the value of some numinous experience beyond the workaday world of the farm against which the poem is set, an experience which is directly compared to that of the creative act itself. The child's act of naming ('Moon!') parallels the artist's act of capture.[12] The poem is so satisfying not only because of its finely self-sustaining economy, but also because, with its lovely sense of the mystery and wonder residing in the everyday and actual, it can be seen as successfully fusing the objective with the subjective, bridging that notorious chasm between outer and inner worlds.

Unfortunately, this successful fusion is not universal in Hughes's work. It is all very well to speak of poetic materials emerging from some remote and mysterious psychic source and shaping the poem's form organically from within, to employ the metaphor of inspiration by some force or 'Muse'. There is the Romantic tradition in support, the Coleridgean notion of an organically shaping spirit. But that act of naming by the child exemplifies the Saussurean arbitrariness of signs; it is the human mind which imparts meaning by differentiating 'moon' from other items, and if child equals poet, the latter *makes* the poem's signifying system in an analogous way. Whatever else it may be, writing a poem is demonstrably an objective, selecting, constructing act of mind. As we've seen, Graves, one of Hughes's mentors, always recognized this; his view of poetic creation stresses the active co-presence of the Muse-inspired emotion and of the craftsman's controlling, refining, formalizing 'reason'. And the presence of Hughes the maker is always strongly felt. There is a distinctive manner of hammering out the poem; one hears the hammer-blows in the successions of clanging consonants, the wordsmith toiling to render his molten material into a wrought artifact, heaving his welters of language into ordered dramatic concentrations like Modernist sculpture. But he is prepared to sacrifice the Gravesian lucidity, the respect for ordinary grammar and syntax, and goes even further than his other mentor Lawrence in freeing up verse-structures. What is needed, he has written, is a 'free poem of sorts where grammar, sentence structure etc., are all sacrificed in an attempt to break fresh and accurate perceptions and words out of the reality of the subject chosen' (*Poetry in the Making*, p. 23).

Auden's two views of the poet, 'as the Possessed and as the Maker', fight a pitched battle in Hughes's work. The sane and practical objectivity of its craftsmanship is in continual conflict with its possession by the spirit, by the poet's wish to cast himself in the role of priest-figure or, to use his own favoured word, shaman. The writer, he has said, is 'affected by the mood and final resolution of his poem, in a final way ... the poem stands there permanent, vivid, and powerful, and tries to make him continue to live in its image'.[13] Any poet might recognize the way a poem tends to detach itself from him once it is finished, but Hughes seems to imply something more: that in the last resort the poem takes itself out of his control and responsibility. He ceases to be the maker, forging the poetry out of his experience; rather, the poetry starts making *him*, starts *being* his experience, a force beyond him, autonomous, impersonal and sacredly undeniable. This is not because poetry and the language out of which it is made are institutions, sets of conventions and codes already present in consciousness; or insofar as they are this, they are a poetic hindrance. The poet can and must escape such socio-cultural constructions to intuit essential meaning. For Hughes, the ultimate unsayable resides in nature, not in the structure of language itself: our logocentrism is what alienates us from nature, it already too much demystifies. Though in a sense, as a materialist, deconstructing idealist myths, Hughes wishes to *re*mystify, to re-invest in the mystery of nature and being. Formally, this manifests itself as a strain in the poetry – sometimes one which rends the poem – arising from the attempt to give shape to the timeless, the inchoate, the elemental. As Ekbert Faas has asked, 'how can such insight into "the world of final reality" be embodied in human language, a medium so much of conscious reasoning and purpose-oriented communication?' (p. 44).

For Hughes this is just the inadequacy of language; each poem is a version of Eliot's 'raid on the inarticulate':

It is when we set out to find words for some seemingly quite simple experience that we begin to realize what a huge gap there is between our understanding of what happens around us and inside us, and the words we have at our command to say something about it. (*Poetry in the Making*, p. 119)

The poem 'Crow Goes Hunting' constructs a simple parable on this effort to hunt meaning with mere language: Crow 'Decided to try words' but is finally left 'Speechless with admiration' (*Crow*, p. 54). While this collision between 'words' and 'final reality' helps generate the poetry's peculiar force, the poetry seldom quite recovers: it moves, as I shall discuss, towards some precarious halfworld. It is self-evident, moreover, that should the gap between nature and human consciousness ever heal completely, the act of the conscious mind which is the writing of a poem would disappear (along with all recognizably human acts). Actually, of course, that complete healing is only ever an hypothesis; figures like Wodwo and Crow represent the irremediable process of breach between nature and consciousness. What the poems dramatize *is* the striving of the mind not just to observe exactly, but to grasp nature imaginatively, to experience it inwardly, acknowledging its inalienable otherness, but trying to capture whatever recognitions can echo across the gulf. The artistic imagination, Hughes has said, involves an attempt to reconcile a collision of inner and outer (Faas, p. 191): another Romantic position restated. It may be that the presentation of this drama is what we can most value about Hughes's art, but the drama is full of unresolved tensions – between the mystic and the natural, between the timeless and the historico-social, between submitting to inspiration and taking responsibility for one's own creative endeavours, between language as a social institution and the poet's occult power to recreate the world by 'naming', between poetic structures which perform their content in plural, open-ended, resonantly suggestive ways, and the poem as closed system enunciating a single oracular truth.

Robert Langbaum has discussed the way Ted Hughes develops Lawrence's anti-anthropocentrism to go far beyond an earlier modern nature poet such as Robert Frost:

In ... 'Pike' ... Ted Hughes makes even more apparent than Lawrence his resistance to the pathetic fallacy; for Hughes intensifies both the nonhumanness and the gorgeousness of his fish ... In the end, Hughes takes just the leap Frost does not take in 'Design'. For the pike are turned into an idea of menace – of a slow, waiting time outside our sense of time, of a terror outside the reality framed by our petty human contrivances. (pp. 115–16)

Reading Hughes's 'Snowdrop' we are obviously in a different world from that of Wordsworth's celandine, his perception of the birds in 'Thrushes' or 'Skylarks' is radically other than Keats's of his nightingale or Shelley's of *his* skylark. Indeed,

'Skylarks' – in part, it seems, a metaphor for Sylvia Plath's art – knowingly plays on the discrepancies:

> O song, incomprehensibly both ways –
> Joy! Help! Joy! Help!
>
> (*Selected Poems*, p. 103)

This is not benevolent nature, or nature as a source of moral uplift, romantic joy, or idealist inspiration:

> Terrifying are the attent sleek thrushes on the lawn ...
>
> (*Selected Poems*, p. 57)

'Lawn' slips in with the effect of an ironic nod to complacent suburban life, but the thrushes are evoked with an explosive intensity which makes the forms our civilized human world has evolved appear irrelevant. And nature is conspicuously not expressed in terms of the *natural*; the poem employs language of the machine – even of the war-machine: 'More coiled steel than living', 'Triggered', 'bullet and automatic / Purpose', 'Strikes too streamlined'. I think this poem exemplifies the risk involved in Hughes's attempts to make language and verse-form enact the near-overwhelming of human order by 'feral' forces. Isn't there something wilful about Hughes's way of looking at such familiar, almost domestic creatures, an effect of exaggeration in the assault on conventional sensibilities? The poem's stridency doesn't allow a fantastical or comic response (as some of the *Crow* poems do), and hence there seems too much strain put on that congruence with our ordinary sense of phenomena which arguably poetry must observe if it is to maintain its hold on us. So I'm not sure that these thrushes become for us the embodiments of inhuman and ruthless savagery Hughes would have us perceive them (pike, perhaps, are a different matter). The poem goes on to represent the shark as displaying the same single-minded purpose as the thrushes; everywhere we look in nature, except in the case of man, those remorseless energies are apparent – though Mozart's mind, apparently, was *super*human in its concentration. Certainly the poem, in the Lawrentian manner, makes us look at nature in a less human-centred way, and makes us ponder the vulnerability of humanity in its introspective self-absorption. But if thrushes and sharks are *un*human, they are so in the manner of machines (that note is *not* Lawrentian), most particularly those machines of impersonal destruction used in warfare; they act (in an ambiguous phrase) 'beyond sense', with the utmost efficiency, to satisfy single-purpose ends (does Mozart really fit here?). To what extent and in what sense, though, *is* 'efficiency' an attribute of nature? The pike which destroy each other would seem to be an example of that careless wastefulness, that huge margin for accident, apparently built into nature's economy. Indeed, the term in this sense does not appear to have come into its own before the eighteenth century; the concept is associated with the onset of mass-manufacture by man. Still, the shock of Hughes's poetry derives in large part from this unexpected concatenation of the mechanical and the natural. Hughes's snowdrop is 'Brutal ... Her pale head heavy as metal'. In the work of Ted Hughes no less than of his wife Sylvia Plath something has entered poetry which was not there before the Second World War. Though in Plath this is more particularly manifested as a pervasive sense of wounding and persecution, she echoes the same experience of living in a mechanical and warring universe; when Hughes and Plath look at nature they do so in a way which seems to announce that nature can never again be seen with pastoral innocence.[14] In an odd way, to extend Langbaum's point, the pathetic fallacy is re-invented; nature is seen with an eye conditioned by man's own violence and inhuman mechanicism.

This, Hughes would no doubt contend, is the inevitable culmination of man's determination to reject nature. For it is only the rational humanist viewpoint that conceives nature as savage; nature itself, as Hughes dramatizes, for example, in 'Hawk Roosting', simply is and simply acts, is not conscious of its own savagery any more than it can form concepts of death or suffering. The hawk's cruelty and arrogance, the 'senseless' cannibalism of the pike, are entirely natural; man's ravaging of the universe to serve his own ends is something else. As I suggested in an earlier chapter, in an almost Manichaean way for Hughes (he has delved into Manichaean lore) nature's malevolence is merely its otherness, and must be treated with, cannot be overmastered or subjected to our moralism. But how can poetry, and its medium language, avoid being themselves products of the humanized vision? In order to show us nature thinking (in 'Hawk Roosting'), 'what I had in mind was that in this hawk Nature is thinking. Simply Nature' (Faas, p. 199) Hughes has to make nature think with a partially and *selectively* human consciousness (the hawk thinks of killing but never of its own death). This seems to illustrate that man's view must in some way be anthropomorphic, that, as Auden perceived, the gulf between man and nature is intrinsic. Secondly, Hughes's imagination, with its vitalist vision, belongs to that Romantic tradition which repudiates the mechanical, utilitarian and rational: that it should come to the contradictory point of perceiving nature as mechanism would seem to reflect an impasse of the Romantic imagination.

This is not to deny that Hughes can make extraordinary use of mechanical and industrial imagery, whether to suggest the sheer materiality and non-intellectuality of the natural universe, or for other effects. In 'The Owl Flower' from *Cave Birds* 'A coffin spins in the torque' (p. 58); *Gaudete* makes use of phrases like 'vast cantileverings of star-balance'.[15] Some astonishing love poetry from *Cave Birds*, in which male and female create each other, fitting together each other's bodies like pieces of Meccano, succeeds in gleaning tenderness from images which would seem to belong more to the activities of electricians and construction workers:

> Now she has brought his feet, she is connecting them
> So that his whole body lights up ...
>
> (*Selected Poetry*, p. 140)

(The mass-produced, manufactured woman in Sylvia Plath's 'The Applicant', of which one is reminded, has a quite different effect; the feeling is corrosive, not lyrical. However, there is clearly mutual influence in this use of a sort of mechanical dismemberment of the human body which appears in poems by both Plath and Hughes. See also, for example, 'Crow's

Battle Fury', *Crow*, p. 67. Hughes has commented on Plath's 'central experience of a shattering of the self, and the labour of fitting it together again' (Faas, p. 180).) Where Auden (if sometimes with a certain explicit nostalgia for *outmoded* forms of technology) accepts the machine as a dominant factor in modern life in a matter-of-fact way and then looks at how this revises our options, Hughes's imagination seems at once dramatically possessed by, yet at odds with, the industrial-technological experience. Consider lines like these, again from *Gaudete*:

> But he knows everything he looks at,
> Even the substance of his fingers, and the near-wall of his
> skin,
> He knows it vibrant with peril, like a blurred speed-vibration.
> He knows the blood in his veins
> Is like heated petrol, as if it were stirring closer and closer to
> explosion,
> As if his whole body were a hot engine, growing hotter
> Connected to the world, which is out of control ...
>
> (p. 49)

In this imagery of the internal combustion engine Hughes is paradoxically striving to convey the changeling Reverend Lumb's intimation of elemental forces (which are, we note, growing 'out of control' – threatening to overwhelm his humanized 'mind'). The grip such imagery has on Hughes's imagination helps make him seem radically 'modern', and helps, too, offset any suspicion that what his poetry is offering is just a beefed-up version of the old myth of a rural England. But he is always attracted by images of explosive energy and force, whether natural or man-made – sometimes, one feels, for their own sake. If he sees clearly the insufficiency of that old-fashioned myth to assuage the extremity of the modern condition, the apocalyptically framed rhetoric with which he struggles to be free of all 'modern industrial civilization' involves sometimes brings him in danger of a lurid nihilism, however he may try to distance this through myth and irony. Hughes very well perceives in 'Thrushes' that man is distinguished from nature by just his susceptibility to the non-

functional, by being subject to doubt and obstruction; a man
dreams or imagines, perpetrates the creative or visionary act
which 'worships itself' without use or purpose, and has an
infinitely capacious mind which is also infinitely tortured by
desires and fears. The poem may wish to show man frail and
impotent beside nature, but Hughes's own premises still seem
to allow the traditional case for the unique value of human
consciousness. The effect is of an element of distortion and
self-contradiction, of a failure to resolve the antithesis between
a limiting instinctuality in nature and a limiting intellectuality
in man. Man and nature have *not* been brought closer together.

Now and then Hughes seems to approach the attitude to
civilization which Lawrence puts into the mouth of Rupert
Birkin in *Women in Love*:

Birkin looked at the land, at the evening, and was thinking: 'Well, if
mankind is destroyed, if our race is destroyed like Sodom, and there is
this beautiful evening with the luminous land and trees, I am satis-
fied. That which informs it all is there, and can never be lost. After
all, what is mankind but just one expression of the incomprehensible.
And if mankind passes away, it will only mean that this particular
expression is completed and done ... Humanity is a dead letter.
There will be a new embodiment, in a new way. Let humanity
disappear as quick as possible.'[16]

Perhaps the fish which prey on each other in 'Pike', together
with the boy's preternatural sense of dark powers in nature
(poetry in this Romantic-Symbolist line seeks to convey to us
feelings beyond articulation, Eliot's 'depths of feeling into
which we cannot peer'), suggest the way nature's oblivious
destructiveness may overtake our human world if we do not
learn to come to some accommodation with it. I've noted that
Hughes's poems are laden with hints of mysterious nature
(Birkin's 'incomprehensible') biding its time, waiting to wrest
back its dominion from arrogant man. But it's difficult to avoid
remarking the blind mindlessness of the fish: they are 'nature
thinking', or rather, *not* thinking. Our response might be that
nature needs human consciousness as much as human
consciousness needs nature. Hughes's poetic argument,
however, sometimes implies the contrary: man has shown, by

his destructive tyranny, that nature is better off without him. It is ironic that what started with the Romantics, in their turning 'back' to nature, as a great poetic movement against de-humanization apparently culminates in a desire *for* de-humanization, though this is the logical outcome of the element of anti-humanism (the escape from personality, art for the Machine Age, Hulme, Vorticism and so on) which was always endemic to the Modernist evolution from, and reaction against, Romanticism. Perhaps Hughes's poetry only means to map the way the gap between man and nature has become too wide, with the result that mindless destructiveness is gradually taking our planet over. But much of the pre-seventies poetry suffers from the strain involved in Hughes's not quite seeing *how* man and nature have the potential to interact positively, healingly: he only feels that man suppresses the elemental forces at his peril, that this leaves him living in a waste land.

But ultimately both Lawrence and Hughes want to see man and nature reconciled, brought into closer communion, as the boy in 'Pike' communes with 'Darkness beneath night's dark-ness'. It is in *Crow, Gaudete* and other works of the seventies that Hughes sets about evolving a myth-system, apocalyptic and arcane like Yeats's, but more directly and avowedly on the model of Robert Graves's; Hughes and Plath studied *The White Goddess* together. The character Crow, a mythical embodiment of that part of reality which seems beyond the control of the Judaeo-Christian God, the God of *Genesis* (God's *nightmare*), both represents that, it seems implied, with which we must come to terms, and (in the later part of the cycle) points towards the self-humbling ordeal by which that coming-to-terms is to be enacted. (It is hard to say exactly what Crow 'is' since he is used in an opportunistic way somewhat like Swift's Gulliver for ironically inverting and negating our customary view of things.) The cycle also seems to show the primordial emergence of human consciousness (another embryonic process) as comically uncalculated but perhaps, after all, some kind of cosmic necessity. *Crow* builds on those ideas of a God not in control of his own creation or of a God essentially a projection of humanity's own needs which furnished Hardy

with his relentless ironies; it sees this humanist God as only a
very partial paradigm of the creative principle. In 'A Childish
Prank' God is so wearied trying to figure out the logic of his
creation of the two sexes that he falls asleep. While he sleeps,
the extra-moral and extra-spiritual Crow, in a parody of the
way the 'Worm' or serpent caused carnality to come into the
world, instils man and woman with the demon of unassuage-
able sexual hunger. It is perhaps as good a mythologizing of the
psychology of desire as any, but while the *Crow* poems' ironic
commentary on the delusiveness of our ideation is at times
brilliantly mordant and comic, at other times it seems a grossly
rhetorical and too starkly fatalistic attempt to uncover a single
undeniable truth about the source and nature of things. And if
Crow is an attempt at the greater scope offered by a structural
myth, the sequence does not appear to be complete, is certainly
not resolved.

Some critics, however, see *Crow* as not so much uncompleted
as the opening trope in a much larger design. *Prometheus on his
Crag, Gaudete, Cave Birds* and perhaps other poems or series of
poems are all part of this design. Here is an emulation of the
Gravesian 'one story and one story only', each poem a report
from a timeless realm beyond history on a single unchanging
reality, though for Hughes, we should remember, the super-
historical, what he calls 'the other world', is entirely material.
We have seen that Hughes conceives of a 'fundamental poetic
event' which by implication all true poems dramatize; his view
that Plath's poems form 'a single work' reminds one of Graves's
insistence on the intrinsic unity of his *Collected Poems*. This
carries perhaps the same dangers; for all the restless exploration and expansion of the single theme, it is shaped, arguably,
by a reductive and narrowing vision. That fascination with
relentless single-mindedness which had been epitomized in
'Thrushes' readily offers itself, after the death of Sylvia Plath,
as a subjective strategy for the poet himself; mere survival is
now what matters most for Hughes, and is best ensured by a
driving singleness of intent and focus. In 'The Howling of
Wolves', written a few weeks after Sylvia Plath's death, the
wolves 'must live', however blindly and uncomprehendingly.

Crow is not, any more than 'God', all-powerful, and when he arrogantly challenges the sources of cosmic power he is made to suffer the ordeal of all hubristic heroes. Above all, however, he is a survivor. The Promethean or Herculean theme now becomes uppermost for Hughes. But his poems had always tended to work themselves out both too vaguely and too reductively; his restless moving on from one poetic try to another is, I think, a strategy of aggressive expansionism as the best form of self-defence, and disallows that kind of concentration of complexities (however static and tentative), that realization of and acquiescence in a plural reality, one finds, for example, in Larkin.

Of course, each repetition ought to bring an increment of meaning. *Gaudete*, through its bizarre narrative, part naturalistic, part deconstructive and anti-realist (surreal, ritualistic), does go further than the earlier poems in offering signposts to what forms the healing interactions of man and nature, of the individual and the cosmos, might take, in doing so, as the title suggests, asserting the renewed possibility of joy – that Romantic joy to be discovered in an ecstatic ritual purging of utilitarian and rationalistic consciousness. The vision is as extreme as Lawrence's, but this is *not*, after all, Birkin's world in which humanity has disappeared: the point of the narrative is in the way nature tries to reclaim humanity for its own purposes, purposes which it seems cannot be fulfilled *without* humanity. The poem unites Eliot's Waste Land myth with Graves's myth of the White Goddess. And since the Goddess is conceived as an actual archetype deep within the unconscious as well as a version of the Grail, her re-animation in the conscious mind will restore the wholeness of the human psyche. The 'shattering of the self' Hughes saw in Plath clearly has to do both with the perceived instability of self, and a Lawrence-like disintegrating of self to discover the new. This is not in fact achieved in the narrative; but the means to the joy is envisioned. In the Epilogue the poet-hero can as yet only chant his lament, but he intimates, in a kind of annunciation, the 'letting in' to this 'Horrible world' of 'The untouched joy' (p. 194). That the narrative centres upon a changeling priest echoes Hughes's belief in the priest-role of the poet: he re-endorses the Romantic notion of the poet as seer or 'shaman'. (He referred to Emily Dickinson, for example, as 'a priestess'.) *Gaudete* posits a changeling religion, primitivist ritualism to supersede increasingly effete and irrelevant humanist Christianity.

However, isn't the narrative somewhat circumscribed by the restriction of its setting, largely, to country life – almost, indeed, to a pastiche of country life? It seems a general problem in the world of Hughes's poetry that the human communities implicated are almost always those of farm or village, not the communities in which most modern people live. To this extent, perhaps, the old rural myth is still too much felt. One wonders, too, whether the wholesale buying-in of World Myth necessarily brings enlarged significance. And it is difficult to see that the religious content of *Gaudete* will strike most people as 'real' or 'true'; at best it is likely to appear brilliantly fantastic. The creature from another world embroiled in rituals of bloodshed and mayhem is wholly familiar in present-day genres of fantasy. This may indicate that Hughes is indeed in touch with some widely felt psychic appetite, but one of which we may well be deeply distrustful. The narrative is vivid, full of characteristically keen detail, comic and satirical, but the sheer firepower of Hughes's writing can't hide the melodrama, and poets like MacNeice, Auden, Gunn and Larkin, with their representations of tawdry urban commercialism, are arguably in more real engagement with the hungers which fuel modern life. Moreover, doesn't this mutation of the poetic into the religious entail a sort of breaking of the contract between poet and reader? Whether or not, in primeval human communities, poetry was intertwined with magic and religion, it seems as unrealistic to suggest that the institution of poetry can return to that condition as that modern communities can return to hunter-gatherer social economies. Such twentieth-century poet-priests as Andrew Young and R. S. Thomas are, I think, quite clear about this; they see the two roles as distinct, though some overlap may permissably occur, and the Christian Auden believed that art is a worldly activity only indirectly admitting 'spiritual' content.[17] A devotional poet – one thinks of what

George Herbert is said to have written to his mother: 'my poor abilities in poetry, shall be all and ever consecrated to God's glory' – may offer his poems to the world as a testimony of his faith, and may even, while composing, feel them to be personal devotional acts. But not only must he scrupulously avoid the heresy of considering them as sacred texts, he must also acknowledge that their being wrought as poems imbues them with a different status, one in the domain of art where the devotional content loses its privileges. Even the sacred text is always only a text, subject to the same conditions as any text, privileged only within certain institutional discursive frames; and in any case, within what frame does Hughes's singular religion fit?

But what if that not fitting is just its power? What if to contend that poetry and religion are separate categories of human expression is symptomatic of that very sickness, that loss of coherence, from which modern civilization suffers? It is precisely in response to this that Hughes proposes a reinstatement of a seamless unity of the poetic and the sacred, of a kind which our loss of faith in the chimerical God of *Genesis* actually facilitates. Hughes's mythopoeic poetry continuously seeks to cross the barrier. The *Cave Birds* sequence celebrates a symbolic execution reminiscent of various religious myths. In 'The Executioner' the verse is formally spaced and measured, the voice has a note of priestly incantation:

> Fills up
> Sun, moon, he fills them up
>
> With his hemlock –
> They darken
>
> He fills up the evening and the morning, they darken
> He fills up the sea
>
> He comes in under the blind filled-up heaven
> Across the lightless filled-up face of water ...
>
> (*Cave Birds*, p. 22)

Biblical rhythms and phrasings are echoed and parodied somewhat as Blake or Lawrence did in their visionary recastings of Christian iconography; the method 'recalls the heretical inversions of Judaeo-Christian cosmology in *Crow*' (Faas, p. 141). The hypnotic and trance-like effects resemble those I analysed in Graves's 'Instructions', though the line is freer like Lawrence's, suggesting a similarly extreme venture into the new rather than a Gravesian reworking of the traditional. Some passages of this kind of writing by Hughes do succeed, I think, in suggesting the 'mystical'. It is done partly by the incantatory repetition, partly by suppressing some of the grammatical logic and the kinds of logic of experiential association which belong to ordinary social and sensory existence:

> The tap drips darkness darkness
> Sticks to the soles of your feet ...

Indeed, the interspersing of liturgical-sounding rhetoric with reminders of the reader's ordinary world – 'roads', 'tap', 'mirror', 'your friends' – achieves a double effect: it both destabilizes the familiar (as it is so often thought poetry must) and familiarizes the strange world of the poem. Since Ezra Pound we routinely look for the hard and concrete in poetry; it is a sustaining strength of Hughes's writing that it never drifts off into the abstract or ethereal, and this helps give his 'mystical' passages a compelling quality. The effect here is to suggest that the mystical is something materially experienced; there is taking place in the concrete here and now that dying into new life which is the subject of this poem as it is of some of the most compelling of Lawrence's and Graves's. And while the hard and aggressive textures of Hughes's verse banish the Eliotish indefinition and evasiveness, those passages in *Four Quartets* where Eliot can achieve an intensity making the physical seem incandescent with a quality of the numinous, parallel this interfusion in 'The Executioner' of the ordinary here and now and 'the powers of the other world' (in Hughes's own phrase). Where the opening lines of 'Little Gidding' are suffused with an unnatural light intimating the *super*natural, the whole of 'The Executioner' is eerily 'filled up' by the 'dripping' darkness with the extraordinary effect of a sort of inverted illumination. Leonard Baskin's drawing which accompanies the text is of a giant raven, a vast opaque smudge of smothering blackness.

Cave Birds is a reiteration of the quest and renewal theme which Eliot made his own in *The Waste Land*. A protagonist – the 'you' of 'The Executioner' – undergoes a process of extinction of consciousness, dismemberment and renewal. The sequence, enigmatically subtitled 'An Alchemical Cave-Drama', is fragmentary and riddle-like, has to be pieced together by the reader, like the esoteric texts of the alchemists but also, of course, like the Modernist poem it is: its meanings must be produced by the reader. (Perhaps also 'alchemical' because seeking *fusion* – of a questor with his lost bride.) The narrative links in the chain are, in the printed version, suppressed; though at its first performance at the Ilkley Literature Festival in May 1975, Hughes provided a commentary developing the story. As with *Crow* there *is* a complete story, but for Hughes these stories are only 'a quarry – a way of getting the poems . . . of getting a big body of ideas and energy moving on a track' (Faas, p. 213). The sequence also enacts, Gifford and Roberts suggest, a subjective drama, 'a drama of inner voices' (p. 200). If Eliot's *œuvre*, revolving through many assumed voices, represents an inner autobiography in which his personal and psychological problems are addressed and finally brought to resolution through acceptance of a religious faith, Hughes seems to have gone on a somewhat analogous journey. If it is now well known that Eliot's relationship with his wife Vivien played a part in that personal existential crisis the poetry charts, it seems obvious that the events surrounding Hughes's marriage to Sylvia Plath and his personal state of mind in the years following her death can in some part account for the direction his poetic development took. A number of poems allude to a figure identifiably Plath, and the mythic quest for a lost bride shapes the sequences from *Crow* to *Cave Birds*. In *Gaudete*, the failure of Lumb to rescue the beautiful maiden Felicity from the clutches of the hag Maud, that is, death, indeed his complicity, hardly requires explicit interpretation, and in his Epilogue the poet, however cryptically, can only lament his loss and voice his remorse. (Hughes had twice been robbed of a 'bride' by death, in 1963 and in 1969, *Crow* being dedicated to the second, as *The Hawk in the Rain* was inscribed 'To Sylvia'.) And if, as I've said, Hughes's obsessive theme is the estrangement of man from nature, we might remember that 'Nature' is, always has been, female. One might develop this point, of course, in terms of a need in modern humanity to re-integrate the masculine and feminine aspects of the psyche.

Hughes himself has said of Eliot:

I can't believe that he took the disintegration of Western civilization as a theme which he then found imagery and a general plan for. His sickness told him the cause. Surely that was it. He cleaned his wounds and found all the shrapnel. (Faas, p. 204)

This seems to describe a painful subjective drama which can only be voiced by the poet in fragmented and gnomic modes, and only finds alleviation in a private visionary experience which, however, the poet offers dogmatically as general 'truth'. Martin Dodsworth has complained about the damaging effects of Hughes's 'fear and self-division'.[18] We have seen with what acute consciousness, how pervasively and alienatingly, 'self-division', incomplete or split subjectivity, is felt by modern poets. But if fear is natural to existence and to our time, and if poetry is arguably always the product of division in the poet's psyche – one recalls Yeats's famous 'We make ... out of the quarrel with ourselves, poetry' – it is true that Hughes's poetry enacts many kinds of ambivalence, a battle of the divided self, an existential 'drama of consciousness' (Gifford and Roberts), and that its aggression seems powered by deep-rooted fears. Throughout, the poetry creates the experience of a will either to allay the dread by violent capture of that which threatens (assuming the powers of the predator, in the received totemistic reading of the animal poems) or to submit ecstatically to the predatory foe (becoming it by being devoured by it), the latter prevailing after the events of Hughes's personal life in the sixties. The essential link to be made between Eliot and Hughes is in the sense of psychic terror which is for both at the heart of experience – Eliot's 'horror' and void, the 'Darkness beyond night's darkness' which freezes the hair of the boy fishing in 'Pike' and which racks much of Hughes's poetry, imparting to it its fierce and wrenching dynamics. For both, this has to do with the incomprehensibility of consciousness once one looks beyond the shams of 'personality' and socialized routines. *Crow* has been compared to the horror-comic (with some of the limitations that implies): 'a totality of horror is narrowly and intensely insisted'.[19]

> Big terror descends.
>
> A drumming glare, a flickering face of flames.

begins 'The Owl Flower', a culminating poem in *Cave Birds* (p. 58). That here the terror transmutes into a pulsating, embryonic source of the new dramatizes that healing, Lawrence-like coming-to-terms with the dark gods which is Hughes's alternative to Eliot's acceptance of the sacred awe formalized in High Anglican tradition. Eliot, of course, would have rejected Hughes's Lawrentian neo-paganism, but I think Eliot could have identified with the way Hughes's work, like his own, conveys a sense of having stood at the brink and peered into the heart of darkness. In this, both speak 'clairvoyantly' to their time, in whatever bizarre or eccentric trappings they may dress their speech. (It is perhaps worth remembering that Hughes's poetry was first published by Eliot at Faber and Faber.) Both, moreover, arrived at the position that waiting it out, suffering the worse, enduring, was the only course. And in both the vision is radical, it disallows the comforts of that easy liberal humanism against which Eliot, in his prose writings, was constantly on the attack.

Even Auden and MacNeice, we've seen, though deeply 'liberal' in feeling, worried about liberalism's seeming inadequacies, and the rejection of liberal complacency takes new forms in the post-Second-World-War context. Hughes commented to Ekbert Faas that since he was of a slightly younger generation, he did not share

the post-war mood of having had enough . . . enough rhetoric, enough overweening push of any kind, enough of the dark gods, enough of the id, enough of the Angelic powers and the heroic efforts to make new worlds. They'd seen it all turn into death camps and atomic bombs. All they wanted was to get back into civvies and get home to the wife and kids ... But it set them dead against negotiation with anything outside the cosiest arrangement of society. (Faas, p. 201)

This is symptomatic of that reaction against the unexcitingly ameliorative spirit of post-war Britain to which, for example, Alvarez's influential 1962 anthology *The New Poetry*, with its commendation of Hughes's poetry as true to the facts of contemporary history, belongs. What is notable is the sense of extremity. The expressionistic techniques which Hughes and certain other poets developed in contrast to the formalism of the 'Movement' created the effect of a crisis of civilization beyond all conventional alleviation, and of anxiety about adequacy of response and feeling in the face of this. Hughes was joint founder of the magazine *Poetry in Translation*, and Eastern European writers were often felt to be somehow more serious, to have more authentic kinds of experience to express, than life in the ('cosy') western democracies allowed. Hughes's 'Six Young Men', for example, or Jon Silkin's 'Death of a Son', appear to echo such work in a sort of relentless confronting of the facts of death and loss without recourse to complacent comfortings. At the same time, Larkin's very different poetry, despite Alvarez's famous finding that it perpetuates a 'gentility principle' in English writing, also adopts a profoundly unconsoled stare at 'the shut of loss'. A kind of *Zeitgeist* seems at work in this pervasive refusal of solace (even Christianity, I've noted, is in R. S. Thomas's case unconsolatory).

Yet, compelling and strange as it is, the inhuman oracular voice of *Cave Birds* seems to me to speak not only from the margins of history, but of poetry itself; its consciousness floats free (and I take it this is the point) of relatedness and connection. Its gnomic, surrealist and aphoristic figures efface at once the localizing effects of the personal speaking voice and its power of direct shared communicability. It is as a voice, Auden declared, that poetry 'acts' and survives. The distinctive voice (e.g. Hardy, Edward Thomas, Larkin) sustains and structures the poem, defines a shared history (because, as Auden so well understood, it is itself an aggregation of historical pressures), speaks with humanized directness to the reader while encompassing all manner of shifts, nuances, ambiguities responding to the pluralities and contradictions of experience. Even in *Four Quartets* we keep being reminded of a personal poetic consciousness despite the impersonally revolving patterns. Voice in this sense, it seems to me, though itself inevitably a stylization, is more than just a formal element in the discourse of poetry; it has to do with the degree of intensity with which we attend to the poem. Though Hughes deliberately abandoned what he saw, in some of his early work, as the academicized obscurities of poetry which fits New Critical formulae, he gradually replaced them with the riddling and the gnomic. *Cave Birds* has its mythic coherence, but it is essentially hermetic, enclosed, baffling access; that extra-human oracular voice belongs to the world of a wholly esoteric vision, one which sees both personality and history as impasse.

If we turn from *Cave Birds* to a piece such as 'A March Calf' from *Season Songs* (1976), we are back, surely with a mode of poetic realization which speaks to wider recognitions:

Right from the start he is dressed in his best – his blacks and
  his whites
Little Fauntleroy – quiffed and glossy,
A Sunday suit, a wedding natty get-up,
Standing in dunged straw

Under cobwebby beams, near the mud wall,
Half of him legs,
Shining-eyed, required nothing more
But his mother's milk come back often.[20]

I don't think I am seeking to reduce a large visionary enterprise, of something like Blakean dimensions, to comfortable and manageable terms. It is not so much that the arrangement of four-line stanzas allows us to get our formal bearing more readily than the less stable, more radical and unnerving structures of *Crow* or *Cave Birds*. For those, radical formal strategies had to be devised: in *Crow*, for example, the verse must attempt to mime a consciousness which lacks any structure of a kind known to us.[21] Its narrowing exploitation of 'common devices in oral poetry from the pre-literate world' (Thwaite, p. 59) is a means of expressing the rawness of a pre-humanized, pre-literate consciousness. And only unintelligent readers will want never to be unnerved. Nor is it entirely that the absence of the oracular or priestly voice makes us feel that here is poetry which has no 'design upon us'. More essentially, it is the skill and inventiveness with which the creature's 'thisness' is placed before us, in experiential terms we can recognize ('cobwebby beams'), the stanza-form made to contribute to the dynamics of mimetic realization. Our reading can be unencumbered here with the totemistic or mythic apparatus to a certain extent, I think, imposed by critics – with Hughes's collusion – *post hoc* on the poetry; we respond to the exemplary, indispensable vivid phrase distilling a perception, the aptness of verse-movement (the calf's tottering eagerness). Not only is the calf seen with the nicest precision, but all its unknown 'otherness' is captured, in a way which makes us assent to the proposition that there is a whole universe beyond the human of which we are only part and of which we need to take account. A world not necessarily arcane but indisputably 'other', with the implication (as in 'The Bull Moses') that the mass of consciousness precedes, envelops and survives beyond mere selfhood or personality, becomes immediate rather than 'visionary'.

Yet at the same time the poem's formal devices, as in formalist descriptions of art cleansing perception through deformation, imbue a familiar world with the intensity of something newly experienced. In such poems Hughes is masterly at combining recognition and shock. Like 'Full Moon and Little Frieda' part of the poem's strength derives from its firm location in the working life of the farm: Hughes is never better than when he is writing out of the direct experience of farming life, his intimacy with his material imparting an almost casual sureness of touch. That very subject-matter which I've suggested is a restriction also furnishes strengths. After all, the farm is the place where man and nature most intimately *do* meet.[22] Both these poems achieve a near-perfect marriage of an everyday reality and of a quality of mystery and wonder. They may seem to have a certain child-like or 'Georgian' simplicity beside the large apocalyptic dramas ('A March Calf' is one of the poems supposedly written for children, though one suspects here a ploy to put such poems out of competition with the ambitions of the mythic sequences), but this is, of course, a sophisticated simplicity, a concentration of art: the witty application of the 'Little Fauntleroy' and 'Sunday suit' ideas, the swift elisions of child, 'moon' and 'artist' in 'Little Frieda'. Every detail exactly and economically right, 'Little Frieda' bridges the subjective–objective gulf to retrieve, in perfectly resolved form, that experience of 'joy' at which the Romantics had always aimed.

Yet neither of these is an anti-humanist poem. Both take in their stride and capitalize upon the fact that the creative act is bound to humanize, and that 'to humanize' means locating in an historical and cultural context. The calf can only be created with that sharply recognizable immediacy because it plays upon óur ordinarily human, culturally mediated experience of Sunday suits and wedding get-ups, and of the irrepressibility of hopefulness. Looking back over Hughes's poetry we see that this has always been the case. 'The Thought Fox' is as much about the human creative act and about human perceptions of foxes ('warily a lame / Shadow lags ...'), as about an alien fox-ness. 'Egg-Head' and 'Thrushes' are metaphorically and even explicitly didactic; they are human moralities. As I have argued throughout, it is difficult to see how poetry can matter to us without this concretely human, and because human inescapably historical, context.

By the end of the seventies, in *Moortown Elegies*, the problem the poetry enacts crystallizes not so much as that of the division between man and nature as that between the urban and the rural experience. Indeed, the value of Hughes's farming poems may not be that they illuminate a healing of the rift between man and nature, but that the poetry imparts a vivid reality to that concentrated specialization of human activity which farming increasingly is: something, for most of us, outside our direct experience. The poems prove, after all, a way for us to experience that which is other, they challenge solipsism and subjectivism, arguably the true creative by-products of the anguish the poet has undergone in his personal life.[23] However, coming even further forward in time, to the salmon-fishing poems in *The River* (1983), we encounter something like a reversion to traditional nature poetry. (Birds and fish: a never-ending litany of these two kinds of creature out of the human element.) 'That Morning' could be taken simply for pantheism, a hymn to nature. Yet another modern poet, it appears, has been journeying; has reached, in fact, the end of a quest – 'So we found the end of our journey' (*Selected Poems*, p. 235: the poems originate in an Alaskan fishing-trip with the poet's son) – has travelled through the darkness, the black vision of Crow, to 'the river of light / Among the creatures of light'. Yet it is still nature poetry with a difference; the salmon are compared to wartime bomber formations; the discarding of the hindrances of 'mind' reaches an apotheosis: the body is 'Separated ... From its doubting thought' to become a 'spirit beacon'. Still there is no transcendentalism, it is still the material body which is sacred, identified with 'spirit'. The river is time 'undergoing itself / In its wheel' (p. 233) suggesting a further echoing of Eliot, and of Graves's use of the Orphic 'weary wheel' motif. But the poet, unlike the Gravesian protagonist, seeks no release from Karma, from the life-death-rebirth wheel; rather, a sacramental submission to it, beyond the hesitations of doubt. History remains essentially a side-issue, but, together with the everyday contemporary world, it is accepted for what it is and suffused with a raptness precariously close in feeling to a traditional, even religiose, sense of the holy.

The River doesn't exactly show Hughes mellowing into a conventional poet, but along with a certain relaxation of the earlier aggressions and indulgences goes a loss of some of the fierce, productive tensions. The source of these tensions in Hughes's best poetry is a sense of the value of human consciousness with its unique perceptions – Little Frieda's amazement at the moon (something of which the Hawk in 'Hawk Roosting' is incapable) – juxtaposed with a desire for being inalienably at one with all matter, becoming subsumed in the invulnerability and survival-power of all that in dumb and blind unconsciousness simply *is*. The drive towards the latter involves in one way a circumscribing and narrowing of vision (though as with orthodox faiths the true believer will not think so); *the experience itself* is not enough, for there is a will to erase the very consciousness of the experience which gives the experiencing subject so much trouble. At such times Hughes even wants to relinquish that minimal state of cognition – knowing one is free from the burden of consciousness – which Coleridge and Edward Thomas desired. Nevertheless, such poetry demands that we recognize the sane contemplation of the extreme as a necessary exercise of the human imagination. There *are* mysteries, voids which our explanations cannot fill; to deny them is another form of closure; and, *pace* Sartre, it is only our uniquely *human* apprehension of void and otherness which makes meaning possible. Moreover, if 'no one exists alone', it is a function of the imagination and its subtleties to reach across the isolating subjectivities, a function which itself gives rise to poems.

Conclusion

What has been widely experienced as a crisis of consciousness has produced a preoccupation in modern poetry with subjective life, partly because any problem of consciousness is of necessity in the subjective realm, and partly because the crisis itself has seemed to these poets the result of a breakdown in the institutions of the outer world. To be conscious means to be conscious of self, and of separation from the other, but the *self*-consciousness of consciousness in the modern period, the acuteness of consciousness in the poet, threaten to overwhelm him, appear at times barely tolerable. This subjective focus tends to underrepresent the extent to which the alienated state of consciousness, the 'ontological insecurity', is socio-historically determined. The problem is signalled by various kinds of contradiction in the poetry: between world and otherworld, 'nature' and 'eternity', poet as 'maker' and as 'oracle', between the presumption in subjects that they are free, autonomous and coherent and the feeling that they are not, between longing for social relatedness and an intensity of self-realization. To an extent, the assigning of inward and 'spiritual', emotional and sensory concerns to poetry takes place as some felt consensual need to correct imbalances in a culture which seems ever more intent on defining itself against positivist and materialist criteria. Certain 'human deficiencies' in the modern world are attributed by Hughes 'to a shifting of the centre of gravity from "man's sense of himself ... his body and his essential human subjectivity", and a surrender of his individuality to an "impersonal abstraction"' (Sagar, *The Achievement of Ted Hughes*, p. 296). This resistance is indispensable; we have seen, though, what difficulties poets have had dealing with the collision between 'totality of self' – the feeling that the self has an almost sacred right and duty to fortify itself against violation by the often crass abstractions of the public and social worlds, to constitute, indeed, an end in itself – and what for shorthand I have called, borrowing from Robert Graves, citizenship.

When Ted Hughes wrote of Keith Douglas that 'He showed in his poetry no concern for man in society' (Faas, p. 171) he did not mean dispraise. Wordsworth 'is an example of both the true poet and the false, the man trusting his gift and producing the real thing, and the man searching for his satisfaction among more popular and public causes' (Faas, p. 164). This pinpoints dangers; nothing I've written, I hope, implies that 'poetry' and 'history' can or should be identical discourses. But that Wordsworth is indeed least compelling when he dutifully attempts a 'public' voice underlines a disability in conceiving poetically of 'man in society'. For Hughes, 'the real thing', the occult 'gift' which makes a true poet, are necessarily incompatible with a public poetry or a poetry of everyday life. Alvarez, a notable champion of intensely inward poetry, said of Auden: 'His business is with the surface of things, not with their real nature' (*The Shaping Spirit*, p. 94). Auden himself had an alternative view, to which his own poetry bears persuasive witness, that 'truth, like love and sleep, resents / Approaches that are too intense' (*New Year Letter, Collected Poems* p. 166). Hughes, I've said, strives to work right through the modern impasse about belief by acknowledging the death of God but directing us instead to the material energies of the universe as the source of the sacred. The drift of my argument, however, has been that Auden's poetry explores a way through that impasse which is more in tune with our late-twentieth-century perceptions by implicitly recognizing that there is no 'real nature of things' but that *we give sense to things*. 'Man is not just *homo sapiens* but *homo significans*: a creature who gives sense to things. Literature offers an example or image of the creation of meaning ...' (Culler, p. 264) Auden found it useful to posit a Redeemer, but I have suggested that this is a focal point around which he can organize existential possibilities, and that in a sense 'it does not matter . . . in what religious sect a man finally finds his home' (p. 264). Such a position is, of course, consistent with a philosophical pluralism, which in any case permits us to see both Auden's and Hughes's poetry as necessary imaginative enterprises.

Hughes's view of how poetry relates to history subtly avoids reductive notions of the 'committed' or 'relevant':

> This flower, this little girl, this little girl, this bird, this old man paddling in a pool . . . all this infatuation with infancy and innocence, what did these have to do with the great issues of the time? Nothing whatsoever, till the spirit that worked through Wordsworth and Coleridge and Blake chose them for its parables. And looking back now, if we wish to see the important issues of those two decades, we see nothing so convincing and enlightening to so many of us, as the spirit which seems to touch us openly and speak to us directly through these poems. (Faas, p. 164)

There is a kind of poetic clairvoyance, and it is in the concretions of poetic image and structure that the content of those 'great issues' can most 'directly' and affectively be read. Something of the kind might be granted even from a cultural materialist point of view, which might attribute the 'clairvoyance' to a necessary circulation of energies between the subjective life of the sensitive, thinking individual and the condition of the time. But in Hughes's formulation, the poet is a vehicle for the 'spirit's' work, feeling himself moved by a supra-psychological power, which does the active 'choosing' of poetic materials. Such a poet, in thrall to the 'real nature' of things (or to its variants the White Goddess, Spiritus Mundi, the Dark Embryo Within), is exempted from the obligation of choice himself. Proselytizing for the Hughesian position, Keith Sagar says:

> The poet is a medium for transmitting an occult charge from the non-human world into the psyche and thence into consciousness . . . Most English poets have drifted into a rational humanism and arrogantly expect us to value their measured musings. (p. 3)

Regained contact with nature, according to *Poetry in the Making*, puts us back in touch with 'prehistoric feelings, satis-

factions' (p. 76), part of ourselves which history has obliterated. Nature is a symbol of what is original and essential, which
it is the poet's task to recover, culture and history being
disruptions of nature's unity. But if the non-human is part of
the otherness our logocentrism has suppressed and may need in
some sense to be retrieved by consciousness if we are to feel less
incomplete, how can it, as a concept or sign, escape human
('rational humanist') discourse (intelligible only in opposition
to humanness, as 'occult charges' signify only in opposition to
positivist cognition)? Suppressing that structure of intelligibility, privileging the non-human and the occult as real and
authentic in a way social existence isn't, is to marginalize the
socio-historical formations ('man in society') which arguably
constitute the very alienation for which the remedy is sought,
and indeed itself sets up an experience of isolation from any
social world. Being a medium for occult charges has obviously
awkward effects upon one's capacity for 'citizenship'.

It is understandable that poets who have undergone particularly difficult or painful experience should adopt forms,
however subtle or complicated, of nostalgia, and that the
inward journey, a desire to retrieve some lost or forgotten truth
within the self, should often be one of those forms. Lawrence in
particular resists imposed social constructions (the 'voices of
my education') and pursues intensifications of inward
consciousness. Lawrence, Graves, Eliot, Yeats all in their
various ways imply that this numinous 'charge' transmitted
into consciousness speaks from some ultimate source which can
claim in a religious way to be the *truth*, and the only kind of
truth which magics words into poetry. It is a nostalgic desire
for origin or centre of a sort which serves closure, provides
certainty. Nowhere are the alienating effects of a false or
illusive subjectivity more evident than in the disembodied,
disorientated voices which haunt Eliot's poetry: this subjectivity obliterates history, and the compensatory reaching for
'impersonality' and later for the nostalgia of faith only consolidates the disconnection from history. However, the work of
MacNeice, Larkin or Gunn (mostly founded upon urban
rather than country life) appears to posit that meaning is not

God-given, or immanent in nature, but is made, the 'work of man'. In any case, why should Lawrence, or Graves, or Hughes, with their Romantic primitivism, be so intent on convincing us that man's first state was his best? Or Eliot's seventeenth century stand as a model, however subtly modified, for a late-twentieth-century society? 'Our psychological problems cannot be solved by a regression to a past state in which they had not yet been brought into being' (William Barrett, see p. 58).

However, if poets are always seeking a centred and ordered whole in themselves and in the world around them (to fix time, to escape death) which is perhaps counter to the nature of consciousness and of the material universe itself, hence often only compounding their own 'suffering', it is difficult to see how life can be lived otherwise – to conceive of radically anarchic states as humanly viable. To *think* Lawrence's 'chaos', say, or Barthes's critical hedonism, is intellectually, even emotionally, liberating, but the need for pattern, for some nucleus or focal point around which to organize, will always be felt. (Lawrence knew very well that people cannot live in chaos, hence his veering to the opposite, almost desperately counterweighing, premise in the 'leadership' novels.) The situation of poets in the present century has often left no recourse but to make this their own lives (including, among other elements, *places* in those lives); they do feel that their 'individual lives have profound meaning and worth' (see p. 188). This has the force of a diagnosis and a critique (none more powerful, indeed, than Lawrence's); in their various writings, the poets discussed all apply acute intelligence to characterizing a cultural and philosophical crisis arising, ultimately, from the Cartesian split and the bourgeois-capitalist hegemony. Moreover, all are concerned with putting together a personal *modus vivendi* in the face of that crisis, a concern crucially generating the poetry, and I do not see how one can without misrepresentation produce readings which do not take account of this. (Poetry, of course, has always been much concerned with 'how to live'.) If the contradictions in the poetry are entailed in the crisis of the culture (if they are not, much of my case falls), and if in some instances, the poets' remedies tend to quackery (Edward Thomas, though, offers no remedy, unless it be 'the experience itself'), this creative undertaking still provides much matter for celebration.

For these reasons, as foreseen in my Introduction, I have not allowed any absolute divorce between 'maker' and life, 'personality' and poem, author and text. At a certain level of abstraction these distinctions are inescapable; in the social and psychological practice of reading and writing they must blur, and in critical practice may lead to barren analysis. One can always be sharpening awareness, contesting suppression and closure, but, as MacNeice was so problematically conscious, one must live in the world as given. Few readers ever read, and fewer poets ever wrote, without assuming some reciprocity between life and text; in practice, it is for the tension between the two that people read, and write. Poetry is, as the theorists say, an institution, *écriture*, but it is also a practice of communication, involving a humanizing voice, an effect of personal utterance, upon which it depends for its affective power to make immediate and concrete, to have us attend. What I speak of as recognition is clearly akin to the theorists' 'naturalization'; as Culler says: 'The strange, the formal, the fictional, must be recuperated or naturalized, brought within our ken, if we do not want to remain gaping before monumental inscriptions' (p. 134). Poetry only signifies and matters to us as a dynamic of recognitions and discoveries (Lawrence's assertion that it ' "discovers" a new world within the known world' is in itself wholly apt). 'Poetry' is not a pursuit of some platonically essential meaning ('truth'); it imitates the ordinary communicative functions of language but by the very process of stylizing, by *foregrounding* patterns, forms and conventions, also dislocates them, in ways which yield fresh perceptions and may uncover the deferments which characterize discursive ideologies. (Organic form and its derivative 'free verse', with their ostensibly naturalizing inclination towards the rhythms and idioms of everyday speech, may seek to fuse form and content, but on analysis their stylizations are perfectly evident.)

Auden like Hughes rooted much of his early thinking in

Lawrence and would not disagree about Sagar's 'human deficiencies' and their causes, or his abhorrence of 'impersonal
abstraction'. But what he seems to have understood is that
words do not just choose the poet any more than does some
supra-psychological 'spirit'. The poet is possessed of a linguistic
and cultural 'competence' which empowers him as maker. The
poet's 'voice', necessarily participating in human and social
energies, addresses a world not only as given, but as 'what we
make'. To foreground the plays and idiosyncrasies of this
speaking voice is to subvert, to show that 'no one knows the
final truth' (it is the 'first principle of democracy': see p. 253),
and also that 'no one exists alone', that being 'a free one' is part
of 'the romantic lie in the brain', but that though the self is a
psycho-cultural construction – 'a choice is denied by each
childhood illness' – possession of that voice is a way of getting
into the gaps in those conditioning discourses. The indeterminacy which in Edward Thomas is passively held where it is and
savoured is supplanted by Yeats ambivalently and Auden
unreservedly with an active pluralism. The indeterminate is
then seen as a field of creative opportunity; poetry may exemplify that we can organize meaning in the face of absurdity, take
part in shaping the history which shapes us. Perhaps, indeed,
this *is* how art relates to 'action'; 'the work of art', Stephen
Greenblatt has written, 'is not the passive surface on which this
historical experience leaves its stamp but one of the creative
agents in the fashioning and re-fashioning of this experience'.[1]
Though fully aware of the often necessary solitariness of the
poet, and of his superfluity and economic inutility in a
capitalist-technological environment, Auden even after his
'change of heart' could assert that 'In our age, the mere
making of a work of art is itself a political act' (*The Dyer's Hand*,
p. 88). If seeming to resemble the view of the poem as heroic
act, an *end* in itself, this importantly repudiates it; the poem is
plugged into a circuit, not absolute and unilateral.

Hughes, of course, is quite aware of some such reciprocity,
and of the dangers of imbalance.

It is only logical to suppose that a faculty developed specially for
peering into the inner world might end up as specialized and destruc-

tive as the faculty for peering into the outer one ... So what we need, evidently, is a faculty that embraces both worlds simultaneously ... This really is imagination. (Faas, p. 191)

The laws of the inner and outer worlds 'are not contradictory at all; they are one all-inclusive system' (p. 192). The rhetoric, nevertheless, is all the time pulling away from balance; the claims of the outer world are swallowed up by the more urgent reality of 'spirit'. The offer to *include* everything must tend towards a suppression of openness and plurality: there is 'one story and one story only'. If one were to theorize imagination as the pursuit of the other in order to remake conscious its relation to the subject, or the relation between inner and outer, the kind of (recognizably Coleridgean) description Hughes gives would be apt enough. The imagination is 'simply one of the characteristics of being alive in these mysterious electrical bodies of ours, and the difficult thing is not to pick up the information but to recognize it – to accept it into consciousness' (*Poetry in the Making*, p. 123). But this information about the other is mystic, mystifyingly coded, and the role assigned to the imagination is 'acceptance', a form of passivism. Shakespeare, certainly, had supposed that 'imagination bodies forth / The forms of things unknown, the poet's pen / Turns them to shapes' (*A Midsummer Night's Dream* v.i), but if this is playfully ambiguous (in its context) about the sources of inspiration, the poet is credited with an active and volitional power of shaping. Quite as much an arduous nurturing of the imagination as a condition of fully 'being alive' is Auden's understanding of the need to place what inner 'charges' suggest to us in a critical frame – that that *also* is an act of the imagination. Experience is not of value in itself, but as a field in which human will and reason are called upon to exercise their freedom, whether as an act of 'worldly duty' or as a 'leap of faith'. Auden wanted us to recognize information about the (psychologically) diseased or (theologically) fallen nature of our instinctuality, its corruptiveness. Seductive claims for a single, 'all-inclusive' truth all too often mark the sadist or the fanatic, mask eruptions of the psychopathic or the totalitarian, to be deconstructed only by something like Auden's passionate rationality. Ethical and social rationalizations such as keeping promises and showing compassion, and the practice of love in its full Audenesque continuum from Eros to Agape, require imaginative qualities too.

Hughes is right: being alive in these 'electrical bodies of ours' certainly is 'mysterious'. Thomas is right: between us, nature and man, 'still we breed a mystery'. Just as self is not co-incidental with consciousness, consciousness is not co-incidental with life: it remains a 'problem', it resists positivist explanation. I cannot put this better than in some sentences from a book on Emily Dickinson by John Robinson. The 'real mystery' is not

in being born and dying (starting and stopping) but in coming to consciousness. Not merely being alive but knowing that you are alive, not eating but being able to think about eating, having thoughts which can be sent – or will wander – outside the immediate moment: this is the mystery. It is not one to be resolved by the biochemical analysis of mechanism ... Nor is the mystery of consciousness to be resolved by pointing out that its content and its processes are power-fully shaped by historical circumstances. It can initiate change; it is not determined.[2]

'What are days for?' asks Larkin's poem, 'They come, they wake us ... ' There is a difference between being passively alive (which is an unbroken flow, even when we sleep) and consciousness, which divides the flow up into 'days' in which we look for something active to do, where options present them-selves (if very limited options, in the view of Larkin the sceptic). The Romantic-modern tradition is not simply obscurantist when it exalts a power in consciousness to intuit and create, a power of 'imagination'. But this then becomes a metaphysic, the Romantic myth of 'poetry' and 'the poet' (there is a myth of 'literature' in general, some would say, but prose drama and narrative were never mythicized in this overt way). This quest for the fixation, the essentialism, of myth, aiming at 'ultimate collectivity ... beyond and above community', suppresses con-crete material and social relatedness, throws the emphasis on the haunting insubstantiality of consciousness and on its power to estrange, so that it is felt as a burden, a source of pain.

That 'measured musings', to return to Sagar's mocking alliteration, seeks in its conjunction of terms to explode a contradiction: the inspirations of the Romantic muse cannot be 'measured'. But precisely there the myth is manifest. If 'musing' relates to the metaphor of being touched by a 'muse', by a sense of the marvellous, it need not connote a low-temperature state, but the poetry arises – including Hughes's poetry – when that is cast into measures: measuring is shaping, giving sense to; it is also taking the measure of things, unfolding lies. Measured musing – the verbal formalization of a charged sense of mystery, interlocking it with the field of historical and social process, a negotiation between and interfashioning of the existential and the historical – is exactly what poetry is.

Notes

INTRODUCTION

1 *Apocalypse*, London, Granada, 1981 (1st edn 1931), p. 44.
2 *Modern Poetry and the Tradition*, Chapel Hill, University of North Carolina Press, 1965, p. xxvii.
3 Ed. Richard Ellman and Charles Feidelson, *The Modern Tradition. Backgrounds of Modern Literature*, New York, Oxford University Press, 1965, p. 685.
4 Herbert Read, *The True Voice of Feeling. Studies in English Romantic Poetry*, London, Faber and Faber, 1953, p. 98.
5 Robert Langbaum, *The Modern Spirit. Essays on the Continuity of Nineteenth and Twentieth-Century Literature*, London, Chatto and Windus, 1970, p. vii.
6 Roland Barthes, *Mythologies*, St Albans, Paladin paperback, 1973, p. 143. For a consise discussion of myth in literature see K. K. Ruthven, *Myth*, London, Methuen, 1976.
7 Frank Kermode, *Romantic Image*, London, Routledge and Kegan Paul, 1957, pp. 2–6.
8 Ed. G. F. Maine, *The Works of Oscar Wilde*, London, Collins, 1948, p. 981.
9 M. L. Rosenthal, *The Modern Poets. A Critical Introduction*, New York, Oxford University Press, 1960, p. 167
10 Quoted by Michael H. Levenson, *A Genealogy of Modernism. A Study of English Literary Doctrine 1908–1922*, Cambridge, Cambridge University Press, 1984, p. ix.
11 Marilyn Butler, *Romantics, Rebels and Reactionaries*, Oxford, Oxford University Press, 1981, p. 143.
12 Raymond Williams, *The Country and the City*, London, Chatto and Windus, 1973, p. 246.
13 *Modern Poetry. A Personal Essay*, Oxford, Oxford University Press, 1960, (1st edn 1938), p. 1.
14 In his essay on Emily Dickinson, quoted by Vivian R. Pollak in

Dickinson. The Anxiety of Gender, Ithaca and London, Cornell University Press, 1984, p. 17.

15 Allan Rodway, *The Romantic Conflict*, London, Chatto and Windus, 1963, p. vii.

16 Ed. Edward Mendelson, *The English Auden*, London, Faber and Faber, 1977, p. 354.

17 Can one conceive at all of human consciousness or society without the impulse for 'order'? Clearly industrial capitalism has a need for special kinds of ordering, and what we most commonly perceive in present western society as principles of order are, like so much else of human need, bourgeois appropriations. A *pluralism* of orders should instead be thought of.

18 Frank Kermode, *The Classic*, London, Faber and Faber, 1975, p. 121. Writing at the same time as Kermode, Jonathan Culler suggested that what we do when we read poetry is always to seek some totality of organization, and that 'the richest organization compatible with the data is to be preferred' (*Structuralist Poetics*, London, Routledge and Kegan Paul, 1975, p. 174).

19 In an interview in *P. N. Review 74*, 16, 6 (1990), 13.

20 'Humanism' also needs liberating from its assimilation to bourgeois ideology; there is a larger humanism, or other humanisms.

21 Anthony Easthope, *Times Higher Education Supplement*, 10 April 1987.

CHAPTER 1 D. H. LAWRENCE AND ROBERT GRAVES

1 C. K. Stead, *The New Poetic: Yeats to Eliot*, London, Hutchinson, 1964, p. 88.

2 *Rhythm*, March 1913, p. xvii.

3 Ed. Timothy Rogers, *Georgian Poetry 1911–1922: The Critical Heritage*, London, Routledge and Kegan Paul, 1977, p. 72.

4 R. H. Ross, *The Georgian Revolt. Rise and Fall of a Poetic Ideal 1910–1922*, London, Faber and Faber, 1967, p. 33.

5 Daniel Hoffman, *Barbarous Knowledge. Myth in the Poetry of Yeats, Graves and Muir*, London and New York, Oxford University Press, 1967, p. 16 (Hoffman gives a most perceptive account of Graves's work).

6 For this point of T. E. Hulme's doctrine see Frank Kermode, *Romantic Image*, p. 128. Much the same kind of distinction seems to have been in Wallace Stevens's mind when he told Robert Frost, 'You write on subjects.' (See Edward Neill, 'Modernism and Englishness: Reflections on Auden and Larkin', *Essays and Studies 1983*, The English Association, p. 80.)

7 Donald Davie's phrase about 'confessional poetry' in *Thomas Hardy and British Poetry*, London, Routledge and Kegan Paul, 1973, p. 54.

8 Pater's statement is in the famous Conclusion to *The Renaissance* (1873): Owen's (to his cousin in 1917) is quoted by Dominic Hibberd, 'Wilfred Owen and the Georgians', *Review of English Studies*, 30, 117 (February 1979), 40.

9 *Required Writing*, London, Faber and Faber, 1983, p. 79.

10 David Perkins, *A History of Modern Poetry. From the 1890s to the High Modernist Mode*, Cambridge, Mass., Harvard University Press, 1976, p. 214.

11 'Chaos in Poetry', in *Selected Literary Criticism*, ed. Anthony Beal, Heinemann, London, 1967, p. 89. Lawrence's comments in the Foreword to *Women in Love* on the importance of the 'struggle for verbal consciousness' are well known.

12 'Georgian Poets', *The Daily Chronicle*, 14 January 1913, p. 4.

13 To judge by Lawrence's comments – 'mean and rather vulgar' – on this kind of realism in Abercrombie's contribution to the second Georgian anthology, quoted by R. H. Ross, p. 151.

14 Originally from *Chambers of Imagery*, quoted here from *Poems and Plays*, London, Bodley Head, 1953, p. 49.

15 'Art and Morality', *The Calendar of Modern Letters*, 2 (1925), 175.

16 Ed. Earl Leslie Griggs, *Collected Letters of Samuel Taylor Coleridge*, 6 Vols. 1956–71, Oxford, Clarendon Press, 1956, Vol. 1, p. 350.

17 Ed. R. George Thomas, *Letters from Edward Thomas to Gordon Bottomley*, London, Oxford University Press, 1968, p. 174.

18 Colin Clarke, *River of Dissolution: D. H. Lawrence and English Romanticism*, New York, Barnes and Noble; London, Routledge and Kegan Paul, 1969, p. 3. Mark Spilka's quarrel with Clarke's thesis in *Novel. A Forum on Fiction*, 4, 3 (Spring 1971), 252–67, should be noted.

19 To his sister Fanny, 17 April 1819. Ed. H. E. Rollins, *The Letters of John Keats 1814–1821*, 2 vols, Cambridge, Mass., Harvard University Press, 1958, Vol. II, p. 56.

20 Frank Kermode discusses this in *Romantic Image*.

21 *Apocalypse*, p. 110.

22 *The Modern Writer and His World*, Harmondsworth, Penguin, 1964, pp. 255–6.

23 *Language as Gesture*, London, Allen and Unwin, 1954, p. 58.

24 Ed. James Gibson, *The Complete Poems*, London, Macmillan, 1976, p. 484. All quotations from Hardy's poetry use this edition and page numbers will be given in the text.

25 'Hardy and "The Lonely Burden of Consciousness: The Poet's

Flirtation with the Void', *English Literature in Transition*, 33, 2 (1980), 90.

26 *The Romantic Survival: A Study in Poetic Evolution*, London, Constable, 1957, p. 64.

27 'Snap-Dragon' had already appeared in *The English Review* and was reprinted with alterations in *Amores*, London, Duckworth, 1916. I quote from the *Georgian Poetry* version.

28 'Lawrence is the foremost emotional realist of the century.' *The Shaping Spirit*, London, Arrow Books, 1963 (1st edn 1958), p. 141.

29 Graham Hough said in his excellent comments on Lawrence's poetry in *The Dark Sun. A Study of D. H. Lawrence* (London, Duckworth, 1956) that Lawrence 'has the Keatsian Negative Capability' (p. 214). Sandra M. Gilbert makes the same point in her admirably full study of Lawrence's poetry, *Acts of Attention*, Ithaca and London, Cornell University Press, 1972, p. 12.

30 Martin Seymour-Smith explains that neurasthenia simply means 'nerve-weakness' and is really another term for battle fatigue or shellshock. See *Robert Graves. His Life and Work*, London, Abacus, 1983, pp. 51, 76. Also see this book for details of Graves's life with Laura Riding.

31 Robert Graves, *Collected Poems 1975*, London, Cassell, 1975, p. 8. All further page references will be given in the text.

32 *Robert Graves and the White Goddess*, Lincoln, Nebraska, University of Nebraska Press, 1972, p. 1. As suggested in my Introduction, the poetic myths of Modernism, even in their Romantic primitivist versions, owe a paradoxical debt to the rationalizing systems of nineteenth-century comparative religion and mythology.

33 Graves's poem first appeared interpolated in his account of the Argonauts, *The Golden Fleece*, London, Cassell, 1944, p. 153. (Published in New York as *Hercules, My Shipmate*.)

34 Blackmur's essay on Lawrence is on pp. 286–300 of *Language as Gesture*. In *Acts of Attention* Sandra M. Gilbert analyses the structures of Lawrence's poetry in detail.

35 *D. H. Lawrence: The Complete Poems*, New York, Viking, Compass, 1971, p. 280. All further page references in the text.

36 Louis MacNeice pointed out: 'the Orphics put on their gravestones: "I have flown out of the sorrowful weary wheel"' (*The Strings are False. An Unfinished Autobiography*, London, Faber and Faber, 1965, p. 32).

37 *The Crowning Privilege*, London, Cassell, 1955, p. 135.

38 *English Poetry 1900–1950. An Assessment*, London, Rupert Hart-Davis, 1971, p. 192.

39 *The Priest of Love*, Harmondsworth, Penguin, 1976, p. 416.

40 'Sex is a creative flow, the excrementory flow is towards dissolution, de-creation ... In the really healthy human being the
distinction between the two is instant, our profoundest instincts
are perhaps our instincts of opposition between the two flows.'

41 *Phoenix II*, London, Heinemann, 1968, pp. 383, 402.

42 *Assorted Articles*, London, Martin Secker, 1930, p. 112.

43 My use here of the terms 'Naturalist' and 'Symbolist' derives in
particular from Edmund Wilson's *Axel's Castle*.

44 The aim of the Romantic ode is 'to transcend and transform the
world, to redeem it from death'. 'If Lawrence did indeed do away
with "the old stable ego of the character", it was in search of a
deeper form of subjectivity ...' (Catherine Belsey, *Critical Practice*,
London and New York, Methuen, 1980, pp. 119, 74).

45 *The Trend of Modern Poetry*, London, Oliver and Boyd, 1934, p. 58.

46 *The White Goddess* first appeared in 1948. I quote the amended
and enlarged edition, London, Faber and Faber, 1961, p. 343.

47 *Irrational Man. A Study in Existential Philosophy*, London, Heinemann, 1967 (1st edn 1958), p. 22.

48 William James, *The Principles of Psychology*, 2 vols, Vol. I, New
York, Henry Holt, 1890, p. 239. William James's writings were
widely read in the formative years of 'modern' poetry and their
concern with the nature and value of subjective consciousness is
closely related to that in the poets I study.

49 In *The Plumed Serpent*, notes Gilbert, 'Lawrence isn't endorsing
"blood-sacrifice", just explaining it' (fn p. 198).

50 'Toward a Definition of Romantic Irony' in *Romantic and Modern.
Revaluations of Literary Tradition*, ed. George Bornstein, Pittsburgh,
University of Pittsburgh Press, 1977, p. 5.

51 'To Juan at the Winter Solstice', *Collected Poems 1975*, p. 137.

52 'Why the Novel Matters', *Selected Literary Criticism*, p. 106.
Compare Virginia Woolf's often quoted remarks on the nature of
consciousness in 'Modern Fiction'.

53 *Bookman*, 44 (April 1913), 47.

CHAPTER 2 MODERN NATURE POETRY AND THE RURAL MYTH

1 For an account of Davies's life see Richard J. Stonesifer, *W. H.
Davies. A Critical Biography*, London, Cape, 1963.

2 John Press, *A Map of Modern English Verse*, London, Oxford
University Press, 1969, p. 116.

3 For details see Joy Grant, *Harold Monro and the Poetry Bookshop*,
London, Routledge and Kegan Paul, 1967.

4 'Critical Note', *Collected Poems of Harold Monro*, London, Cobden-Sanderson, 1933, p. xv.

5 Keith Sagar, *Ted Hughes* (Writers and their Work Series), Windsor, Profile Books, 1981, p. 47.

6 I borrow 'protoreligious' from Robert Langbaum, *The Modern Spirit*, p. 101.

7 At the time this passage was originally written, Michael Kirkham's *The Imagination of Edward Thomas* (Cambridge, Cambridge University Press, 1986) had not appeared, but I note that he makes a similar connection.

8 Ed. Miriam Allott, *John Keats. The Complete Poems*, London, Longman, 1970, p. 45.

9 *After Strange Gods*, London, Faber and Faber, 1934, pp. 62–3. Lawrence is deplored, on similar grounds, as one of the 'foolish prophets' of the time.

10 A. E. Housman, *Collected Poems*, London, Cape, 1939, p. 148.

11 W. H. Davies, *Collected Poems*, London, Cape, 1942, p. 502.

12 Unpublished letter in the collection of King's School, Canterbury. The poem appeared many years later (1939), and I don't mean that it necessarily records the same occasion. The letter of 7 August 1909 is from the same source.

13 See Stonesifer for details.

14 In *Andrew Young. Prospect of a Poet*, ed. Leonard Clark, London, Rupert Hart-Davis, 1957, p. 67.

15 Andrew Young, *Complete Poems*, London, Secker and Warburg, 1974, p. 150.

16 Noted by Christopher Hassall in an essay in *Andrew Young. Prospect of a Poet*, pp. 51–60.

17 *The Observer*, 13 January 1985.

18 In the Introduction to the Faber *Selected Poems of Edward Thomas*, London, 1964. In the brief remarks which follow I am conscious of not having done justice to R. S. Thomas's work or to the notion of the 'provincial'. Thomas has written variously on the problems of the Anglo-Welsh writer, e.g. 'Suicide of the Writer', *Helix* (Melbourne), nos. 5–6 (1980), 129–32.

19 G. B. Cox, 'Welsh Bards in Hard Times'. *The New Pelican Guide to English Literature. 8, The Present*, Harmondsworth, Penguin, 1983, p. 221.

20 *Selected Poems 1946–68*, Newcastle upon Tyne, Bloodaxe, 1986, p. 35.

21 *New Bearings in English Poetry*, Harmondsworth, Penguin, 1963 (1st edn 1932), p. 59.

22 'The Sunlit Vale', *Poems of Many Years*, London, Collins, 1957, p. 117.

23 *Selected Poems 1957–1981*, London, Faber and Faber, 1982, p. 51.

CHAPTER 3 EDWARD THOMAS

1 Ed. R. George Thomas, *Letters from Edward Thomas to Gordon Bottomley*, London, Oxford University Press, 1968, pp. 8–10.

2 *The Icknield Way*, London, Constable, 1913, p. 281. The passage in which this occurs was versified by Thomas in 'Rain'.

3 *Out of Battle. The Poetry of the Great War*, London, Oxford University Press, 1972, p. 90.

4 Ed. R. George Thomas, *The Collected Poems of Edward Thomas*, Oxford, Oxford University Press, 1978, p. 233. Page numbers in the text refer to this edition (pagination in the paperback differs).

5 See Eleanor Farjeon, *Edward Thomas: The Last Four Years*, London, Oxford University Press, 1958, p. 153.

6 *Collected Poems*, p. 107. Note, however, that this edition reads 'stir or stain' in the final line of 'Parting'; the Faber and all other printings I have examined read 'stir or strain', which I have substituted. See R. George Thomas's note to the poem.

7 Page references to Thomas's *Keats* (London, T. C. and E. C. Jack, 1916) are given in the text. Keats's definition is on p. 387 of the Rollins *Letters*, Vol. 1 (1958).

8 William Cooke, *Edward Thomas: A Critical Biography*, London, Faber and Faber, 1970, p. 201.

9 Ed. Rollins, *Letters*, Vol. I, p. 188.

10 *Edward Thomas: A Biography and a Bibliography*, London, Dent, 1937, pp. 9, 11.

11 D. W. Harding's well-known 'A Note on Nostalgia', *Scrutiny*, I, 1 (May 1932), 8–19, influenced my perception of this kind of 'psychological patterning' – the connection in poets between acute sensitivity or 'acute consciousness' and 'regression'. Kirkham (p. xi, see note 14 below) says that Harding no longer holds the view of Thomas expressed there.

12 Ed. Rollins, Vol. 1, p. 287.

13 Thomas wrote to Eleanor Farjeon: 'I suppose every man thinks that Hamlet was written for him, but I *know* he was written for me ...' *Edward Thomas*, p. 12.

14 Since I wrote the articles on Edward Thomas from which this chapter derives, publications relating to him have come thick and fast: R. George Thomas, *Edward Thomas: A Portrait* (Oxford, Clarendon Press, 1985); Michael Kirkham, *The Imagination of Edward Thomas* (Cambridge, Cambridge University Press, 1986);

and (especially interesting) Stan Smith, *Edward Thomas* (London, Faber and Faber, 1986) should be noted.

15 This and further quotations from Thomas's prose are taken for convenience (Thomas published over thirty volumes) from David Wright's *Edward Thomas. Selected Poems and Prose*, Harmondsworth, Penguin, 1981. See p. 57. Unless otherwise indicated, page references for the prose are to this selection.

16 'A Language not to be Betrayed', *Literature and History*, 4 (Autumn 1976), 71.

17 John Lucas, *TLS*, 21 August 1981, p. 961.

18 Philip Larkin, 'Grub Vale', *The Guardian*, 12 February 1970.

19 Ed. Edna Longley, *Poems and Last Poems*, Plymouth, MacDonald and Evans, 1973, p. 139.

20 There is a careful study of Thomas's syntactical peculiarities by Martin Scofield, 'Edward Thomas: Syntax and Self-Consciousness', *English* (Spring 1982), 19–38.

21 Alun Lewis, *Raider's Dawn*, London, Allen and Unwin, 1942, p. 23.

22 By David Parker in 'Edward Thomas: Tasting Deep the Hour', *The Critical Review*, 22 (1980), 44–55. Parker also remarks (p. 45) on 'a kind of hunger for experience itself' in Thomas's poetry.

CHAPTER 4 W. B. YEATS

1 *Collected Poems of W. B. Yeats*, London, Macmillan, 1965, p. 182. Further page references are given in the text.

2 Quoted by A. N. Jeffares in *A Commentary on the Collected Poems of W. B. Yeats*, London, Macmillan, 1968, p. 195. Like all students of Yeats, I am greatly indebted to Jeffares's *Commentary*.

3 *Autobiographies*, London, Macmillan, 1955, p. 273.

4 In *Romantic Image* Frank Kermode takes 'the root signification' of Yeats's Tower to be 'the isolation of the artist' (p. 30). The 'double-shadowed Tower' in Edward Thomas's 'Tears' (*Collected Poems*, p. 75) might be similarly interpreted.

5 In the Introduction to *A Vision*, London, Macmillan, 1962, p. 8.

6 *The Last Romantics*, London, University Paperbacks, 1961 (1st edn 1947), p. 262.

7 *Mythologies*, New York, Macmillan, 1959, p. 331. This might be compared with the emphasis in Walter Benjamin's discussion of Baudelaire on bourgeois-capitalist existence as characterized by momentary aims disconnected from each other. See chapter 6, note 35 below.

8 Quoted Jeffares, p. 116.

9 Some of my earlier comments might suggest that just as Law-rence sought not so much a *totality* of self as an infinite possibility of self, he pursued not so much a *timeless* reality as a perpetual rebirth in time. (Sandra M. Gilbert argues something of the kind, e.g. p. 136.) In its effects, however, this seems to me the same thing, and to be precisely covered by Williams's formu-lations.

10 *The Poetry of W. B. Yeats*, London, Faber and Faber, 1967 (1st edn 1941), p. 108.

11 Catherine Belsey, *Critical Practice*, London, Methuen, 1980, pp. 67, 68.

12 *The Identity of Yeats*, London, Faber paperback, 1964, p. 222.

13 'A General Introduction to my Work', *Essays and Introductions*, London, Macmillan, 1969, p. 509.

14 Quoted Jeffares, p. 202 (no source given).

CHAPTER 5 T. S. ELIOT

1 Peter Ackroyd, *T. S. Eliot*, London, Hamish Hamilton, 1984, p. 107.

2 'Books of the Quarter', *The Criterion*, 12, 44 (July 1933), 682–3.

3 'Critical Note', *Collected Poems of Harold Monro*, London, 1933, pp. xiii–xv.

4 The phrase is F. O. Matthiessen's in *The Achievement of T. S. Eliot: An Essay on the Nature of Poetry*, New York, Oxford University Press, 1958 (1st edn 1935), p. 59.

5 *The Collected Poems and Plays of T. S. Eliot*, Faber and Faber, 1969, p. 38. Unless otherwise indicated, quotations are from this edition, page numbers in the text.

6 L. G. Salinger in 'T. S. Eliot: Poet and Critic', *The Pelican Guide to English Literature* 7, Harmondsworth, Penguin, 1961, p. 333.

7 Introduction to *Pascal's Pensées*, London, Everyman's Library, 1931, p. x.

8 Matthiessen, p. 65.

9 A. D. Moody, *Thomas Stearns Eliot, Poet*, Cambridge, Cambridge University Press, 1979, p. 244.

10 I quote from Leonard Woolf's account of 'the decade before the 1914 war' in *Beginning Again: An Autobiography of the Years 1911–1918*, London, The Hogarth Press, 1972, p. 36.

11 *Poetry and Drama*, 1, 1 (1913), 64.

12 By Glenn Hughes in *Imagism and the Imagists*, Stanford, Stanford University Press, 1931, p. 158. Flint's work is discussed at greater length in my article 'F. S. Flint: Zeppelin into Moon', *Helix*

13/14, Melbourne, 1983, pp. 31–44, from which some of the material used here is adapted.

13 Quoted by Charles Norman, *Ezra Pound*, New York, Macmillan, 1960, p. 114.

14 New York, Dutton paperback, 1958, p. 46 (1st edn 1899, revised 1908, 1919).

15 Ed. Edward Alexander, *John Stuart Mill. Literary Essays*, Indianapolis, 1967, pp. 56, 67.

16 *Literary Essays*, London, Faber and Faber, 1954, p. 9.

17 *Letters*, ed. D. D. Paige, London, Faber and Faber, 1951, p. 91. Compare also Lawrence's 'Before anything I like sincerity' (quoted Gilbert, *Acts of Attention*, p. 53).

18 *The Chapbook*, 9 (March 1920), 18–19. For a useful survey of the background see Clive Scott, 'The Prose Poem and Free Verse', *Modernism*, ed. Malcolm Bradbury and James McFarlane, Harmondsworth, Penguin, 1976, pp. 349–68.

19 Ed. W. J. B. Owen and Jane Worthington Smyser, *The Prose Works of William Wordsworth*, 3 vols, Oxford University Press, 1974, Vol. I, p. 135.

20 *Collected Shorter Poems*, London, Faber and Faber, 1952, p. 119.

21 See Eliot's essay in *A Choice of Kipling's Verse*, London, Faber and Faber, 1941.

22 Lyndall Gordon, *Eliot's Early Years*, Oxford, Oxford University Press, 1977, p. 40.

23 *The Use of Poetry and the Use of Criticism*, London, Faber and Faber, 1964, (1st edn 1933), p. 119.

24 See John Lucas and William Myers, '*The Waste Land* Today', *Essays in Criticism*, 19, 2 (April 1969), 193–209.

25 'Then came Nietzsche. That was my fault. Orage went over the top and so did the group. We all developed supermania. He wanted a Nietzsche circle in which Plato and Blavatsky, Fabianism and Hinduism, Shaw and Wells and Edward Carpenter should be blended, with Nietzsche as the catalytic. An exciting brew ... '. Holbrook Jackson, obituary of A. R. Orage, quoted by Paul Selver, *Orage and the New Age Circle*, London, Allen and Unwin, 1959, p. 87.

26 London, 1929, p. 269. It is, of course, a common observation, e.g.: 'No age has ever been so self-conscious as ours' (William Barrett, *Irrational Man*, p. 20). In my Introduction I have quoted Ellman and Feidelson on modern *cultivation* of self-consciousness.

27 *The Poetry of T. S. Eliot*, London, 1952; Routledge paperback, 1960, pp. 61–3. Rachael, one might add, appears from her name to be Jewish; 'Bleistein with a Cigar' certainly is. So Jews by

association contribute through that spiritually void commercialism which for Eliot they represent to the nightmare of inauthentic being.

28 William V. Spanos, '"Wanna Go Home Baby?"': *Sweeney Agonistes* as Drama of the Absurd', *PMLA*, 85 (1970), 11.

29 'Tradition and the Individual Talent', *The Sacred Wood*, London, Methuen paperback, 1960 (1st edn 1920), p. 58.

30 Introduction to Baudelaire's *Intimate Journals*, London, 1930, p. 21.

31 Some of the points I make in this section and in chapter 6, pp. 223–4 and 226–8, about 'poetry of departures' are repeated and expanded in my article 'Poetry of Departures: Larkin and the Power of Choosing', *Critical Survey*, 1, 2 (1989), 183–93.

32 'Le Voyage', *Baudelaire: Oeuvres Complètes*, Vol. I, Paris, Bibliothèque de la Pléiade, 1961, p. 127.

33 *The Romantic Agony* (1933), Oxford Paperback, 1970, p. 146.

34 *Baudelaire*, Paris, 1947. References to the Gallimard edn, 1963, pp. 226–8. There is a translation by Martin Turnell, London, Horizon, 1949.

35 On Baudelaire and the city see Walter Benjamin, 'On some motifs in Baudelaire', *Illuminations*, 1955, trans. Harry Zohn, New York, Harcourt, Brace & World, 1968, pp. 157–202, and on the connection with Eliot, G. M. Hyde, 'The Poetry of the City', in *Modernism*, ed. Bradbury and McFarlane, Harmondsworth, Penguin, 1976, pp. 337–48.

36 *De Baudelaire au Surréalisme*, Paris, 1933. I quote from the Methuen paperback, 1970, p. 11.

37 See Enid Starkie, *Baudelaire* (1957), Harmondsworth, Penguin, 1971, pp. 65–75.

38 'Edgar Poe: sa vie, ses œuvres'. Preface to Baudelaire's translation of *Histoires extraordinaires*, Paris, Editions Garnier, p. 24.

39 *Countries of the Mind*, London, Oxford University Press, 1937, p. 117.

40 See Peter Ackroyd, e.g. p. 19.

41 Ed. Jacques Crépet, *Charles Baudelaire, lettres inédites à sa mère*, Paris, Louis Conard, 1918, p. 142. Auden was wonderfully precise in *New Year Letter*:

> Trim, dualistic BAUDELAIRE,
> Poet of cities, harbours, whores,
> Acedia, gaslight and remorse ...

(*Collected Poems*, p. 165)

42 *The Modern Poets. A Critical Introduction*, New York, Oxford University Press, 1960, p. 237.

43 Jean-Jacques Rousseau, *Confessions*, trans. J. M. Cohen, Harmondsworth, Penguin, 1953, p. 88.

44 Unsigned review, *The English Review*, November 1911, 723.

45 'The Psychobiographical Approach to Eliot', *The Southern Review*, 6, 1 (1973), 18. A schizoid personality type is one which displays 'aloofness, detachment and a tendency to suppress the outward show of emotion' (*The Fontana Dictionary of Modern Thought*).

46 This trait in Eliot the man has often been commented on, but see e.g. Ackroyd, p. 108.

47 *Meridian. The La Trobe University English Review*, 2, 2 (October 1984), 99, 100.

48 S. E. Hymans, *The Armed Vision*, Vintage paperback, New York, 1955, p. 64.

49 Quoted by F. O. Matthiessen, *The Achievement of T. S. Eliot*, p. 6.

50 'East Coker', ll.186–9. Line numbers for quotations from *Four Quartets* are those of the Faber paperback, 1944. *Four Quartets* is on pp. 171–98 of *The Complete Poems and Plays*.

51 *Modern Poetry and the Tradition*, p. ix.

52 *The Mirror and the Lamp*, New York, Oxford University Press, 1953, p. 124.

53 A. D. Moody makes a similar point regarding these lines: 'That is to affirm ... just the immediate experience itself; and it is to affirm, moreover, not any value in experience, but just its being a valuation of ourselves' (pp. 214–15).

54 'Burnt Norton', 4–5. It is hardly feasible to annotate every nuance and possibility in passages from *Four Quartets*, such is the subtlety of this text. 'Unredeemable' here is audaciously enigmatic. It would seem, as I've said, to refer to our incapacity to 'redeem' time, our being victims of it. But it is difficult to avoid the Christian connotations of 'redeem'. Does Eliot mean to suggest that if there had been only eternity (all time eternally present), not human history, there would have been no coming of Christ to redeem humanity, a reference to the Christian paradox of the Fortunate Fall.

55 'Dissociation in Time', helpfully brought to our notice by Bernard Bergonzi in *T. S. Eliot: Four Quartets. A Casebook*, London, Macmillan, 1969, p. 251.

56 The desire of Faulkner's Quentin Compson in *The Sound and the Fury* to 'freeze' time is but one example of many comparable instances in modern literature.

57 *The Sacred Wood*, Methuen paperback, 1960, p. 49.

58 I need not go into Eliot's own problems concerning 'desire' of a sexual kind. Peter Ackroyd and Lyndall Gordon are informative.

59 L. G. Salingar, 'T. S. Eliot', p. 334. See G. M. Hyde on 'unreality' in the city.

CHAPTER 6 LOUIS MACNEICE AND W. H. AUDEN

1 *The Sense of Movement*, London, Faber and Faber, 1957, p. 33.

2 *Unreal City. Urban Experience in Modern European Literature and Art*, Manchester, Manchester University Press, 1985, p. 4.

3 *The Cave of Making*, Oxford, Oxford University Press, 1982, pp. 151, 134. Marsack's title is from Auden's poem in memory of MacNeice. A valuable book despite my disagreement on this point.

4 A review by Stephen Wall, 'Louis MacNeice and the Line of Least Resistance', *The Review*, 11–12 (1964), 91–4, makes a similar case, declining to take the more usual view of MacNeice's development.

5 Quoted by Barbara Coulton in *Louis MacNeice in the BBC*, London, Faber and Faber, 1980, p. 152.

6 Ed. E. R. Dodds, *The Collected Poems of Louis MacNeice*, London, Faber and Faber, 1966. Page numbers in the text are for this collection.

7 *Louis MacNeice*, (Writers and Their Work no. 187), London, Longmans, Green, 1965, p. 29.

8 London, 1960 edn, pp. 14–15. Benjamin suggests that 'the technique of Impressionist painting, whereby the picture is garnered in a riot of dabs of colour, would be a reflection of the experiences with which the eyes of a big city-dweller have become familiar' (*Illuminations*, p. 199).

9 See for example Robyn Marsack, p. 24.

10 Second edn, Oxford, Oxford University Press, 1968, p. 54.

11 'Louis MacNeice', *A Poetry Chronicle. Essays and Reviews*, London, Faber and Faber, 1973, p. 32. 'Bagpipe Music', 'Les Sylphides' and 'Snow' are so well known and widely anthologized that further quotation seems unnecessary.

12 Julian Gitzen in 'Louis MacNeice: The Last Decade', *Twentieth Century Literature*, 14, 3 (October 1968), 133–41, is informative about MacNeice's use of the journey motif.

13 See Robyn Marsack, p. 45 and note p. 155.

14 *Louis MacNeice. A Study*, London, Faber and Faber, 1988, p. 63.

15 *Louis MacNeice: Sceptical Vision*, Dublin and New York, Gill and MacMillan, 1975, p. 10. A parallel is suggested here with the two

Thomases' ambiguous Anglo-Welshness, and possibly with Eliot's Anglo-Americanism.

16 London, Faber and Faber, 1965, p. 220.

17 'Louis MacNeice Remembered', *Quarto*, 6 (May 1980), 14.

18 'In the Salt Mines', *Ireland and the English Crisis*, Newcastle upon Tyne, Bloodaxe, 1984, pp. 80–4.

19 *Varieties of Parable*, Cambridge, Cambridge University Press, 1965, p. 140.

20 *The Poetry of Louis MacNeice*, Leicester, Leicester University Press, 1972.

21 'Experiences With Images', quoted by Terence Brown, p. 134.

22 See Allan Rodway's commentary on 'Snow' in *The Craft of Criticism*, Cambridge, Cambridge University Press, 1982, pp. 111–13.

23 *W. H. Auden. A Biography*, London, Unwin Paperback, 1983, p. 156.

24 Ed. Edward Mendelson, *W. H. Auden Collected Poems*, London, Faber and Faber, 1976, p. 183. Unless otherwise indicated I quote from this edition of the poems.

25 Ed. Edward Mendelson, *The English Auden. Poems, Essays and Dramatic Writings 1927–1939*, London, Faber and Faber, 1977, p. 367.

26 A. Alvarez, *The Shaping Spirit*, London, Arrow Books, 1963, p. 95.

27 Allan Rodway, *A Preface to Auden*, London and New York, Longman, 1984, p. 98.

28 *The Enchaféd Flood*, New York, Random House, 1950, p. 21.

29 *W. H. Auden*, Oxford, Blackwell, 1985, p. 46. Smith's case about Auden is one of the best yet made and I must acknowledge his influence on several points.

30 Justin Replogle, *Auden's Poetry*, London, Methuen, 1969, p. 6.

31 Ed. Edward Mendelson, *W. H. Auden Selected Poems*, London, Faber and Faber, 1979, p. 88. Mendelson's *Collected* remains true to the editions of his poems prepared by Auden himself in not including 'September 1, 1939'. The *Selected* does a great service in reviving both this and 'Spain', as well as a number of other poems suppressed by Auden, and in printing original texts (as does *The English Auden*).

32 Quoted from an article in *Theology* by John Fuller, *A Reader's Guide to W. H. Auden*, London, Thames and Hudson, 1970, pp. 222, 232.

33 William Barrett, *Irrational Man*, p. 15.

34 'Vespers' enacts a varation on this dialectic, one between the 'arcadian' and 'utopian' sides of consciousness, making use of the

Yeatsian term 'Anti-type'. The two 'cannot resist meeting / to remind the other ... of that half of their secret which he would most like to forget ...' (p. 484).

35 Quoted by Carpenter, p. 277.

CHAPTER 7 TED HUGHES

1 See Ekbert Faas, *Ted Hughes: The Unaccommodated Universe*, Santa Barbara, Black Sparrow Press, 1980, p. 206. This book anthologizes many of Hughes's most illuminating statements about poets and poetry and I have drawn on it extensively.

2 See Stuart Hirschberg, *Myth in the Poetry of Ted Hughes*, Portmarnock, Co. Dublin, Wolfhound Press, 1981, for a detailed study of these motifs.

3 For convenience, except where otherwise indicated, I quote from *Ted Hughes. Selected Poems 1957–1981*, Faber and Faber, London, 1982. 'The Thought-Fox' is on p. 13.

4 *Poetry in the Making*, London, Faber and Faber, 1967. Paperback, 1969, p. 20.

5 Terry Gifford and Neil Roberts in *Ted Hughes. A Critical Study*, London, Faber and Faber, 1981, establish this point: correctly, I think, though they point out that Hughes sometimes refers to 'materialism' in the common negative sense (pp. 14–17).

6 *Cave Birds*, London, Faber and Faber, 1978, p. 42. I propose this reading without being fully confident of it. The *Cave Birds* poems date originally from 1975, but were published in revised form in 1978, and I think are best regarded as coming after *Gaudete* (1977).

7 Quoted by Faas, p. 183.

8 Quoted by Faas, p. 15.

9 For Williams this severing was necessary just so that he could make the vital connection with his new world, his America.

10 Seamus Heaney has made this connection with Eliot more technically: see 'Hughes and England', *The Achievement of Ted Hughes*, ed. Keith Sagar, Manchester, Manchester University Press, 1983, p. 14.

11 See 'Capturing Animals', *Poetry in the Making*.

12 See Keith Sagar, *The Achievement of Ted Hughes*, p. 297, on 'naming' in this poem.

13 *Ibid.*, p. 267: quoted by Craig Robinson from a recording for the Critical Forum Series, Norwich Tapes Ltd, 1978.

14 Hughes has said that his imagination was formed by the *First World War*, experienced through his father's stories (Hughes was

born in 1930). But one can hardly see his poetry as belonging with the poetry of *that* war or its aftermath.

15 *Gaudete*, London (1977), Faber paperback, 1979, p. 50. See also Gifford and Roberts on 'machinery', p. 225.

16 *Women in Love*, Harmondsworth, Penguin, 1960, p. 65.

17 In his poem 'Priest and Peasant' R. S. Thomas writes:

> And so you work
> In the wet fields and suffer pain
> And loneliness as a tree takes
> The night's darkness, the day's rain;
> While I watch you, and pray for you . . .
>
> > (*Song at the Year's Turning*, London,
> > Rupert Hart-Davis, p. 109)

The poet is not seen as a mediator of sacred truths, an oracle; he is little more than a passive observer of God's bleak mysteries. Auden's dedicatory verse for his *Collected Poems* suggests that in a strict sense it may be wrong for a Christian to write poetry at all.

18 'Ted Hughes and Geoffrey Hill: An Antithesis', *The New Pelican Guide 8*, Harmondsworth, Penguin, 1983, p. 287.

19 Anthony Thwaite, *Poetry Today. A Critical Guide to British Poetry 1960–1984*, London, Longman, 1985, pp. 59–60.

20 *Selected Poems*, p. 143. Numerous other poems could be cited in illustration of this point.

21 Hirschberg's broad distinction between poems 'modelled on the quatrain' and those which basically employ 'the single line as stanza' (p. 8) opens the way to my larger point.

22 This is interestingly discussed by Craig Robinson in *The Achievement of Ted Hughes*, pp. 257–84.

23 Or perhaps, as Graham Bradshaw has put it, these are poems which 'the "myth" or "symbolic fable" . . . has served to liberate'. See his review of Faas, '"Flash Vision": Ted Hughes and the New Aesthetic', *The Cambridge Quarterly*, 10, 2 (1981), 172–8. His comments on Faas's misdating of some of the *Wodwo* poems should also be noted.

CONCLUSION

1 Ed. Stephen Greenblatt, *Representing the English Renaissance*, Berkeley and London, University of California Press, 1988, p. viii.

2 *Emily Dickinson. Looking to Canaan*, London, Faber and Faber, 1986, p. 86.

Select bibliography

•

The following are book-length materials, including biographical and critical studies and the editions of poets' works, which have been most used in the preparation of the text. Critical studies of individual poets have not been included, as these are too many.

Abrams, M. H., *The Mirror and the Lamp: Romantic Theory and Critical Tradition*, New York, Oxford University Press, 1953

Ackroyd, Peter, *T. S. Eliot*, London, Faber and Faber, 1984

Alvarez, A., *The Shaping Spirit*, London, Arrow Books, 1963; 1st edn Chatto and Windus, 1958

Auden, W. H., *Collected Poems*, ed. Edward Mendelson, London, Faber and Faber, 1976

The Dyer's Hand, London, Faber and Faber, 1963

The English Auden: Poems, Essays and Dramatic Writings 1927–1939, ed. Edward Mendelson, London, Faber and Faber, 1977

The Enchaféd Flood or *The Romantic Iconography of the Sea*, New York, Vintage Books, 1967; 1st edn 1950

Selected Poems, ed. Edward Mendelson, London, Faber and Faber, 1979

Barthes, Roland, *Mythologies*, selected and translated from the French by Annette Lavers, St Albans, Paladin, 1973 (Paris, Editions de Seuil, 1957)

Baudelaire, Charles, *Baudelaire: œuvres complètes*, Paris, Bibliothèque de la Pléiade, 1961

Bayley, John, *The Romantic Survival: A Study in Poetic Evolution*, London, Constable, 1957

Belsey, Catherine, *Critical Practice*, London and New York, Methuen, 1980

Benjamin, Walter, *Illuminations*, ed. and with an Introduction by Hannah Arendt, trans. Harry Zohn, New York, Harcourt, Brace and World, 1968. Originally published in Germany by Suhrkamp Verlag, 1955.

Bennett, Tony, *Formalism and Marxism*, London, Methuen, 1979

Blackmur, R. P., *Language as Gesture*, London, Allen and Unwin, 1954

Bornstein, George, ed. *Romantic and Modern: Revaluations of Literary Tradition*, Pittsburgh, University of Pittsburgh Press, 1977

Bradbury, Malcolm and James McFarlane, eds. *Modernism, 1890–1930*, Harmondsworth, Penguin, 1976

Brooks, Cleanth, *Modern Poetry and the Tradition*, Chapel Hill, University of North Carolina Press, 1965; 1st edn 1939

Butler, Marilyn, *Romantics, Rebels and Reactionaries: English Literature and Its Background 1760–1830*, Oxford, Oxford University Press, 1981

Carpenter, Humphrey, *W. H. Auden: A Biography*, London, Unwin Paperbacks, 1983; 1st edn 1981

Coffman, Stanley K., *Imagism: A Chapter for the History of Modern Poetry*, Norman, University of Oklahoma Press, 1951

Cooke, William, *Edward Thomas: A Critical Biography 1878–1917*, London, Faber and Faber, 1970

Culler, Jonathan, *Structuralist Poetics: Structuralism, Linguistics and the Study of Literature*, London, Routledge and Kegan Paul, 1975

Davie, Donald, *Thomas Hardy and British Poetry*, London, Routledge and Kegan Paul, 1973

Eliot, T. S., *The Collected Poems and Plays of T. S. Eliot*, London, Faber and Faber, 1969

    The Letters of T. S. Eliot, Vol. I. 1898–1922, ed. Valerie Eliot, London, Faber and Faber, 1988

    Selected Essays, London, Faber and Faber, 3rd edn 1951. Other prose works by Eliot are cited in the text.

    The Waste Land: A Facsimile and Transcript, ed. Valerie Eliot, London, Faber and Faber, 1971

Ellman, Richard and Charles Feidelson, eds. *The Modern Tradition: Backgrounds of Modern Literature*, New York, Oxford University Press, 1965

Faas, Ekbert, *Ted Hughes: The Unaccommodated Universe*, Santa Barbara, Black Sparrow Press, 1980

Farjeon, Eleanor, *Edward Thomas: The Last Four Years*, London, Oxford University Press, 1958

Fraser, G. S., *The Modern Writer and His World*, Harmondsworth, Penguin, 1964

Fuller, John, *A Reader's Guide to W. H. Auden*, London, Thames and Hudson, 1970

Gordon, Lyndall, *Eliot's Early Years*, Oxford, Oxford University Press, 1977

    Eliot's New Life, Oxford, Oxford University Press, 1988

Graves, Robert, *Collected Poems 1975*, London, Cassell, 1975

The Crowning Privilege, London, Cassell, 1955; Penguin, 1959

Goodbye to All That, London, Cape, 1929; Penguin, 1960

The White Goddess: A Historical Grammar of Poetic Myth, London, Faber and Faber, 1948; amended and enlarged 1961

Graves, Robert and Hodge, Alan, *The Long Week-End: A Social History of Great Britain 1918–1939*, London, Faber and Faber, 1941

Hamburger, Michael, *The Truth of Poetry: Tensions in Modern Poetry from Baudelaire to the 1960s*, London, Weidenfeld and Nicolson, 1969; Penguin, 1972

Hamilton, Ian, *A Poetry Chronicle: Essays and Reviews*, Faber and Faber, 1973

Hardy, Thomas, *The Complete Poems*, ed. James Gibson, London, Macmillan, 1976

Harmer, J. B., *Victory in Limbo: Imagism 1908–1917*, New York, St Martins' Press, 1975

Hoffman, Daniel, *Barbarous Knowledge: Myth in the Poetry of Yeats, Graves and Muir*, London and New York, Oxford University Press, 1967

Hough, Graham, *The Last Romantics*, London, University Paperbacks, 1967; 1st edn 1941

Housman, A. E., *The Name and Nature of Poetry*, The Leslie Stephen Lecture delivered at Cambridge 9 May 1933, London, Cambridge University Press, 1933

Hughes, Glenn, *Imagism and the Imagists*, Stanford, Stanford University Press, 1931; London, Bowes and Bowes, 1960

Hughes, Ted., *Cave Birds*, London, Faber and Faber, 1978

Crow, London, Faber and Faber, 1972

Gaudete, London, Faber and Faber, 1977

Poetry in the Making, London, Faber and Faber, 1967

Selected Poems 1957–1981, London, Faber and Faber, 1982

Jeffares, Norman, *A Commentary on the Poems of W. B. Yeats*, London, Macmillan, 1968

Kermode, Frank, *The Classic: The T. S. Eliot Memorial Lectures*, London, Faber and Faber, 1975

Romantic Image, London, Routledge and Kegan Paul, 1957

Langbaum, Robert, *The Modern Spirit: Essays on the Continuity of Nineteenth and Twentieth-Century Literature*, London, Chatto and Windus, 1970

The Poetry of Experience, London, Chatto and Windus, 1957; Penguin, 1974

Lawrence, D. H., *Apocalypse*, London, Granada, 1981; 1st edn 1931

The Complete Poems, ed. V. da Sola Pinto and Warren Hughes, New York, Viking, Compass, 1971

Selected Literary Criticism, ed. Anthony Beal, London, Heinemann, 1967

Lehmann, A. G., *The Symbolist Aesthetic in France 1885–1895*, Oxford, Blackwell, 1950; 2nd edn 1968

Levenson, Michael H., *A Genealogy of Modernism: A Study of English Literary Doctrine 1980–1982*, Cambridge, Cambridge University Press, 1984

Lucas, John, *Modern English Poetry: From Hardy to Hughes*, London, Batsford, 1986

MacNeice, Louis, *The Collected Poems of Louis MacNeice*, ed. E. R. Dodds, London, Faber and Faber, 1966 and 1979

   Modern Poetry: A Personal Essay, Oxford, Oxford University Press, 1968; 1st edn 1938

   The Poetry of W. B. Yeats, London, Faber and Faber, 1967; 1st edn 1941

   The Strings Are False: An Unfinished Autobiography, London, Faber and Faber, 1965

   Varieties of Parable, Cambridge, Cambridge University Press, 1965

Marsh, Edward, ed. *Georgian Poetry 1911–1912*; *1913–15*; *1916–17*; *1918–19*; *1920–22*, London, The Poetry Bookshop, 1912–22

Martin, Wallace, *The New Age under Orage: Chapters in English Cultural History*, Manchester, Manchester University Press, 1967

Monro, Harold, *Collected Poems*, ed. Alida Monro, with a Preface by Ruth Tomalin, London, Gerald Duckworth, 1970; with a 'Critical Note' by T. S. Eliot and a 'Biographical Note' by F. S. Flint, London, R. Cobden-Sanderson, 1933

Moore, Harry T., *The Priest of Love*, Harmondsworth, Penguin, 1976

Murry, J. Middleton, *Countries of the Mind*, London, Collins, 1922; new edn, Oxford University Press, 1931; The Oxford Bookshelf, 1937

Osborn, Charles, *W. H. Auden: The Life of a Poet*, London, Eyre Methuen, 1980

Perkins, David, *A History of Modern Poetry: From the 1890s to the High Modernist Mode*, Cambridge, Mass., Harvard University Press, 1976

Pound, Ezra, *Literary Essays*, edited and with an introduction by T. S. Eliot, London, Faber and Faber, 1954; paperback 1960

   The Letters 1970–1941, ed. D. D. Paige, London, Faber and Faber, 1951

Praz, Mario, *The Romantic Agony*, London, Oxford University Press, 1933; Oxford paperback, 1970

Press, John, *A Map of Modern English Verse*, London, Oxford University Press, 1969

Raymond, Marcel, *From Baudelaire to Surrealism*, London, Methuen paperback, 1970; first published as *De Baudelaire au Surréalisme*, Paris, 1933

Read, Herbert, *The True Voice of Feeling: Studies in English Romantic Poetry*, London, Faber and Faber, 1953

Rodway, Allan, *The Romantic Conflict*, London, Chatto and Windus, 1963

Rogers, Timothy, ed. *Georgian Poetry 1911–1922: The Critical Heritage*, London, Routledge and Kegan Paul, 1977

Rosenthal, M. L., *The Modern Poets: A Critical Introduction*, New York, Oxford University Press, 1960

Ross, R. H., *The Georgian Revolt: Rise and Fall of a Poetic Ideal 1910–1922*, London, Faber and Faber, 1967

Sagar, Keith, ed. *The Achievement of Ted Hughes*, Manchester, Manchester University Press, 1983

Sartre, Jean-Paul, *Baudelaire*, Paris, Gallimard, 1963; 1st edn 1947

Selver, Paul, *Orage and the New Age Circle*, London, Allen and Unwin, 1959

Seymour-Smith, Martin, *Robert Graves: His Life and Work*, London, Abacus, 1983

Silkin, Jon, *Out of Battle: The Poetry of the Great War*, London, Oxford University Press, 1972

Sisson, C. H., *English Poetry 1900–1950: An Assessment*, London, Rupert Hart-Davis, 1971

Starkie, Enid, *Baudelaire*, Harmondsworth, Penguin, 1971; 1st edn 1957

Stead, C. K., *The New Poetic: Yeats to Eliot*, London, Hutchinson, 1964; Penguin, 1967

Symons, Arthur, *The Symbolist Movement in Literature*, London, Heinemann, 1899; paperback, with an introduction by Richard Ellman, New York, E. P. Dutton, 1958

Symons, Julian, *The Thirties: A Dream Revolved*, London, The Cresset Press, 1960

Thomas, Edward, *The Collected Poems*, ed. R. George Thomas, Oxford, Oxford University Press, 1978

Keats, London, T. C. and E. C. Jack, 1916

Edward Thomas: Selected Poems and Prose, ed. David Wright, Harmondsworth, Penguin, 1981

Thomas, Helen, *As It Was*, London, Heinemann, 1926

World Without End, London, Heinemann, 1931

Thomas, R. George, *Edward Thomas: A Portrait*, Oxford, Oxford University Press, 1985

(ed.) *Letters from Edward Thomas to Gordon Bottomley*, London, Oxford University Press, 1968

Thwaite, Anthony, *Poetry Today: A Critical Guide to British Poetry 1960–1984*, London, Longman, 1985

Timms, Edward and David Kelly, eds. *Unreal City: Urban Experience in Modern European Literature and Art*, Manchester, Manchester University Press, 1985

Williams, Raymond, *The Country and the City*, London, Chatto and Windus, 1973

Woolf, Leonard, *Beginning Again: An Autobiography of the Years 1911–1918*, London, The Hogarth Press, 1972

Yeats, W. B., *Autobiographies*, London, Macmillan, 1955
Collected Poems of W. B. Yeats, London, Macmillan, 1965
Mythologies, London, Macmillan, 1959
A Vision, London, Macmillan, 1962

Index

Individual works are listed under the author's name

332